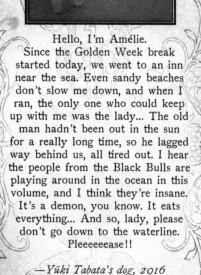

Hello, I'm Amélie.
Since the Golden Week break started today, we went to an inn near the sea. Even sandy beaches don't slow me down, and when I ran, the only one who could keep up with me was the lady... The old man hadn't been out in the sun for a really long time, so he lagged way behind us, all tired out. I hear the people from the Black Bulls are playing around in the ocean in this volume, and I think they're insane. It's a demon, you know. It eats everything... And so, lady, please don't go down to the waterline. Pleeeeeease!!

*—Yūki Tabata's dog, 2016*

### YŪKI TABATA

was born in Fukuoka Prefecture and got his big break in the 2011 Shonen Jump Golden Future Cup with his winning entry, *Hungry Joker*. He started the magical fantasy series *Black Clover* in 2015.

# BLACK CLOVER
## VOLUME 7
### SHONEN JUMP Manga Edition

Story and Art by YŪKI TABATA

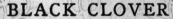

Translation ❀ TAYLOR ENGEL,
HC LANGUAGE SOLUTIONS, INC.

Touch-Up Art & Lettering ❀ ANNALIESE CHRISTMAN

Design ❀ SHAWN CARRICO

Editor ❀ ALEXIS KIRSCH

Printed in the U.S.A.

Published by VIZ Media, LLC
P.O. Box 77010
San Francisco, CA 94107

10 9 8 7 6 5 4 3 2 1
First printing, June 2017

www.shonenjump.com     www.viz.com

SHONENJUMP MANGA

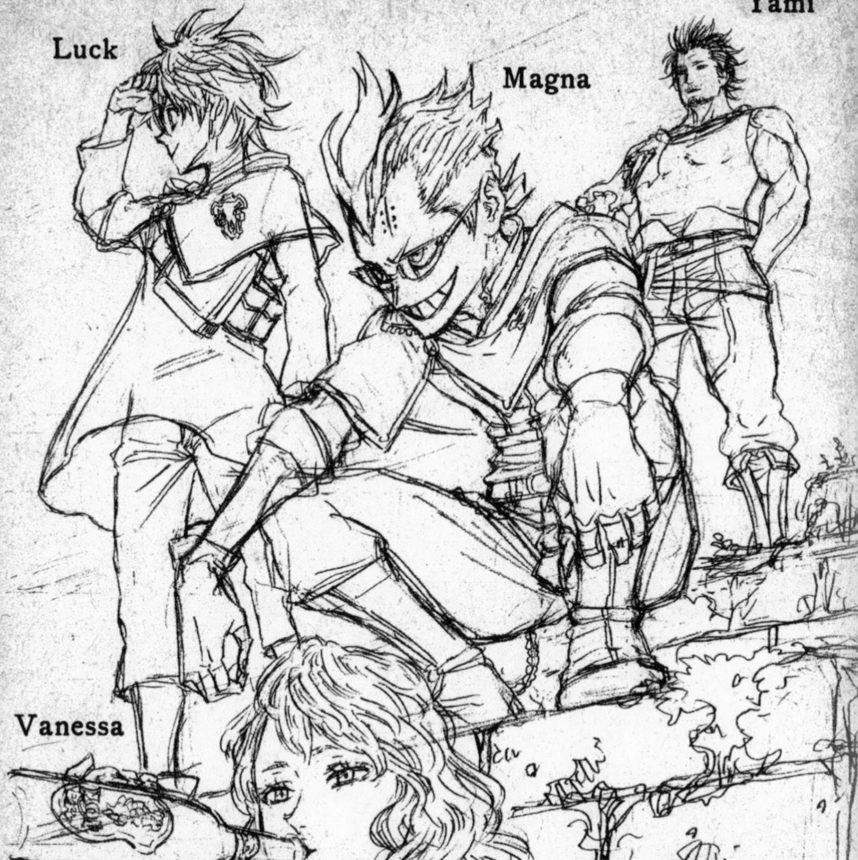

Yami
Luck
Magna
Vanessa


# Black Clover

# 7

YŪKI TABATA

THE MAGIC KNIGHT CAPTAIN CONFERENCE

# Characters

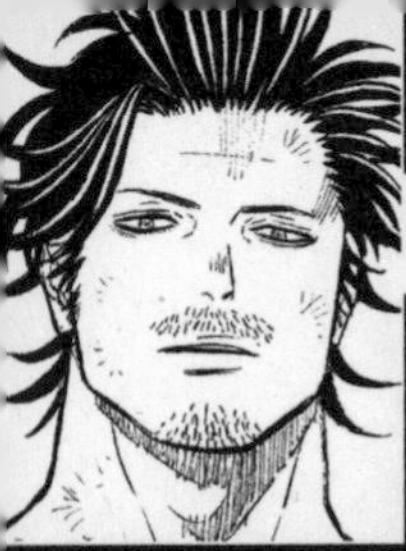

## Yami Sukehiro

Member of:
The Black Bulls
Magic: Dark

A captain who looks fierce and has a hot temper, but is very popular with his brigade.

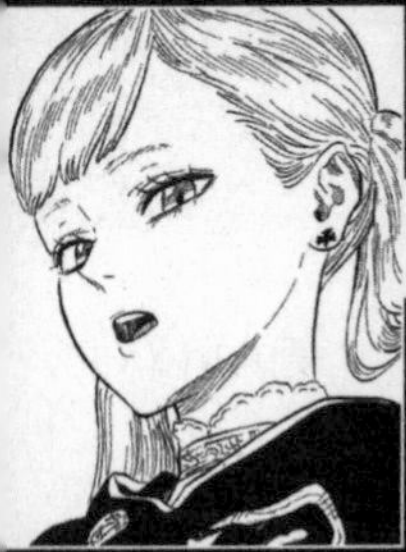

## Noelle Silva

Member of:
The Black Bulls
Magic: Water

A royal. She's really impudent, but can be kind too.

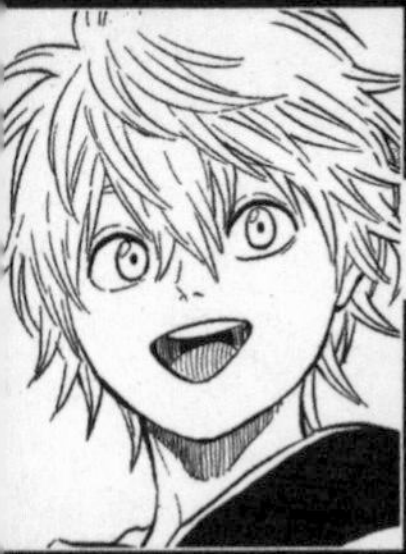

## Luck Voltia

Member of:
The Black Bulls
Magic: Lightning

A battle maniac who smiles constantly and has a problematic personality.

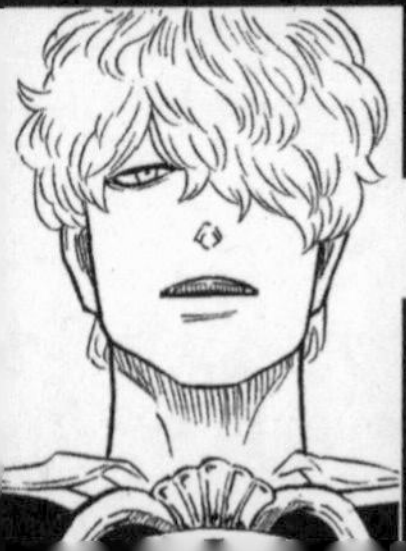

## Gauche Adlai

Member of:
The Black Bulls
Magic: Mirror

A former convict with a blind, pathological love for his little sister.

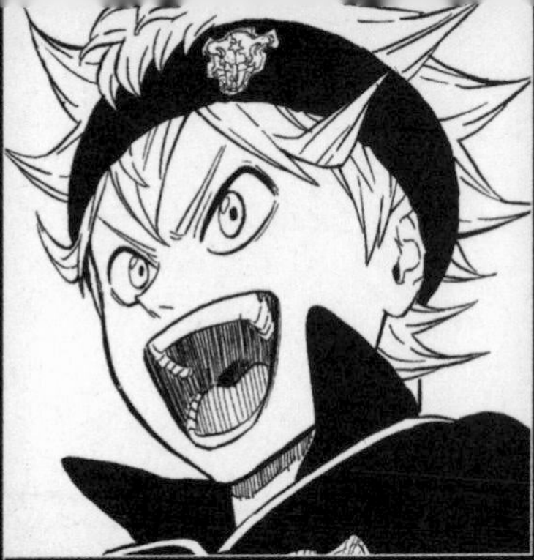

## Asta

Squad: The Black Bulls
Magic: None (Anti-Magic)

He has no magic, but he's working to become the Wizard King through sheer guts and his well-trained body.

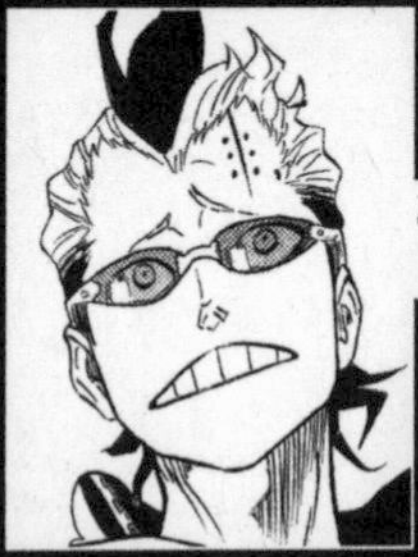

## Magna Swing

Member of:
The Black Bulls
Magic: Flame

He has the temperament of a delinquent, but he's quite manly and good at taking care of others.

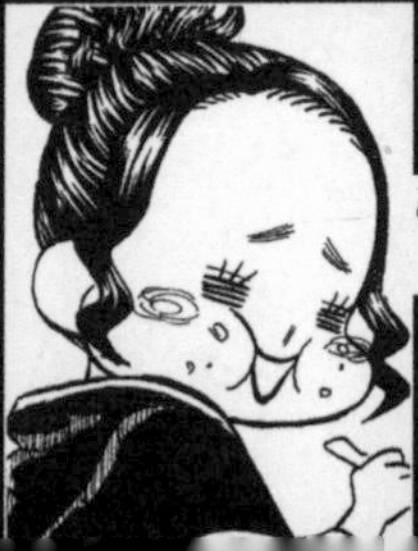

## Charmy Pappitson

Member of:
The Black Bulls
Magic: Cotton

She's small, but she eats like a maniac.

## Vanessa Enoteca

Member of:
The Black Bulls
Magic: ?

A witch with an unparalleled love of liquor who was exiled from a distinguished family.

## Finral Roulacase

Squad:
The Black Bulls
Magic: Spatial

A flirt who likes girls so much it gets in the way of his missions.

## Nozel Silva

Member of:
The Silver Eagles
Magic: Mercury

A proud captain. Noelle's older brother.

## Julius Novachron

Wizard King
Magic: Time

The strongest man in the Clover Kingdom. Also a magic fanatic.

## Jack the Ripper

Member of: The Green Praying Mantises
Magic: Severing

A super-sadist who loves breaking stuff. Does he view Yami as a rival?

## Charlotte Roselei

Member of: The Blue Rose Knights
Magic: Briar

A cool and beautiful captain. She's in love with Yami.

# STORY

In a world where magic is everything, Asta and Yuno are both found abandoned on the same day at a church in the remote village of Hage. Both dream of becoming the Wizard King, the highest of all mages, and they spend their days working toward that dream.

The year they turn 15, both receive grimoires, magic books that amplify their bearer's magic. They take the entrance exam for the Magic Knights, nine groups of mages under the direct control of the Wizard King. Yuno, whose magic is strong, joins the Golden Dawn, an elite group, while Asta, who has no magic at all, joins the Black Bulls, a group of misfits. With this, the two finally take their first step toward becoming the Wizard King...

While fighting Licht, the leader of the Eye of the Midnight Sun, Yami finds himself in trouble when the group's top mages, the Third Eye, join the fray. However, with help from the Magic Knight captains and Asta, Yami manages to drive the enemy away. When Asta returns to the royal capital, he receives a certain

# CONTENTS

**BLACK ❖ CLOVER**

# 7

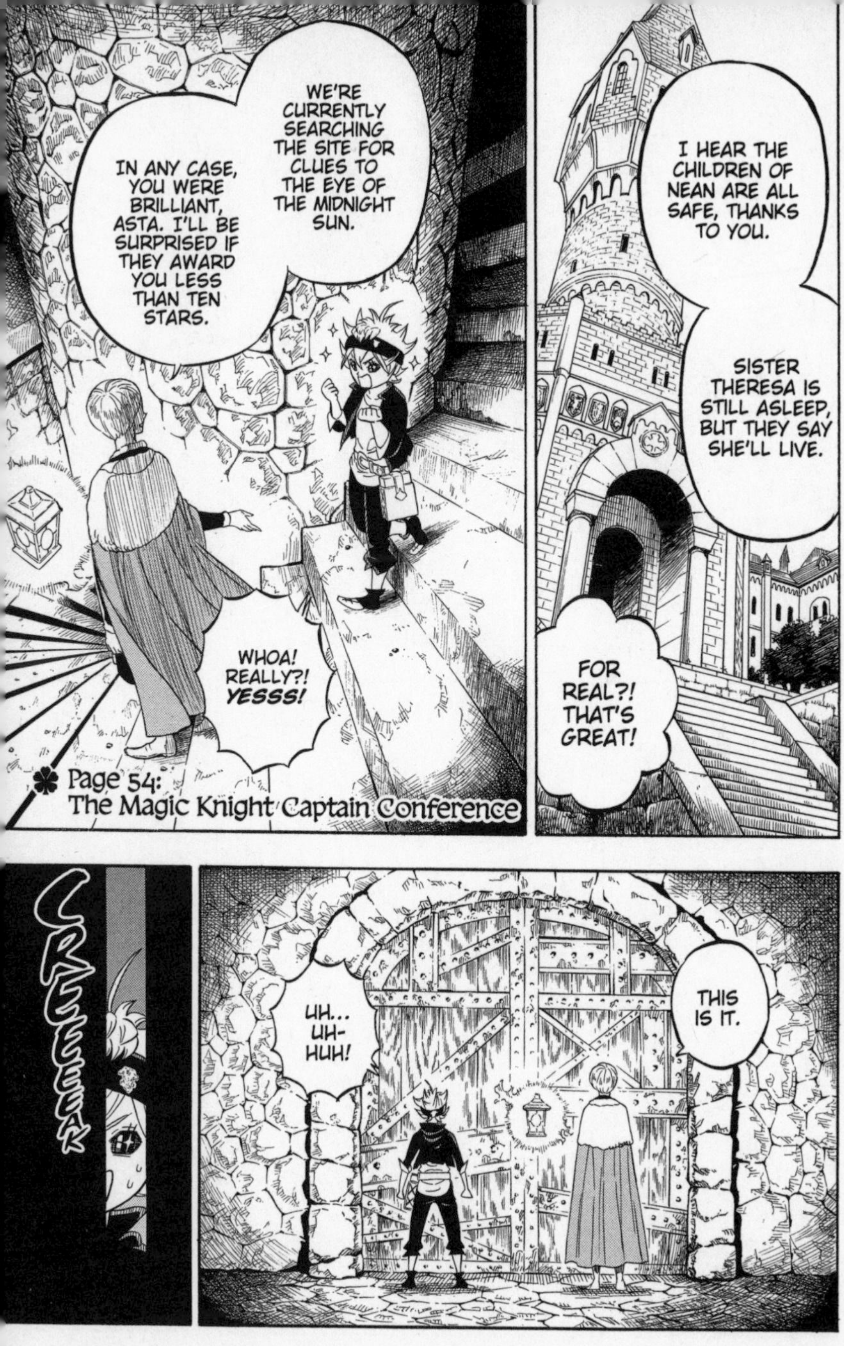
I HEAR THE CHILDREN OF NEAN ARE ALL SAFE, THANKS TO YOU.
SISTER THERESA IS STILL ASLEEP, BUT THEY SAY SHE'LL LIVE.
FOR REAL?! THAT'S GREAT!
WE'RE CURRENTLY SEARCHING THE SITE FOR CLUES TO THE EYE OF THE MIDNIGHT SUN.
IN ANY CASE, YOU WERE BRILLIANT, ASTA. I'LL BE SURPRISED IF THEY AWARD YOU LESS THAN TEN STARS.
WHOA! REALLY?! *YESSS!*
Page 54: The Magic Knight Captain Conference
THIS IS IT.
UH... UH-HUH!
CREEEEAK

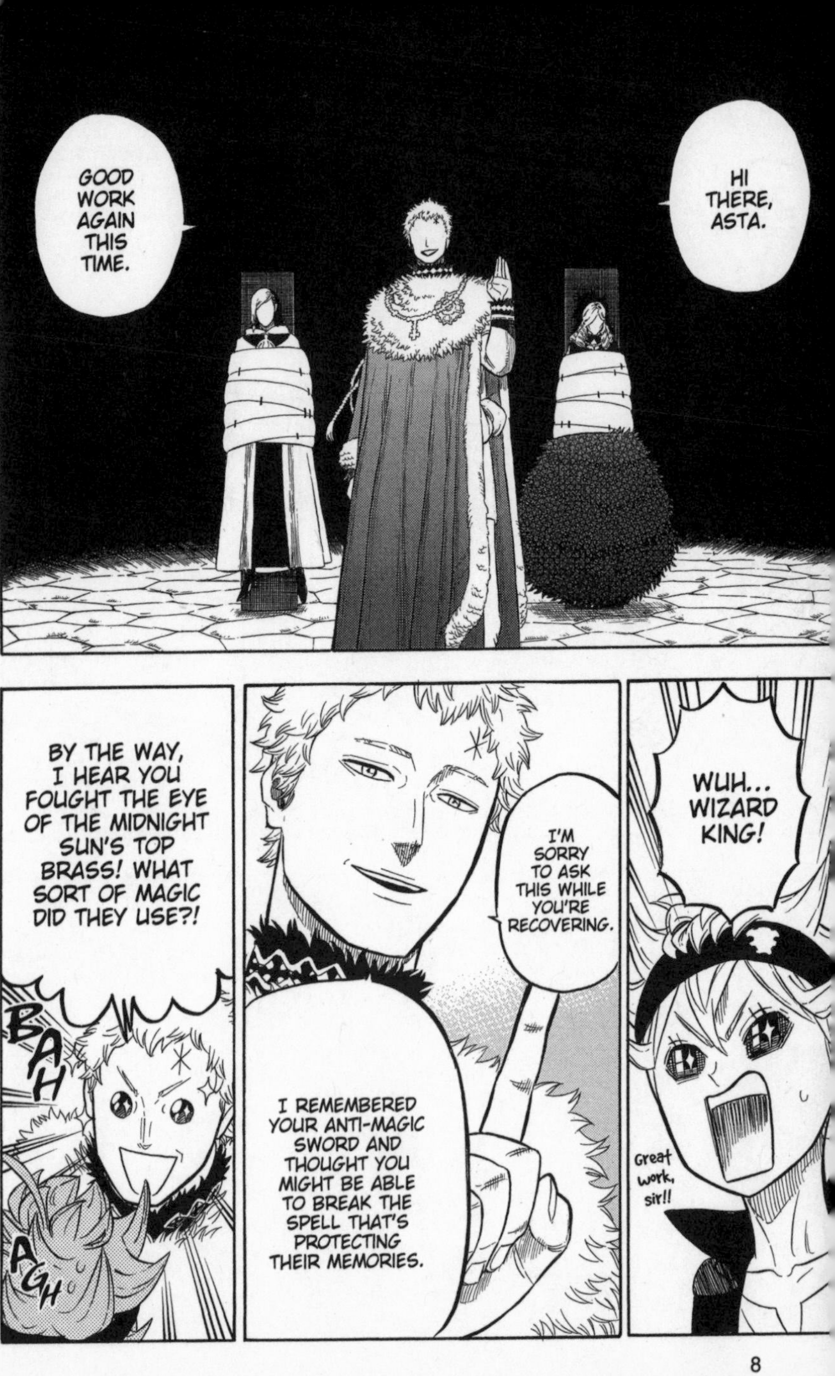
HI THERE, ASTA.
GOOD WORK AGAIN THIS TIME.
WUH... WIZARD KING!
Great work, sir!!
I'M SORRY TO ASK THIS WHILE YOU'RE RECOVERING.
I REMEMBERED YOUR ANTI-MAGIC SWORD AND THOUGHT YOU MIGHT BE ABLE TO BREAK THE SPELL THAT'S PROTECTING THEIR MEMORIES.
BY THE WAY, I HEAR YOU FOUGHT THE EYE OF THE MIDNIGHT SUN'S TOP BRASS! WHAT SORT OF MAGIC DID THEY USE?!
BAH
AGH

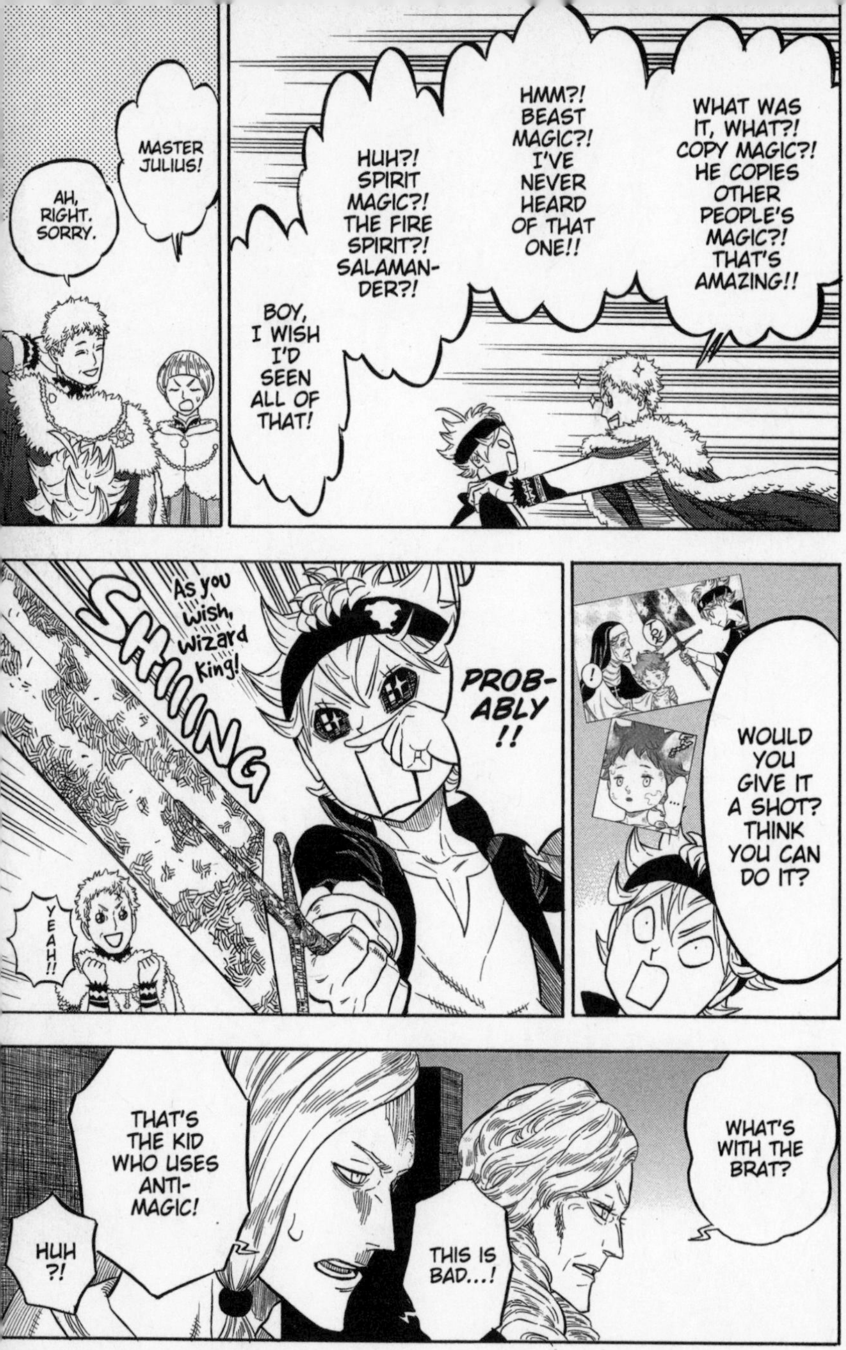
WHAT WAS IT, WHAT?! COPY MAGIC?! HE COPIES OTHER PEOPLE'S MAGIC?! THAT'S AMAZING!!
HMM?! BEAST MAGIC?! I'VE NEVER HEARD OF THAT ONE!!
HUH?! SPIRIT MAGIC?! THE FIRE SPIRIT?! SALAMAN-DER?!
BOY, I WISH I'D SEEN ALL OF THAT!
MASTER JULIUS!
AH, RIGHT. SORRY.
WOULD YOU GIVE IT A SHOT? THINK YOU CAN DO IT?
PROB-ABLY!!
As you wish, wizard King!
SHIIING
YEAH!!
WHAT'S WITH THE BRAT?
THIS IS BAD...!
THAT'S THE KID WHO USES ANTI-MAGIC!
HUH?!

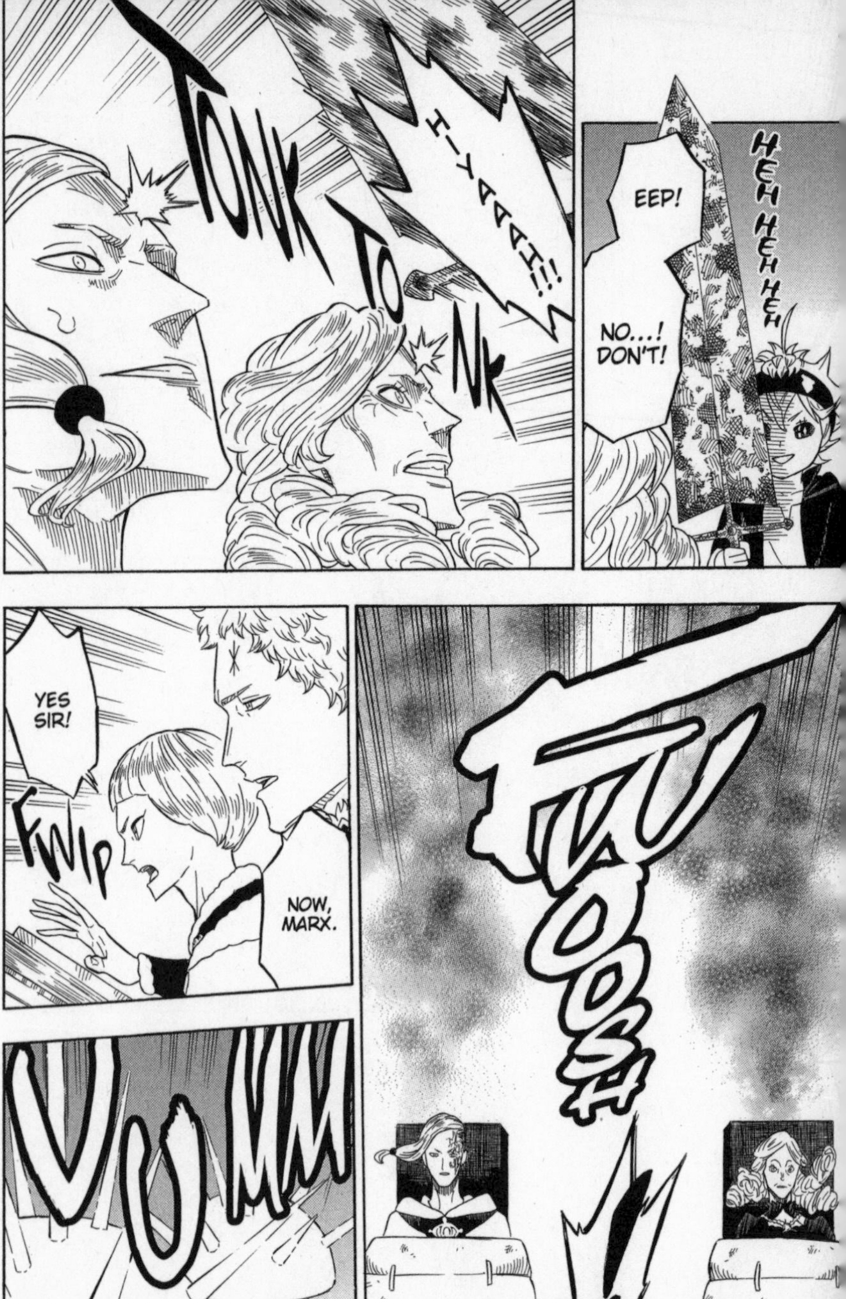
EEP!
NO...! DON'T!
HEH HEH HEH HEH
TONK
HIYAAAH!!!
TONK
FWOOOSH!
NOW, MARX.
YES SIR!
FWIP
VOOMM

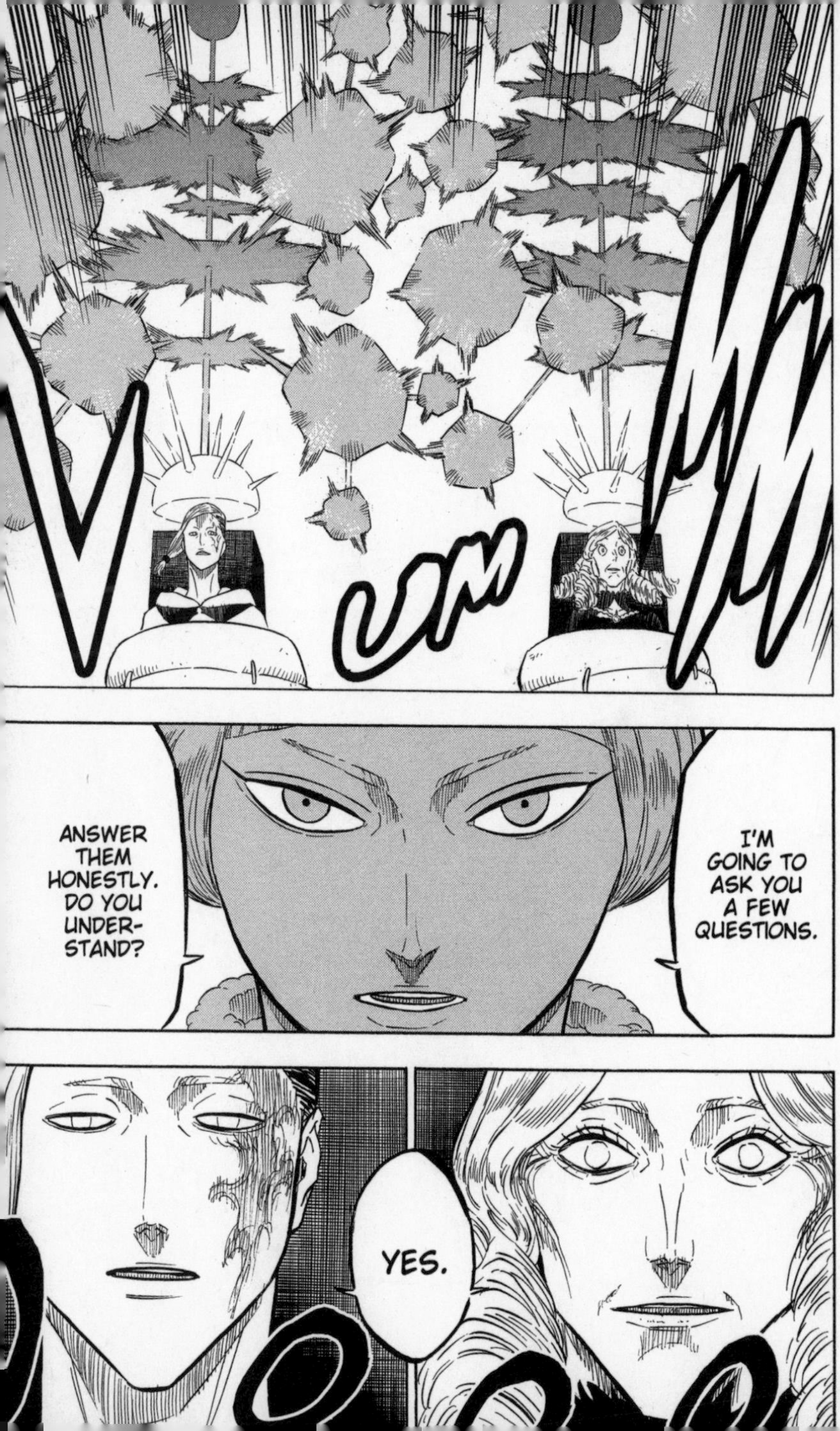
I'M GOING TO ASK YOU A FEW QUESTIONS.
ANSWER THEM HONESTLY. DO YOU UNDER-STAND?
YES.

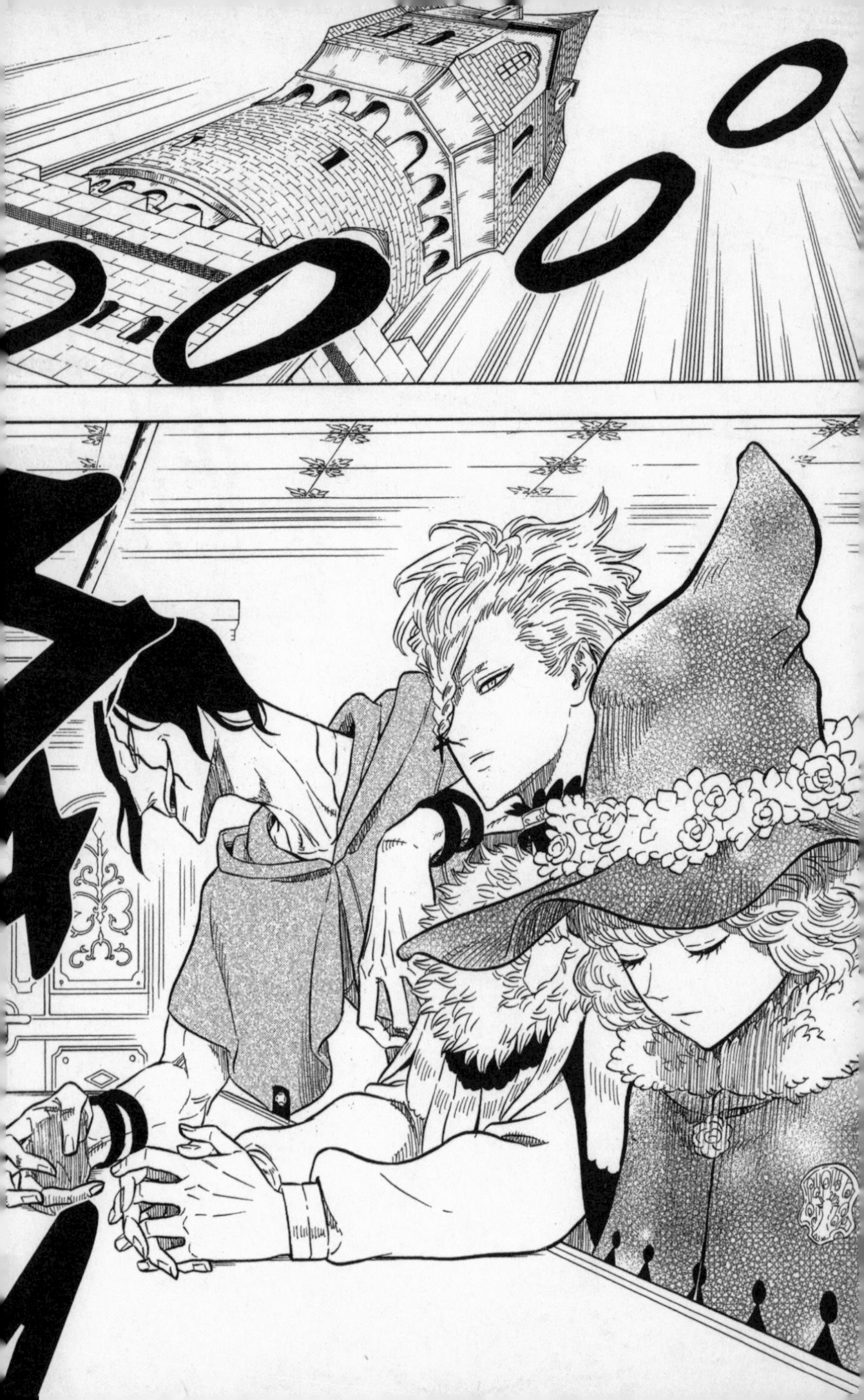

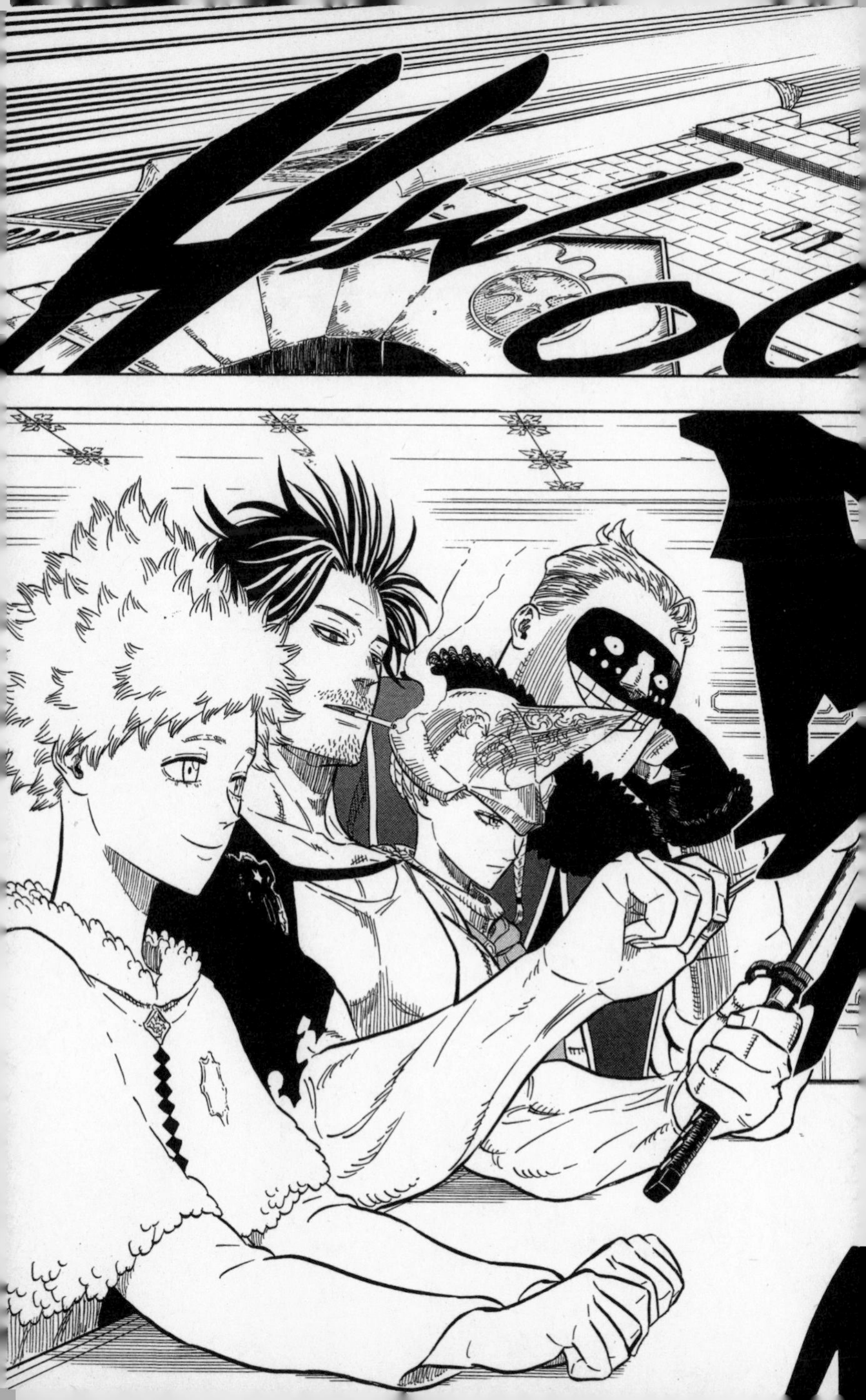
Whoo

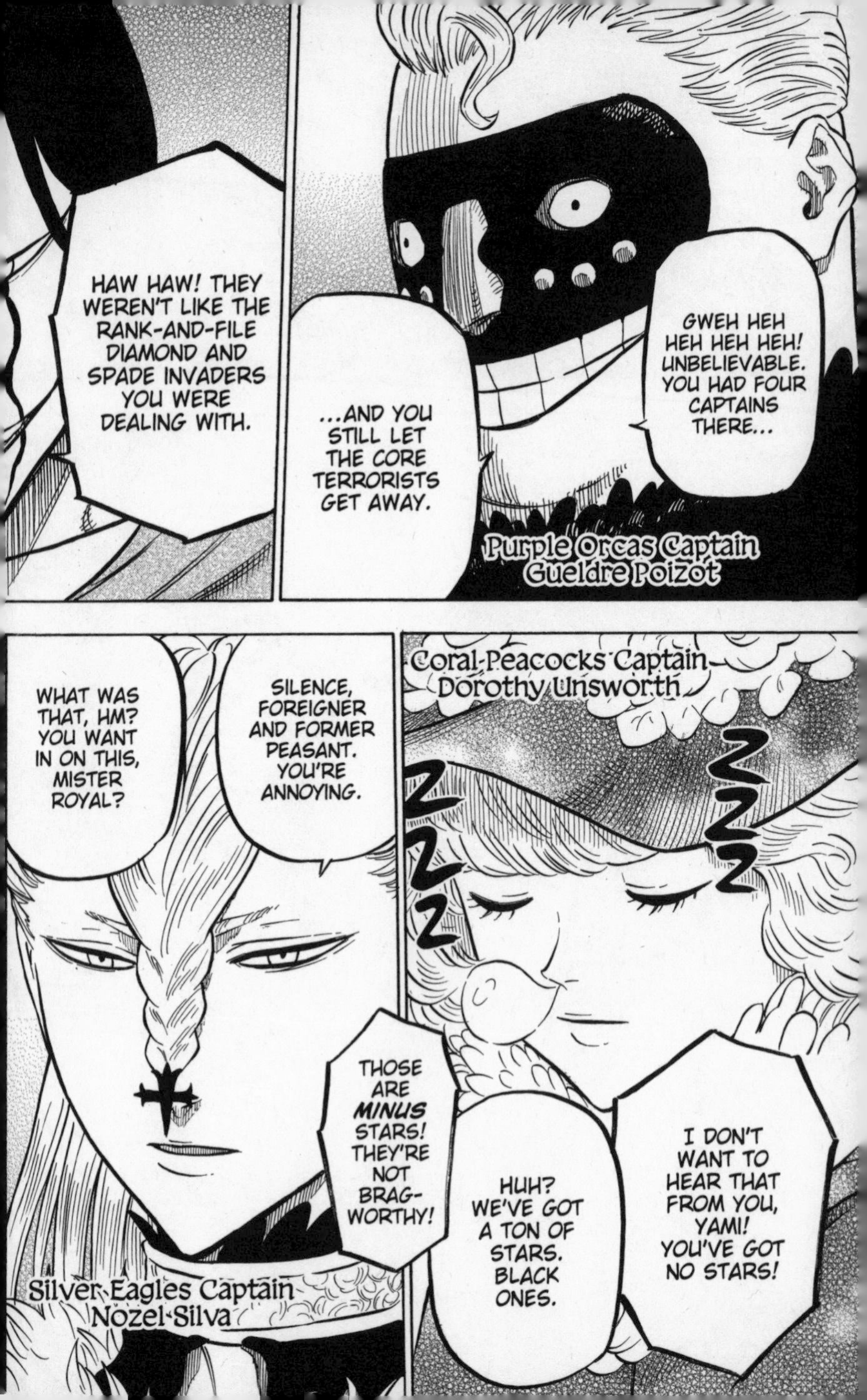
GWEH HEH HEH HEH HEH! UNBELIEVABLE. YOU HAD FOUR CAPTAINS THERE...
...AND YOU STILL LET THE CORE TERRORISTS GET AWAY.
Purple Orcas Captain Gueldre Poizot
HAW HAW! THEY WEREN'T LIKE THE RANK-AND-FILE DIAMOND AND SPADE INVADERS YOU WERE DEALING WITH.
Coral-Peacocks Captain Dorothy Unsworth
ZZZ
I DON'T WANT TO HEAR THAT FROM YOU, YAMI! YOU'VE GOT NO STARS!
HUH? WE'VE GOT A TON OF STARS. BLACK ONES.
THOSE ARE *MINUS* STARS! THEY'RE NOT BRAG-WORTHY!
SILENCE, FOREIGNER AND FORMER PEASANT. YOU'RE ANNOYING.
WHAT WAS THAT, HM? YOU WANT IN ON THIS, MISTER ROYAL?
Silver Eagles Captain Nozel Silva

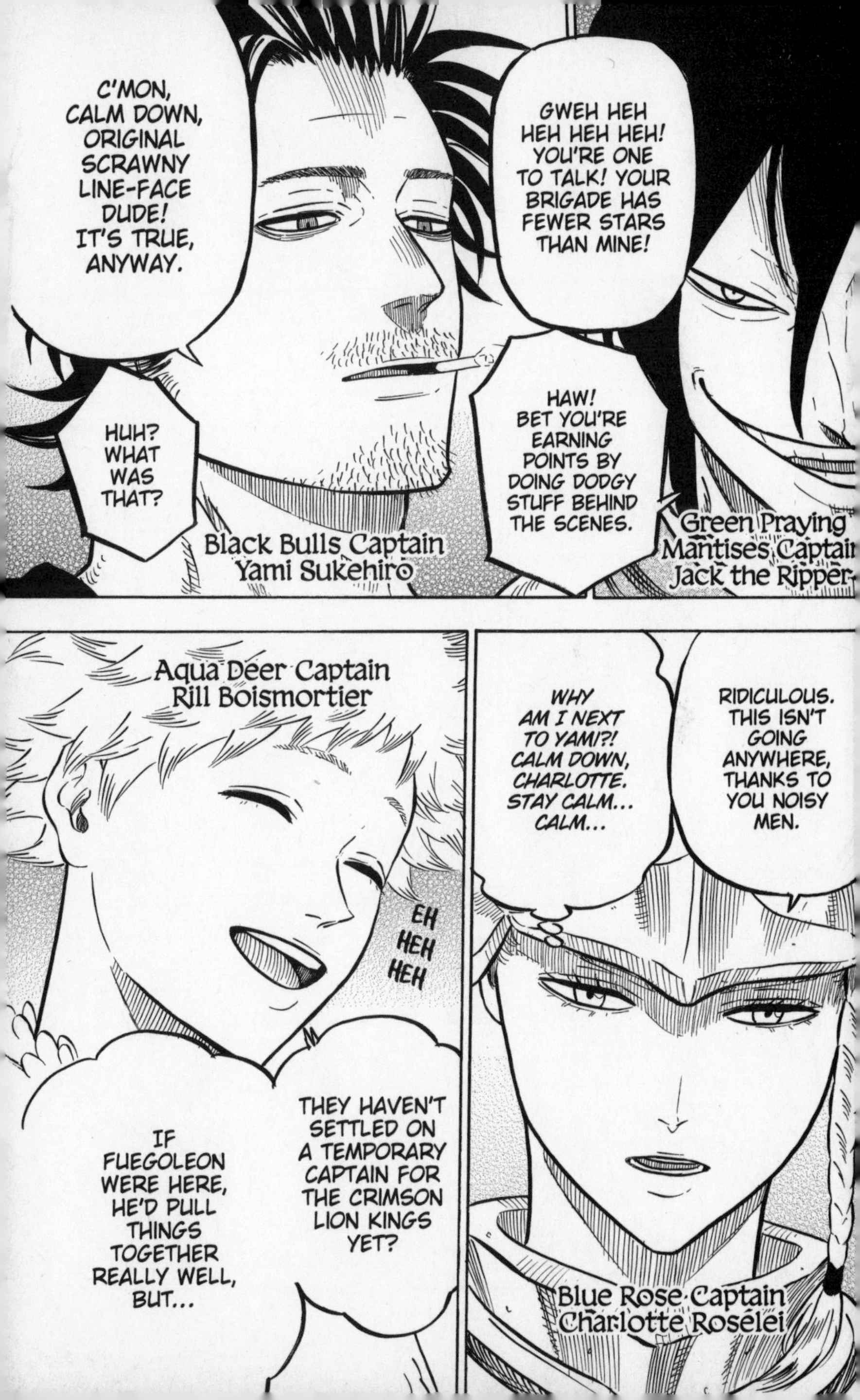
GWEH HEH HEH HEH HEH! YOU'RE ONE TO TALK! YOUR BRIGADE HAS FEWER STARS THAN MINE!
C'MON, CALM DOWN, ORIGINAL SCRAWNY LINE-FACE DUDE! IT'S TRUE, ANYWAY.
Green Praying Mantises Captain Jack the Ripper
HAW! BET YOU'RE EARNING POINTS BY DOING DODGY STUFF BEHIND THE SCENES.
HUH? WHAT WAS THAT?
Black Bulls Captain Yami Sukehiro
RIDICULOUS. THIS ISN'T GOING ANYWHERE, THANKS TO YOU NOISY MEN.
WHY AM I NEXT TO YAMI?! CALM DOWN, CHARLOTTE. STAY CALM... CALM...
Blue Rose Captain Charlotte Roselei
Aqua Deer Captain Rill Boismortier
EH HEH HEH
THEY HAVEN'T SETTLED ON A TEMPORARY CAPTAIN FOR THE CRIMSON LION KINGS YET?
IF FUEGOLEON WERE HERE, HE'D PULL THINGS TOGETHER REALLY WELL, BUT...

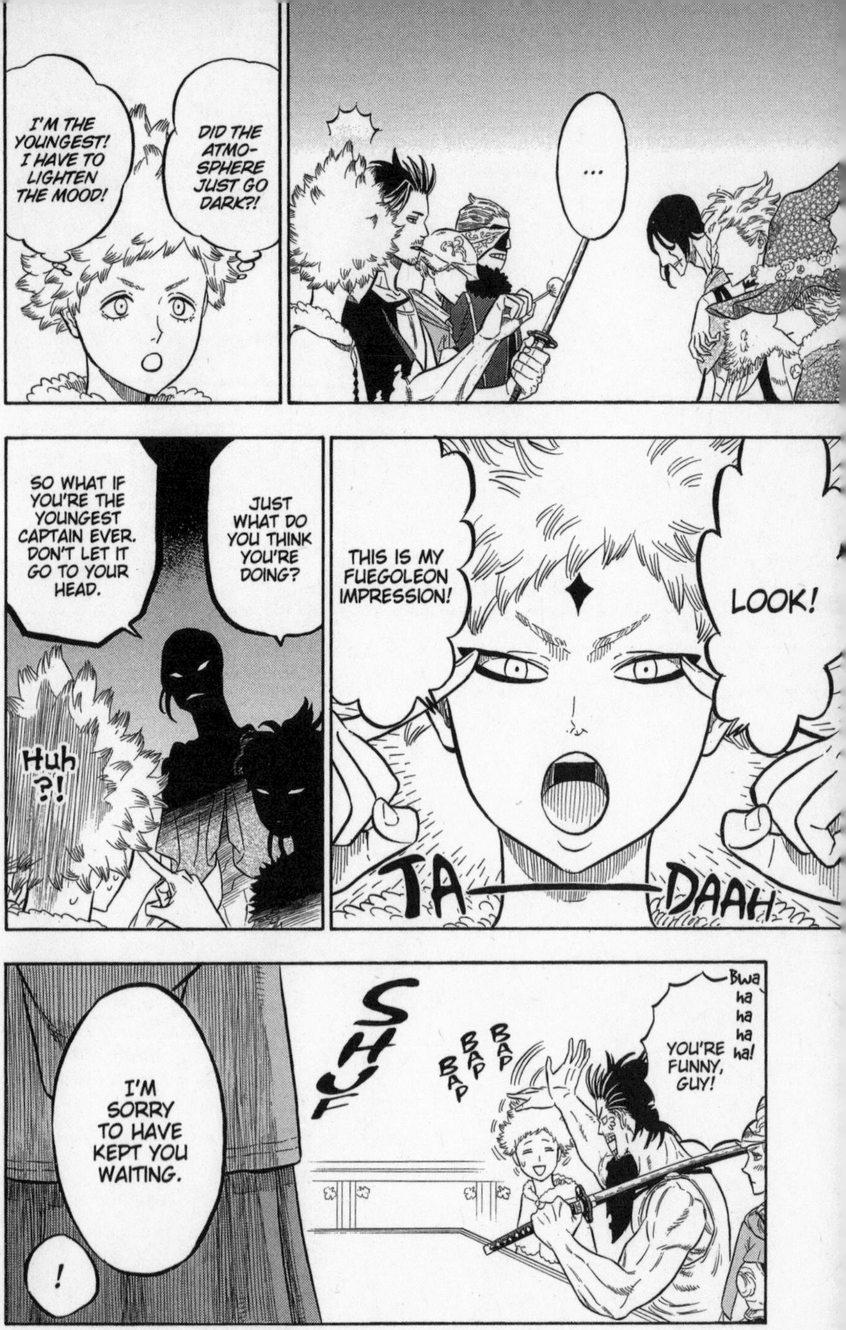
...
DID THE ATMO- SPHERE JUST GO DARK?!
I'M THE YOUNGEST! I HAVE TO LIGHTEN THE MOOD!
LOOK!
THIS IS MY FUEGOLEON IMPRESSION!
TA—DAAH
JUST WHAT DO YOU THINK YOU'RE DOING?
SO WHAT IF YOU'RE THE YOUNGEST CAPTAIN EVER. DON'T LET IT GO TO YOUR HEAD.
Huh ?!
Bwa ha ha ha ha!
YOU'RE FUNNY, GUY!
BAP BAP BAP
SHUF
I'M SORRY TO HAVE KEPT YOU WAITING.
!

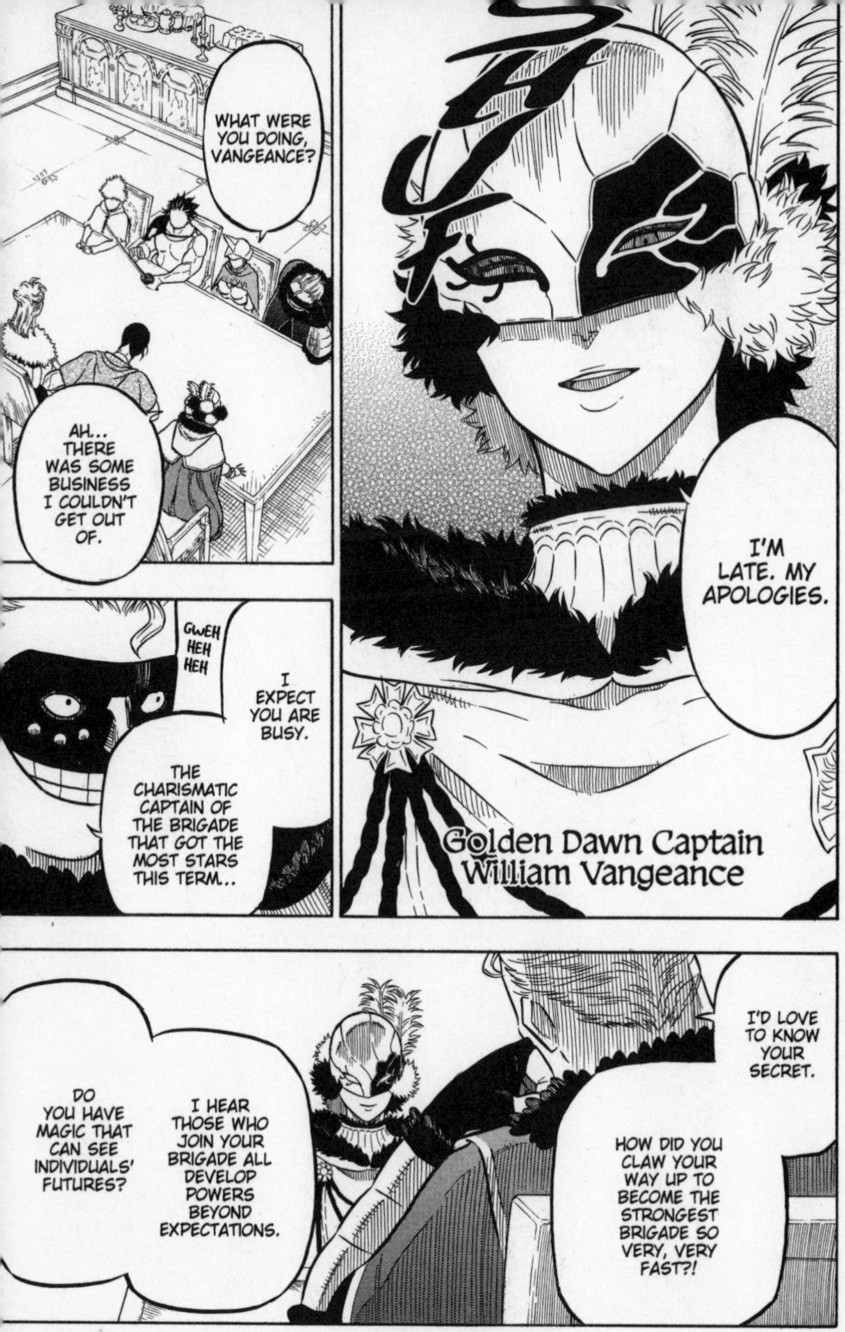
I'M LATE. MY APOLOGIES.
Golden Dawn Captain William Vangeance
WHAT WERE YOU DOING, VANGEANCE?
AH... THERE WAS SOME BUSINESS I COULDN'T GET OUT OF.
GWEH HEH HEH
I EXPECT YOU ARE BUSY.
THE CHARISMATIC CAPTAIN OF THE BRIGADE THAT GOT THE MOST STARS THIS TERM..
I'D LOVE TO KNOW YOUR SECRET.
HOW DID YOU CLAW YOUR WAY UP TO BECOME THE STRONGEST BRIGADE SO VERY, VERY FAST?!
I HEAR THOSE WHO JOIN YOUR BRIGADE ALL DEVELOP POWERS BEYOND EXPECTATIONS.
DO YOU HAVE MAGIC THAT CAN SEE INDIVIDUALS' FUTURES?

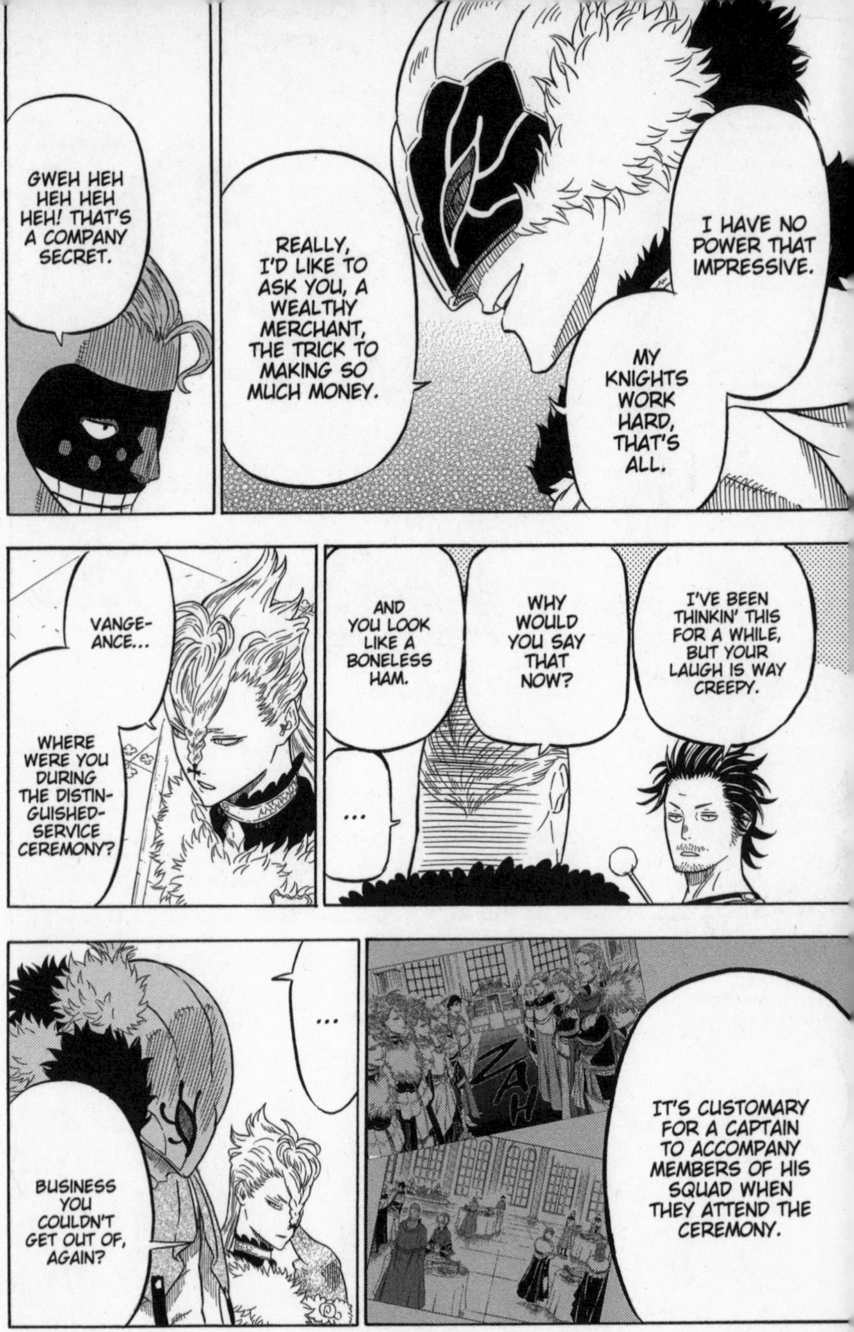
I HAVE NO POWER THAT IMPRESSIVE.
MY KNIGHTS WORK HARD, THAT'S ALL.
REALLY, I'D LIKE TO ASK YOU, A WEALTHY MERCHANT, THE TRICK TO MAKING SO MUCH MONEY.
GWEH HEH HEH HEH HEH! THAT'S A COMPANY SECRET.
I'VE BEEN THINKIN' THIS FOR A WHILE, BUT YOUR LAUGH IS WAY CREEPY.
WHY WOULD YOU SAY THAT NOW?
AND YOU LOOK LIKE A BONELESS HAM.
...
VANGE-ANCE...
WHERE WERE YOU DURING THE DISTIN-GUISHED-SERVICE CEREMONY?
IT'S CUSTOMARY FOR A CAPTAIN TO ACCOMPANY MEMBERS OF HIS SQUAD WHEN THEY ATTEND THE CEREMONY.
ZAH
...
BUSINESS YOU COULDN'T GET OUT OF, AGAIN?

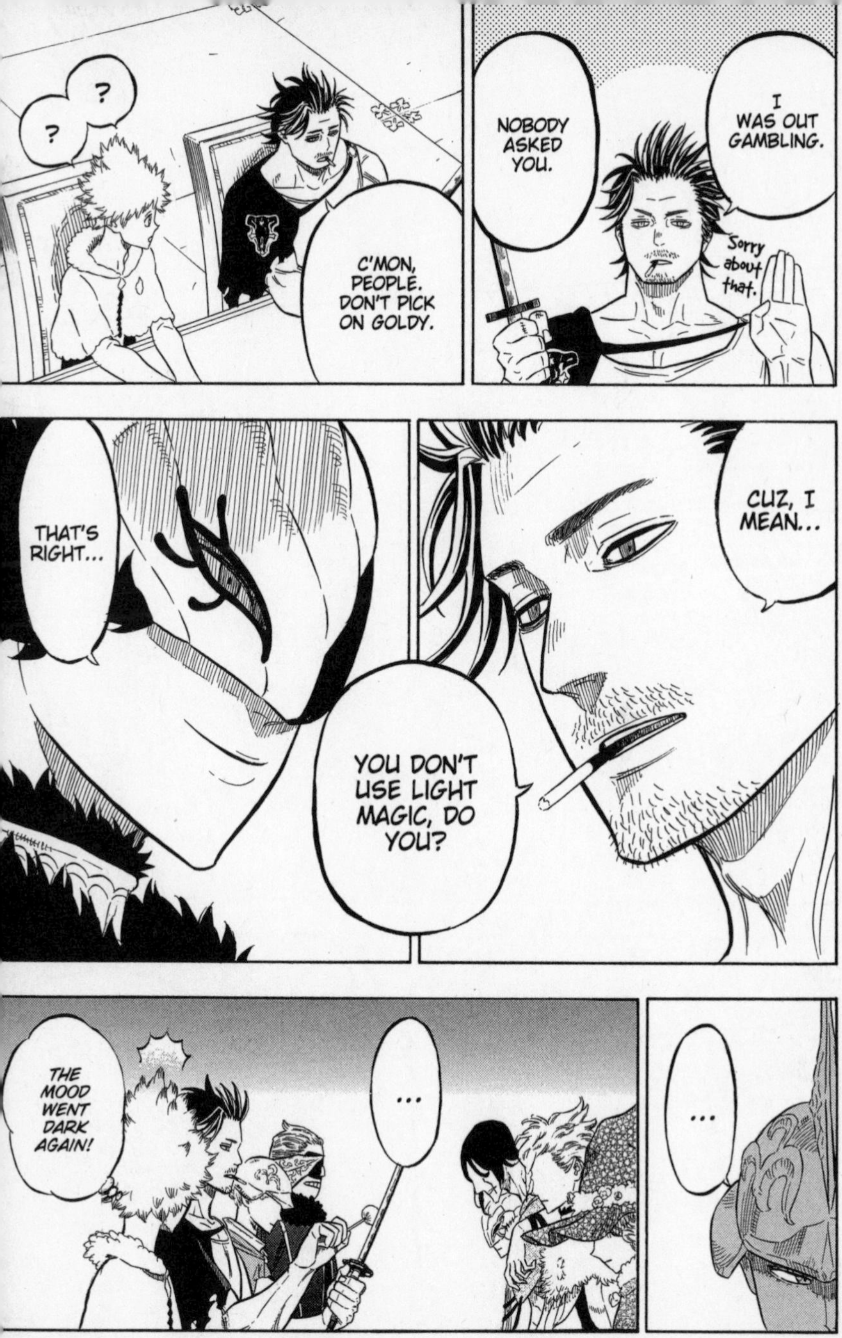
I WAS OUT GAMBLING.
Sorry about that.
NOBODY ASKED YOU.
C'MON, PEOPLE. DON'T PICK ON GOLDY.
? ?
CUZ, I MEAN...
YOU DON'T USE LIGHT MAGIC, DO YOU?
THAT'S RIGHT...
...
...
THE MOOD WENT DARK AGAIN!

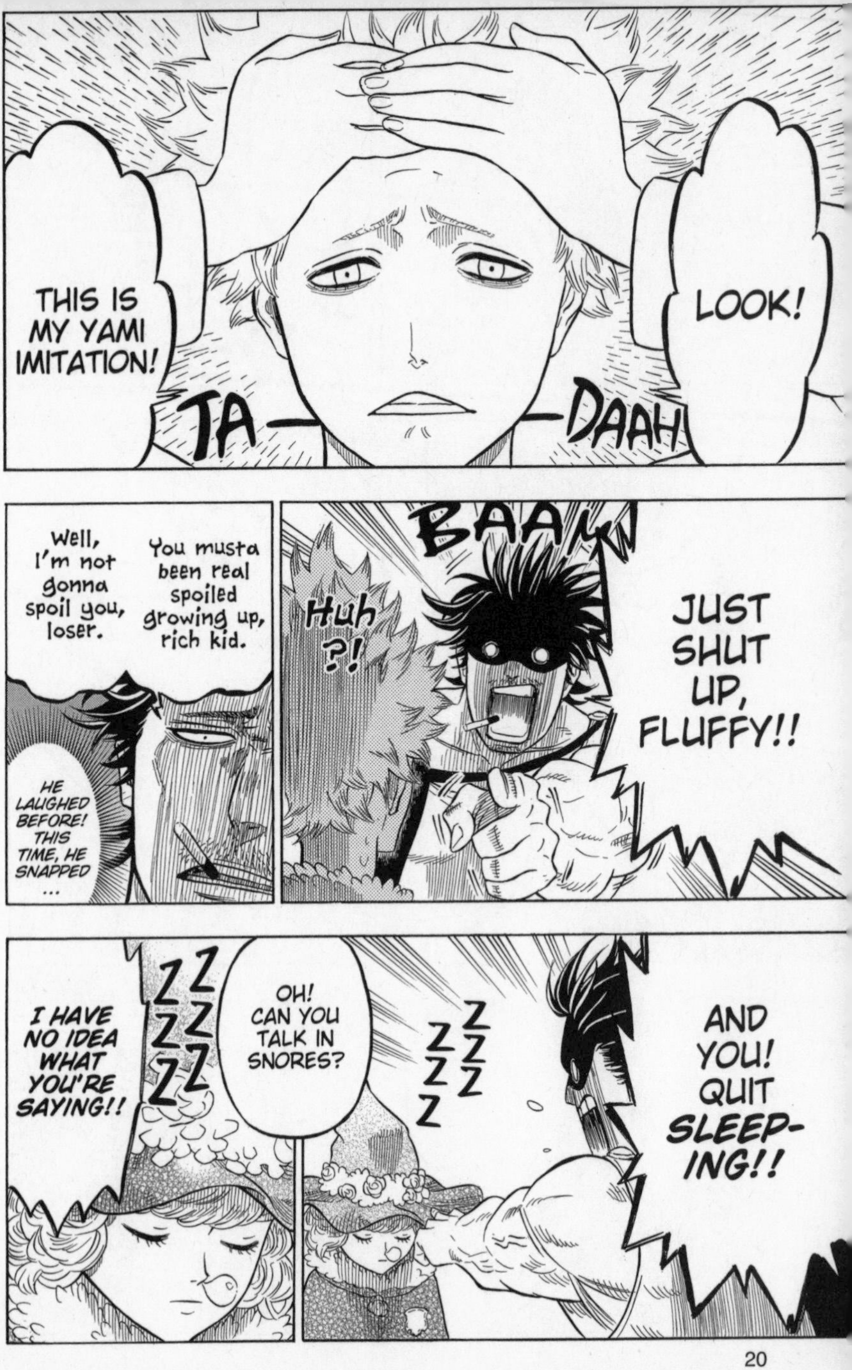
LOOK!
THIS IS MY YAMI IMITATION!
TA— —DAAH
BAAM
JUST SHUT UP, FLUFFY!!
Huh?!
You musta been real spoiled growing up, rich kid.
Well, I'm not gonna spoil you, loser.
HE LAUGHED BEFORE! THIS TIME, HE SNAPPED...
AND YOU! QUIT SLEEPING!!
ZZZZZZZ
OH! CAN YOU TALK IN SNORES?
ZZZZZZ
I HAVE NO IDEA WHAT YOU'RE SAYING!!

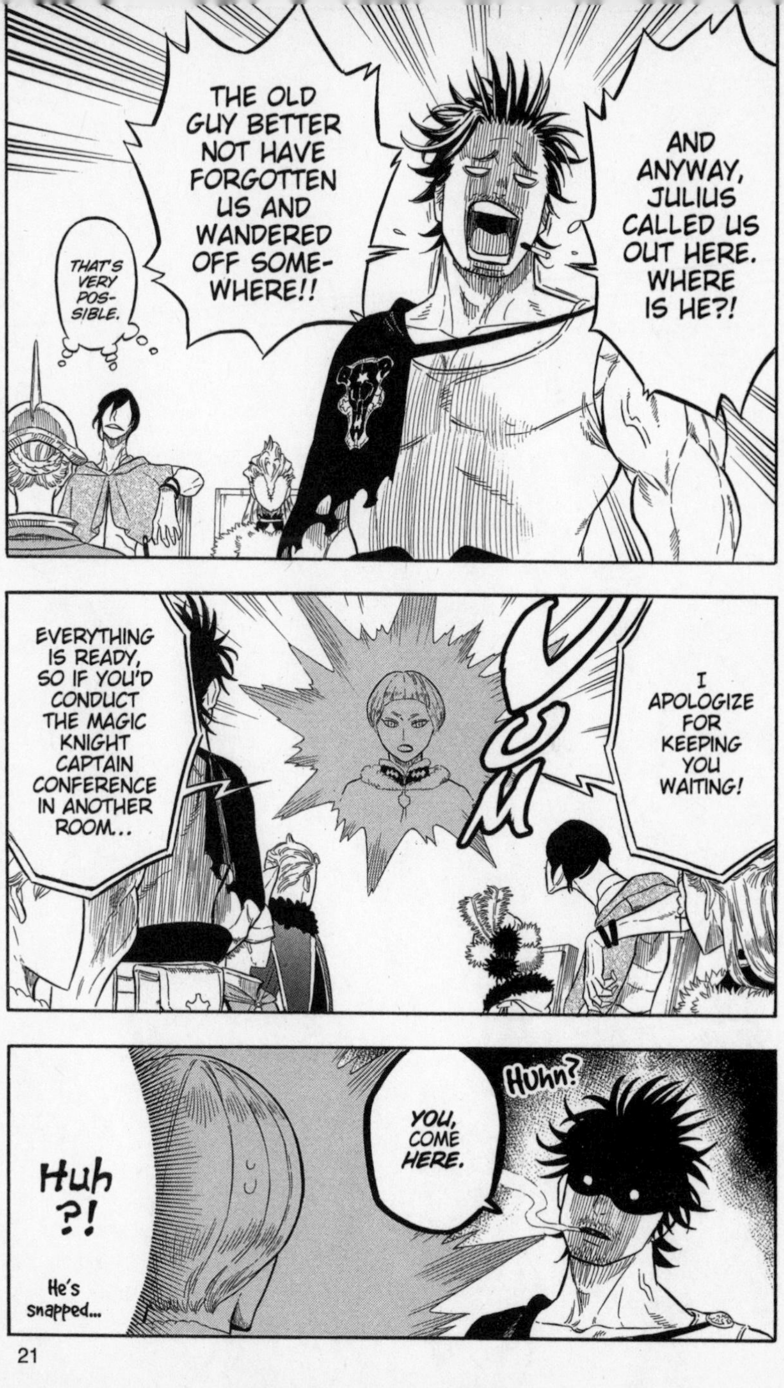
AND ANYWAY, JULIUS CALLED US OUT HERE. WHERE IS HE?!
THE OLD GUY BETTER NOT HAVE FORGOTTEN US AND WANDERED OFF SOME-WHERE!!
THAT'S VERY POS-SIBLE.
I APOLOGIZE FOR KEEPING YOU WAITING!
EVERYTHING IS READY, SO IF YOU'D CONDUCT THE MAGIC KNIGHT CAPTAIN CONFERENCE IN ANOTHER ROOM...
Huhn?
YOU, COME HERE.
Huh ?!
He's snapped...

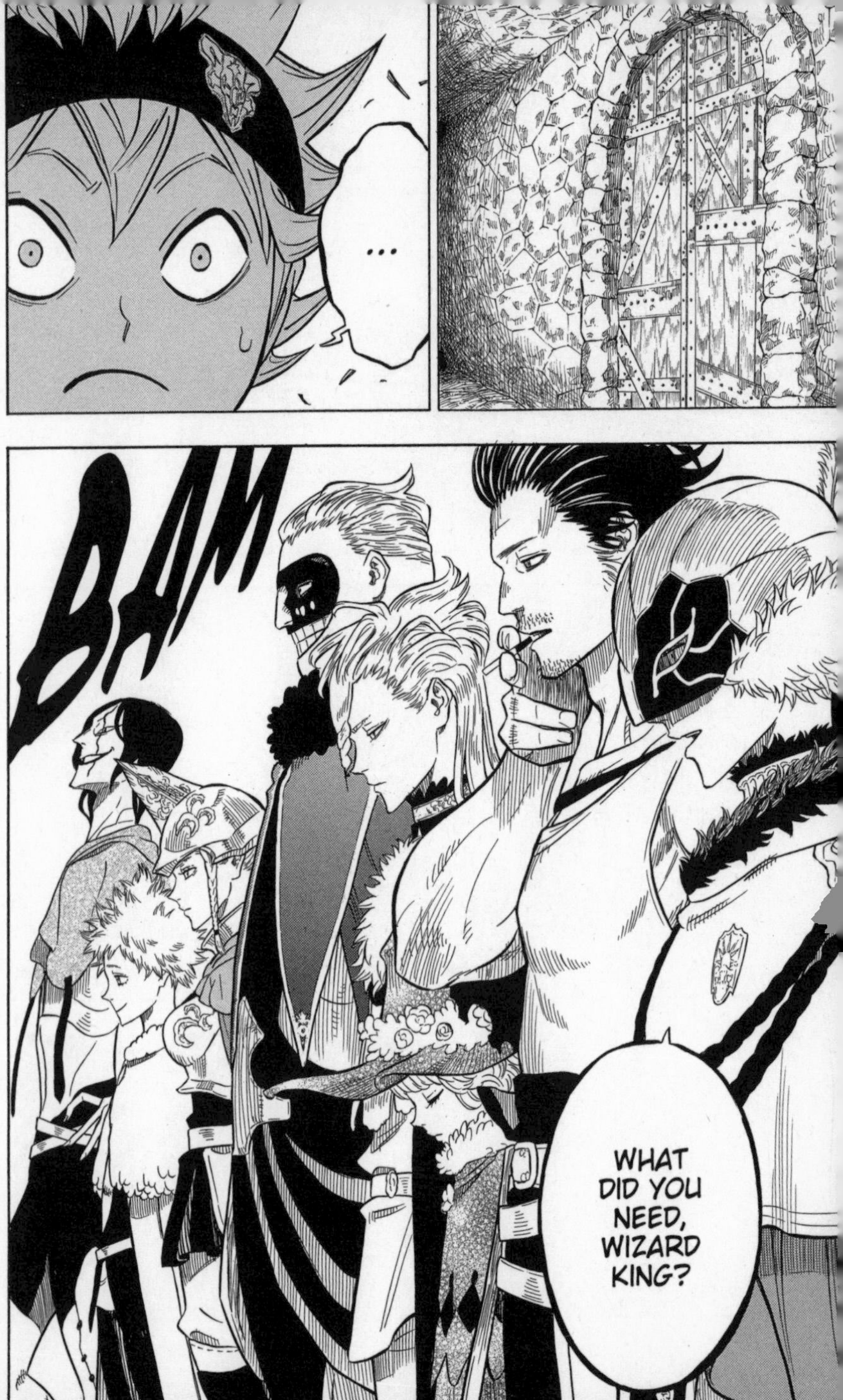
...
BAM
WHAT DID YOU NEED, WIZARD KING?

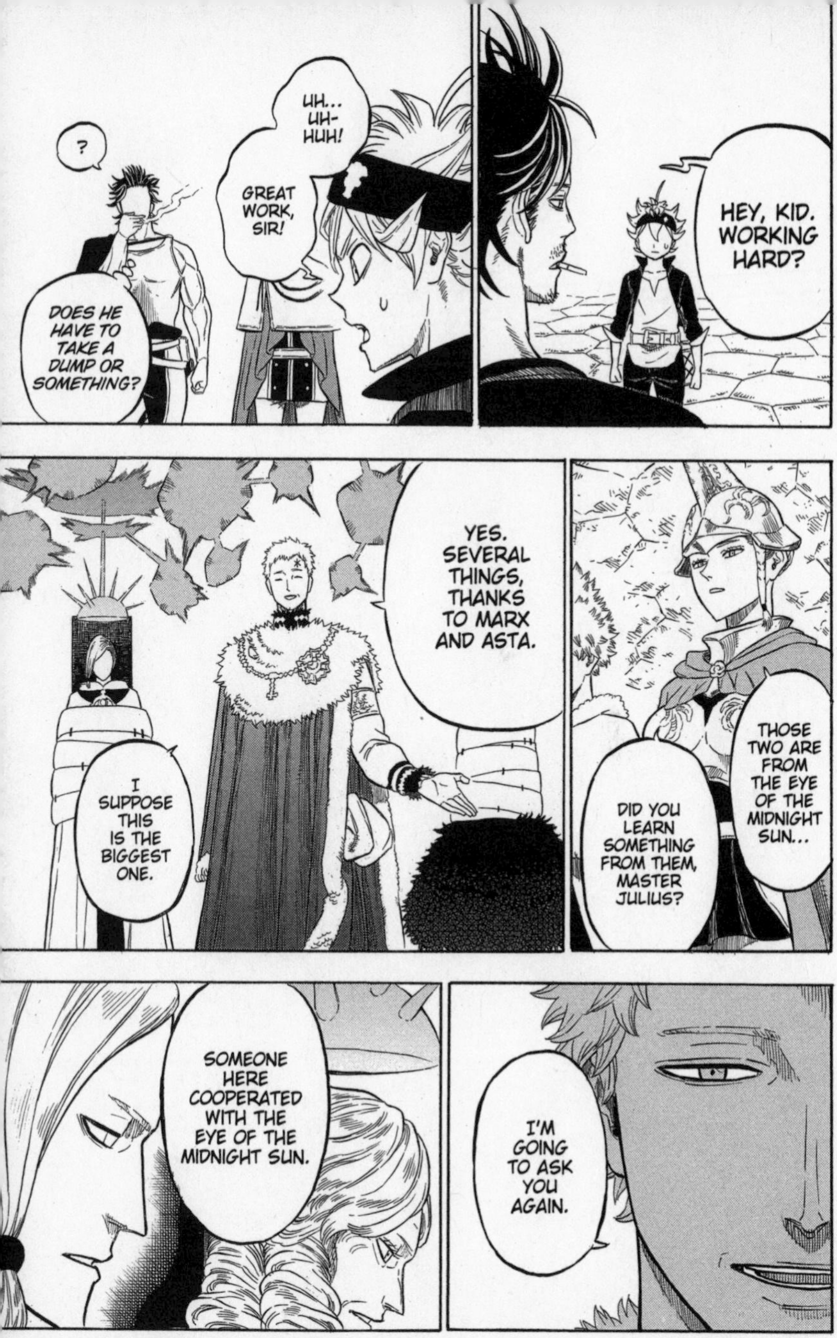
HEY, KID. WORKING HARD?
UH... UH-HUH!
GREAT WORK, SIR!
?
DOES HE HAVE TO TAKE A DUMP OR SOMETHING?
THOSE TWO ARE FROM THE EYE OF THE MIDNIGHT SUN...
DID YOU LEARN SOMETHING FROM THEM, MASTER JULIUS?
YES. SEVERAL THINGS, THANKS TO MARX AND ASTA.
I SUPPOSE THIS IS THE BIGGEST ONE.
I'M GOING TO ASK YOU AGAIN.
SOMEONE HERE COOPERATED WITH THE EYE OF THE MIDNIGHT SUN.

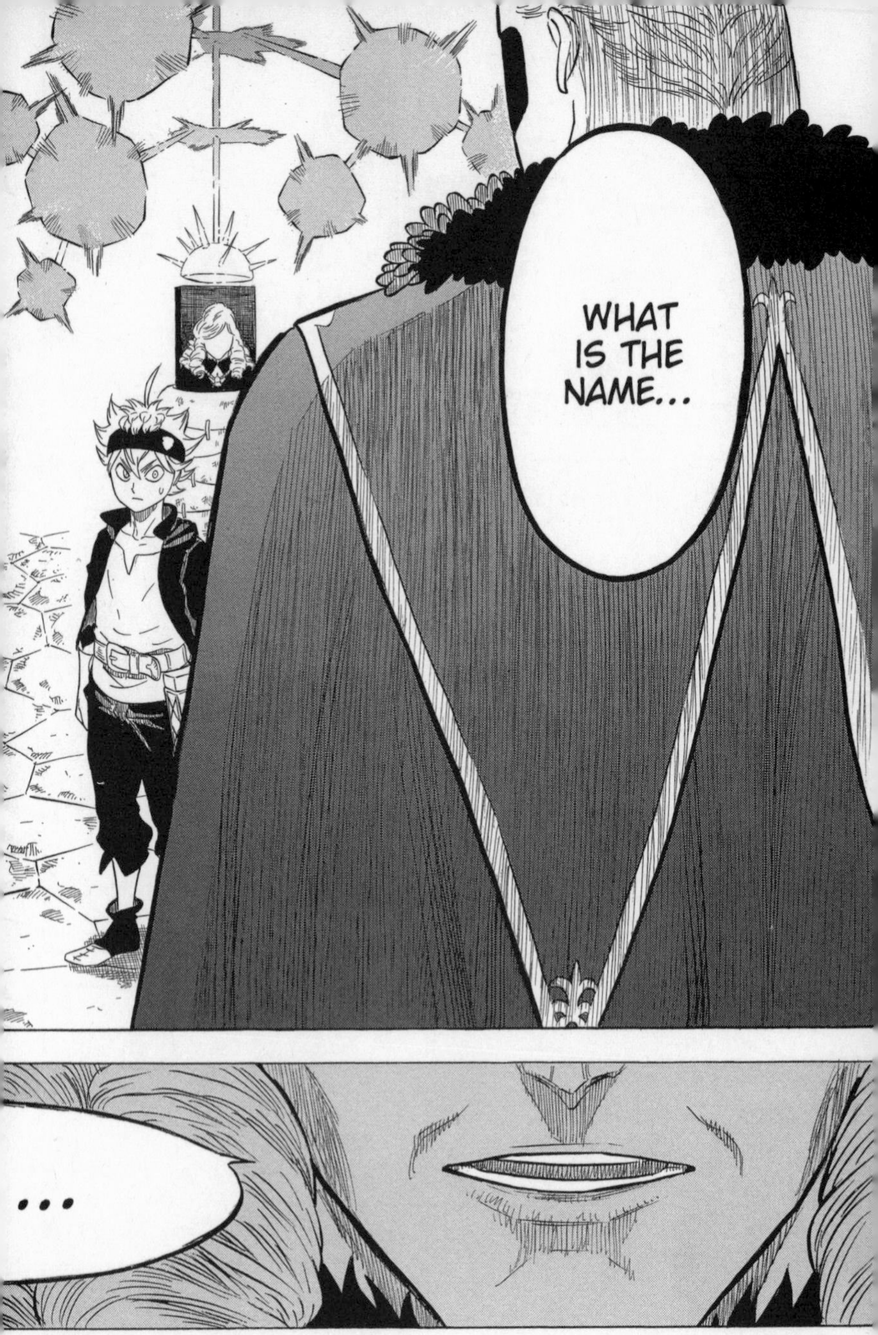
WHAT IS THE NAME...
...

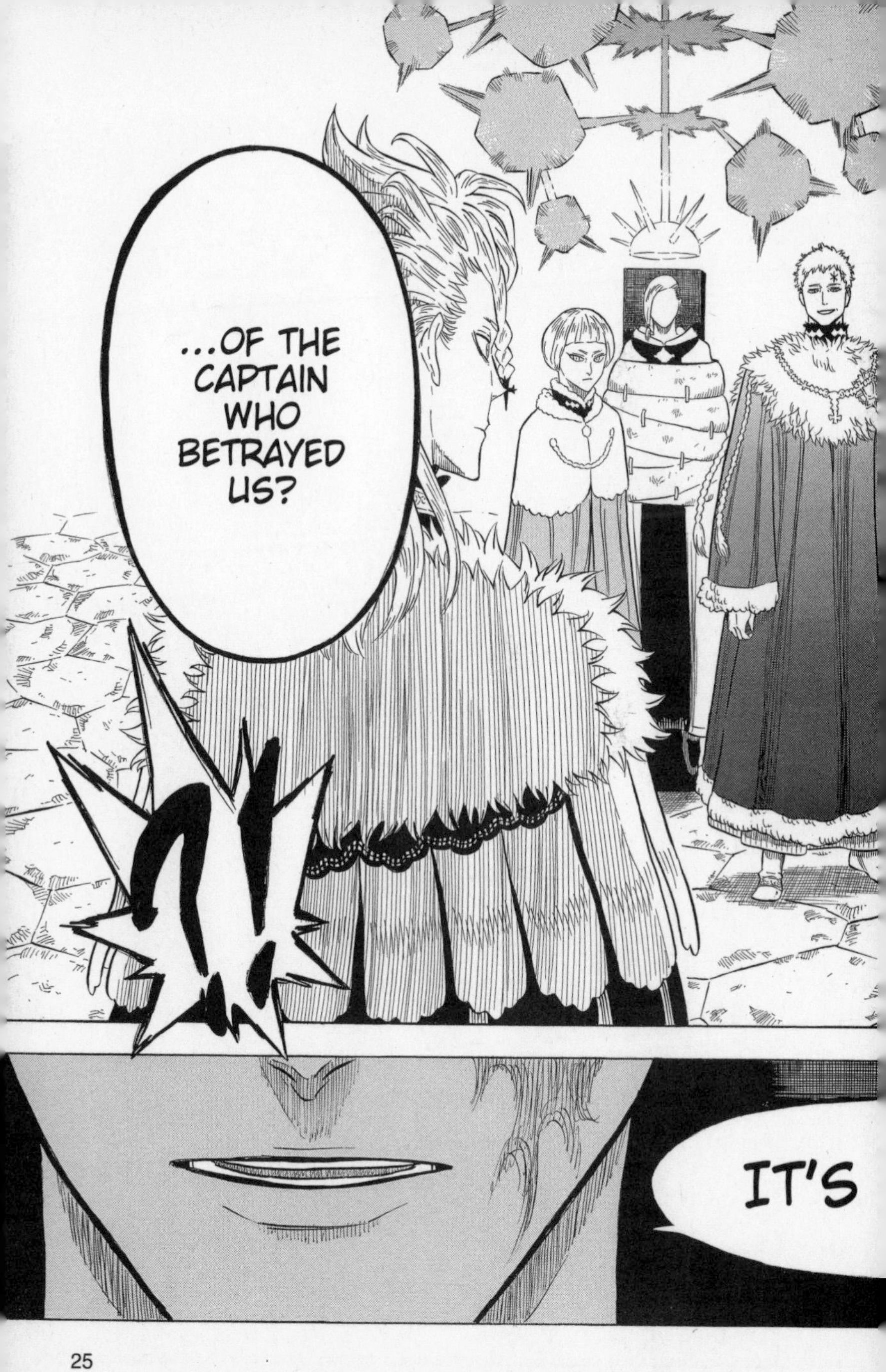
...OF THE CAPTAIN WHO BETRAYED US?
?!
IT'S

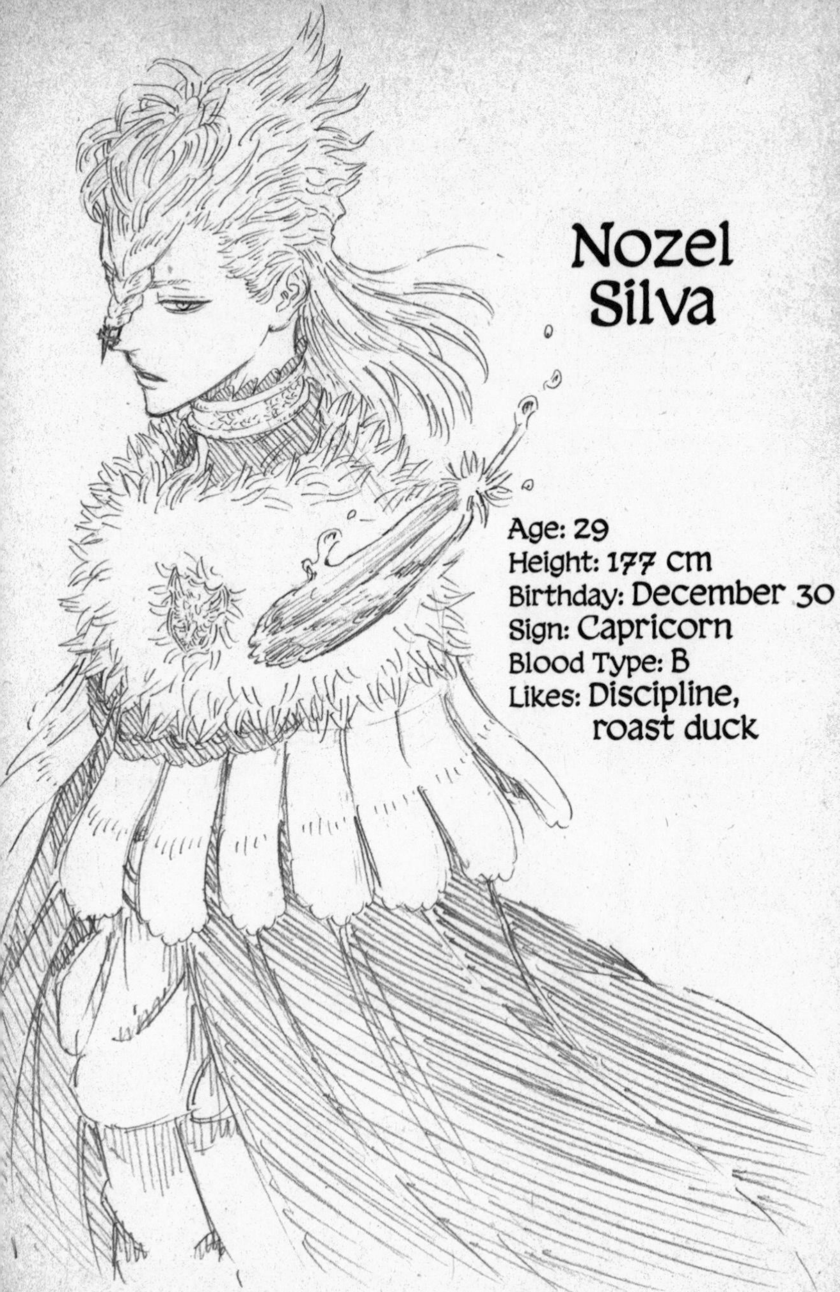

# Nozel Silva

Age: 29
Height: 177 cm
Birthday: December 30
Sign: Capricorn
Blood Type: B
Likes: Discipline, roast duck

Character Profile

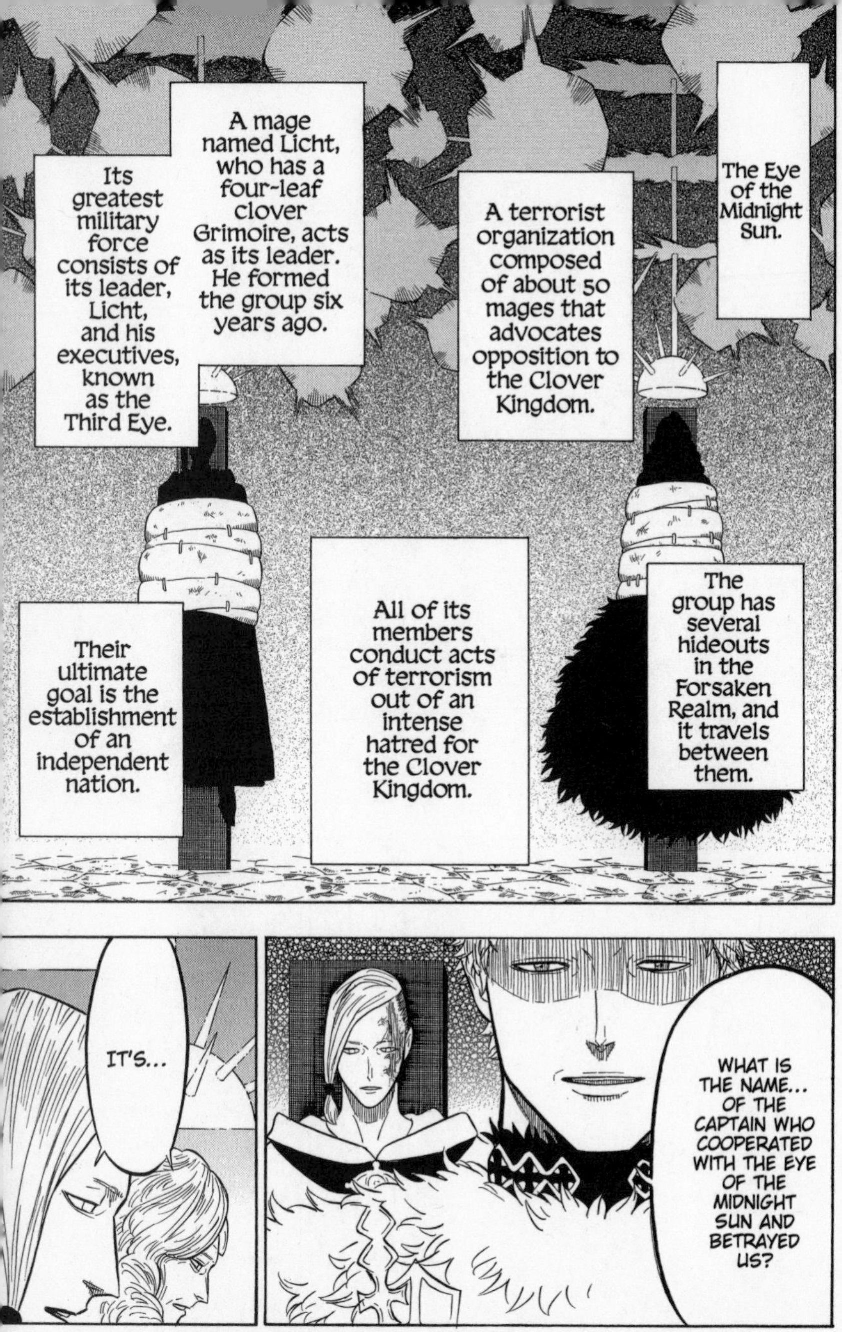
The Eye of the Midnight Sun.
A terrorist organization composed of about 50 mages that advocates opposition to the Clover Kingdom.
A mage named Licht, who has a four-leaf clover Grimoire, acts as its leader. He formed the group six years ago.
Its greatest military force consists of its leader, Licht, and his executives, known as the Third Eye.
The group has several hideouts in the Forsaken Realm, and it travels between them.
All of its members conduct acts of terrorism out of an intense hatred for the Clover Kingdom.
Their ultimate goal is the establishment of an independent nation.
WHAT IS THE NAME... OF THE CAPTAIN WHO COOPERATED WITH THE EYE OF THE MIDNIGHT SUN AND BETRAYED US?
IT'S...



✤ Page 55: The Captains and the Peasant Boy

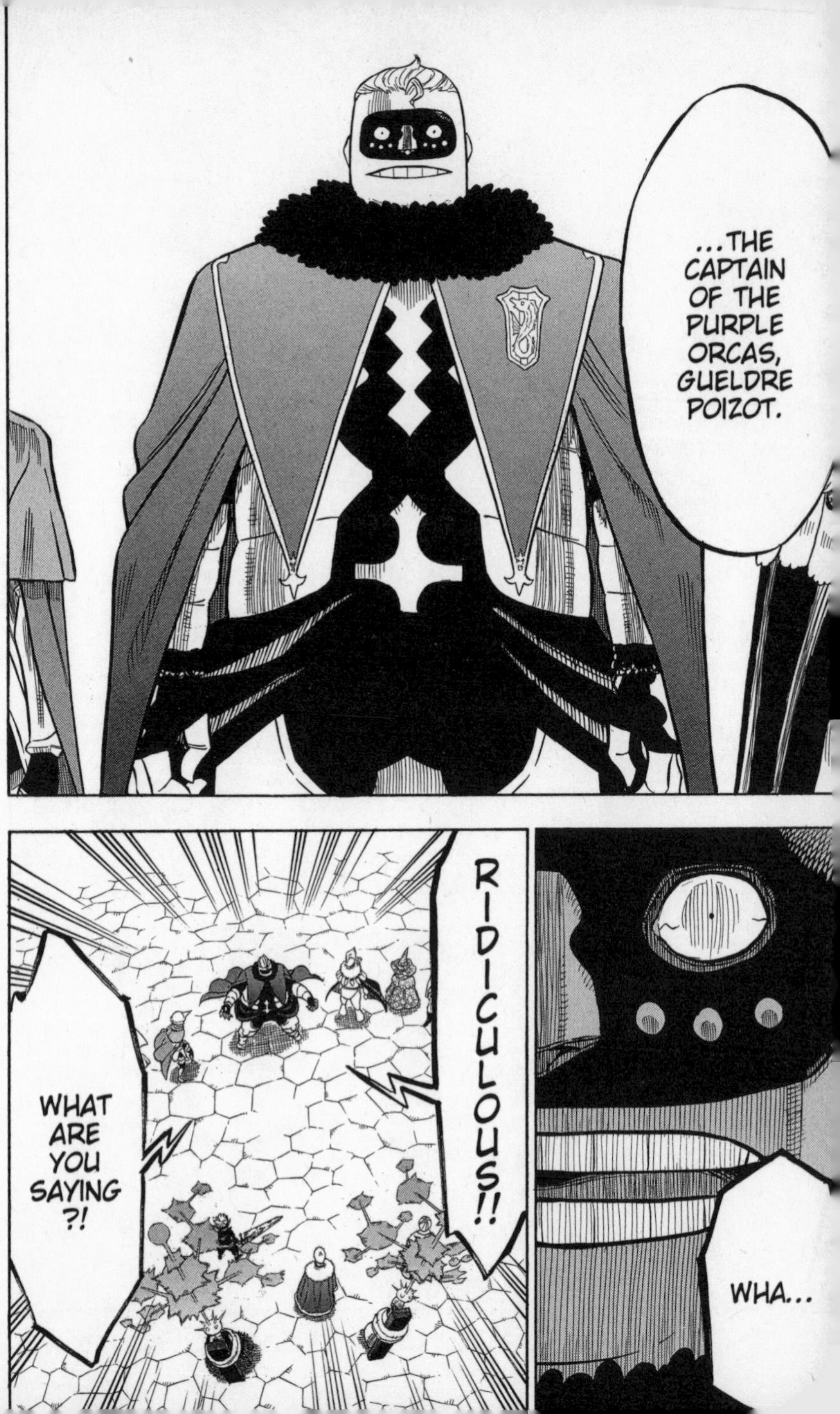
...THE CAPTAIN OF THE PURPLE ORCAS, GUELDRE POIZOT.
WHA...
RIDICULOUS!!
WHAT ARE YOU SAYING?!

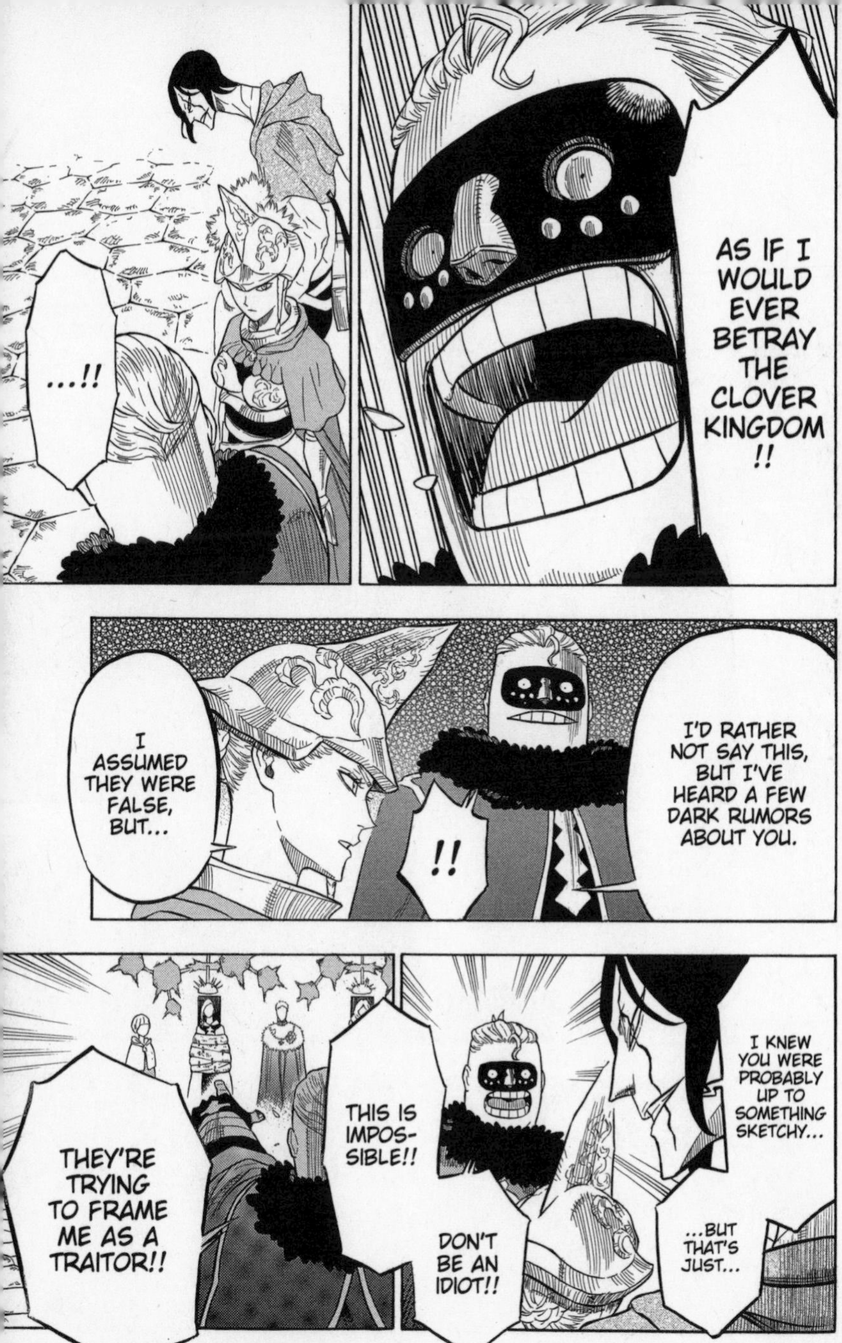
AS IF I WOULD EVER BETRAY THE CLOVER KINGDOM!!
...!!
I'D RATHER NOT SAY THIS, BUT I'VE HEARD A FEW DARK RUMORS ABOUT YOU.
!!
I ASSUMED THEY WERE FALSE, BUT...
I KNEW YOU WERE PROBABLY UP TO SOMETHING SKETCHY...
THIS IS IMPOS-SIBLE!!
...BUT THAT'S JUST...
DON'T BE AN IDIOT!!
THEY'RE TRYING TO FRAME ME AS A TRAITOR!!

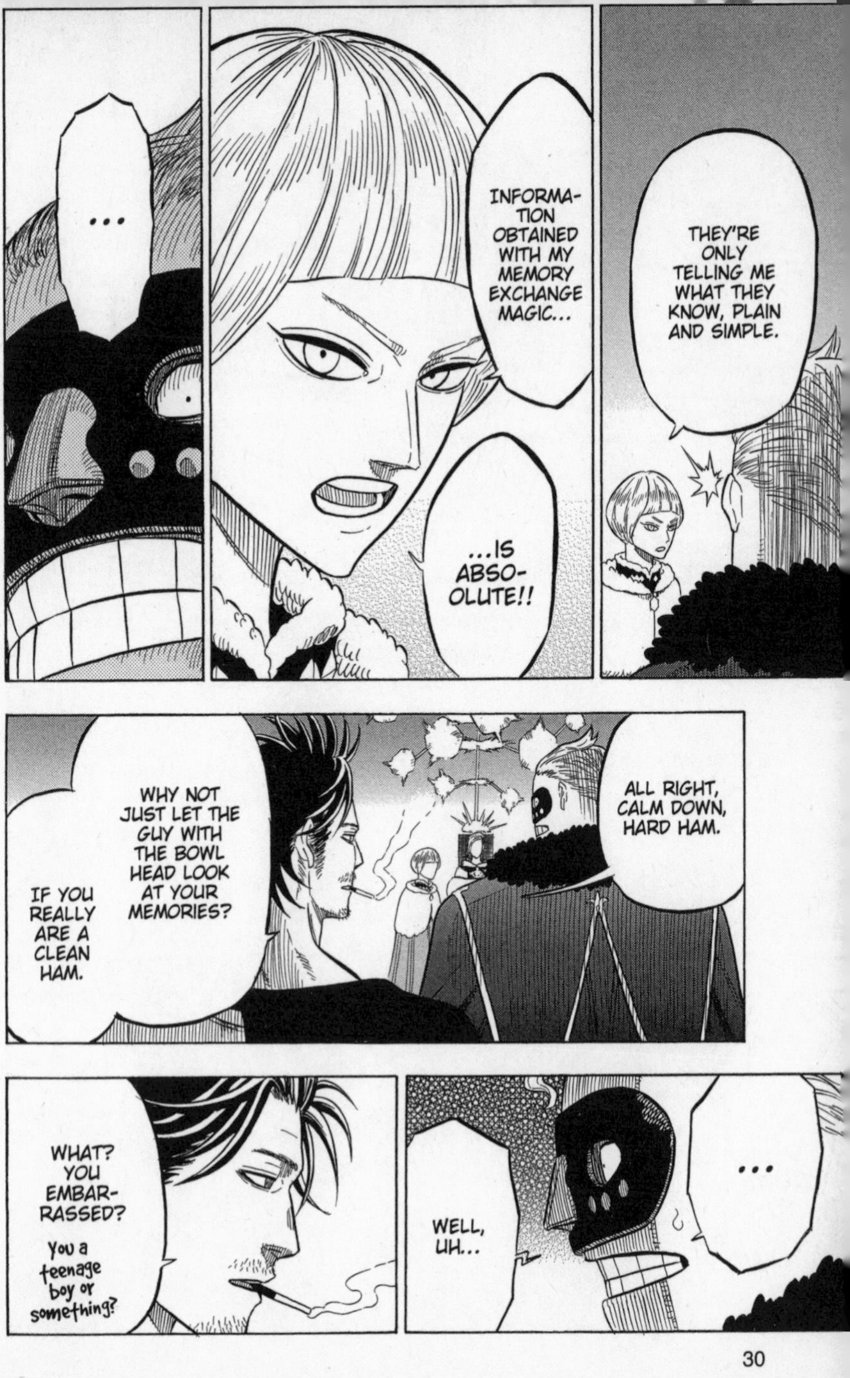
THEY'RE ONLY TELLING ME WHAT THEY KNOW, PLAIN AND SIMPLE.
INFORMATION OBTAINED WITH MY MEMORY EXCHANGE MAGIC...
...IS ABSOLUTE!!
...
ALL RIGHT, CALM DOWN, HARD HAM.
WHY NOT JUST LET THE GUY WITH THE BOWL HEAD LOOK AT YOUR MEMORIES?
IF YOU REALLY ARE A CLEAN HAM.
...
WELL, UH...
WHAT? YOU EMBARRASSED?
You a teenage boy or something?

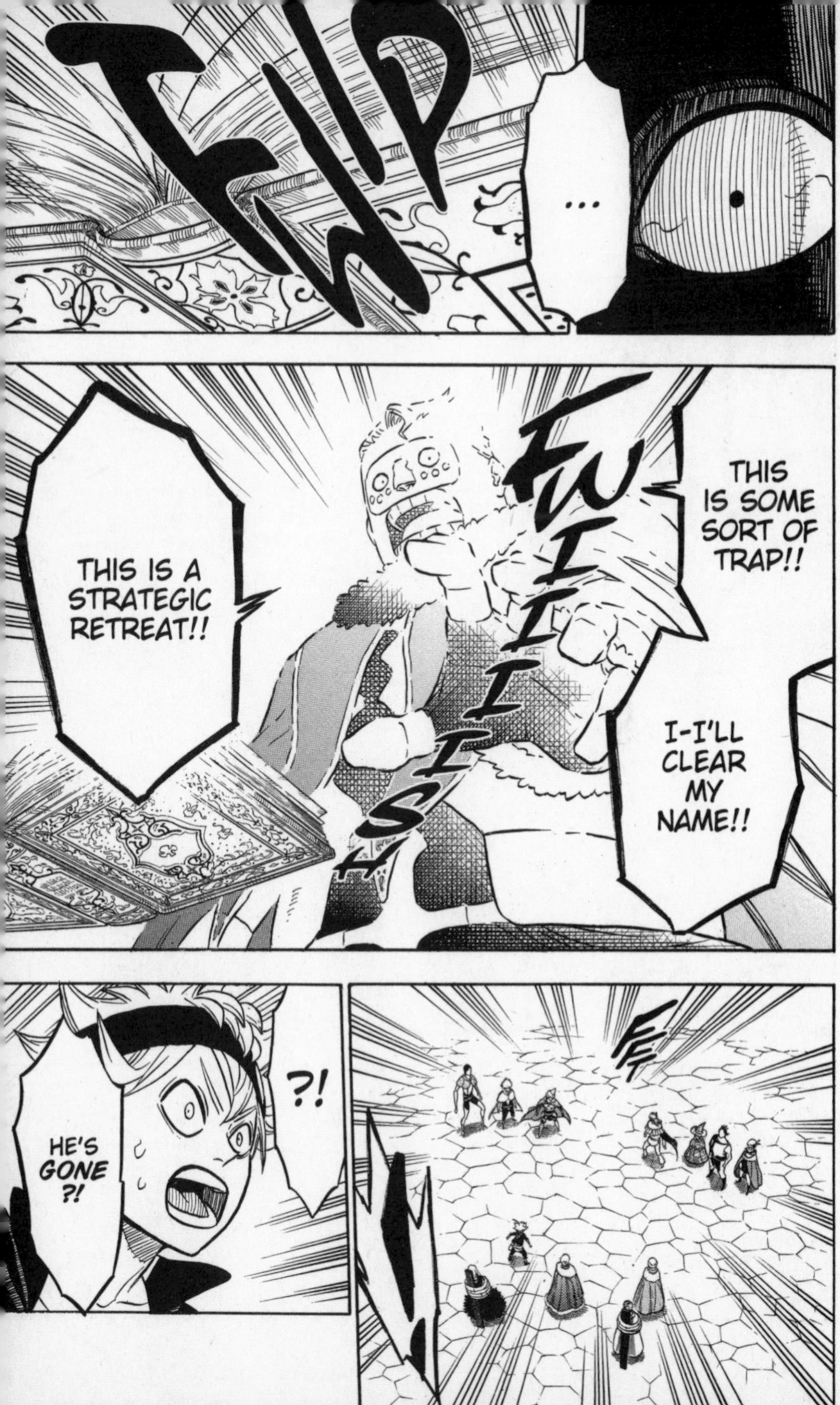
...
THUD
THIS IS SOME SORT OF TRAP!!
I-I'LL CLEAR MY NAME!!
FWIIIIISH
THIS IS A STRATEGIC RETREAT!!
?!
HE'S GONE?!

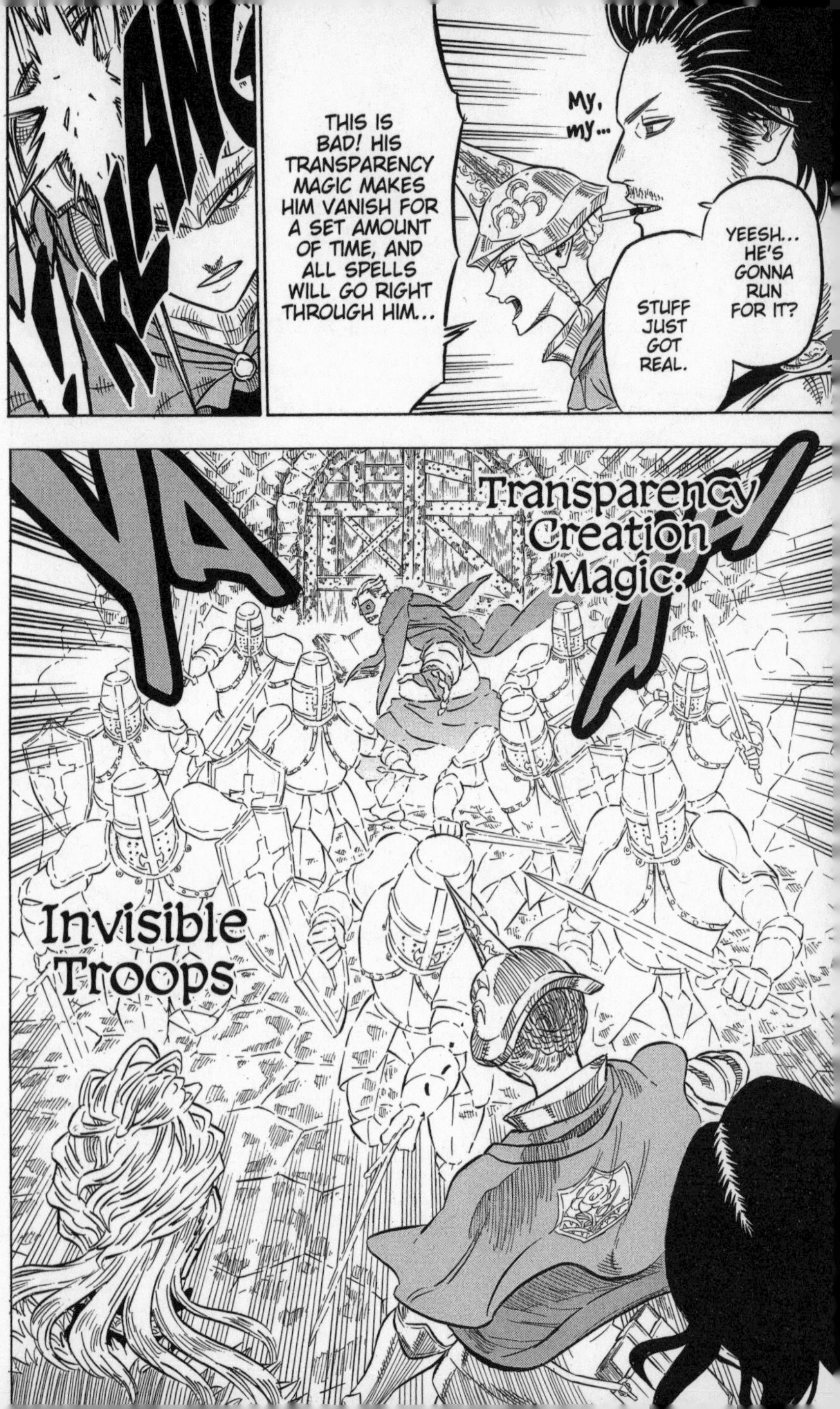
My, my...
THIS IS BAD! HIS TRANSPARENCY MAGIC MAKES HIM VANISH FOR A SET AMOUNT OF TIME, AND ALL SPELLS WILL GO RIGHT THROUGH HIM...
YEESH... HE'S GONNA RUN FOR IT?
STUFF JUST GOT REAL.
Transparency Creation Magic:
Invisible Troops

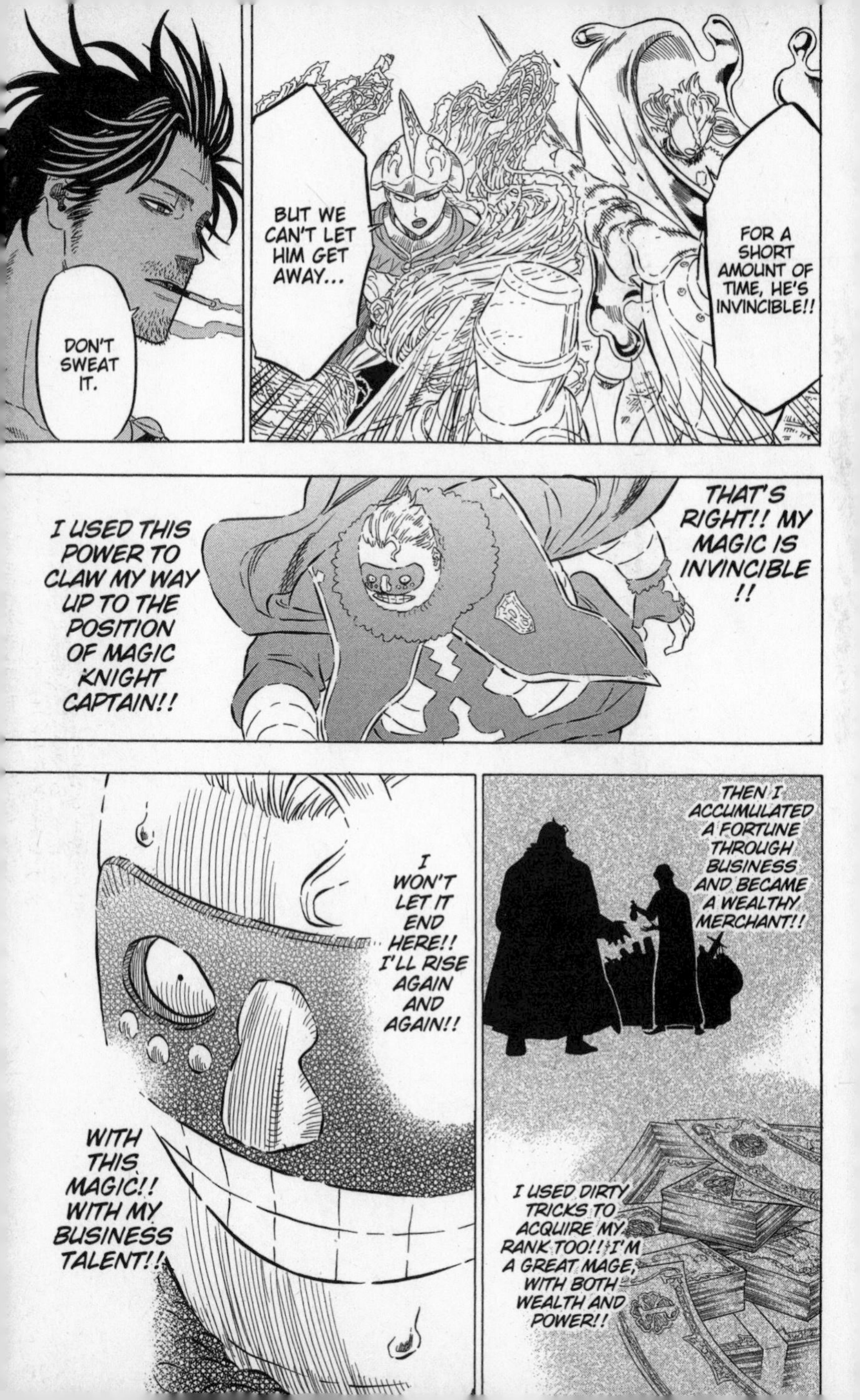
FOR A SHORT AMOUNT OF TIME, HE'S INVINCIBLE!!
BUT WE CAN'T LET HIM GET AWAY...
DON'T SWEAT IT.
THAT'S RIGHT!! MY MAGIC IS INVINCIBLE!!
I USED THIS POWER TO CLAW MY WAY UP TO THE POSITION OF MAGIC KNIGHT CAPTAIN!!
THEN I ACCUMULATED A FORTUNE THROUGH BUSINESS AND BECAME A WEALTHY MERCHANT!!
I USED DIRTY TRICKS TO ACQUIRE MY RANK TOO!! I'M A GREAT MAGE, WITH BOTH WEALTH AND POWER!!
I WON'T LET IT END HERE!! I'LL RISE AGAIN AND AGAIN!!
WITH THIS MAGIC!! WITH MY BUSINESS TALENT!!

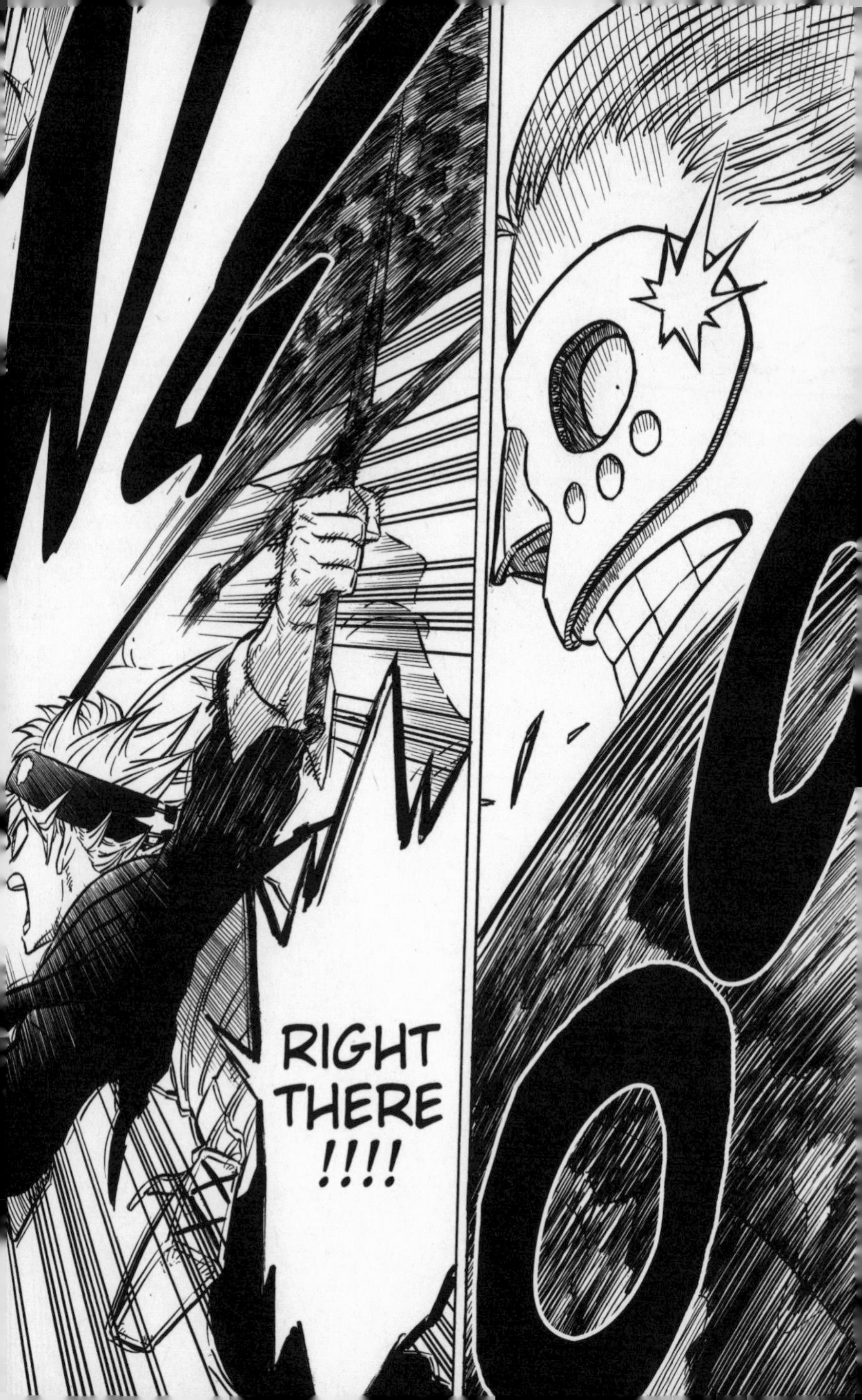
RIGHT THERE !!!!

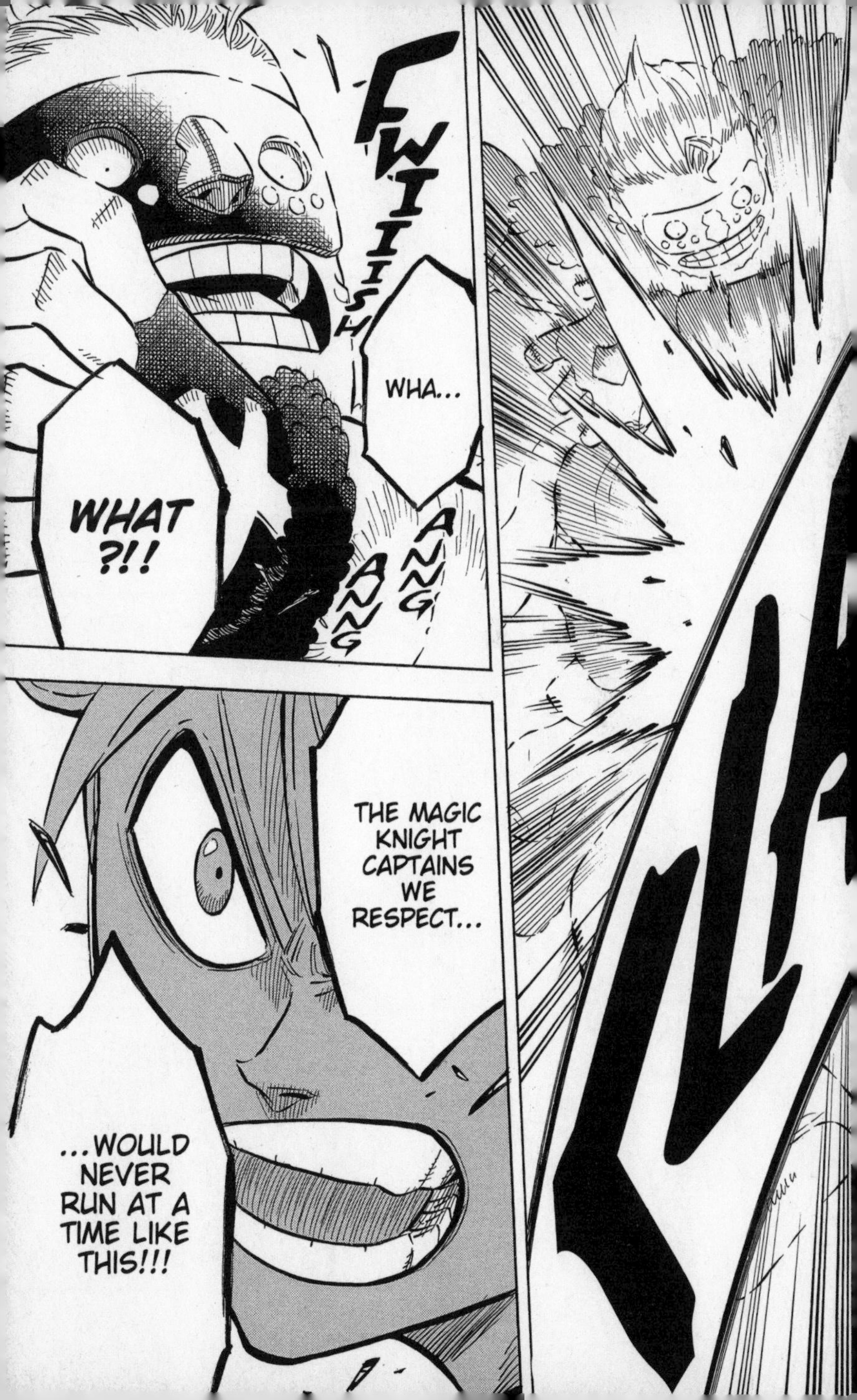
FWIIIISH
WHA...
ANNG
ANNG
WHAT?!!
THE MAGIC KNIGHT CAPTAINS WE RESPECT...
...WOULD NEVER RUN AT A TIME LIKE THIS!!!

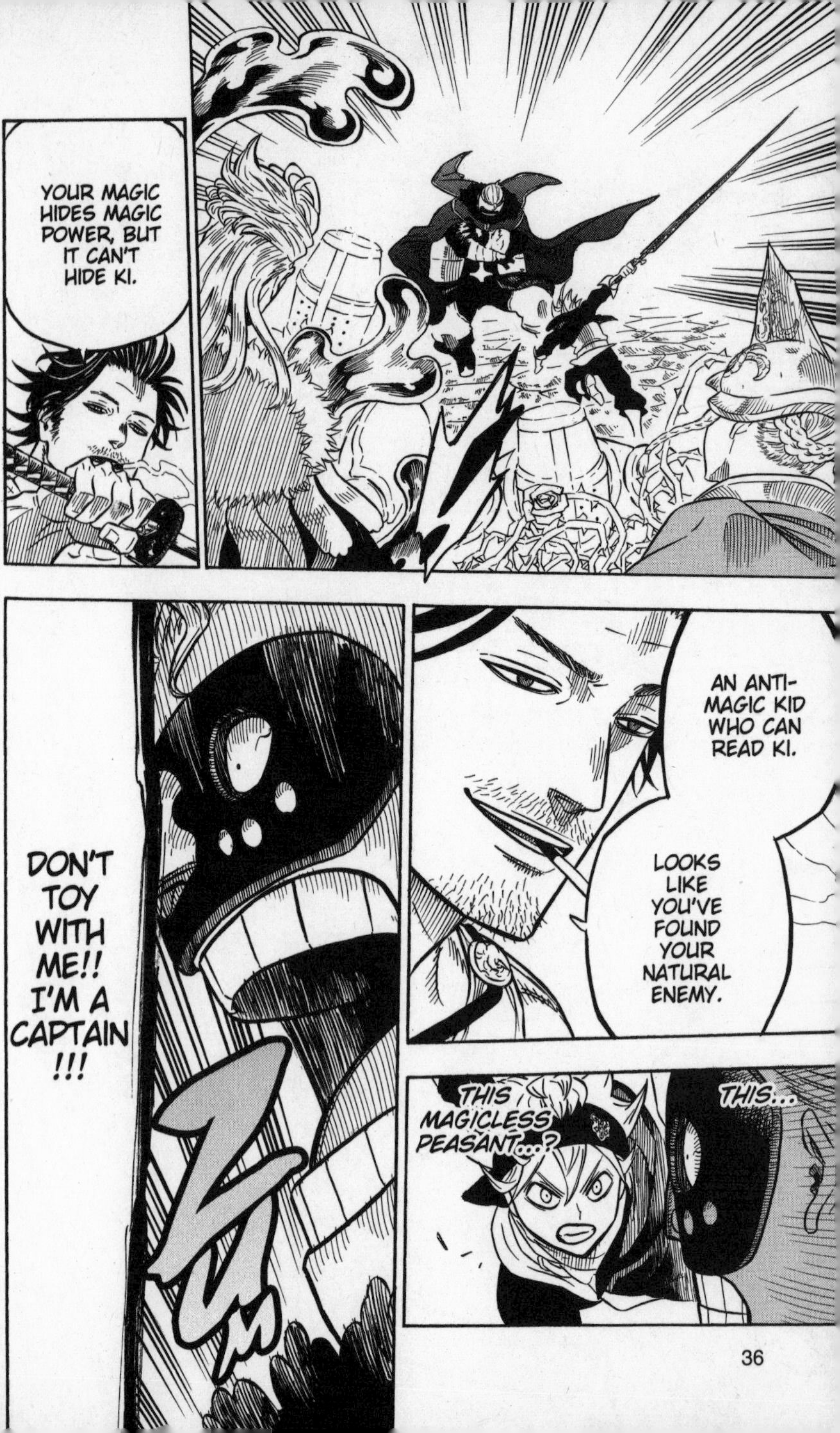
YOUR MAGIC HIDES MAGIC POWER, BUT IT CAN'T HIDE KI.
AN ANTI-MAGIC KID WHO CAN READ KI.
LOOKS LIKE YOU'VE FOUND YOUR NATURAL ENEMY.
THIS...
THIS MAGICLESS PEASANT...?
DON'T TOY WITH ME!! I'M A CAPTAIN!!!

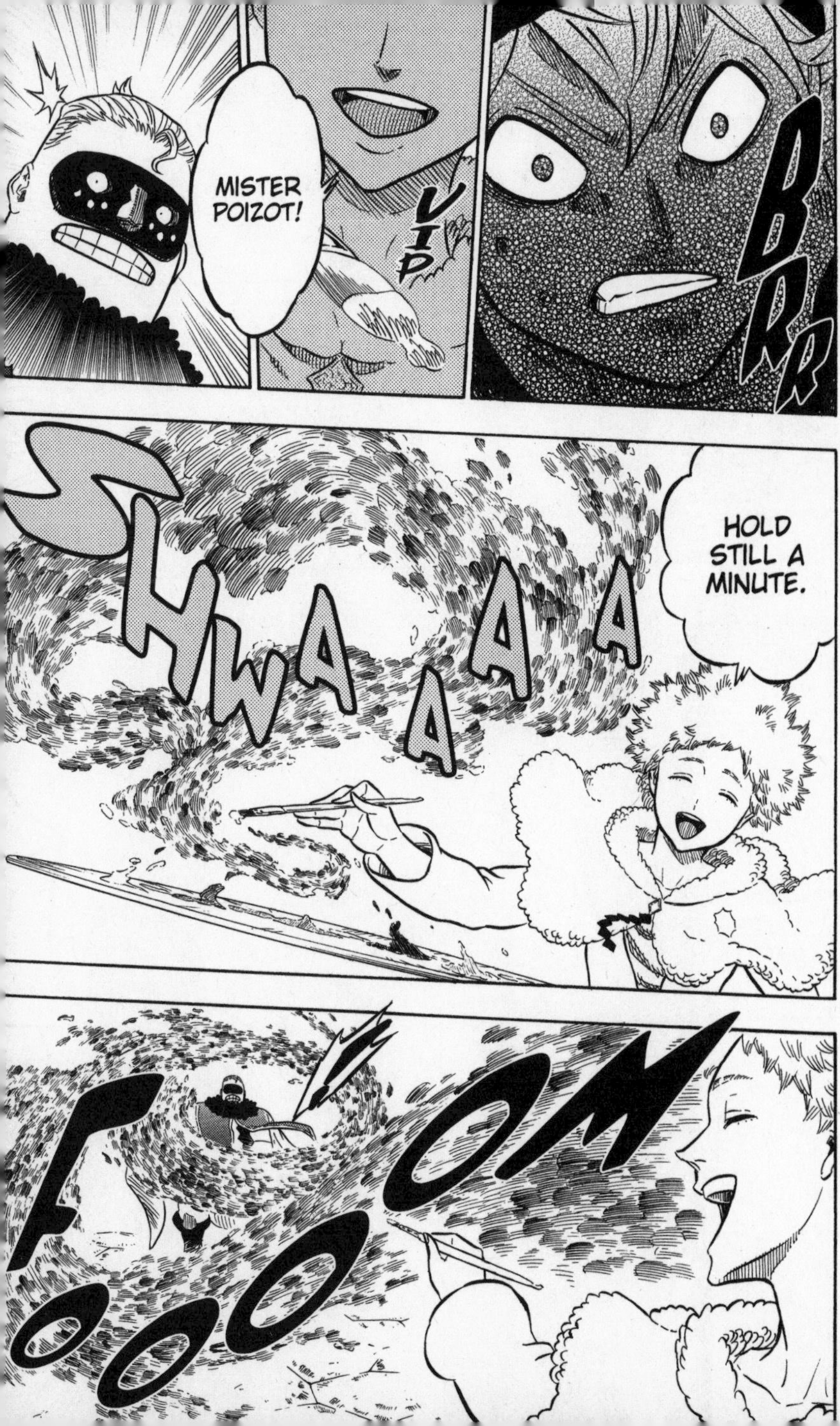
BRRR
VIP
MISTER POIZOT!
HOLD STILL A MINUTE.
SHWAAAAA
FOOOOOM

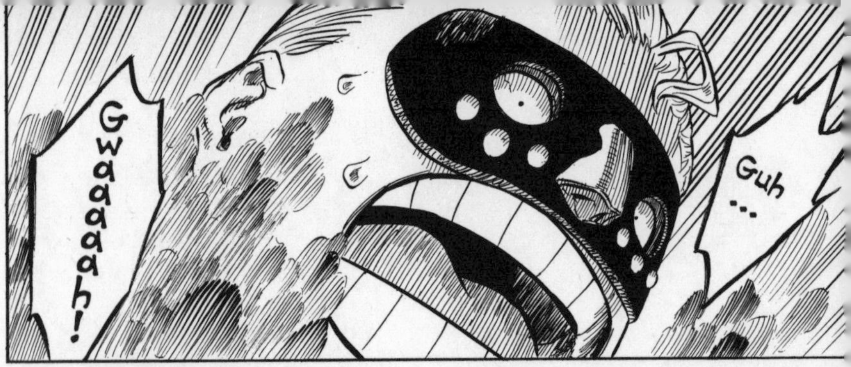
Guh...
Gwaaaaah!

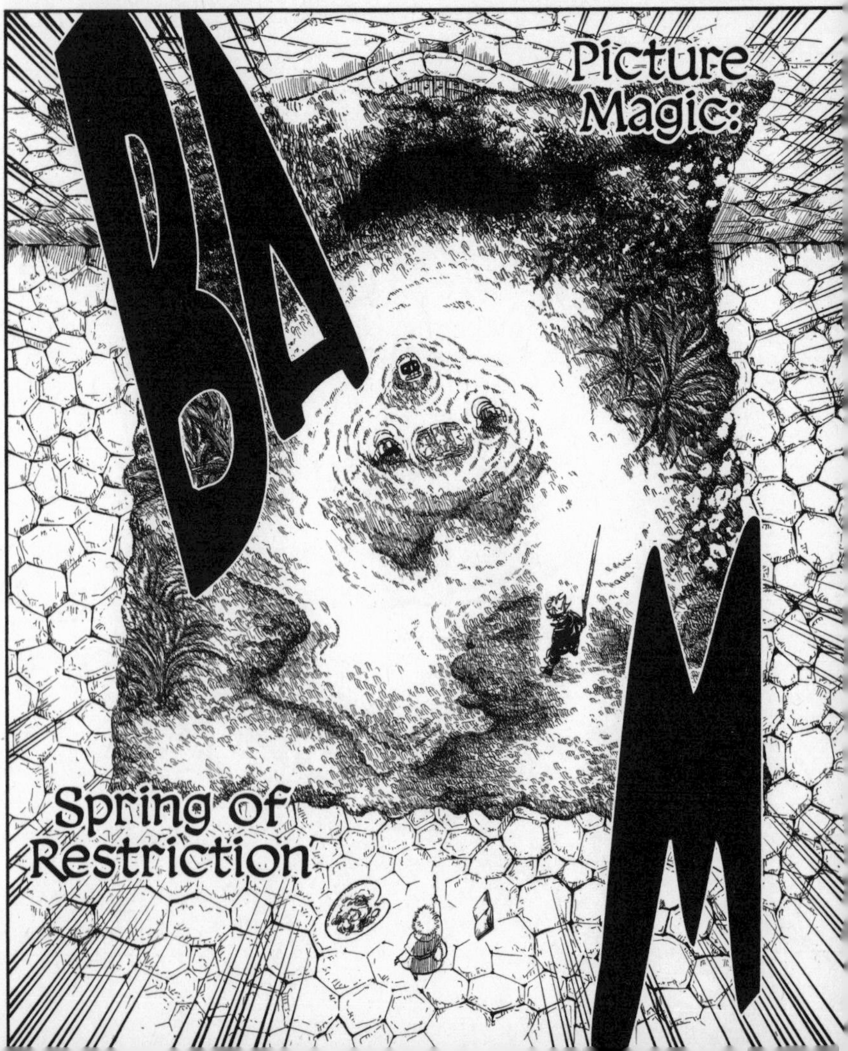
Picture Magic:
Spring of Restriction
BAM

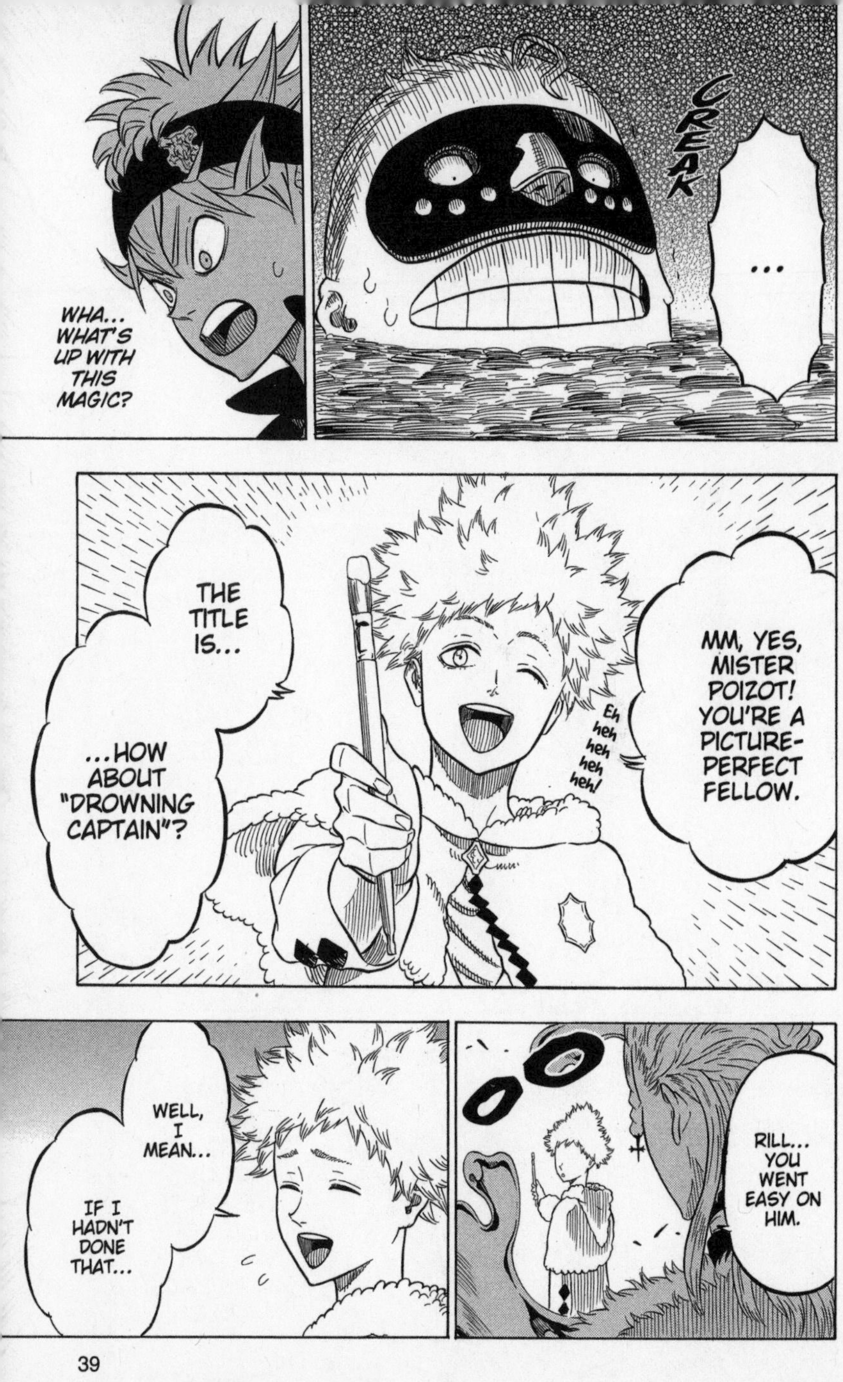
CREAK
...
WHA... WHAT'S UP WITH THIS MAGIC?
MM, YES, MISTER POIZOT! YOU'RE A PICTURE-PERFECT FELLOW.
Eh heh heh heh heh!
THE TITLE IS...
...HOW ABOUT "DROWNING CAPTAIN"?
RILL... YOU WENT EASY ON HIM.
WELL, I MEAN...
IF I HADN'T DONE THAT...

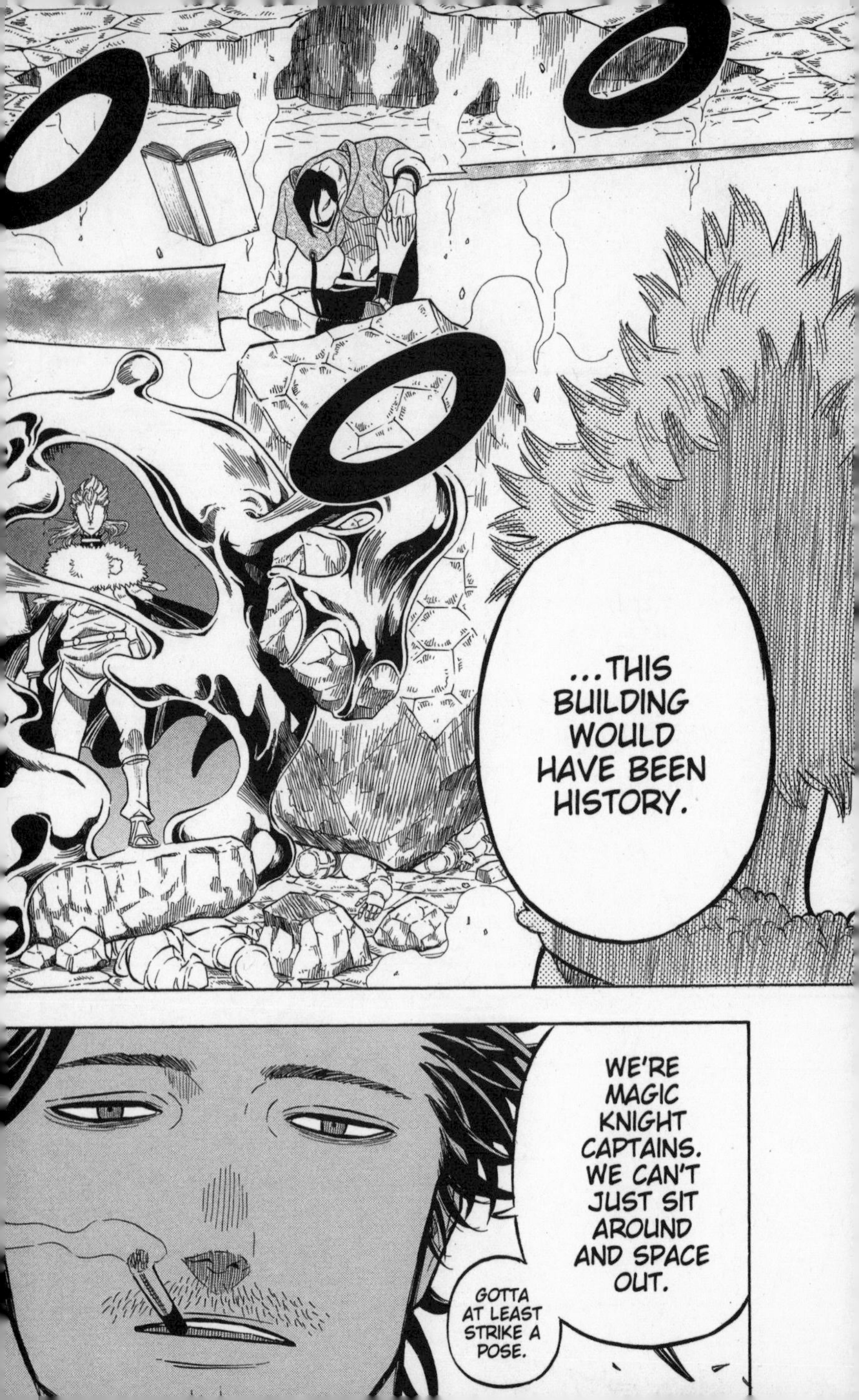
...THIS BUILDING WOULD HAVE BEEN HISTORY.
WE'RE MAGIC KNIGHT CAPTAINS. WE CAN'T JUST SIT AROUND AND SPACE OUT.
GOTTA AT LEAST STRIKE A POSE.

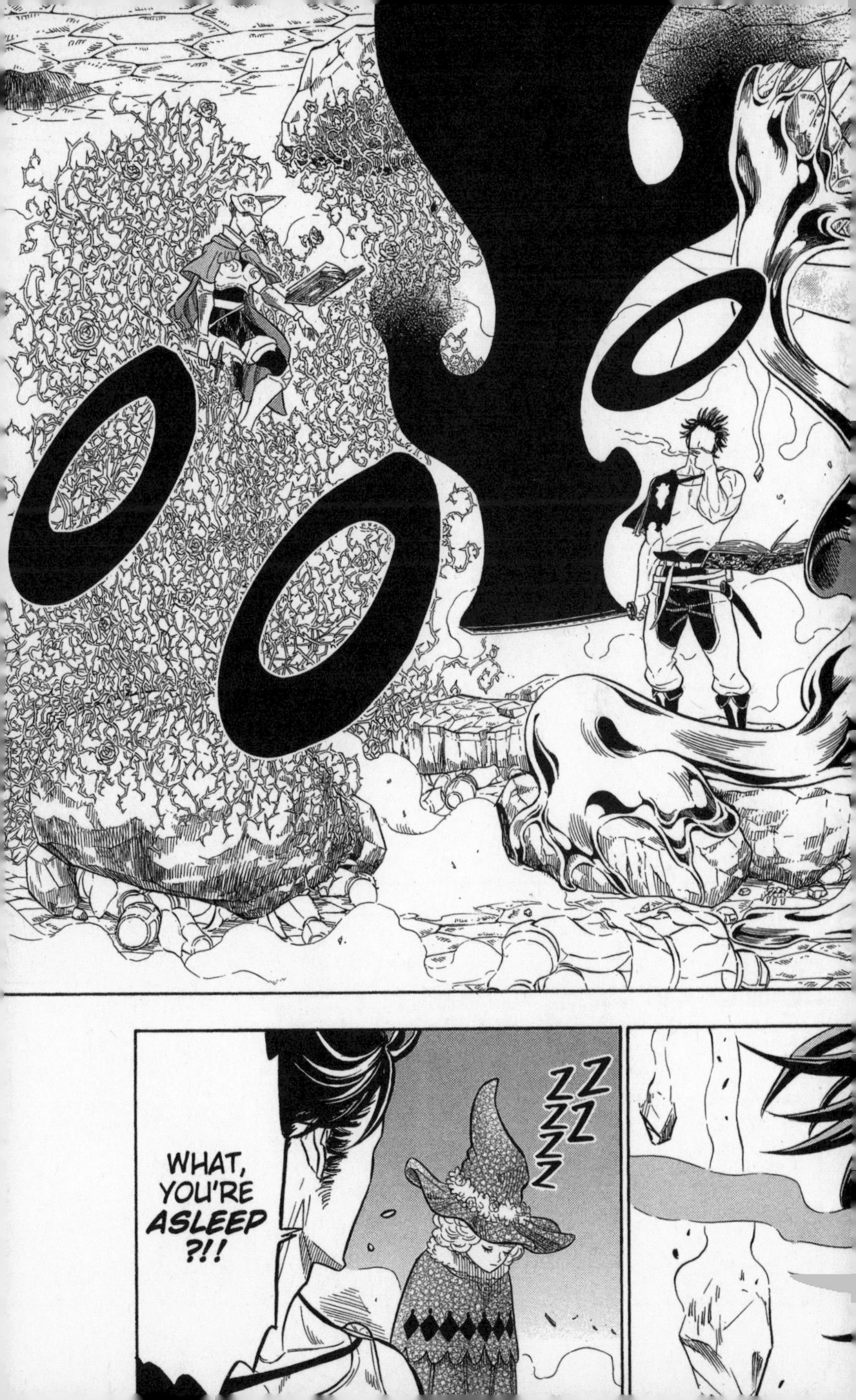
ZZZZZZ
WHAT, YOU'RE ASLEEP ?!!

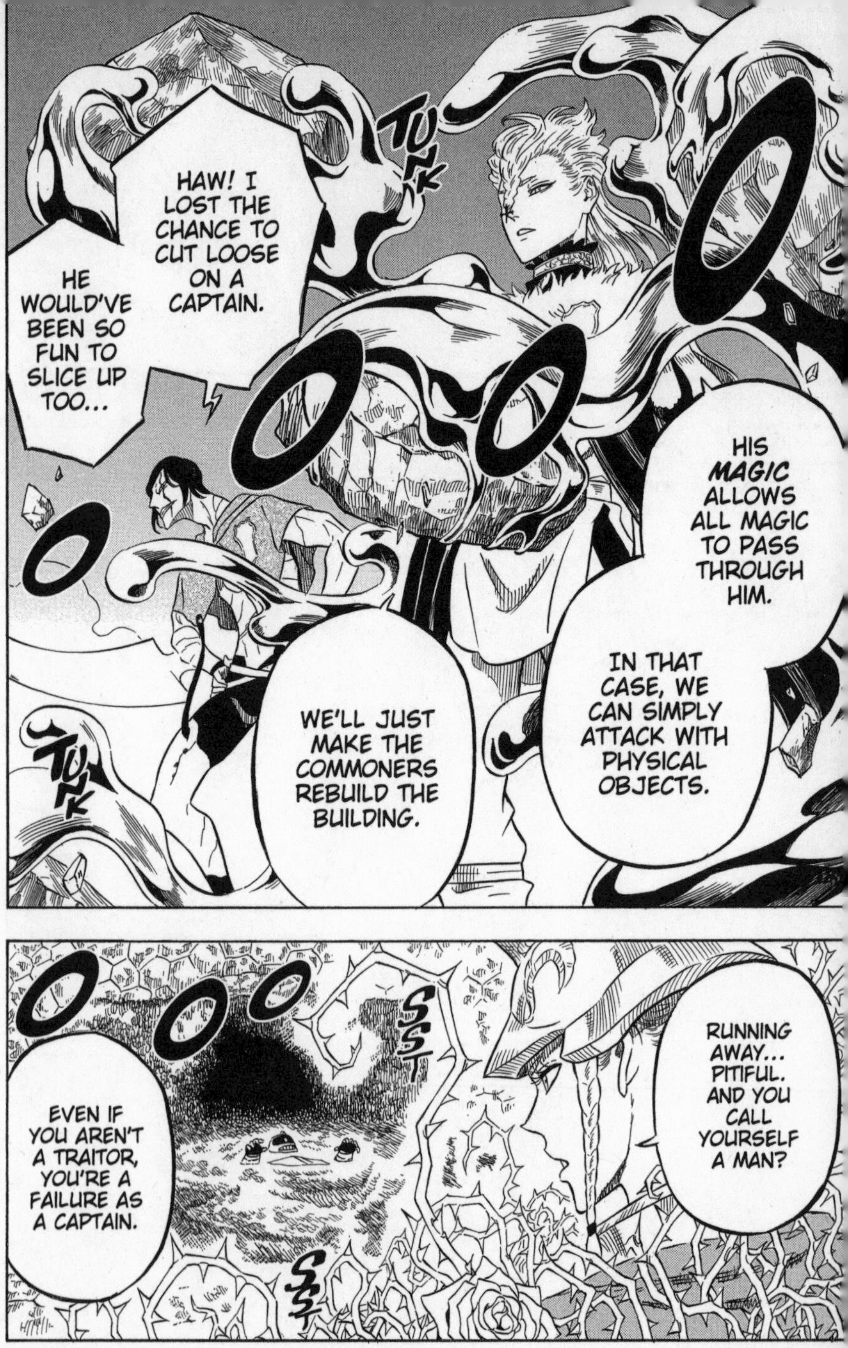
TUNK
HIS MAGIC ALLOWS ALL MAGIC TO PASS THROUGH HIM.
IN THAT CASE, WE CAN SIMPLY ATTACK WITH PHYSICAL OBJECTS.
WE'LL JUST MAKE THE COMMONERS REBUILD THE BUILDING.
HAW! I LOST THE CHANCE TO CUT LOOSE ON A CAPTAIN.
HE WOULD'VE BEEN SO FUN TO SLICE UP TOO...
TUNK
RUNNING AWAY... PITIFUL. AND YOU CALL YOURSELF A MAN?
SSST
EVEN IF YOU AREN'T A TRAITOR, YOU'RE A FAILURE AS A CAPTAIN.
SSST

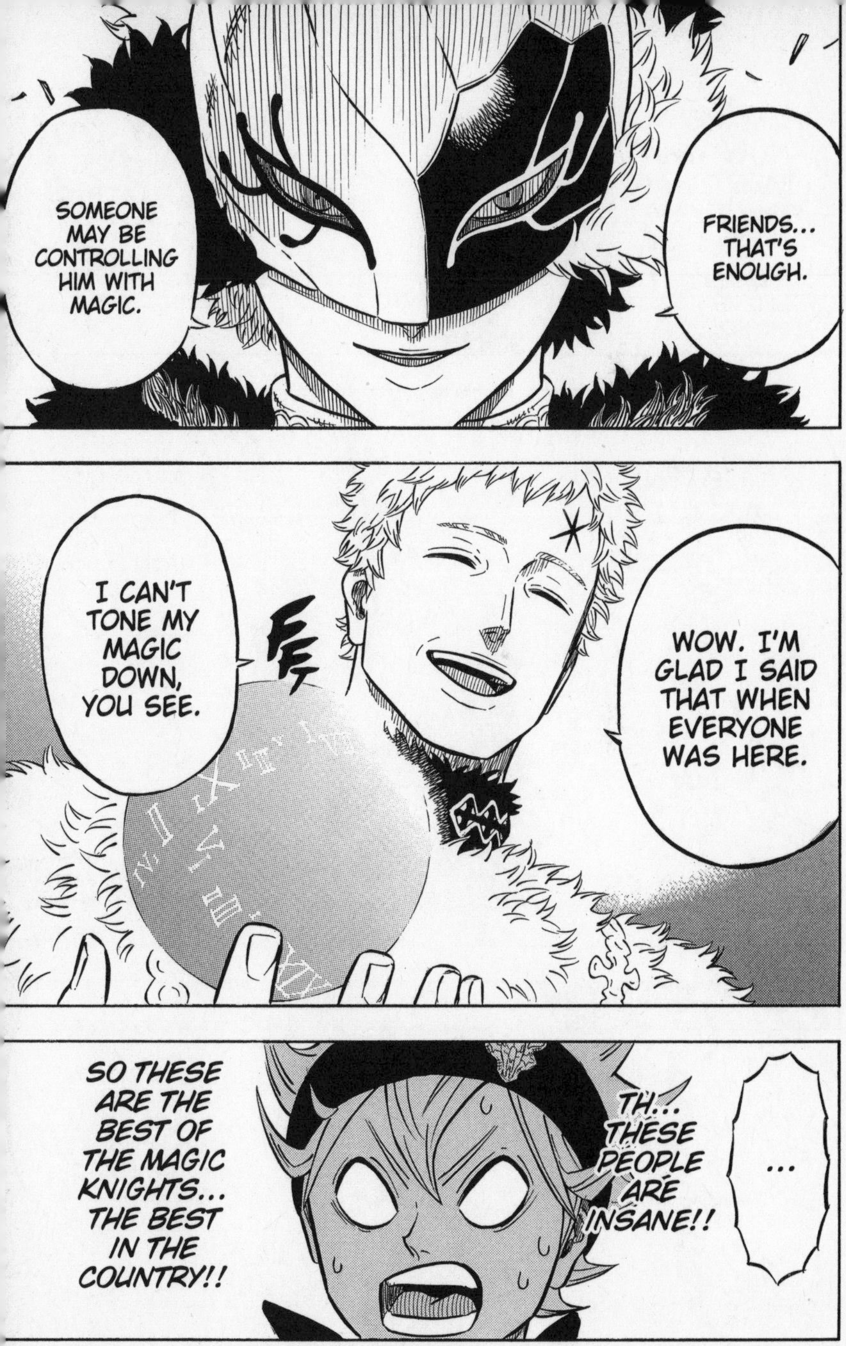
FRIENDS... THAT'S ENOUGH.
SOMEONE MAY BE CONTROLLING HIM WITH MAGIC.
WOW. I'M GLAD I SAID THAT WHEN EVERYONE WAS HERE.
I CAN'T TONE MY MAGIC DOWN, YOU SEE.
...
TH... THESE PEOPLE ARE INSANE!!
SO THESE ARE THE BEST OF THE MAGIC KNIGHTS... THE BEST IN THE COUNTRY!!

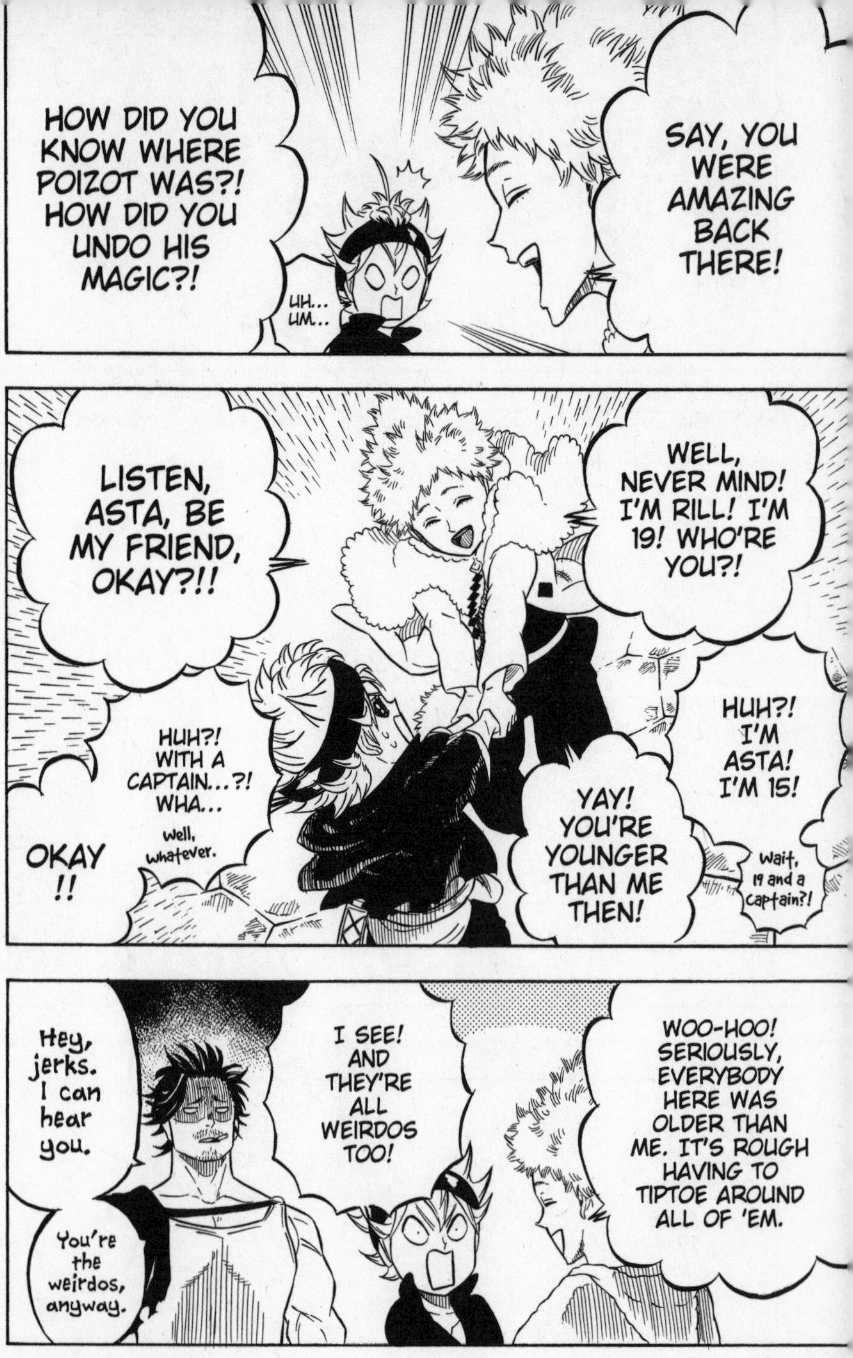
SAY, YOU WERE AMAZING BACK THERE!
HOW DID YOU KNOW WHERE POIZOT WAS?! HOW DID YOU UNDO HIS MAGIC?!
UH... UM...
WELL, NEVER MIND! I'M RILL! I'M 19! WHO'RE YOU?!
HUH?! I'M ASTA! I'M 15!
Wait, 19 and a captain?!
YAY! YOU'RE YOUNGER THAN ME THEN!
LISTEN, ASTA, BE MY FRIEND, OKAY?!!
HUH?! WITH A CAPTAIN...?! WHA...
well, whatever.
OKAY !!
WOO-HOO! SERIOUSLY, EVERYBODY HERE WAS OLDER THAN ME. IT'S ROUGH HAVING TO TIPTOE AROUND ALL OF 'EM.
I SEE! AND THEY'RE ALL WEIRDOS TOO!
Hey, jerks. I can hear you.
You're the weirdos, anyway.

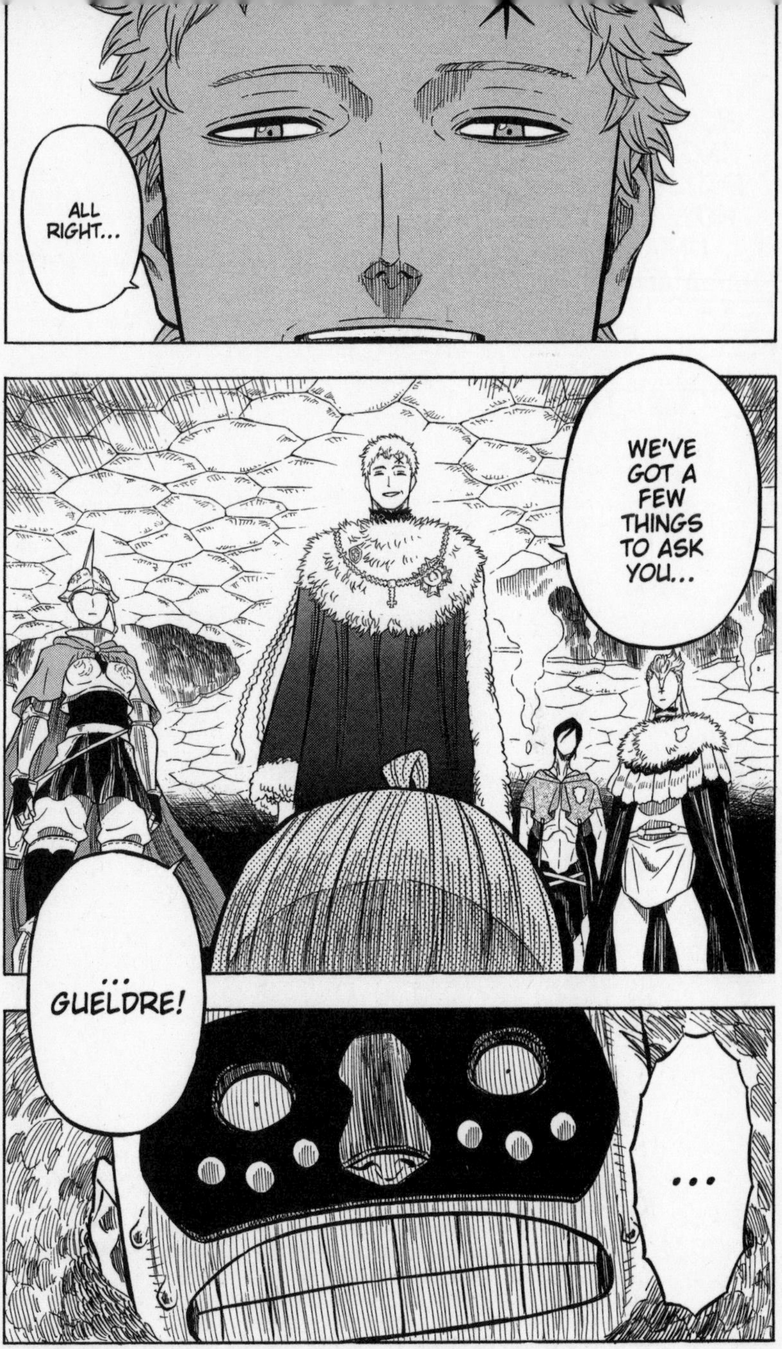
ALL RIGHT...
WE'VE GOT A FEW THINGS TO ASK YOU...
...GUELDRE!
...

# Charlotte Roselei

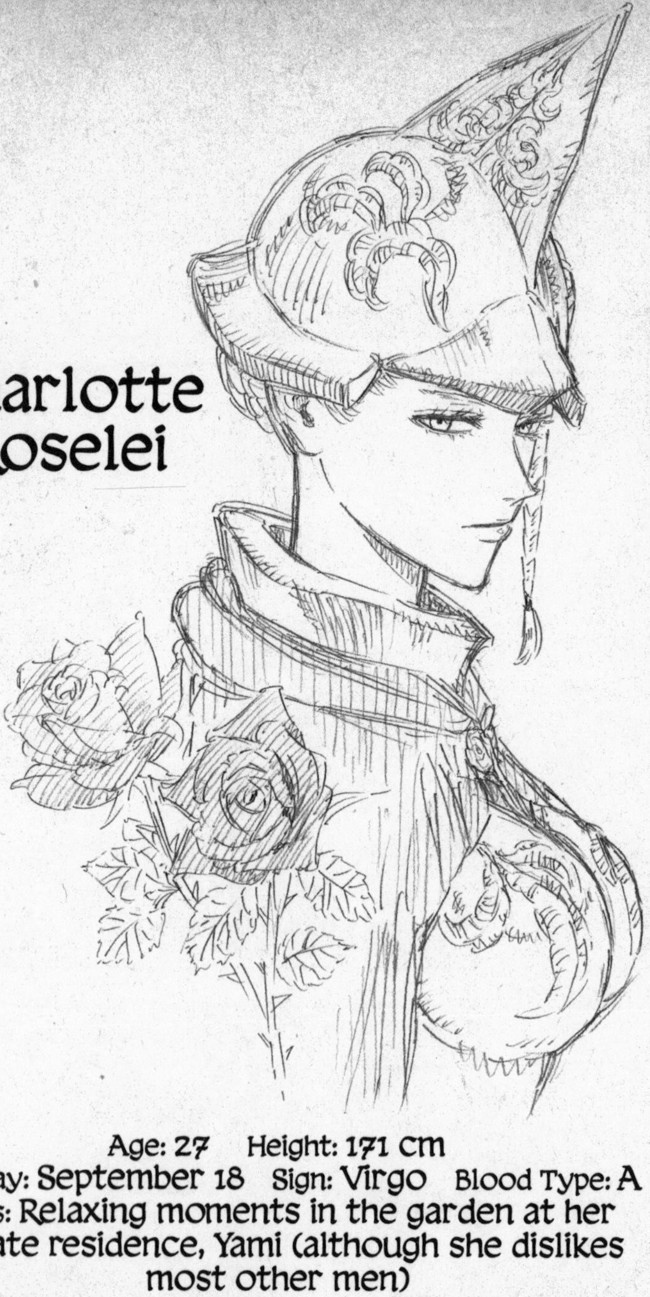

Age: 27 Height: 171 cm
Birthday: September 18 Sign: Virgo Blood Type: A
Likes: Relaxing moments in the garden at her private residence, Yami (although she dislikes most other men)

Character Profile

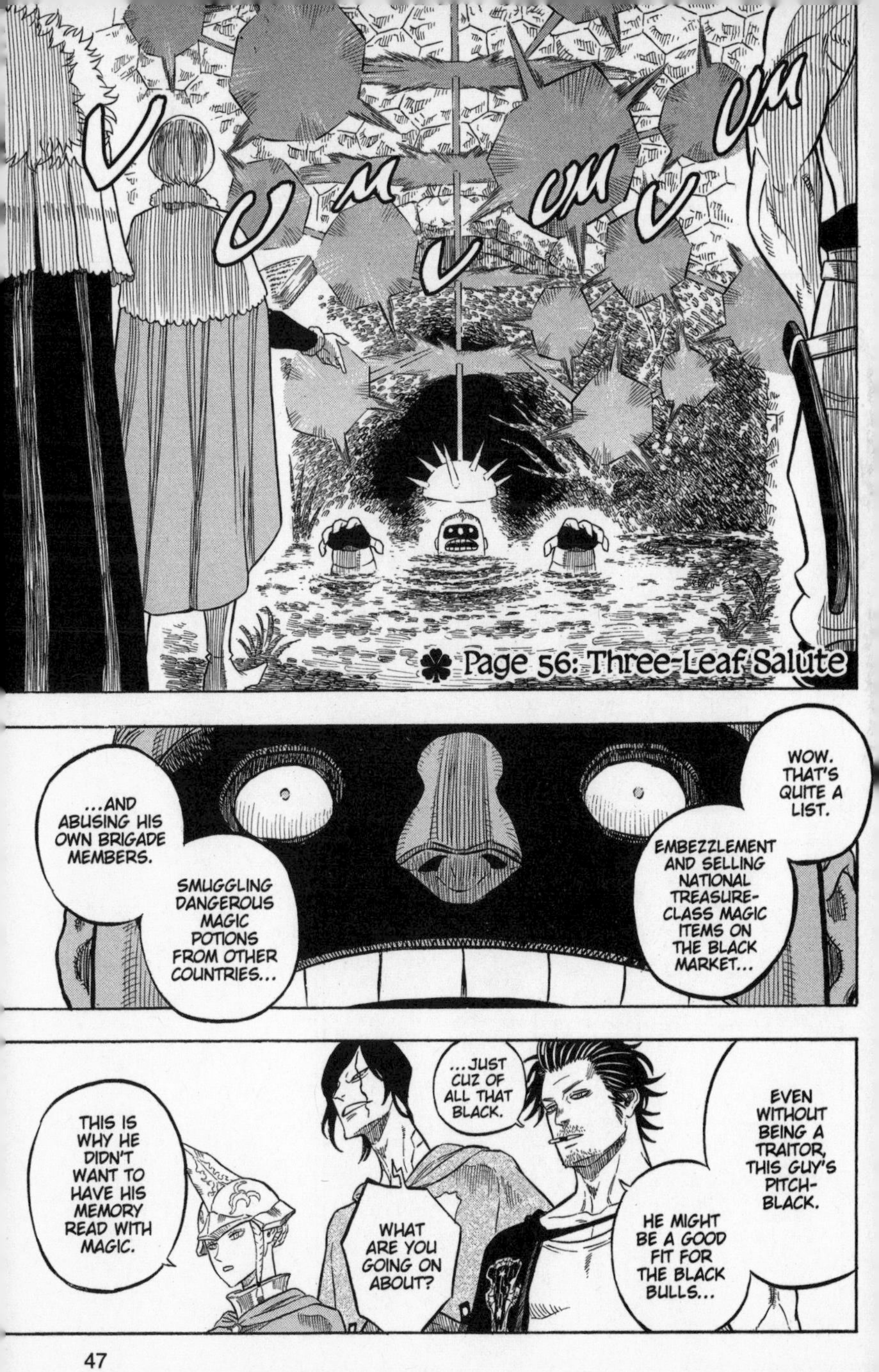
Page 56: Three-Leaf Salute
WOW. THAT'S QUITE A LIST.
EMBEZZLEMENT AND SELLING NATIONAL TREASURE-CLASS MAGIC ITEMS ON THE BLACK MARKET...
SMUGGLING DANGEROUS MAGIC POTIONS FROM OTHER COUNTRIES...
...AND ABUSING HIS OWN BRIGADE MEMBERS.
EVEN WITHOUT BEING A TRAITOR, THIS GUY'S PITCH-BLACK.
HE MIGHT BE A GOOD FIT FOR THE BLACK BULLS...
...JUST CUZ OF ALL THAT BLACK.
WHAT ARE YOU GOING ON ABOUT?
THIS IS WHY HE DIDN'T WANT TO HAVE HIS MEMORY READ WITH MAGIC.

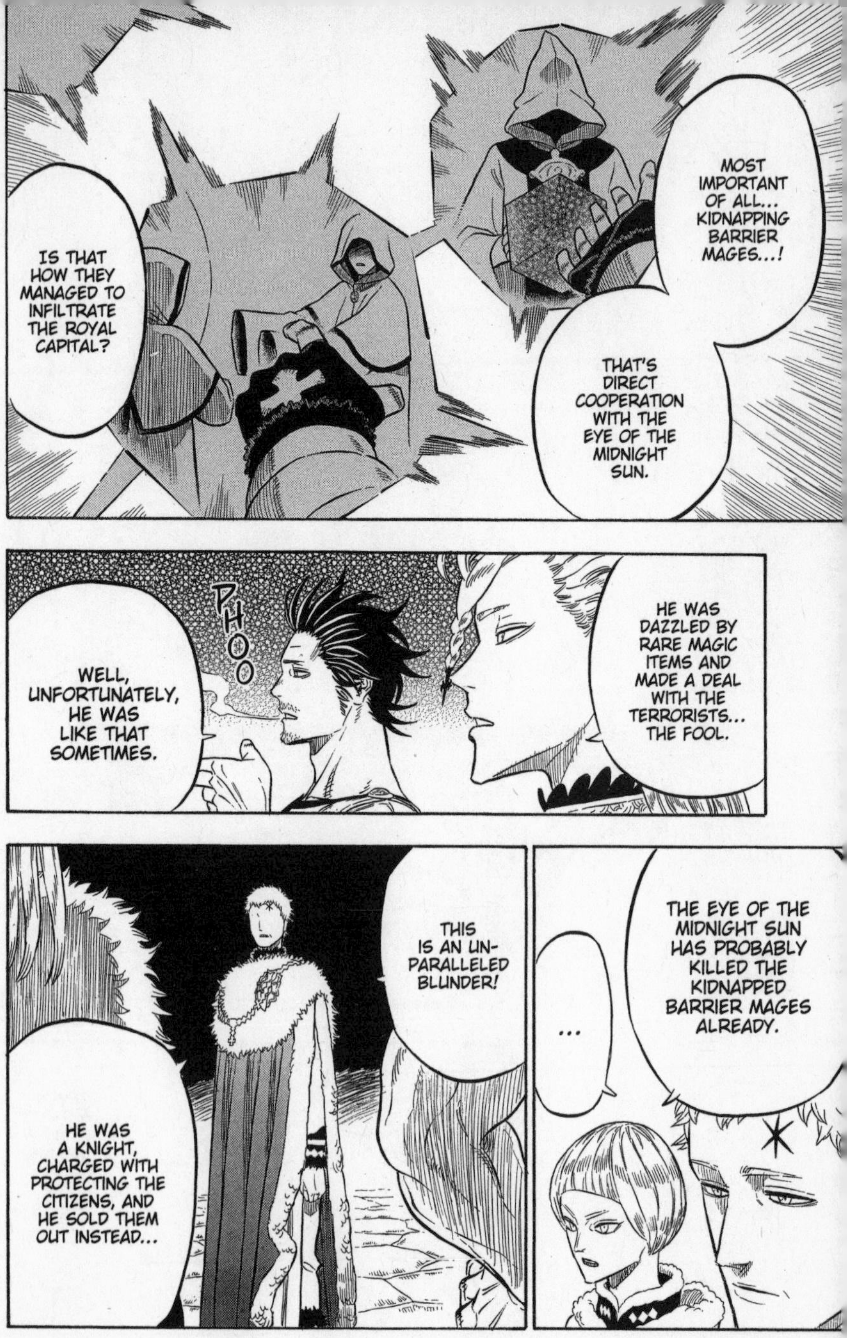
MOST IMPORTANT OF ALL... KIDNAPPING BARRIER MAGES...!
THAT'S DIRECT COOPERATION WITH THE EYE OF THE MIDNIGHT SUN.
IS THAT HOW THEY MANAGED TO INFILTRATE THE ROYAL CAPITAL?
HE WAS DAZZLED BY RARE MAGIC ITEMS AND MADE A DEAL WITH THE TERRORISTS... THE FOOL.
PHOO
WELL, UNFORTUNATELY, HE WAS LIKE THAT SOMETIMES.
THE EYE OF THE MIDNIGHT SUN HAS PROBABLY KILLED THE KIDNAPPED BARRIER MAGES ALREADY.
...
THIS IS AN UN-PARALLELED BLUNDER!
HE WAS A KNIGHT, CHARGED WITH PROTECTING THE CITIZENS, AND HE SOLD THEM OUT INSTEAD...

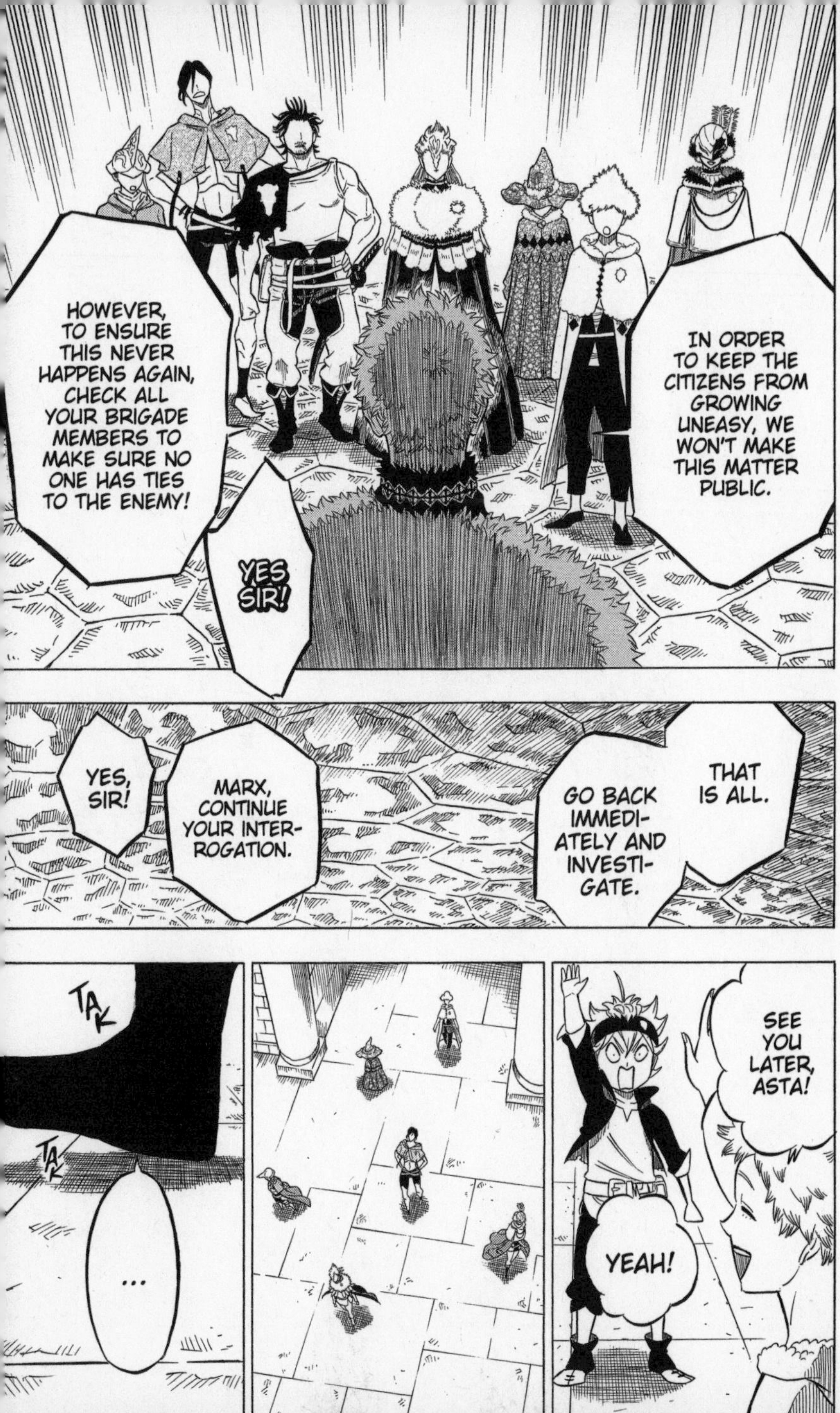
IN ORDER TO KEEP THE CITIZENS FROM GROWING UNEASY, WE WON'T MAKE THIS MATTER PUBLIC.
HOWEVER, TO ENSURE THIS NEVER HAPPENS AGAIN, CHECK ALL YOUR BRIGADE MEMBERS TO MAKE SURE NO ONE HAS TIES TO THE ENEMY!
YES SIR!
THAT IS ALL.
GO BACK IMMEDI-ATELY AND INVESTI-GATE.
MARX, CONTINUE YOUR INTER-ROGATION.
YES, SIR!
SEE YOU LATER, ASTA!
YEAH!
TAK
TAK
...

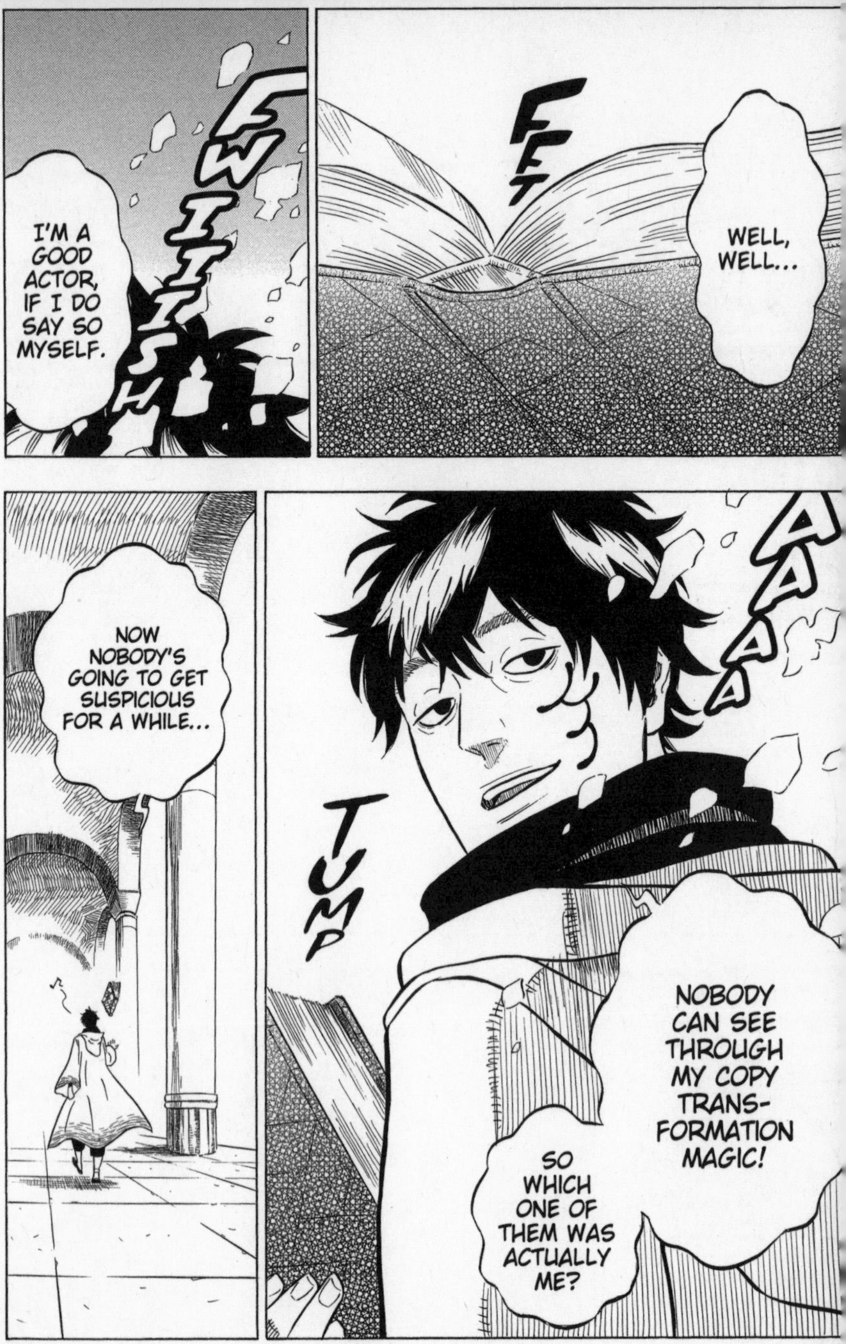
FFT
WELL, WELL...
FWIISH
I'M A GOOD ACTOR, IF I DO SAY SO MYSELF.
AAAAA
TUMP
NOBODY CAN SEE THROUGH MY COPY TRANS-FORMATION MAGIC!
SO WHICH ONE OF THEM WAS ACTUALLY ME?
NOW NOBODY'S GOING TO GET SUSPICIOUS FOR A WHILE...

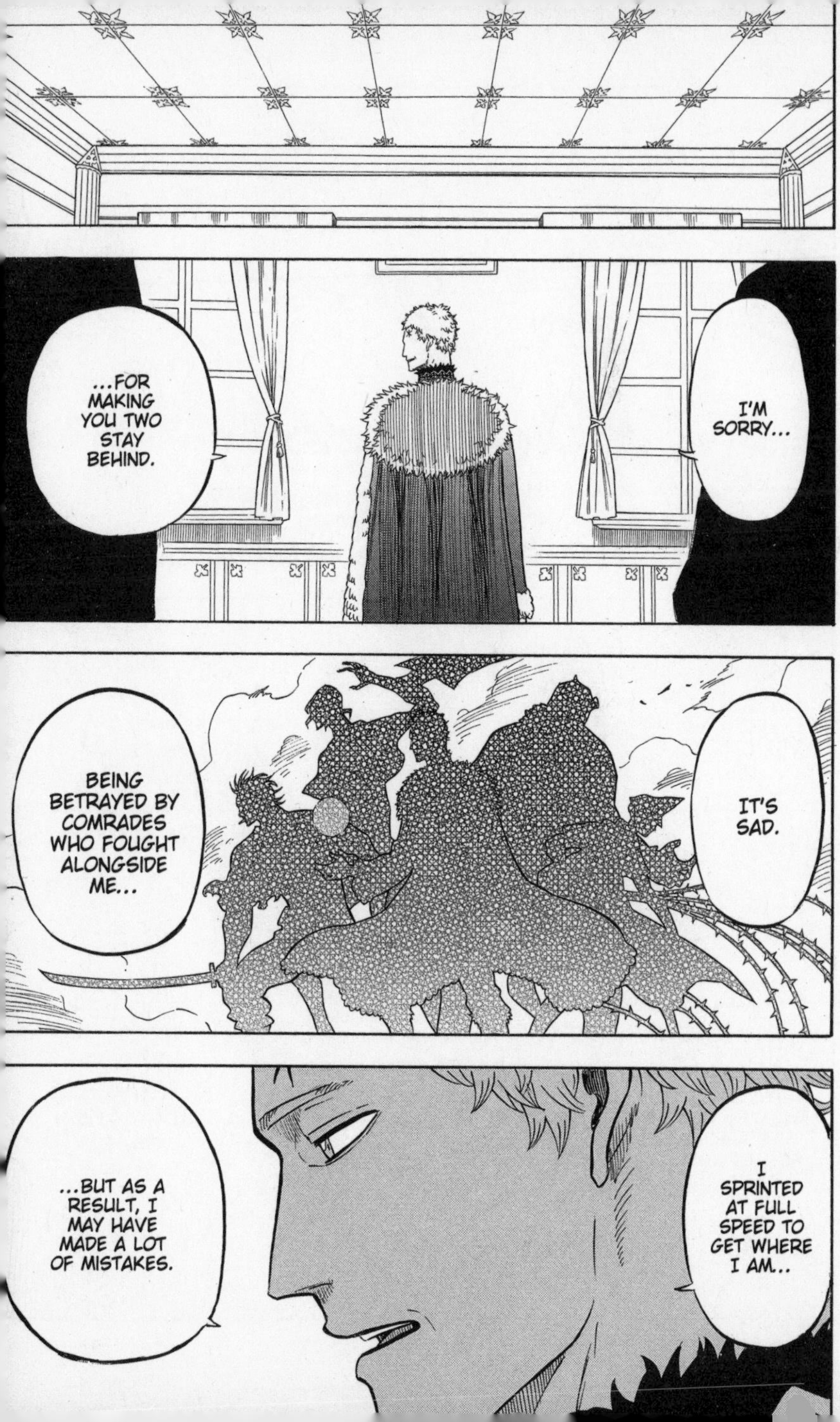
I'M SORRY...
...FOR MAKING YOU TWO STAY BEHIND.
IT'S SAD.
BEING BETRAYED BY COMRADES WHO FOUGHT ALONGSIDE ME...
I SPRINTED AT FULL SPEED TO GET WHERE I AM..
...BUT AS A RESULT, I MAY HAVE MADE A LOT OF MISTAKES.

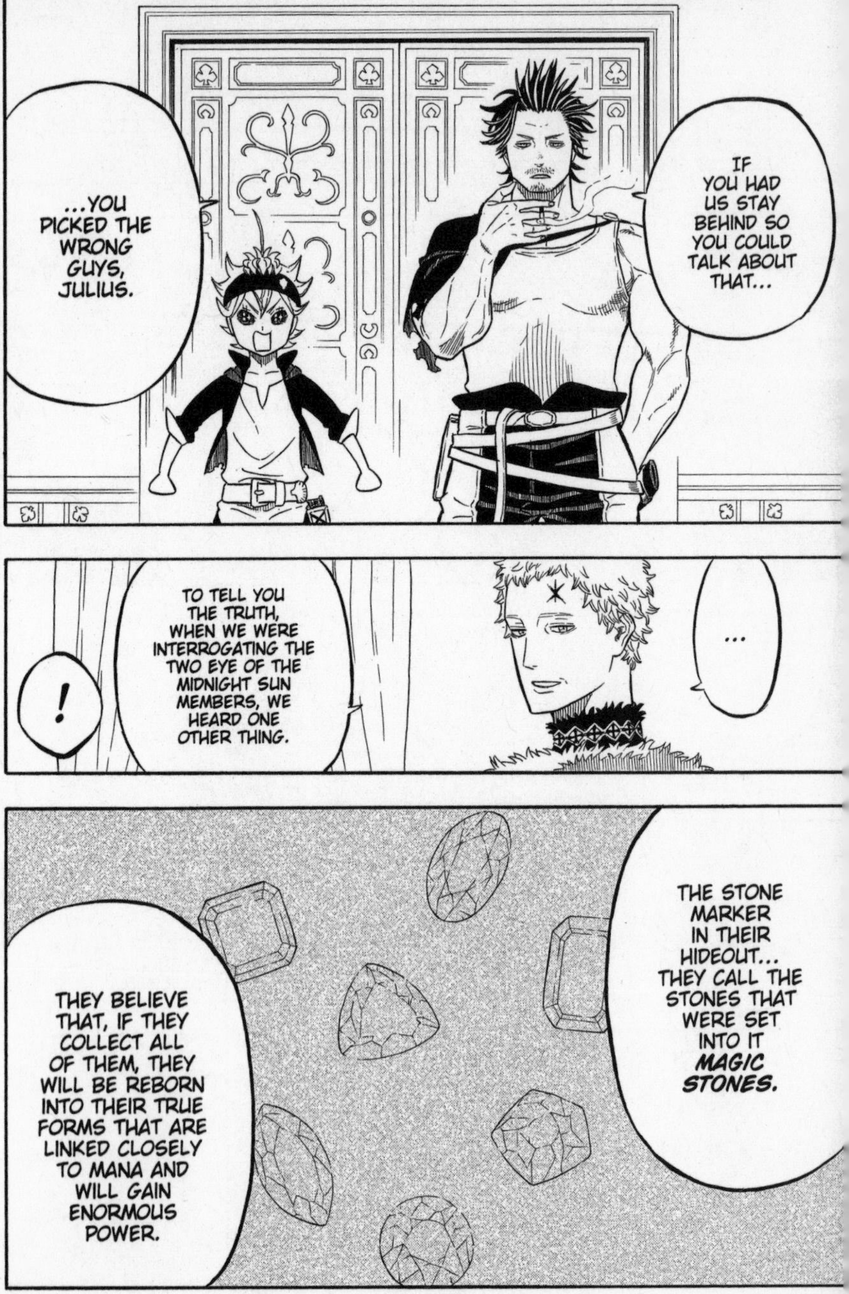
IF YOU HAD US STAY BEHIND SO YOU COULD TALK ABOUT THAT...
...YOU PICKED THE WRONG GUYS, JULIUS.
...
TO TELL YOU THE TRUTH, WHEN WE WERE INTERROGATING THE TWO EYE OF THE MIDNIGHT SUN MEMBERS, WE HEARD ONE OTHER THING.
!
THE STONE MARKER IN THEIR HIDEOUT... THEY CALL THE STONES THAT WERE SET INTO IT *MAGIC STONES.*
THEY BELIEVE THAT, IF THEY COLLECT ALL OF THEM, THEY WILL BE REBORN INTO THEIR TRUE FORMS THAT ARE LINKED CLOSELY TO MANA AND WILL GAIN ENORMOUS POWER.

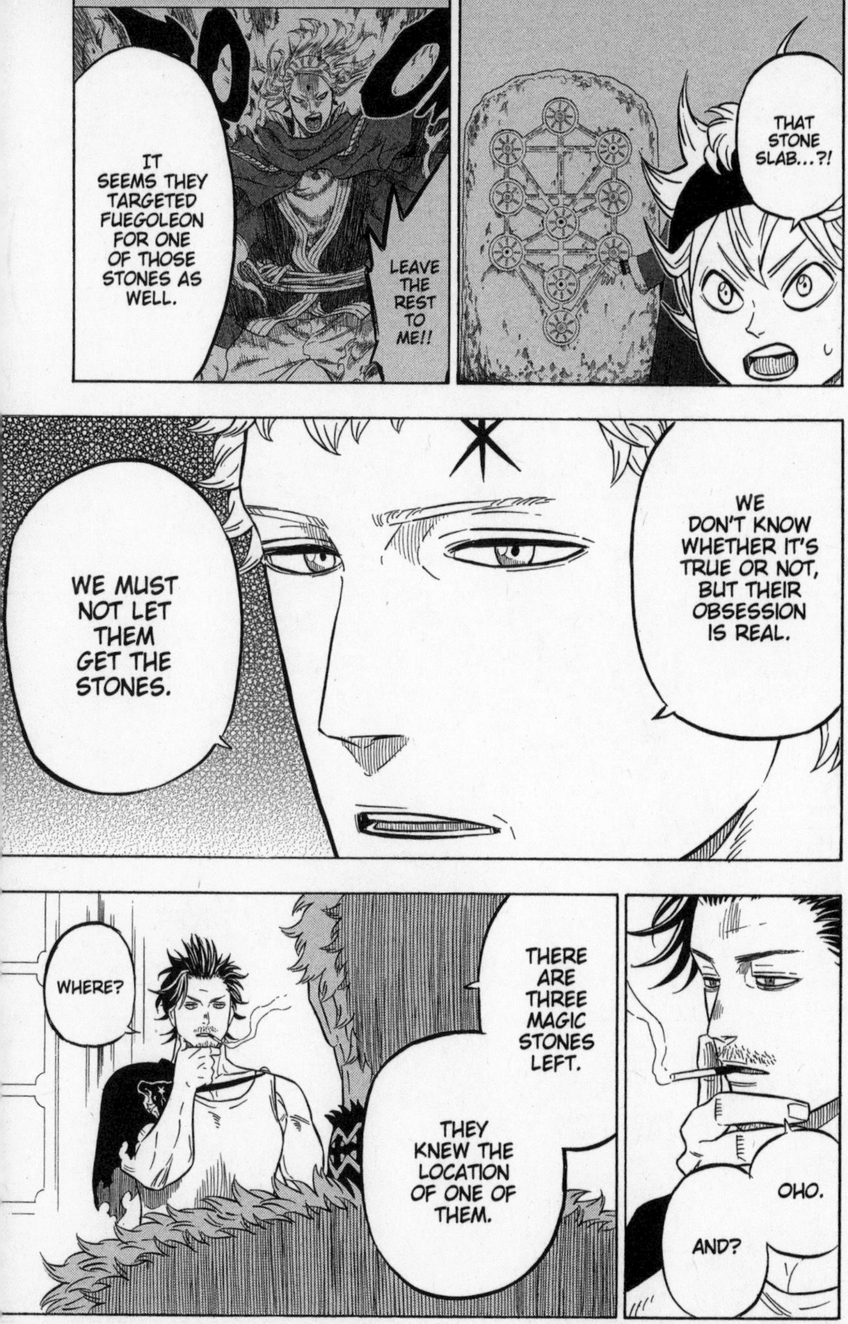
THAT STONE SLAB...?!
IT SEEMS THEY TARGETED FUEGOLEON FOR ONE OF THOSE STONES AS WELL.
LEAVE THE REST TO ME!!
WE DON'T KNOW WHETHER IT'S TRUE OR NOT, BUT THEIR OBSESSION IS REAL.
WE MUST NOT LET THEM GET THE STONES.
OHO.
AND?
THERE ARE THREE MAGIC STONES LEFT.
THEY KNEW THE LOCATION OF ONE OF THEM.
WHERE?

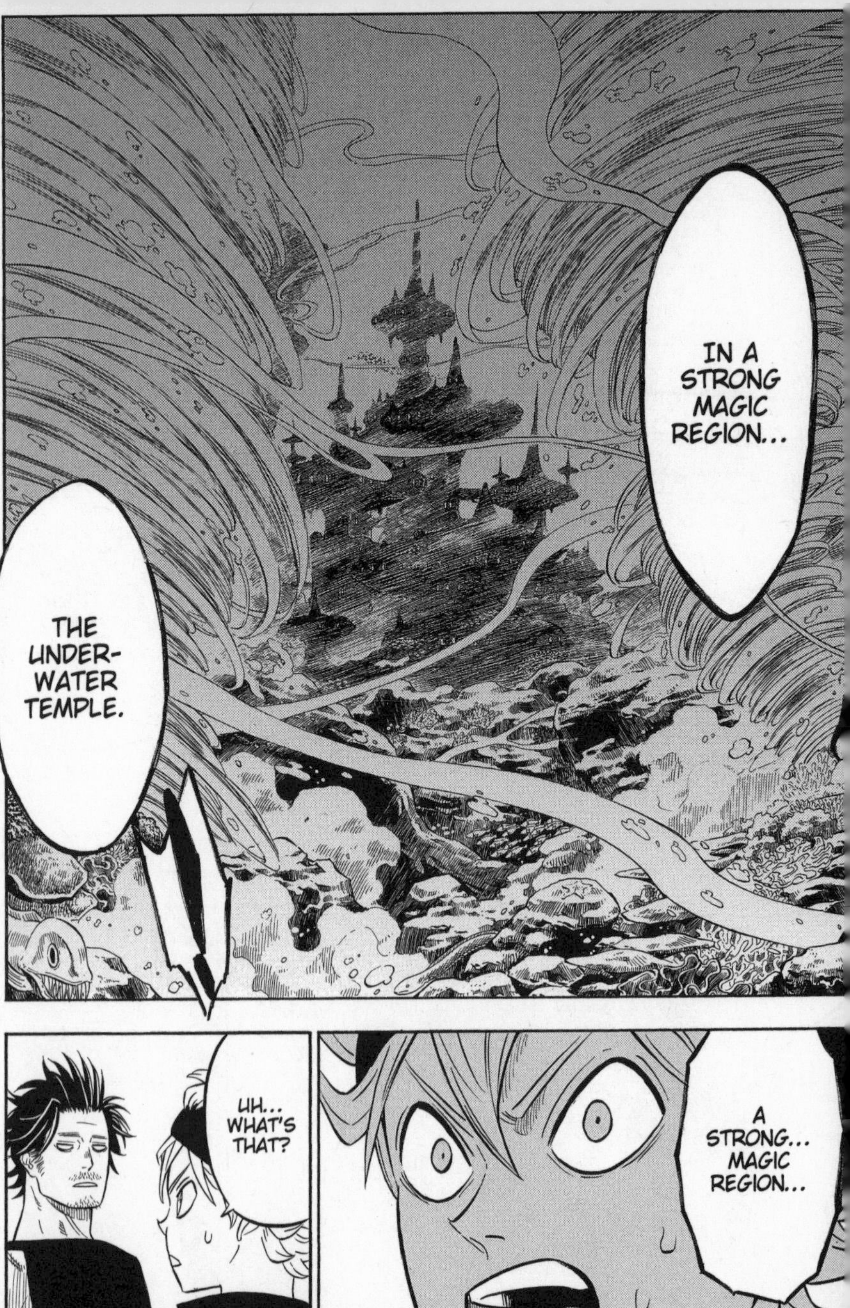
IN A STRONG MAGIC REGION...
THE UNDER-WATER TEMPLE.
A STRONG... MAGIC REGION...
UH... WHAT'S THAT?

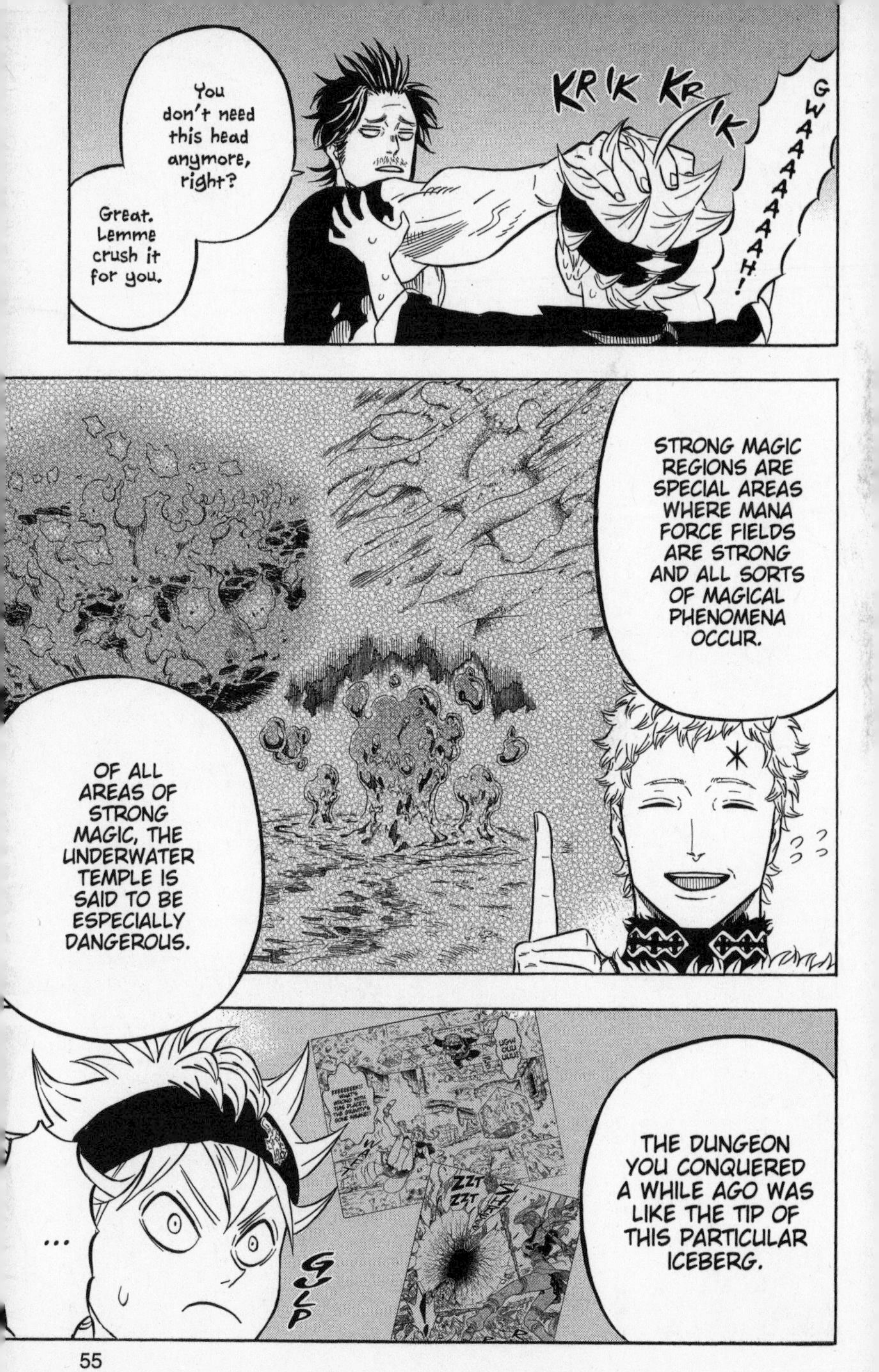
GWAAAAAAAAAH!
KRIK KRIK
You don't need this head anymore, right?
Great. Lemme crush it for you.
STRONG MAGIC REGIONS ARE SPECIAL AREAS WHERE MANA FORCE FIELDS ARE STRONG AND ALL SORTS OF MAGICAL PHENOMENA OCCUR.
OF ALL AREAS OF STRONG MAGIC, THE UNDERWATER TEMPLE IS SAID TO BE ESPECIALLY DANGEROUS.
THE DUNGEON YOU CONQUERED A WHILE AGO WAS LIKE THE TIP OF THIS PARTICULAR ICEBERG.
ZZT ZZT
GULP
...

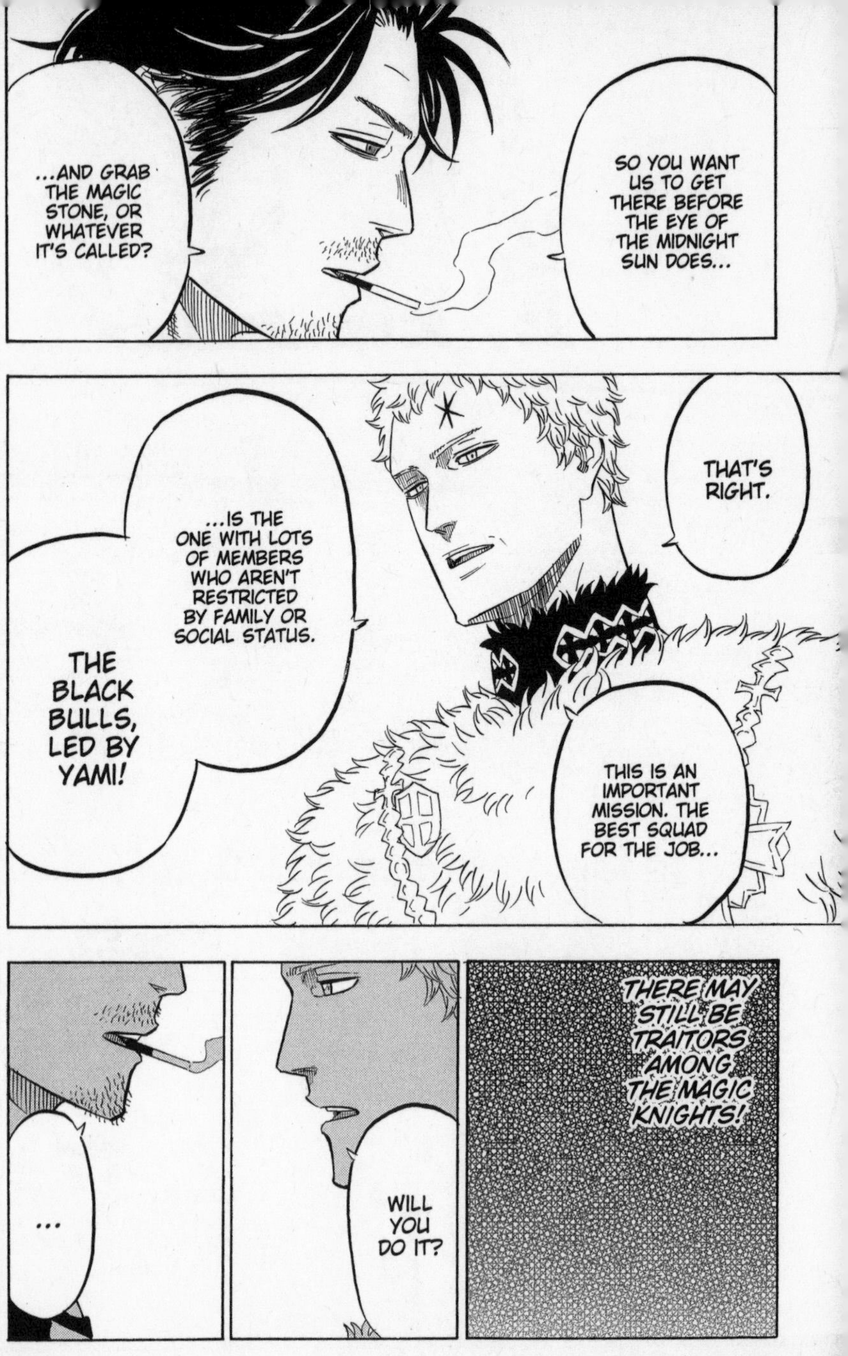
SO YOU WANT US TO GET THERE BEFORE THE EYE OF THE MIDNIGHT SUN DOES...
...AND GRAB THE MAGIC STONE, OR WHATEVER IT'S CALLED?
THAT'S RIGHT.
THIS IS AN IMPORTANT MISSION. THE BEST SQUAD FOR THE JOB...
...IS THE ONE WITH LOTS OF MEMBERS WHO AREN'T RESTRICTED BY FAMILY OR SOCIAL STATUS.
THE BLACK BULLS, LED BY YAMI!
THERE MAY STILL BE TRAITORS AMONG THE MAGIC KNIGHTS!
WILL YOU DO IT?
...

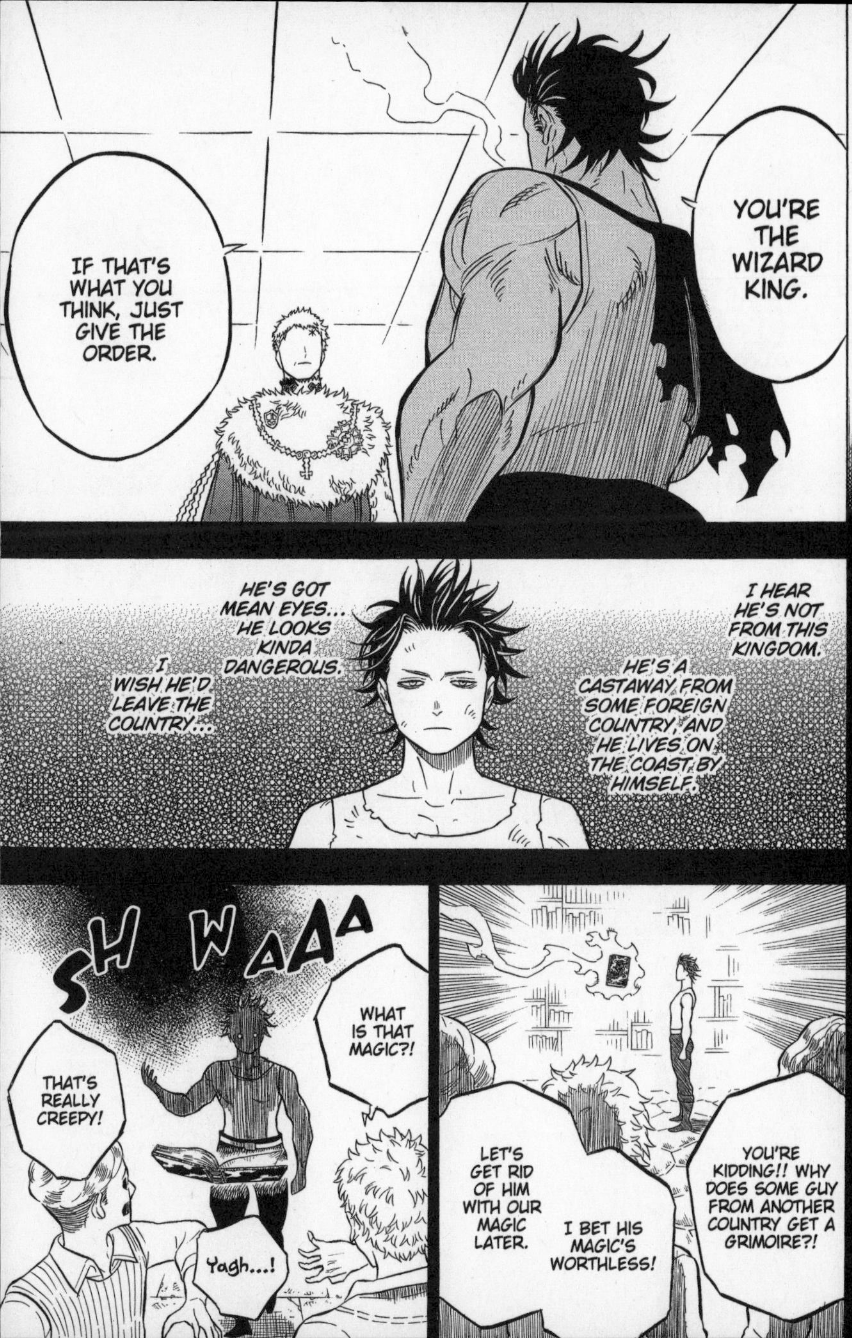
YOU'RE THE WIZARD KING.
IF THAT'S WHAT YOU THINK, JUST GIVE THE ORDER.
I HEAR HE'S NOT FROM THIS KINGDOM.
HE'S A CASTAWAY FROM SOME FOREIGN COUNTRY, AND HE LIVES ON THE COAST BY HIMSELF.
HE'S GOT MEAN EYES... HE LOOKS KINDA DANGEROUS.
I WISH HE'D LEAVE THE COUNTRY...
YOU'RE KIDDING!! WHY DOES SOME GUY FROM ANOTHER COUNTRY GET A GRIMOIRE?!
I BET HIS MAGIC'S WORTHLESS!
LET'S GET RID OF HIM WITH OUR MAGIC LATER.
SHWAAA
WHAT IS THAT MAGIC?!
THAT'S REALLY CREEPY!
Yagh...!

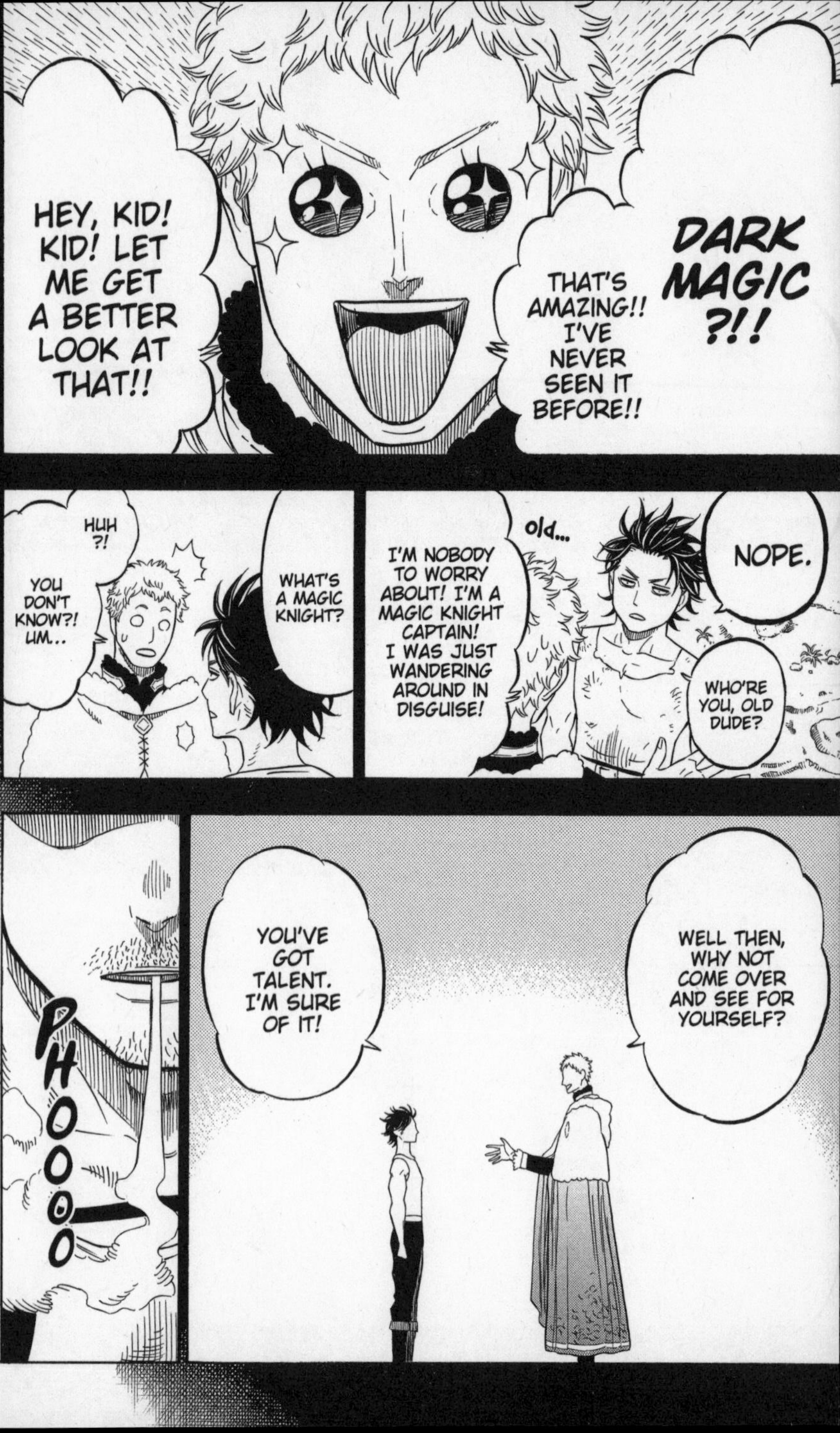
DARK MAGIC ?!!
THAT'S AMAZING!! I'VE NEVER SEEN IT BEFORE!!
HEY, KID! KID! LET ME GET A BETTER LOOK AT THAT!!
NOPE.
WHO'RE YOU, OLD DUDE?
old...
I'M NOBODY TO WORRY ABOUT! I'M A MAGIC KNIGHT CAPTAIN! I WAS JUST WANDERING AROUND IN DISGUISE!
WHAT'S A MAGIC KNIGHT?
HUH ?!
YOU DON'T KNOW?! UM...
WELL THEN, WHY NOT COME OVER AND SEE FOR YOURSELF?
YOU'VE GOT TALENT. I'M SURE OF IT!
PHOOOOO

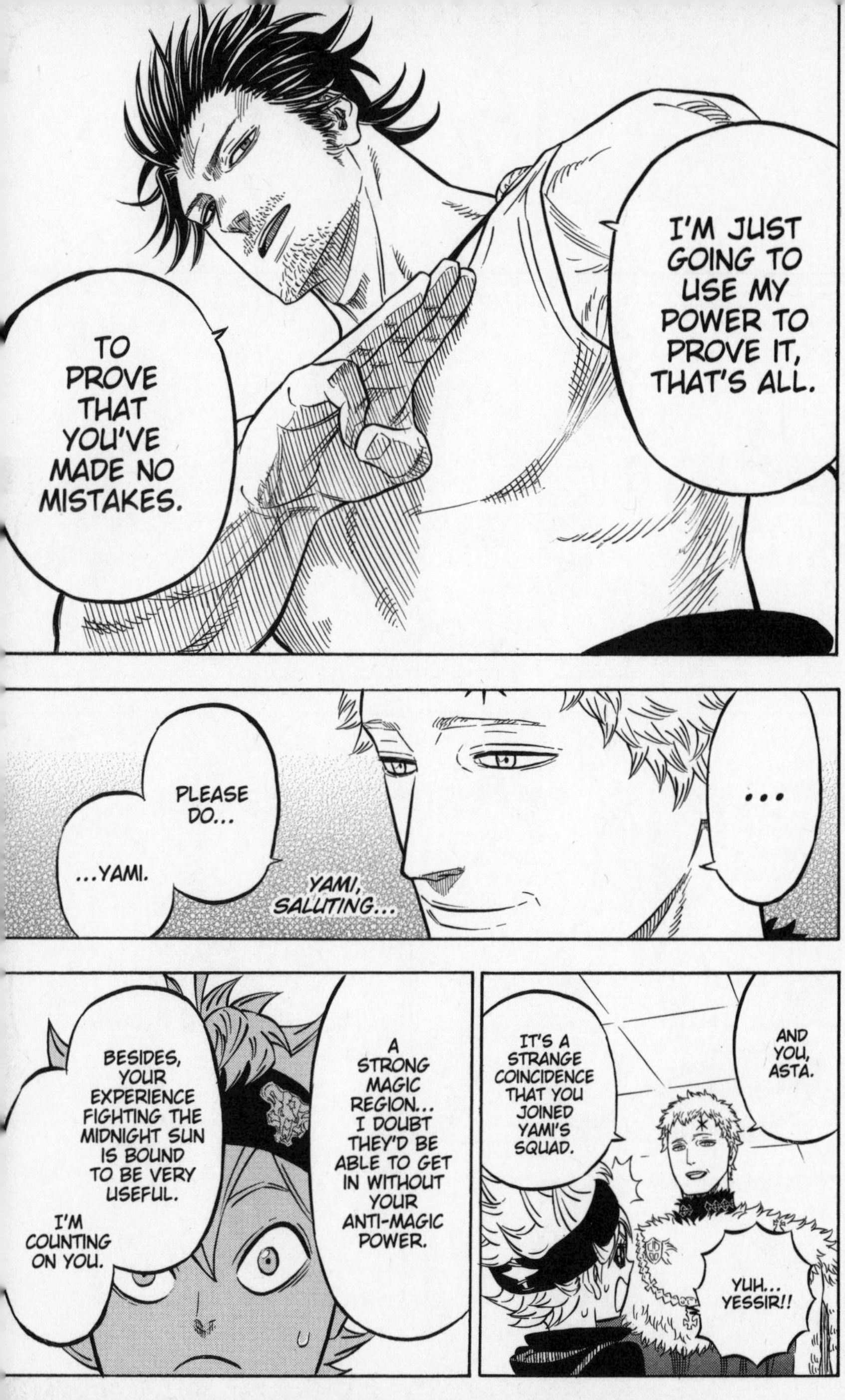
I'M JUST GOING TO USE MY POWER TO PROVE IT, THAT'S ALL.
TO PROVE THAT YOU'VE MADE NO MISTAKES.
...
YAMI, SALUTING...
PLEASE DO... ...YAMI.
AND YOU, ASTA.
IT'S A STRANGE COINCIDENCE THAT YOU JOINED YAMI'S SQUAD.
YUH... YESSIR!!
A STRONG MAGIC REGION... I DOUBT THEY'D BE ABLE TO GET IN WITHOUT YOUR ANTI-MAGIC POWER.
BESIDES, YOUR EXPERIENCE FIGHTING THE MIDNIGHT SUN IS BOUND TO BE VERY USEFUL.
I'M COUNTING ON YOU.

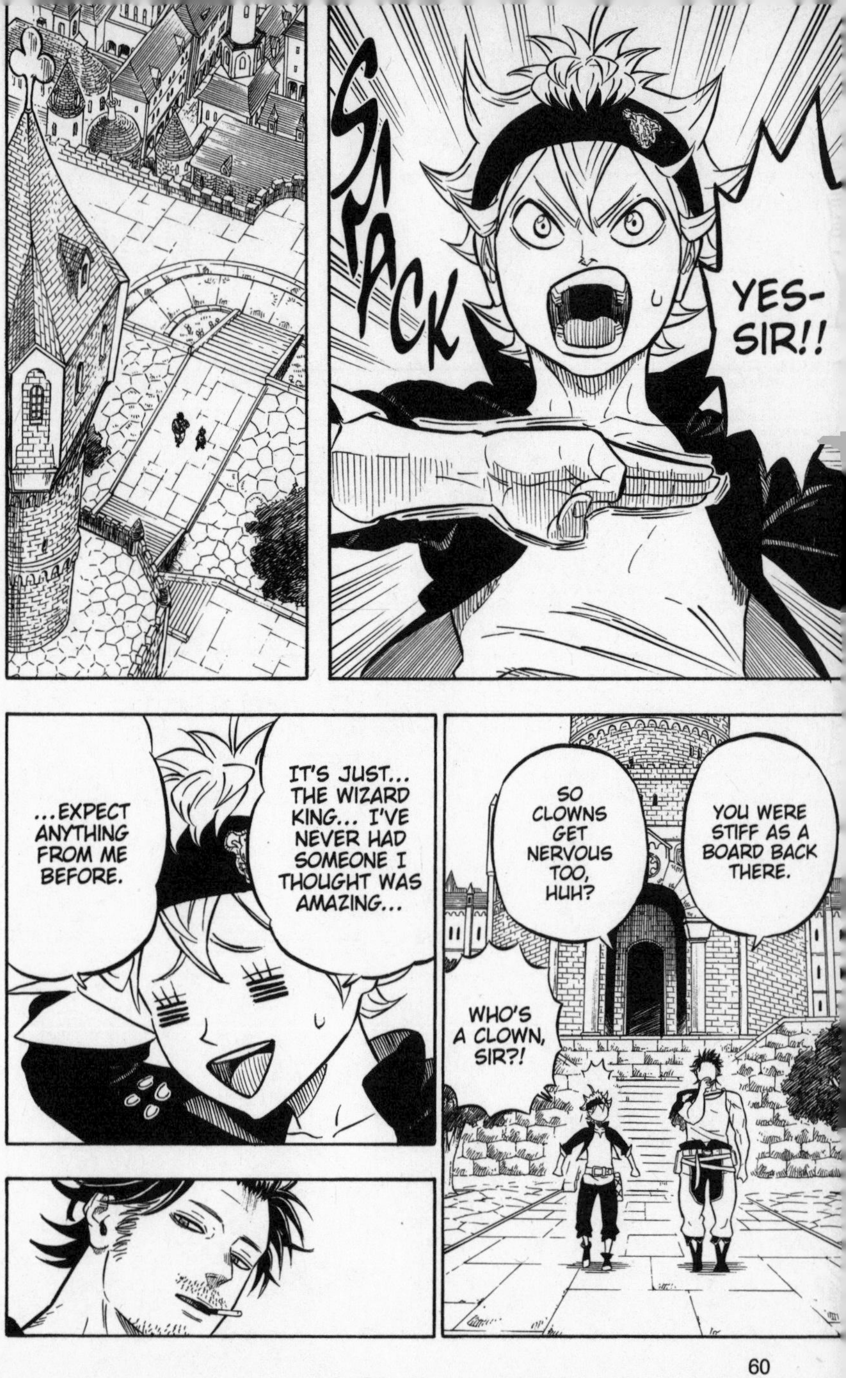
YES-SIR!!
SMACK
YOU WERE STIFF AS A BOARD BACK THERE.
SO CLOWNS GET NERVOUS TOO, HUH?
WHO'S A CLOWN, SIR?!
IT'S JUST... THE WIZARD KING... I'VE NEVER HAD SOMEONE I THOUGHT WAS AMAZING...
...EXPECT ANYTHING FROM ME BEFORE.

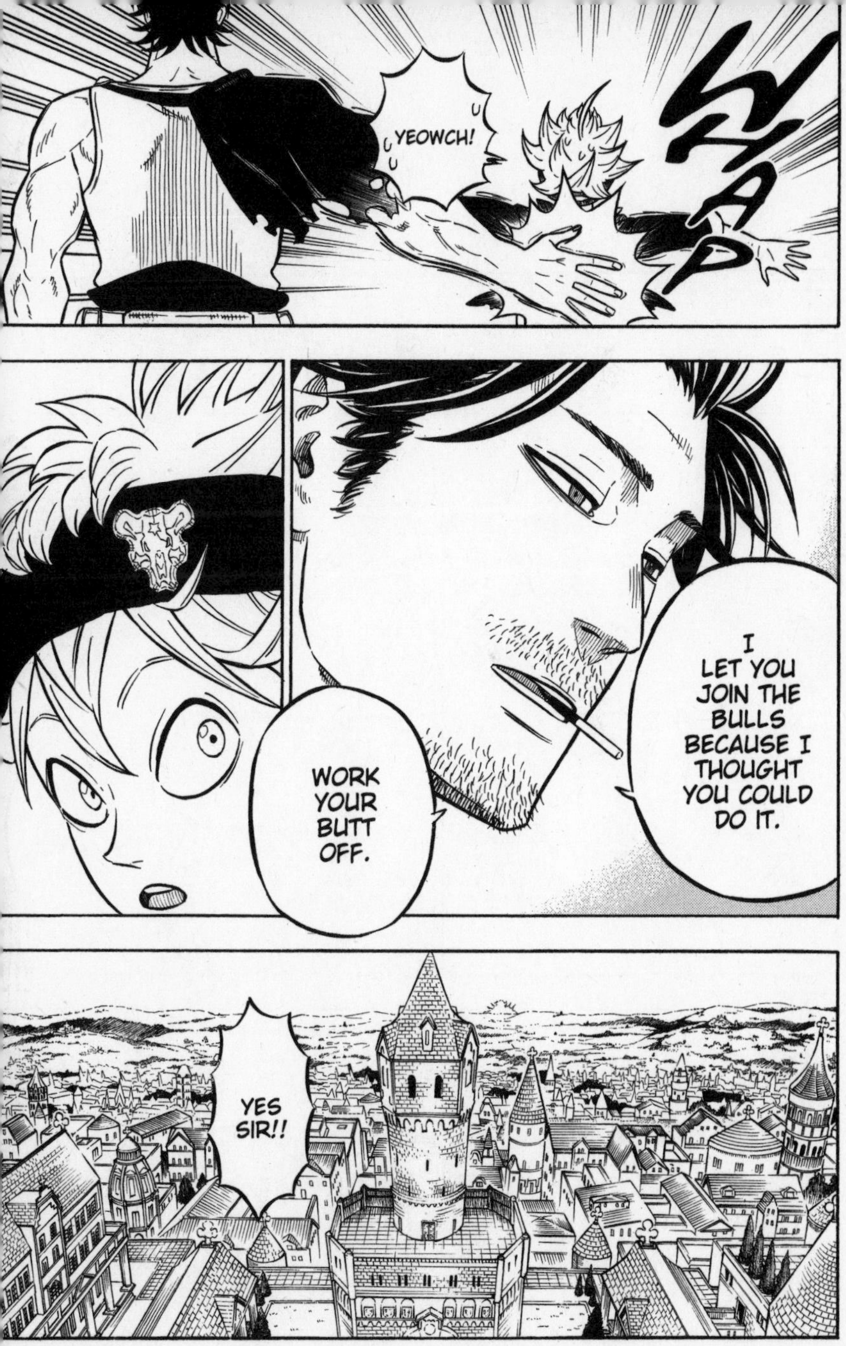
WHAP
YEOWCH!
I LET YOU JOIN THE BULLS BECAUSE I THOUGHT YOU COULD DO IT.
WORK YOUR BUTT OFF.
YES SIR!!

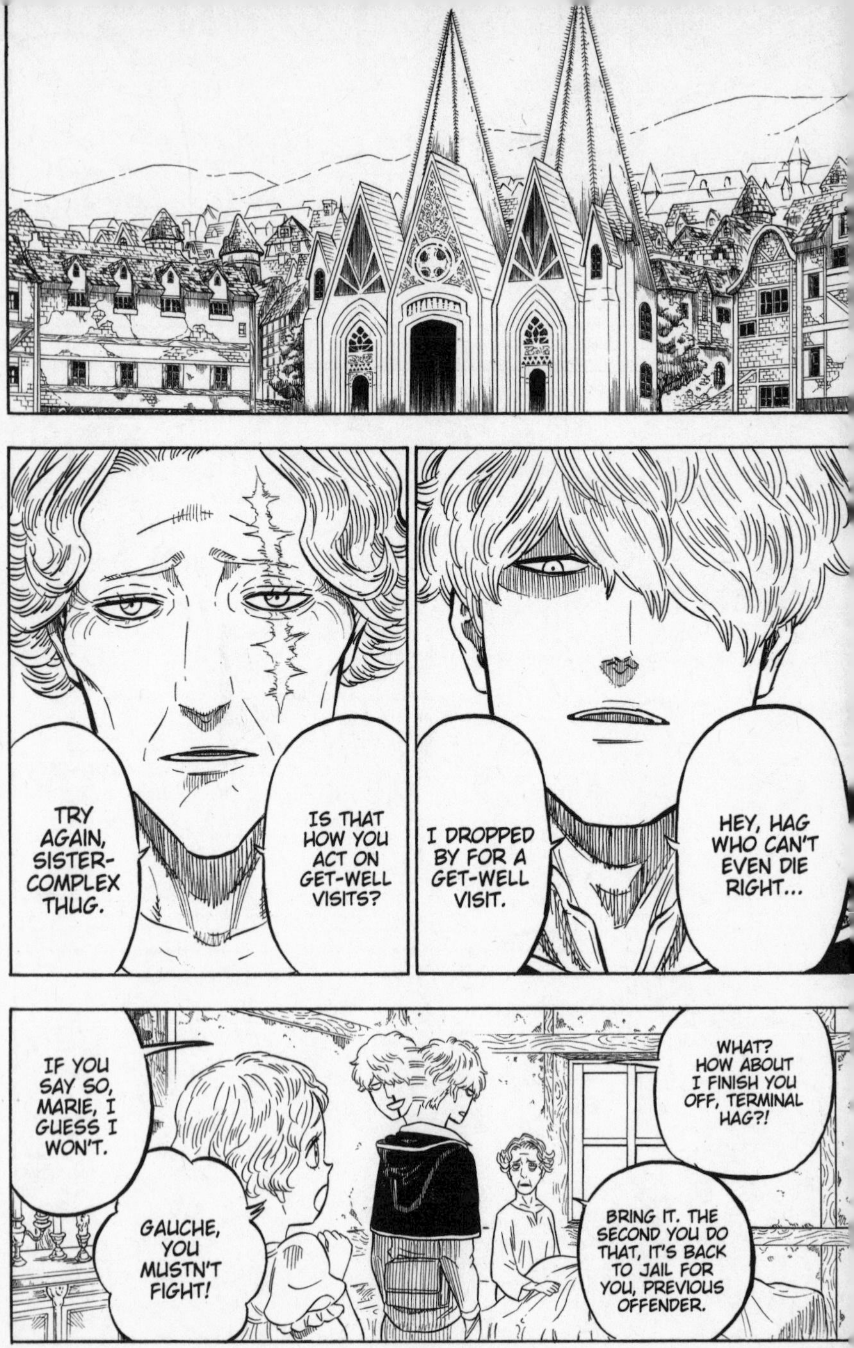
HEY, HAG WHO CAN'T EVEN DIE RIGHT...
I DROPPED BY FOR A GET-WELL VISIT.
IS THAT HOW YOU ACT ON GET-WELL VISITS?
TRY AGAIN, SISTER-COMPLEX THUG.
WHAT? HOW ABOUT I FINISH YOU OFF, TERMINAL HAG?!
BRING IT. THE SECOND YOU DO THAT, IT'S BACK TO JAIL FOR YOU, PREVIOUS OFFENDER.
GAUCHE, YOU MUSTN'T FIGHT!
IF YOU SAY SO, MARIE, I GUESS I WON'T.

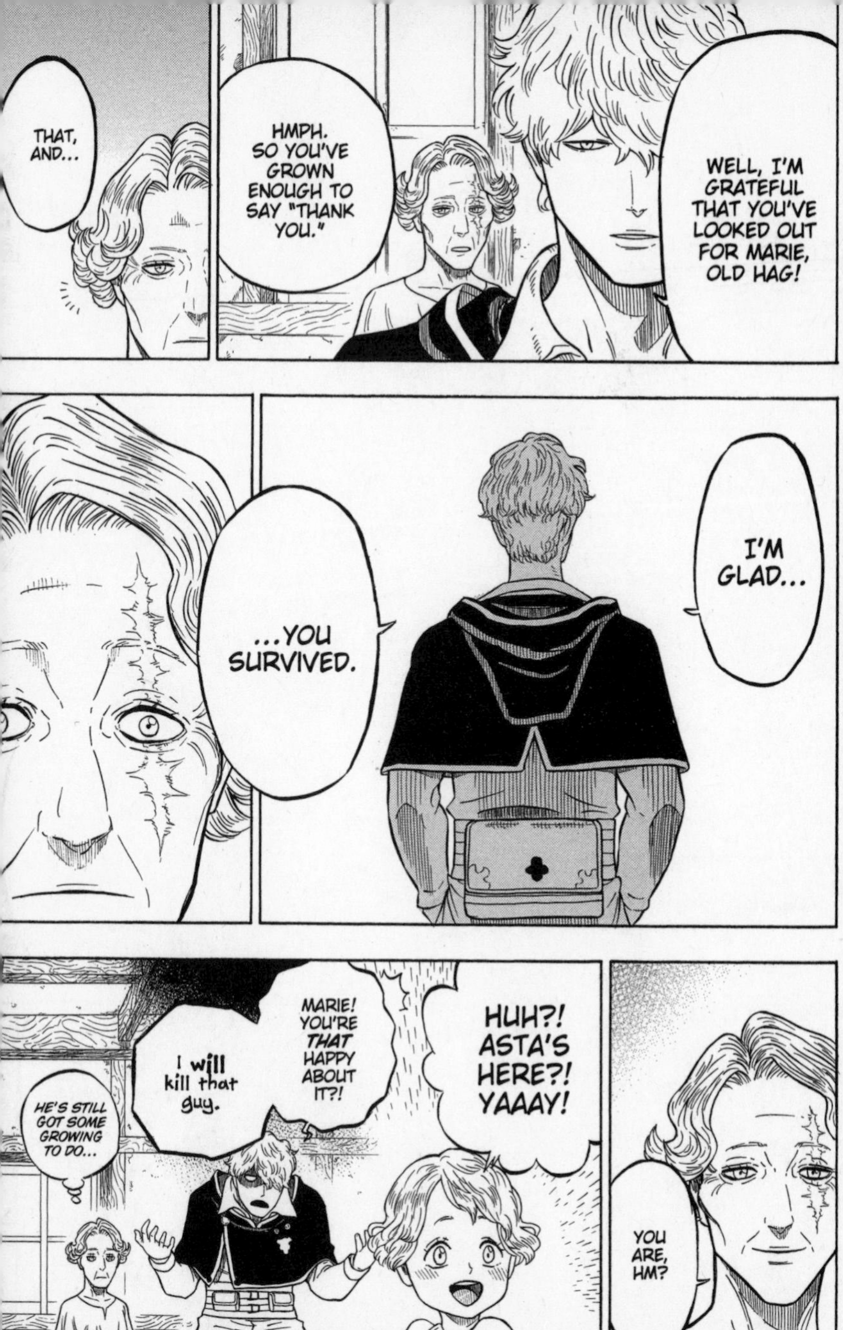
WELL, I'M GRATEFUL THAT YOU'VE LOOKED OUT FOR MARIE, OLD HAG!
HMPH. SO YOU'VE GROWN ENOUGH TO SAY "THANK YOU."
THAT, AND...
I'M GLAD...
...YOU SURVIVED.
YOU ARE, HM?
HUH?! ASTA'S HERE?! YAAAY!
MARIE! YOU'RE *THAT* HAPPY ABOUT IT?!
I will kill that guy.
HE'S STILL GOT SOME GROWING TO DO...

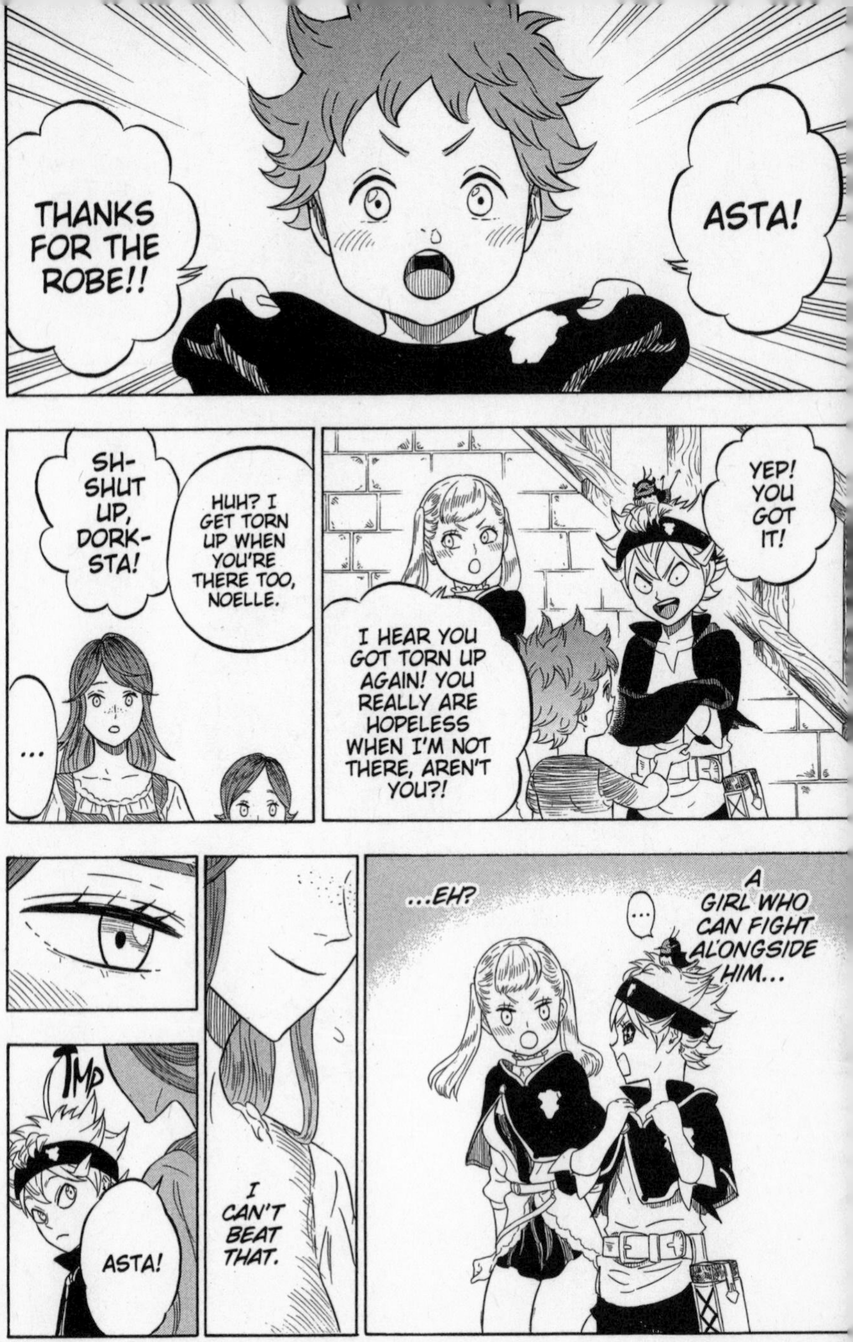
ASTA!
THANKS FOR THE ROBE!!
YEP! YOU GOT IT!
I HEAR YOU GOT TORN UP AGAIN! YOU REALLY ARE HOPELESS WHEN I'M NOT THERE, AREN'T YOU?!
HUH? I GET TORN UP WHEN YOU'RE THERE TOO, NOELLE.
SH-SHUT UP, DORK-STA!
...
A GIRL WHO CAN FIGHT ALONGSIDE HIM...
...
...EH?
I CAN'T BEAT THAT.
TMP
ASTA!

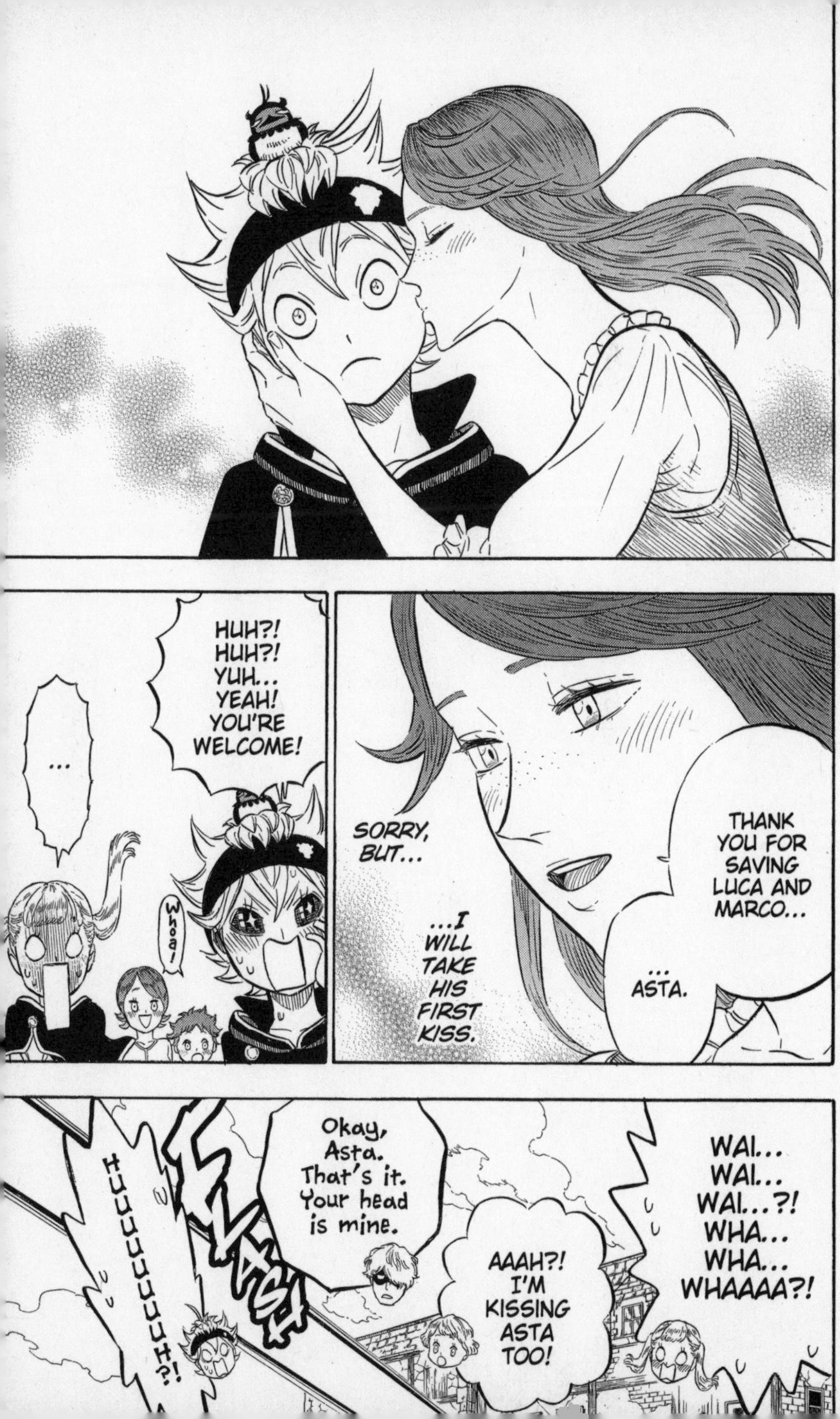
THANK YOU FOR SAVING LUCA AND MARCO...
... ASTA.
SORRY, BUT...
...I WILL TAKE HIS FIRST KISS.
HUH?! HUH?! YUH... YEAH! YOU'RE WELCOME!
...
Whoa!
WAI... WAI... WAI...?! WHA... WHA... WHAAAA?!
AAAH?! I'M KISSING ASTA TOO!
Okay, Asta. That's it. Your head is mine.
HUUUUUUUUH?!

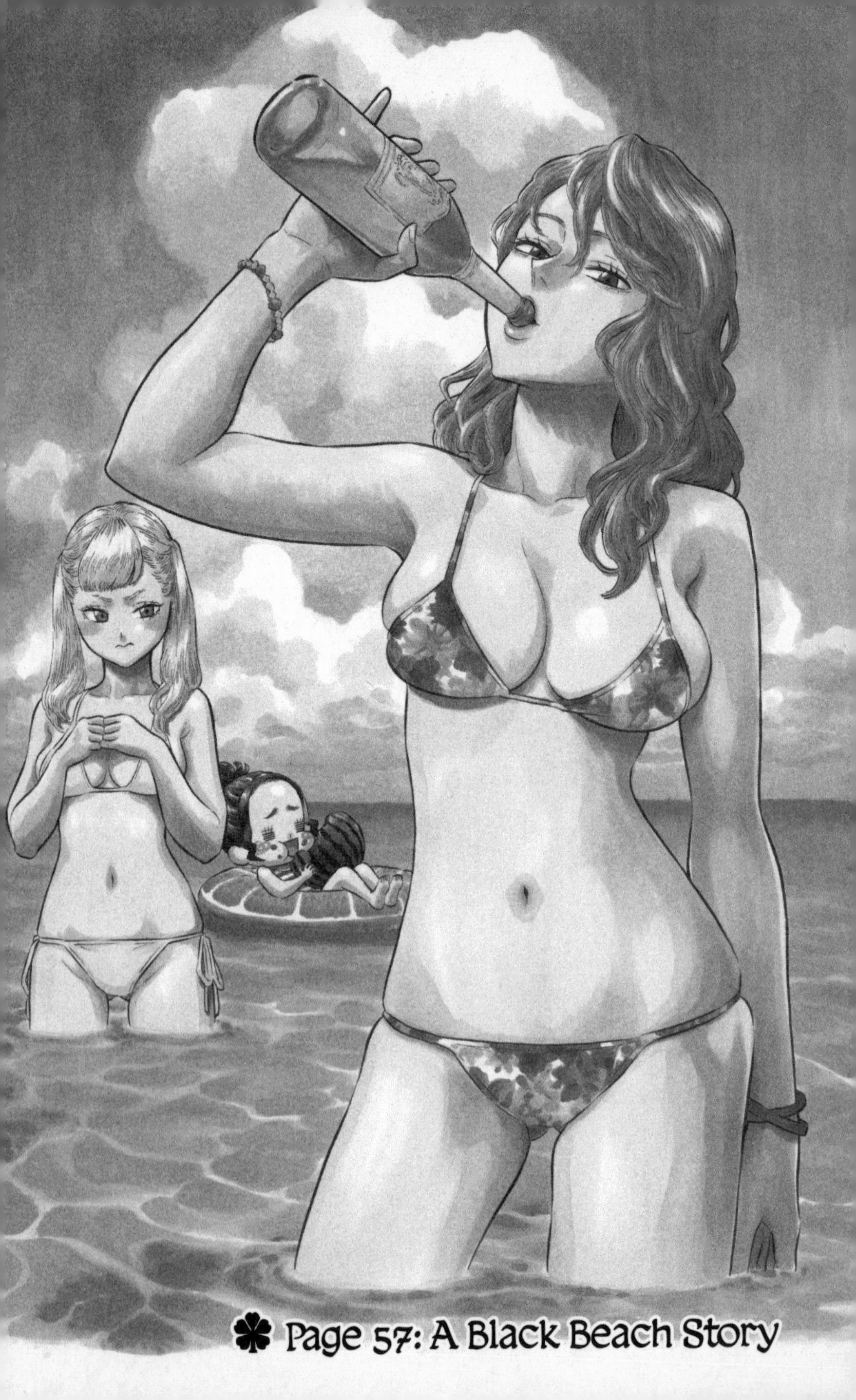

# Page 57: A Black Beach Story

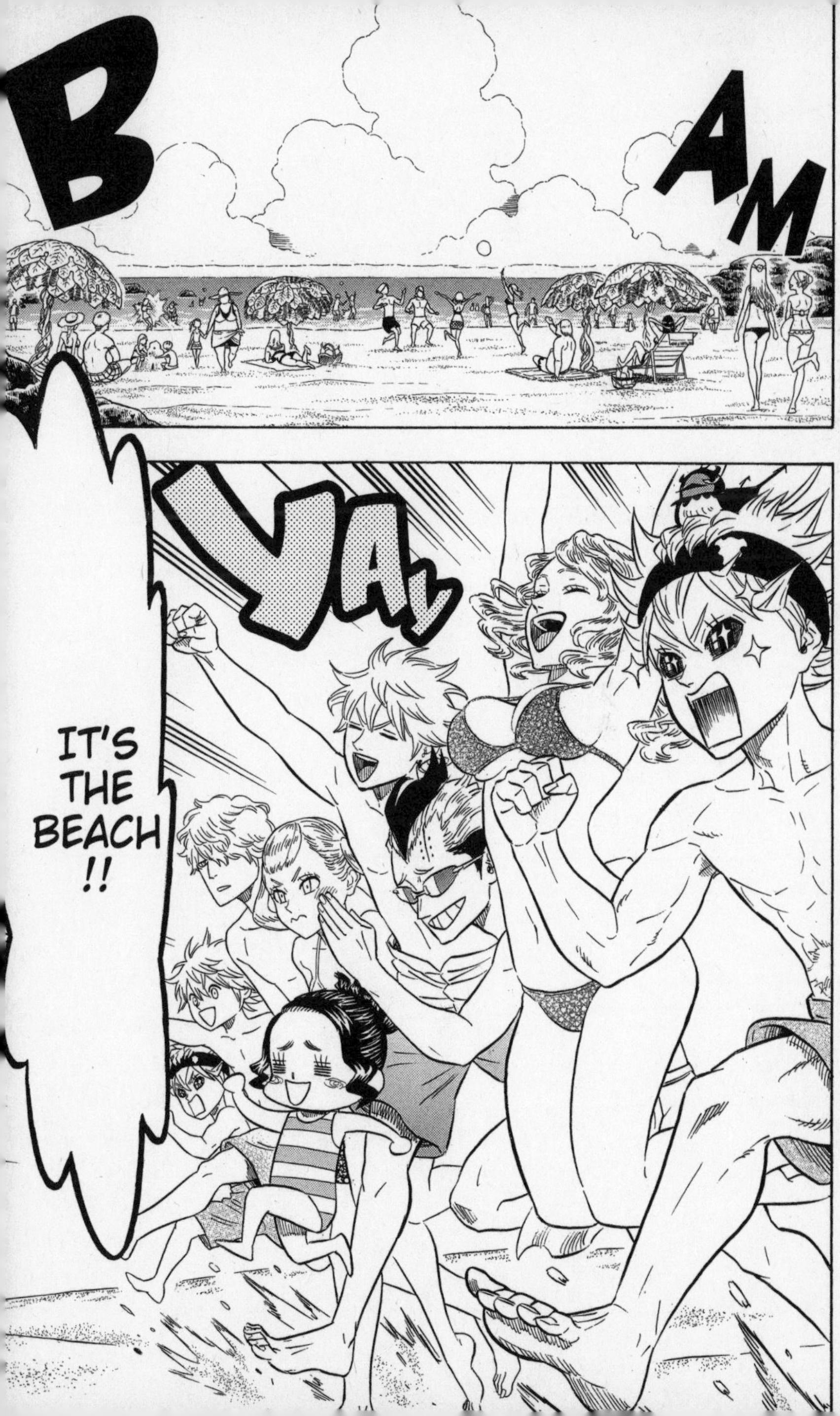
BAM
YA
IT'S THE BEACH!!

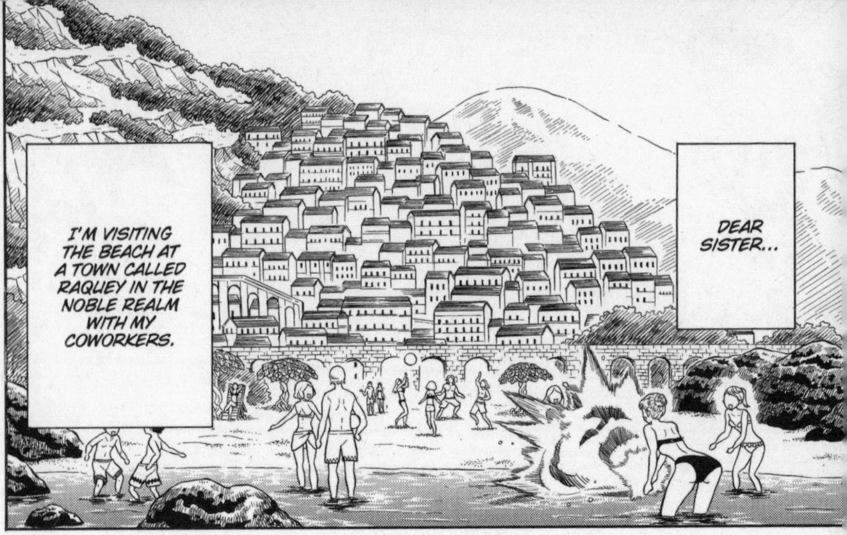
DEAR SISTER...
I'M VISITING THE BEACH AT A TOWN CALLED RAQUEY IN THE NOBLE REALM WITH MY COWORKERS.

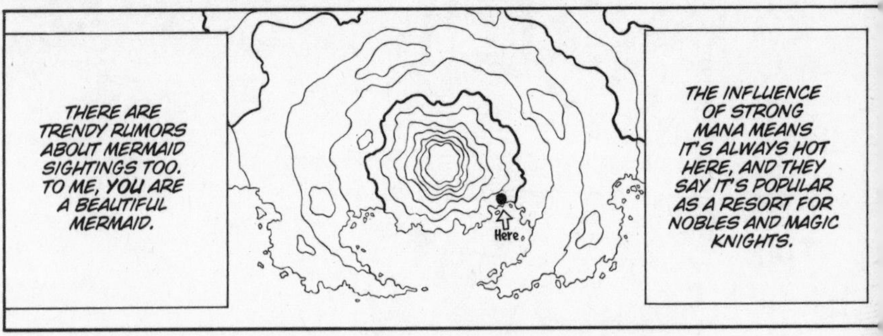
THE INFLUENCE OF STRONG MANA MEANS IT'S ALWAYS HOT HERE, AND THEY SAY IT'S POPULAR AS A RESORT FOR NOBLES AND MAGIC KNIGHTS.
Here
THERE ARE TRENDY RUMORS ABOUT MERMAID SIGHTINGS TOO. TO ME, YOU ARE A BEAUTIFUL MERMAID.

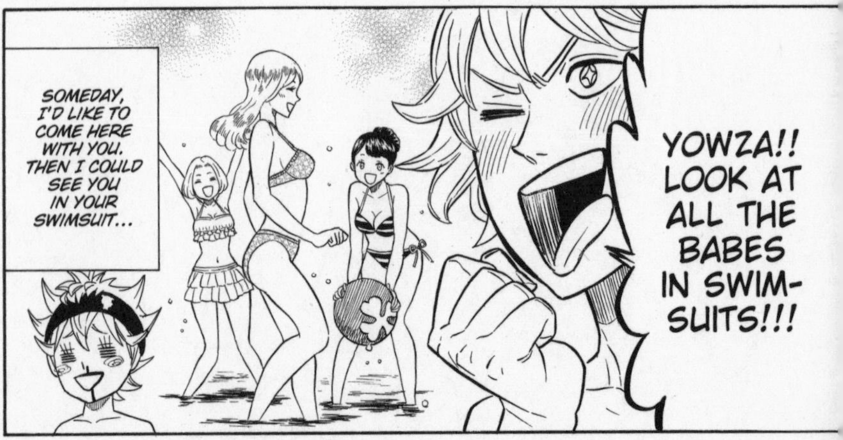
YOWZA!! LOOK AT ALL THE BABES IN SWIM-SUITS!!!
SOMEDAY, I'D LIKE TO COME HERE WITH YOU. THEN I COULD SEE YOU IN YOUR SWIMSUIT...

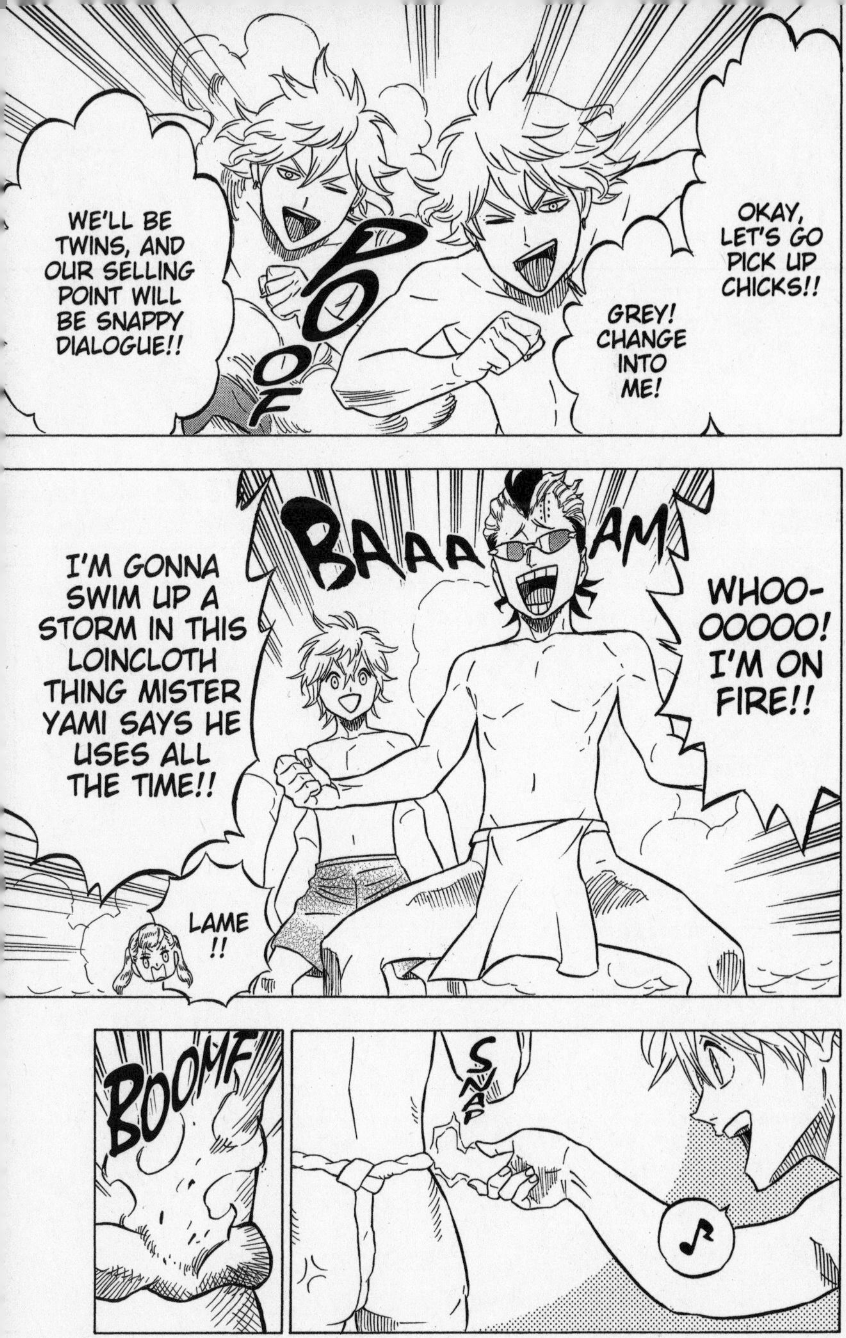
OKAY, LET'S GO PICK UP CHICKS!!
GREY! CHANGE INTO ME!
POOF
WE'LL BE TWINS, AND OUR SELLING POINT WILL BE SNAPPY DIALOGUE!!
WHOO-OOOOO! I'M ON FIRE!!
BAAAAM
I'M GONNA SWIM UP A STORM IN THIS LOINCLOTH THING MISTER YAMI SAYS HE USES ALL THE TIME!!
LAME !!
SNAP
♪
BOOMF

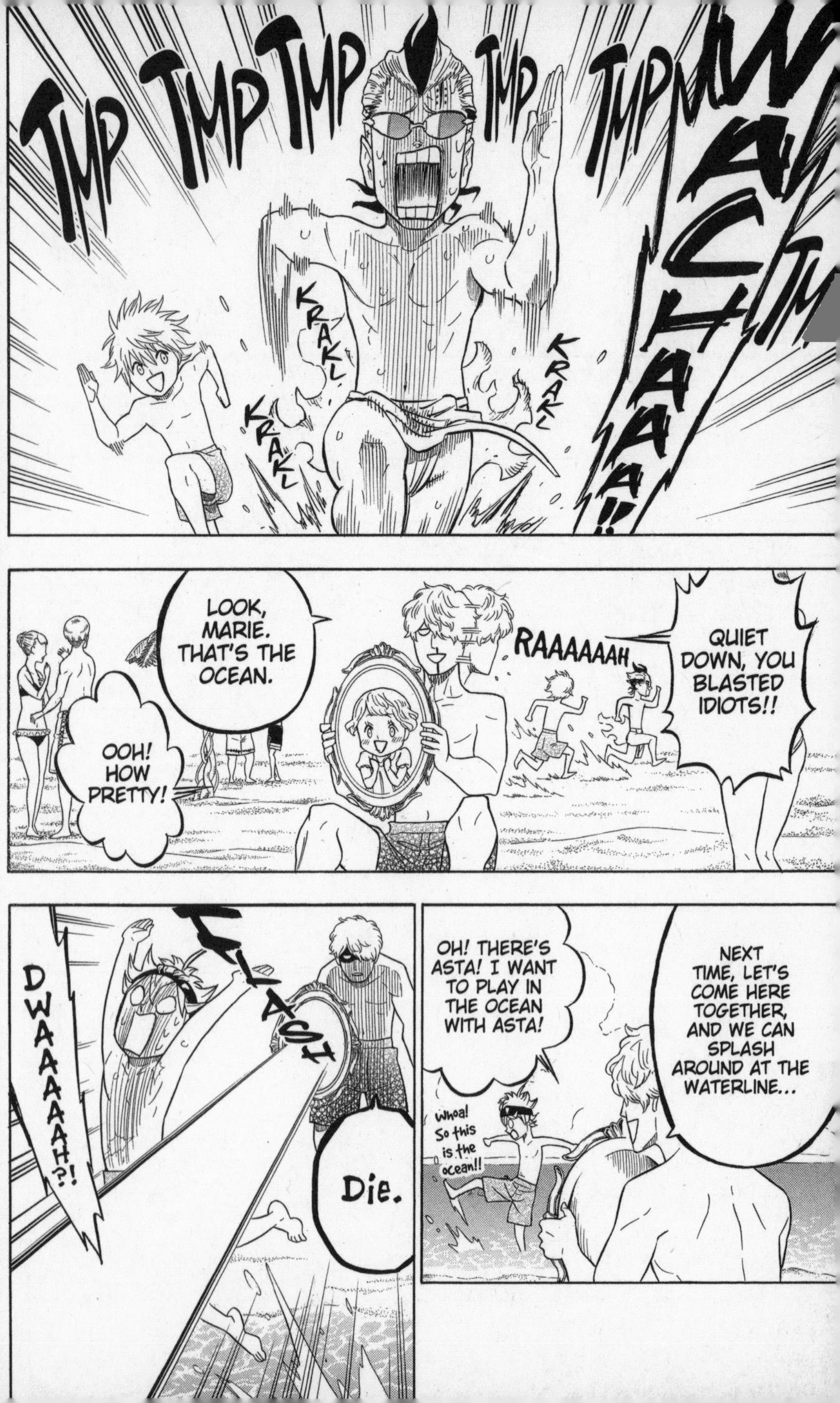
TMP
TMP
TMP
TMP
TMP
KRAKL
KRAKL
KRAKL
QUIET DOWN, YOU BLASTED IDIOTS!!
RAAAAAAH
LOOK, MARIE. THAT'S THE OCEAN.
OOH! HOW PRETTY!
NEXT TIME, LET'S COME HERE TOGETHER, AND WE CAN SPLASH AROUND AT THE WATERLINE...
OH! THERE'S ASTA! I WANT TO PLAY IN THE OCEAN WITH ASTA!
Whoa! So this is the ocean!!
FLASH
DWAAAAAAH?!
Die.

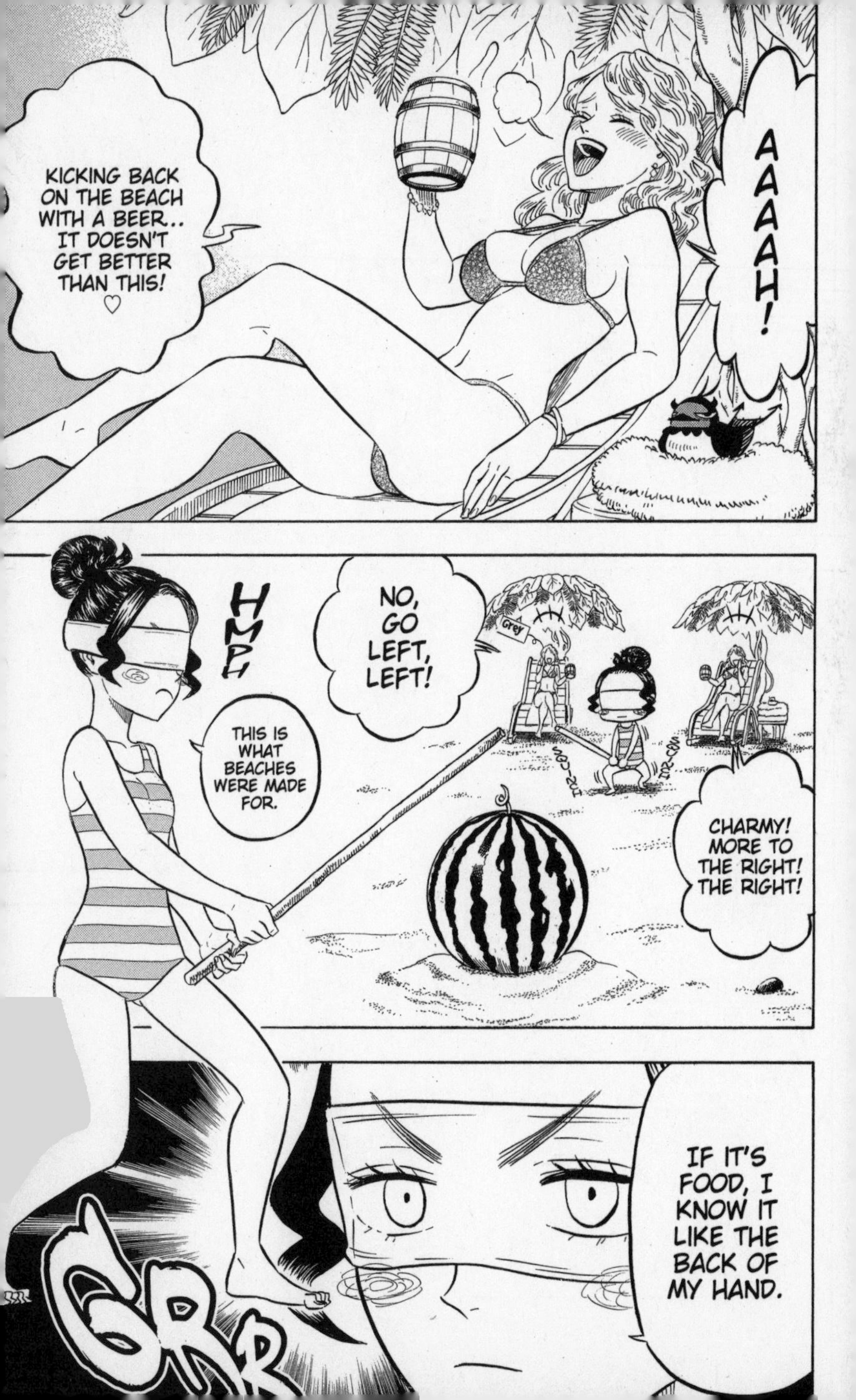

AAAAAH!
KICKING BACK ON THE BEACH WITH A BEER... IT DOESN'T GET BETTER THAN THIS! ♡
Grey
NO, GO LEFT, LEFT!
CHARMY! MORE TO THE RIGHT! THE RIGHT!
HMPH
THIS IS WHAT BEACHES WERE MADE FOR.
IF IT'S FOOD, I KNOW IT LIKE THE BACK OF MY HAND.
GRR

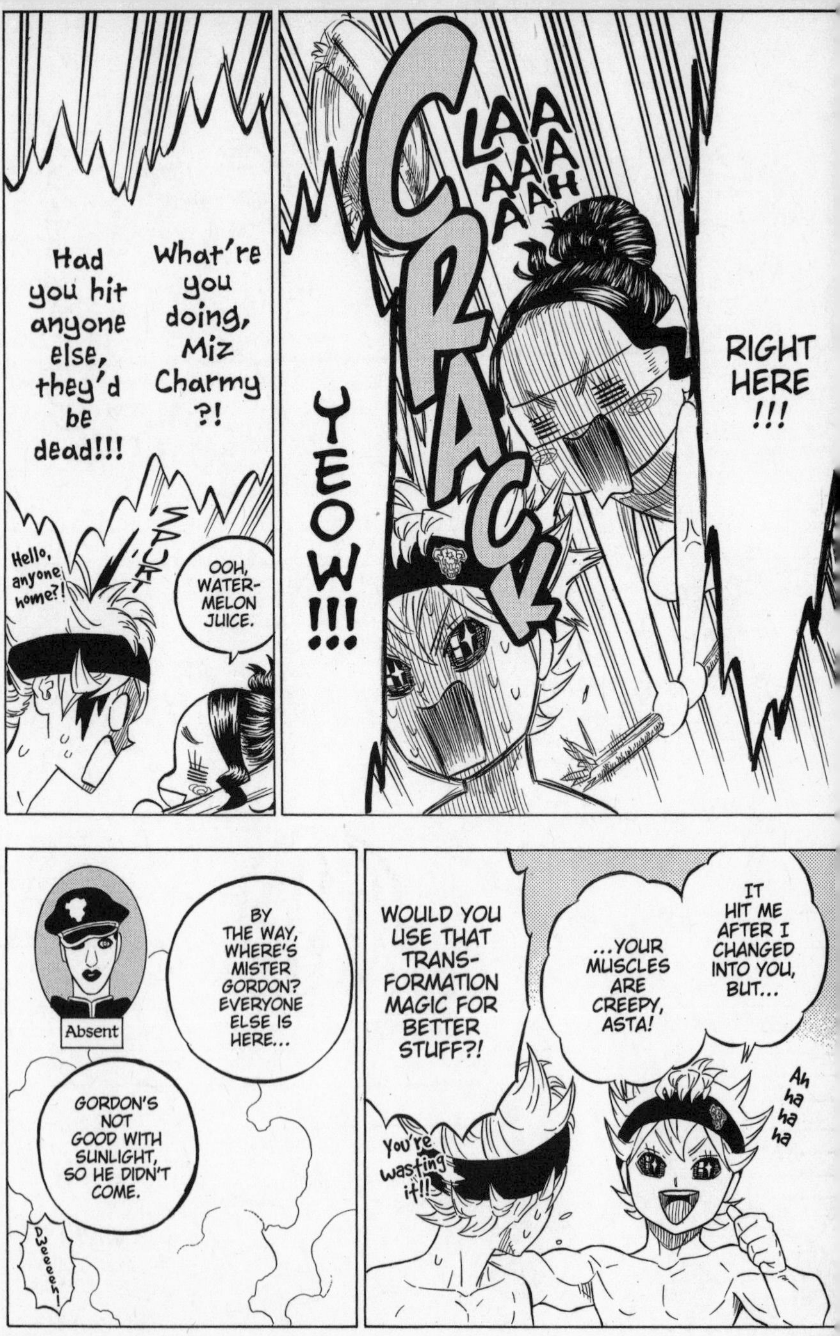
RIGHT HERE!!!
CLAAAAAAAAAH
CRACK
YEOW!!!
What're you doing, Miz Charmy?!
Had you hit anyone else, they'd be dead!!!
SPURT
OOH, WATER-MELON JUICE.
Hello, anyone home?!
IT HIT ME AFTER I CHANGED INTO YOU, BUT...
...YOUR MUSCLES ARE CREEPY, ASTA!
Ah ha ha ha
WOULD YOU USE THAT TRANS-FORMATION MAGIC FOR BETTER STUFF?!
You're wasting it!!
BY THE WAY, WHERE'S MISTER GORDON? EVERYONE ELSE IS HERE...
Absent
GORDON'S NOT GOOD WITH SUNLIGHT, SO HE DIDN'T COME.
Dweeeeen!

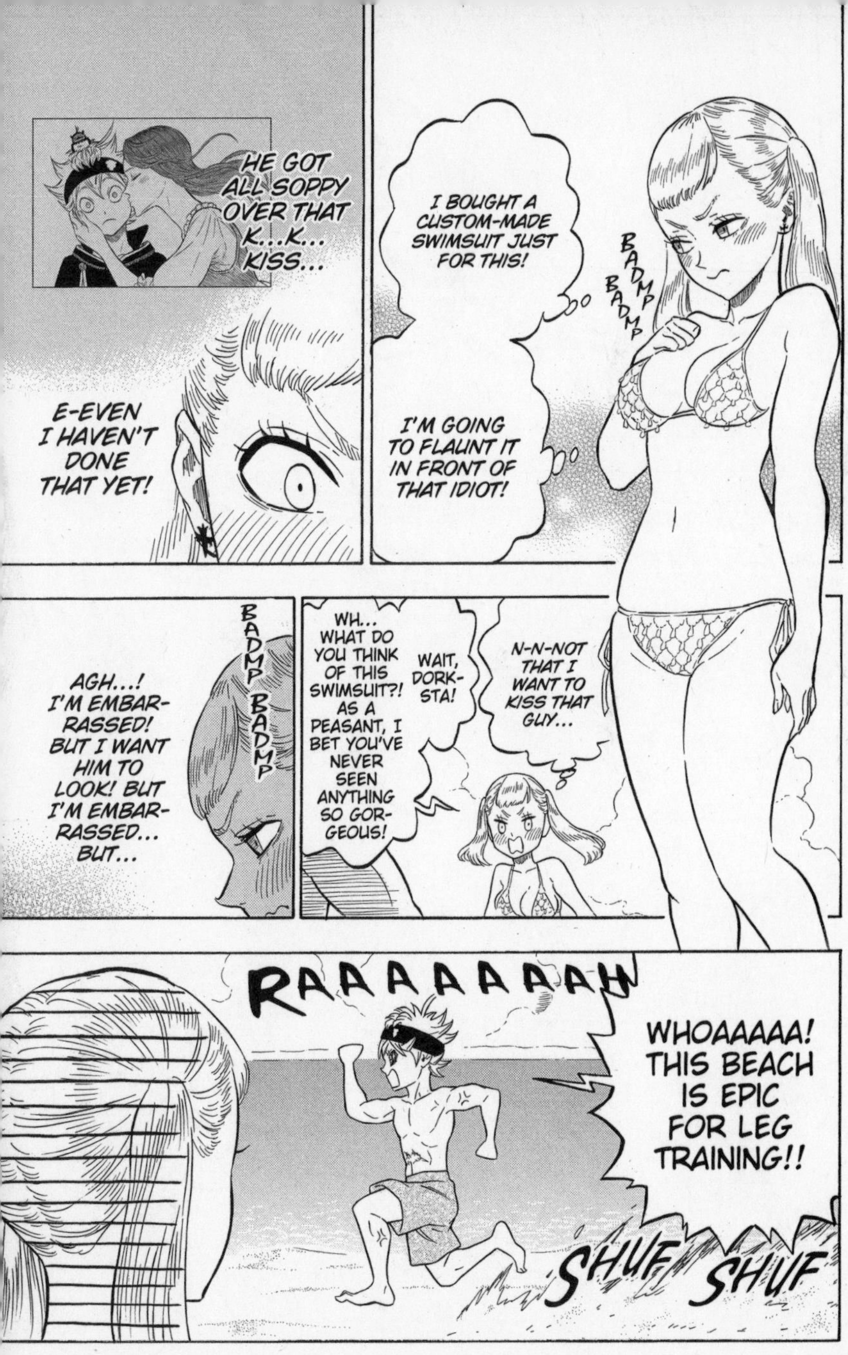
I BOUGHT A CUSTOM-MADE SWIMSUIT JUST FOR THIS!
BADMP BADMP
I'M GOING TO FLAUNT IT IN FRONT OF THAT IDIOT!
HE GOT ALL SOPPY OVER THAT K...K... KISS...
E-EVEN I HAVEN'T DONE THAT YET!
N-N-NOT THAT I WANT TO KISS THAT GUY...
WAIT, DORK-STA!
WH... WHAT DO YOU THINK OF THIS SWIMSUIT?! AS A PEASANT, I BET YOU'VE NEVER SEEN ANYTHING SO GOR-GEOUS!
BADMP BADMP
AGH...! I'M EMBAR-RASSED! BUT I WANT HIM TO LOOK! BUT I'M EMBAR-RASSED... BUT...
RAAAAAAAH
WHOAAAAA! THIS BEACH IS EPIC FOR LEG TRAINING!!
SHUF SHUF

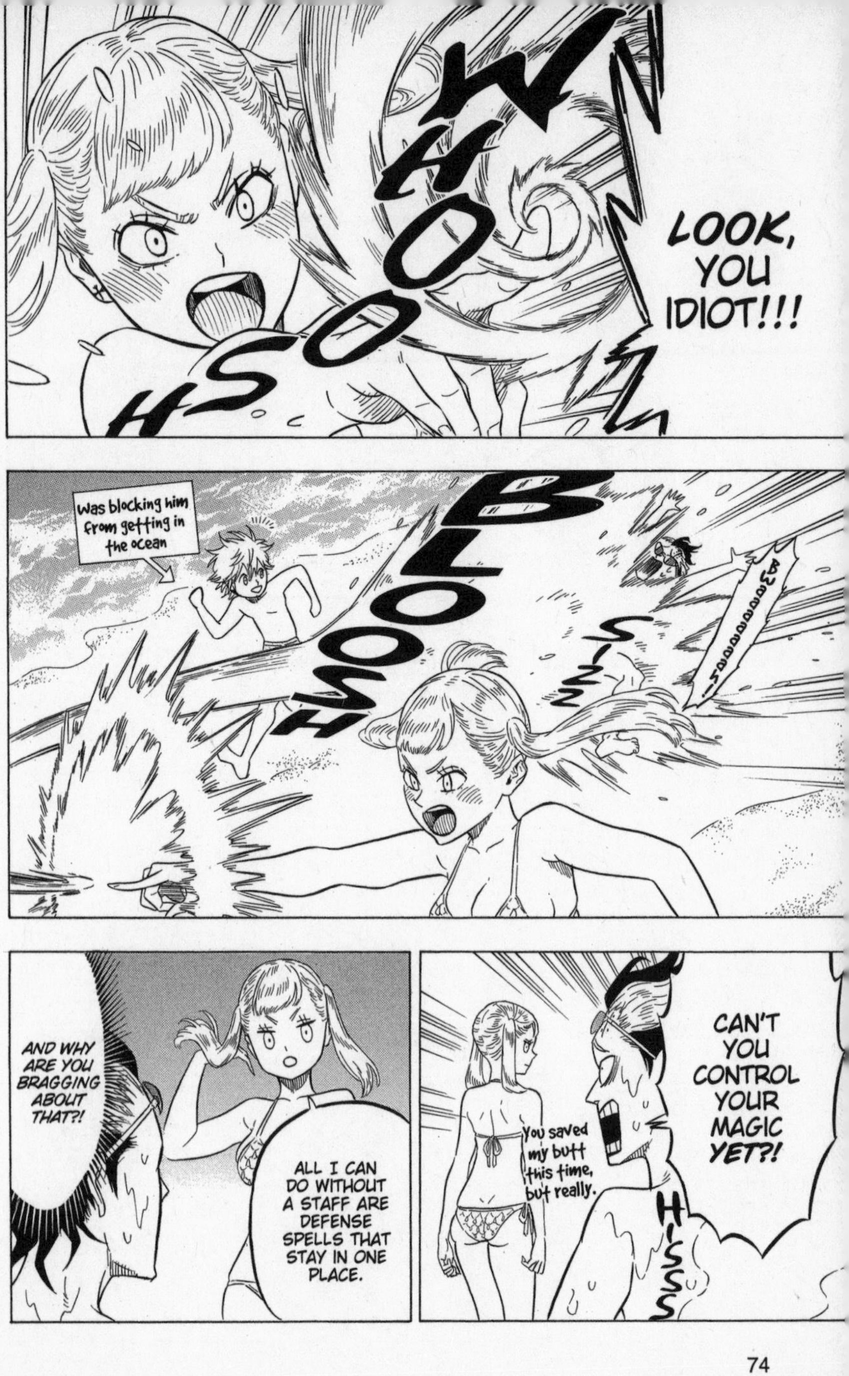
WHOOSH
LOOK, YOU IDIOT!!!
BLOOSH
BWAAAAAAAAAAS!
SIZZ
Was blocking him from getting in the ocean
CAN'T YOU CONTROL YOUR MAGIC YET?!
You saved my butt this time, but really.
HISSS
ALL I CAN DO WITHOUT A STAFF ARE DEFENSE SPELLS THAT STAY IN ONE PLACE.
AND WHY ARE YOU BRAGGING ABOUT THAT?!

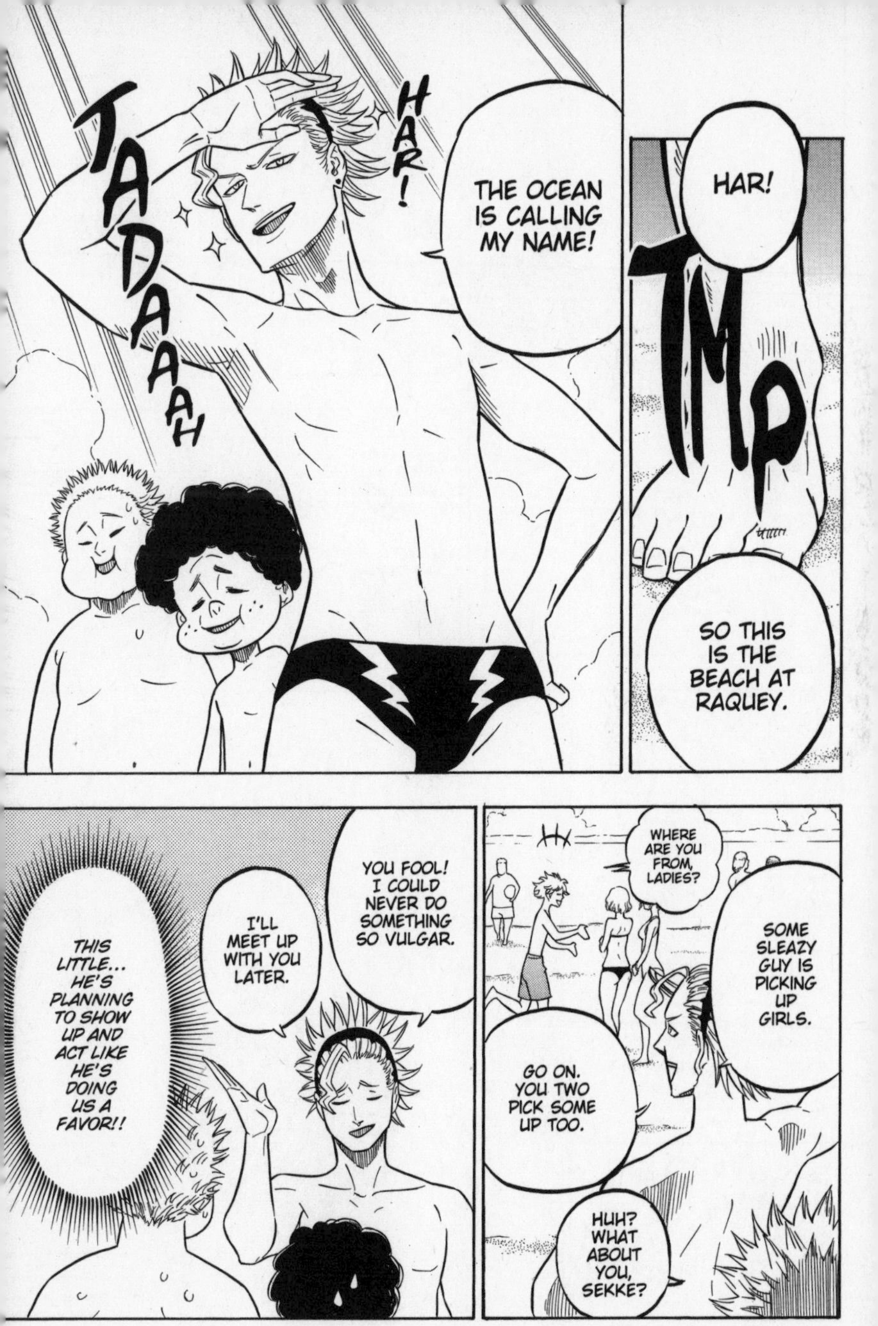
HAR!
TMP
SO THIS IS THE BEACH AT RAQUEY.
HAR!
THE OCEAN IS CALLING MY NAME!
TADAAAAH
WHERE ARE YOU FROM, LADIES?
SOME SLEAZY GUY IS PICKING UP GIRLS.
GO ON. YOU TWO PICK SOME UP TOO.
HUH? WHAT ABOUT YOU, SEKKE?
YOU FOOL! I COULD NEVER DO SOMETHING SO VULGAR.
I'LL MEET UP WITH YOU LATER.
THIS LITTLE... HE'S PLANNING TO SHOW UP AND ACT LIKE HE'S DOING US A FAVOR!!

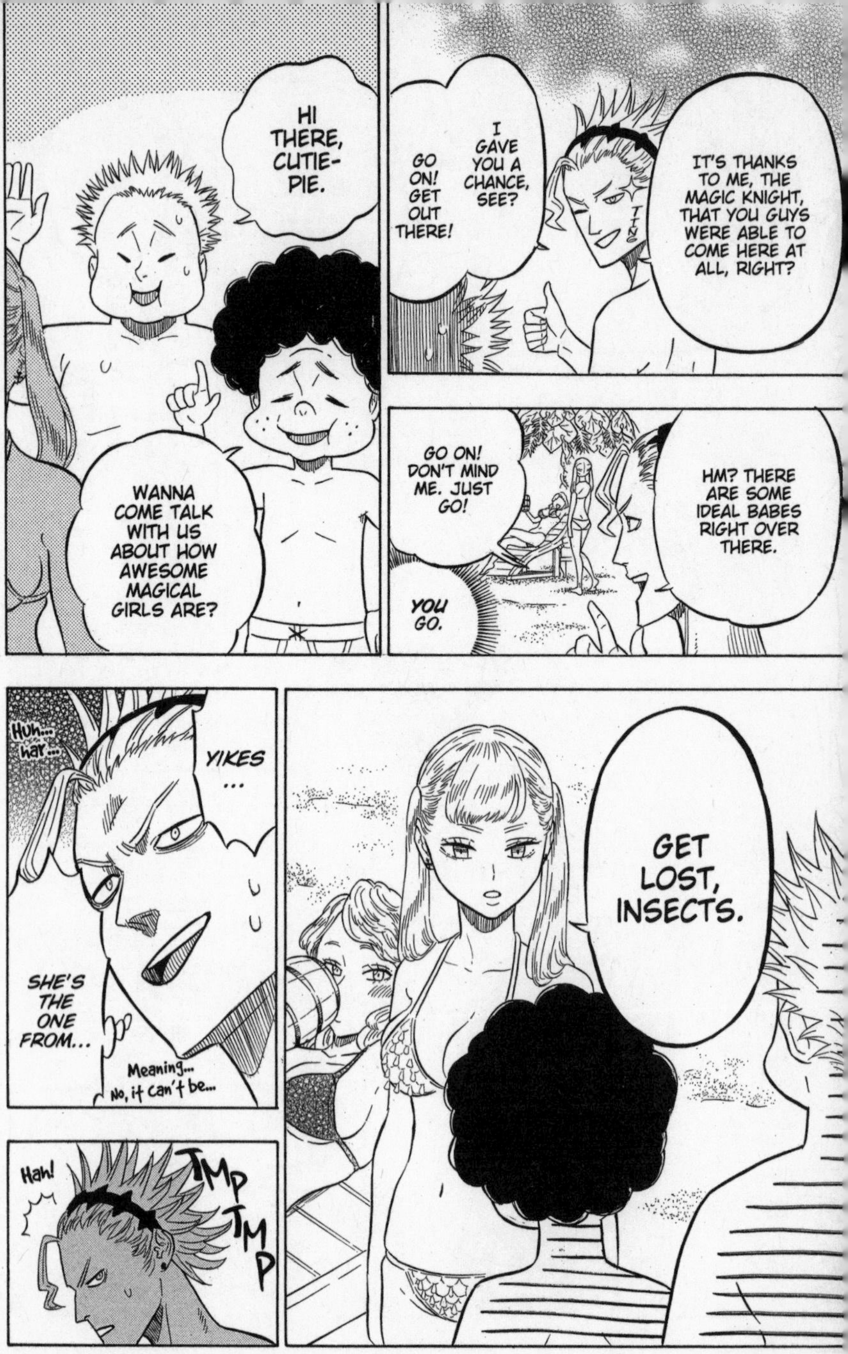
IT'S THANKS TO ME, THE MAGIC KNIGHT, THAT YOU GUYS WERE ABLE TO COME HERE AT ALL, RIGHT?
TING
I GAVE YOU A CHANCE, SEE?
GO ON! GET OUT THERE!
HM? THERE ARE SOME IDEAL BABES RIGHT OVER THERE.
GO ON! DON'T MIND ME. JUST GO!
YOU GO.
HI THERE, CUTIE-PIE.
WANNA COME TALK WITH US ABOUT HOW AWESOME MAGICAL GIRLS ARE?
GET LOST, INSECTS.
YIKES...
Huh... har...
SHE'S THE ONE FROM...
Meaning... No, it can't be...
Hah!
TMP TMP

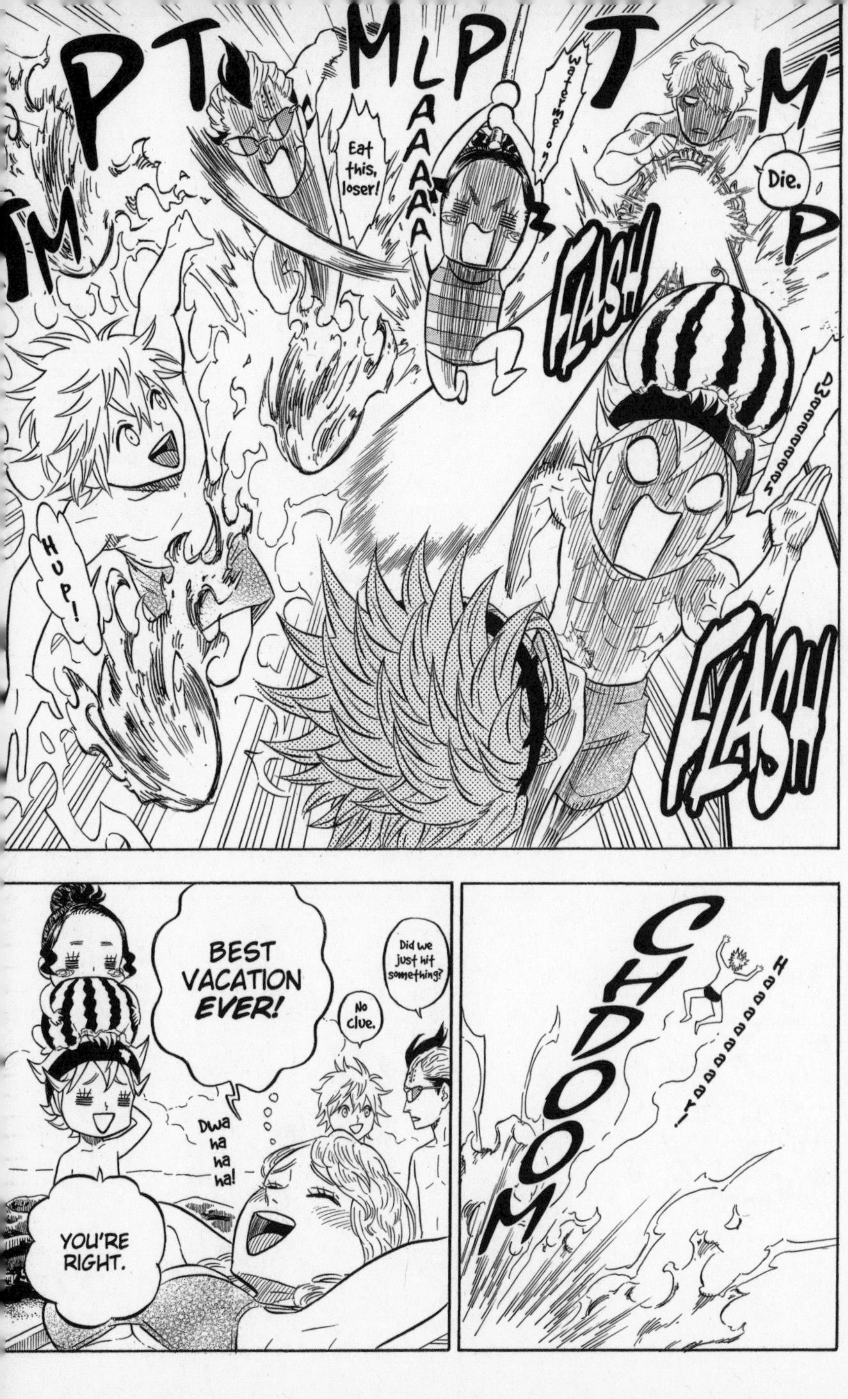
Die.
watermelon!
LAAAAAAA
Eat this, loser!
ZASH!
Dwaaaaaaaaa
HUP!
ZASH!
CHDOOM
Haaaaaaaaaaa!
Did we just hit something?
No clue.
BEST VACATION EVER!
Dwa ha ha ha!
YOU'RE RIGHT.

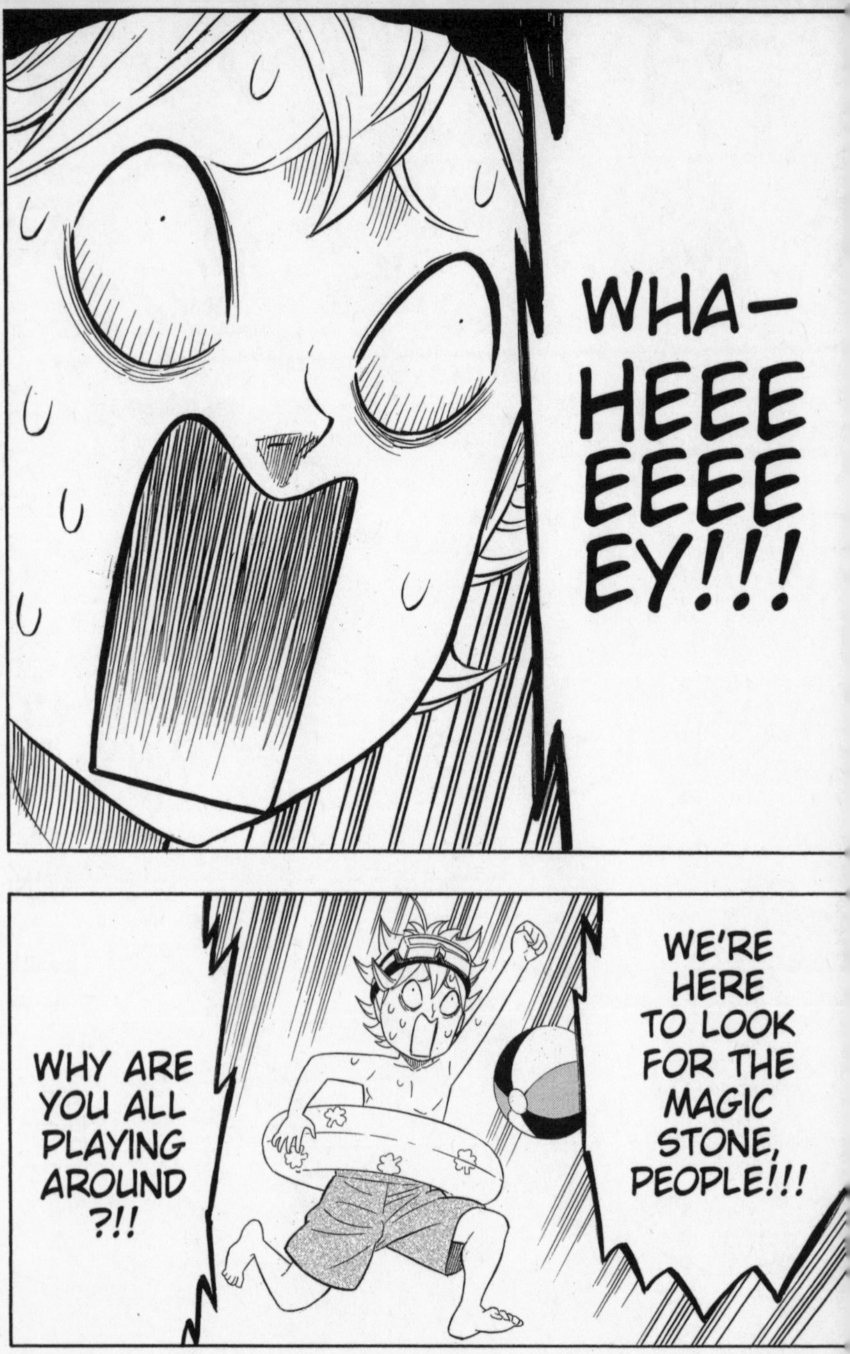
WHA-HEEEEEEEEY!!!
WE'RE HERE TO LOOK FOR THE MAGIC STONE, PEOPLE!!!
WHY ARE YOU ALL PLAYING AROUND?!!

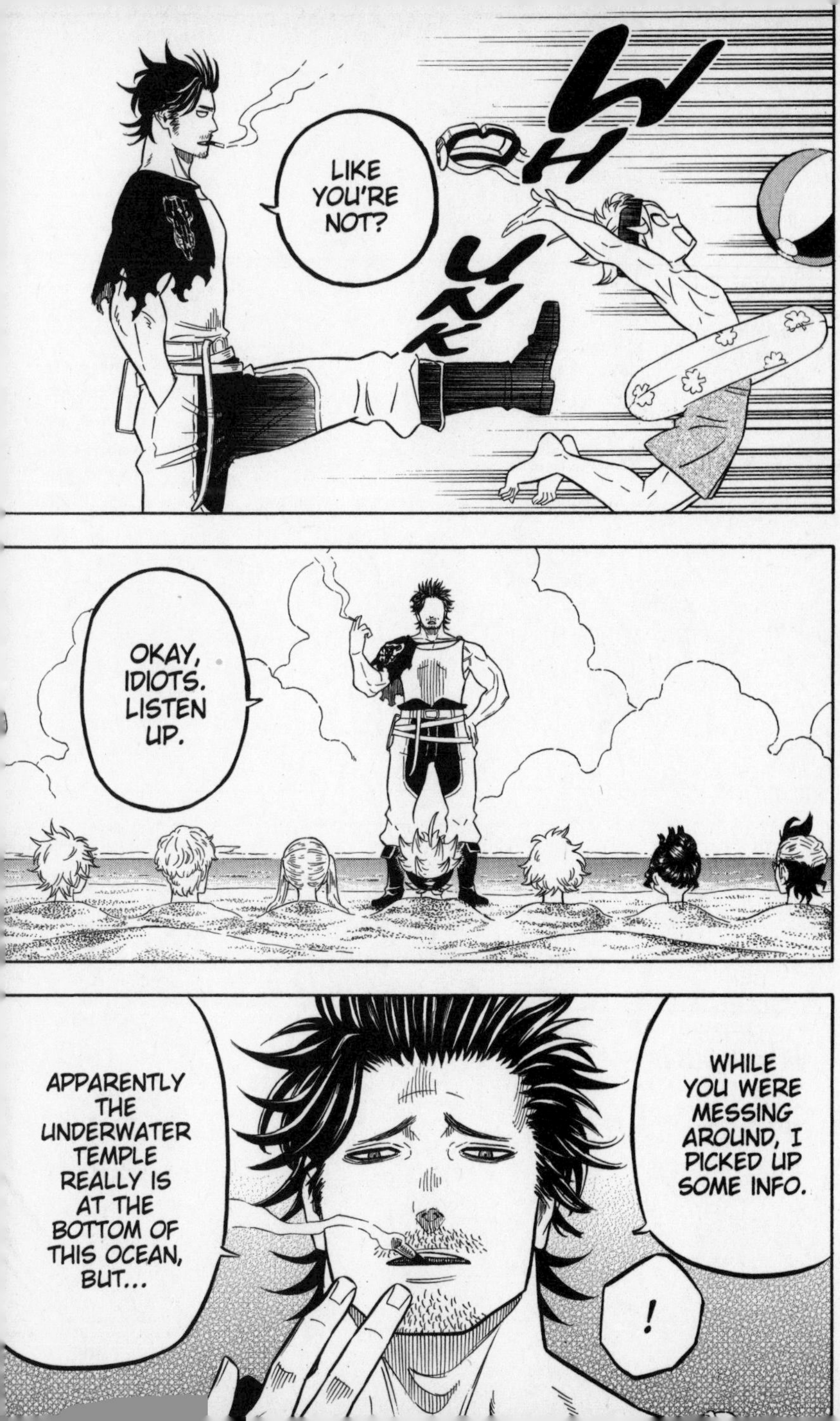
WHUNK
LIKE YOU'RE NOT?
OKAY, IDIOTS. LISTEN UP.
WHILE YOU WERE MESSING AROUND, I PICKED UP SOME INFO.
APPARENTLY THE UNDERWATER TEMPLE REALLY IS AT THE BOTTOM OF THIS OCEAN, BUT...
!

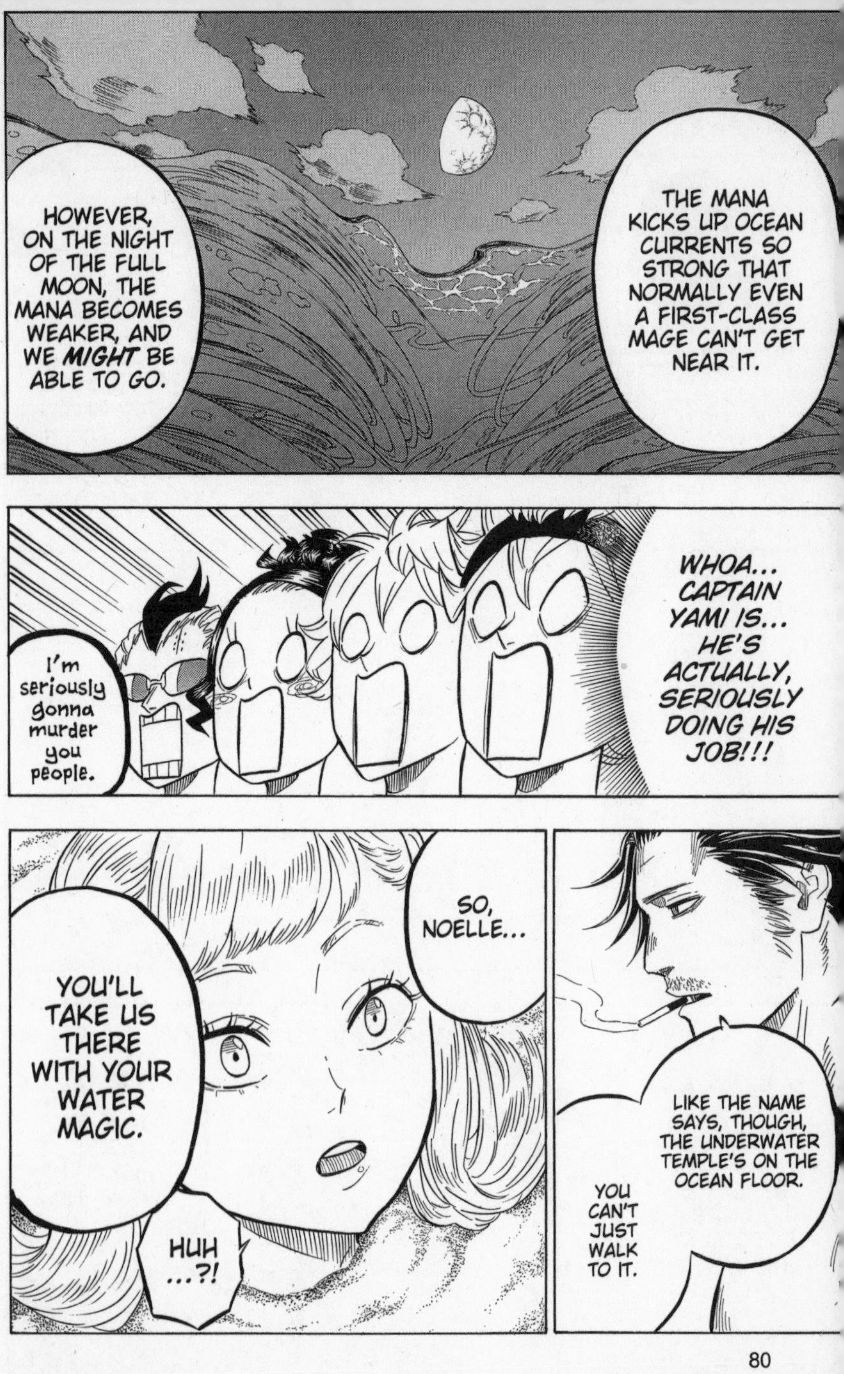
THE MANA KICKS UP OCEAN CURRENTS SO STRONG THAT NORMALLY EVEN A FIRST-CLASS MAGE CAN'T GET NEAR IT.
HOWEVER, ON THE NIGHT OF THE FULL MOON, THE MANA BECOMES WEAKER, AND WE *MIGHT* BE ABLE TO GO.
WHOA... CAPTAIN YAMI IS... HE'S ACTUALLY, SERIOUSLY DOING HIS JOB!!!
I'm seriously gonna murder you people.
LIKE THE NAME SAYS, THOUGH, THE UNDERWATER TEMPLE'S ON THE OCEAN FLOOR.
YOU CAN'T JUST WALK TO IT.
SO, NOELLE...
YOU'LL TAKE US THERE WITH YOUR WATER MAGIC.
HUH ...?!

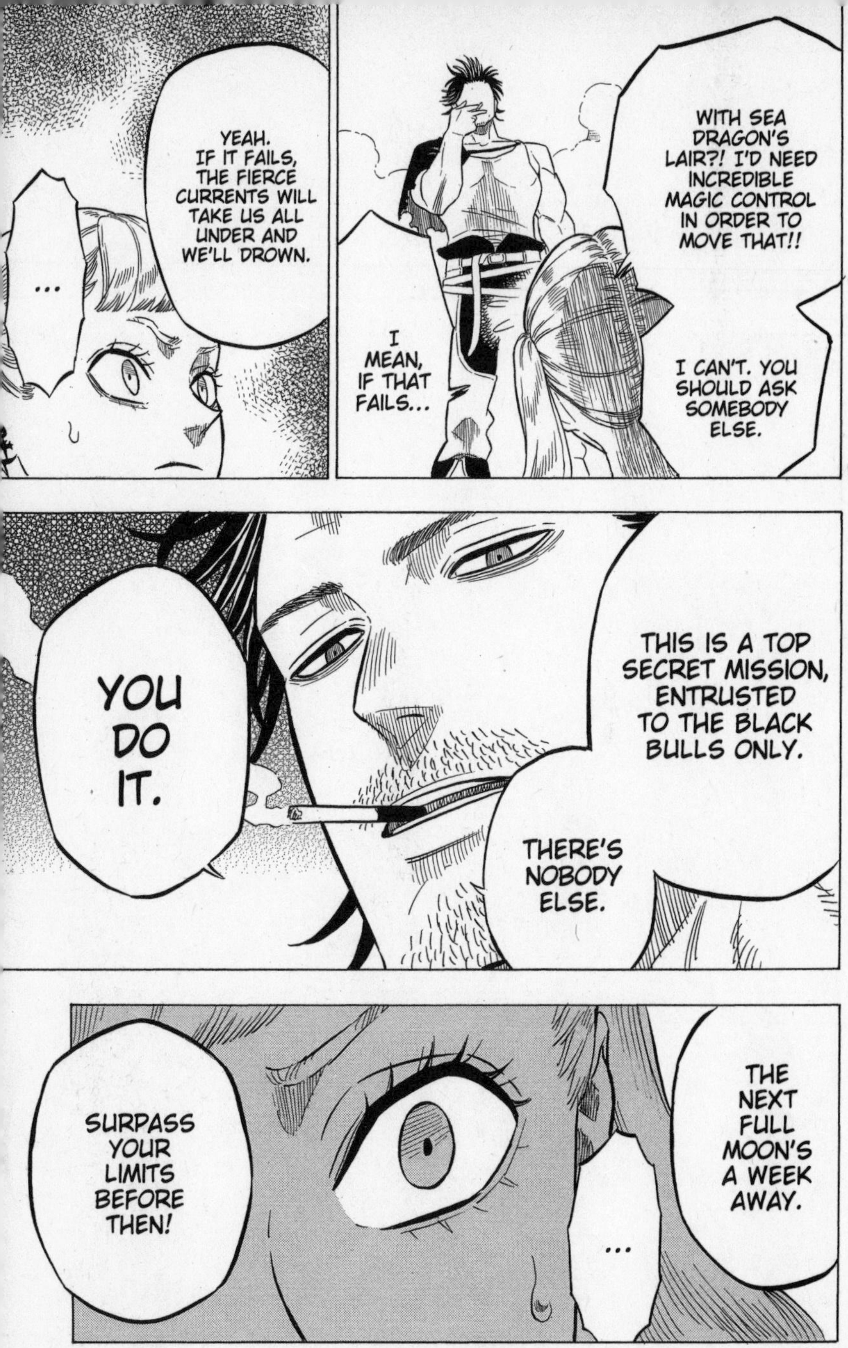
WITH SEA DRAGON'S LAIR?! I'D NEED INCREDIBLE MAGIC CONTROL IN ORDER TO MOVE THAT!!
I CAN'T. YOU SHOULD ASK SOMEBODY ELSE.
I MEAN, IF THAT FAILS...
YEAH. IF IT FAILS, THE FIERCE CURRENTS WILL TAKE US ALL UNDER AND WE'LL DROWN.
...
THIS IS A TOP SECRET MISSION, ENTRUSTED TO THE BLACK BULLS ONLY.
THERE'S NOBODY ELSE.
YOU DO IT.
THE NEXT FULL MOON'S A WEEK AWAY.
...
SURPASS YOUR LIMITS BEFORE THEN!

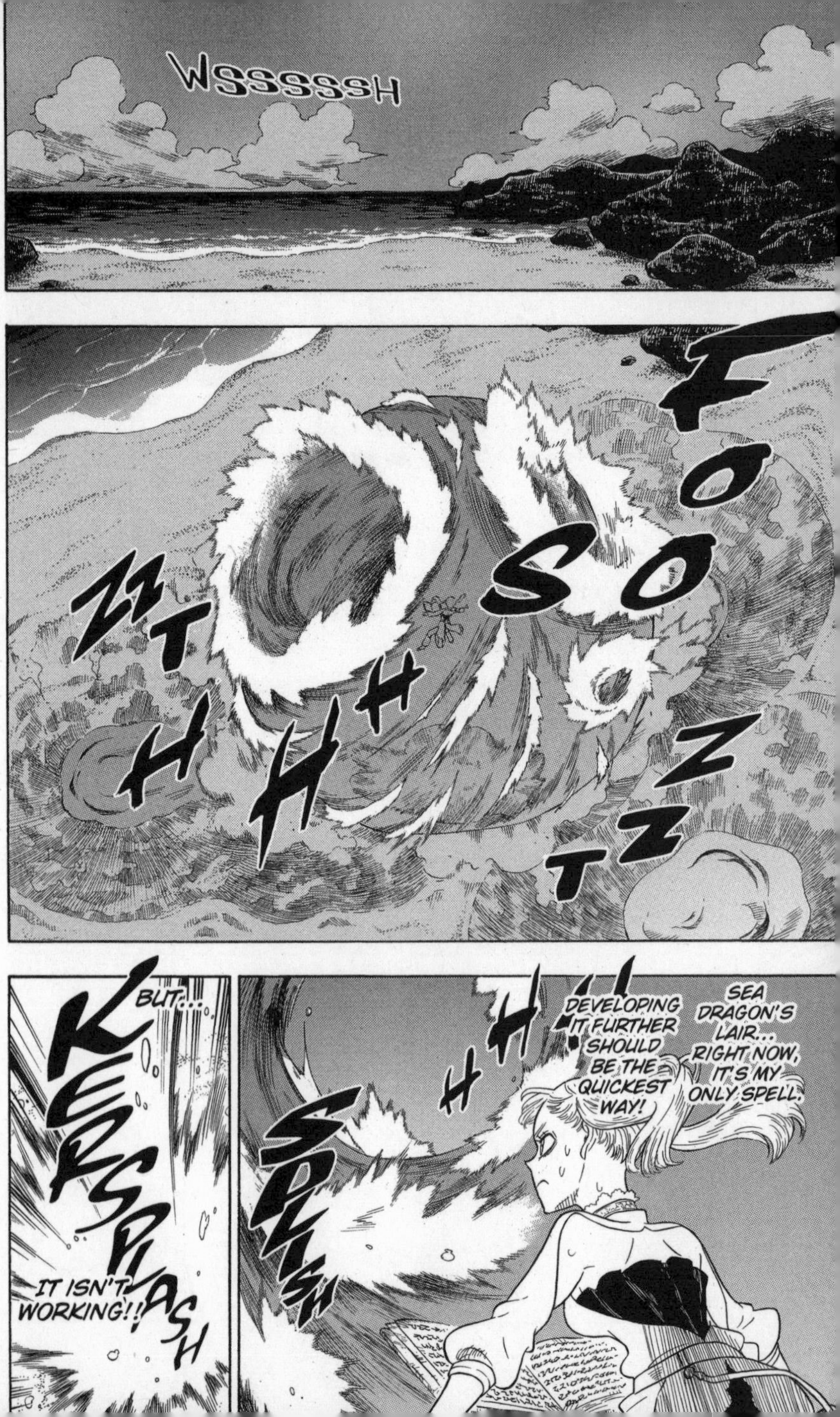
WSSSSSSH
SEA DRAGON'S LAIR... RIGHT NOW, IT'S MY ONLY SPELL.
DEVELOPING IT FURTHER SHOULD BE THE QUICKEST WAY!
SPLASH
BUT...
KERSPLASH
IT ISN'T WORKING!!

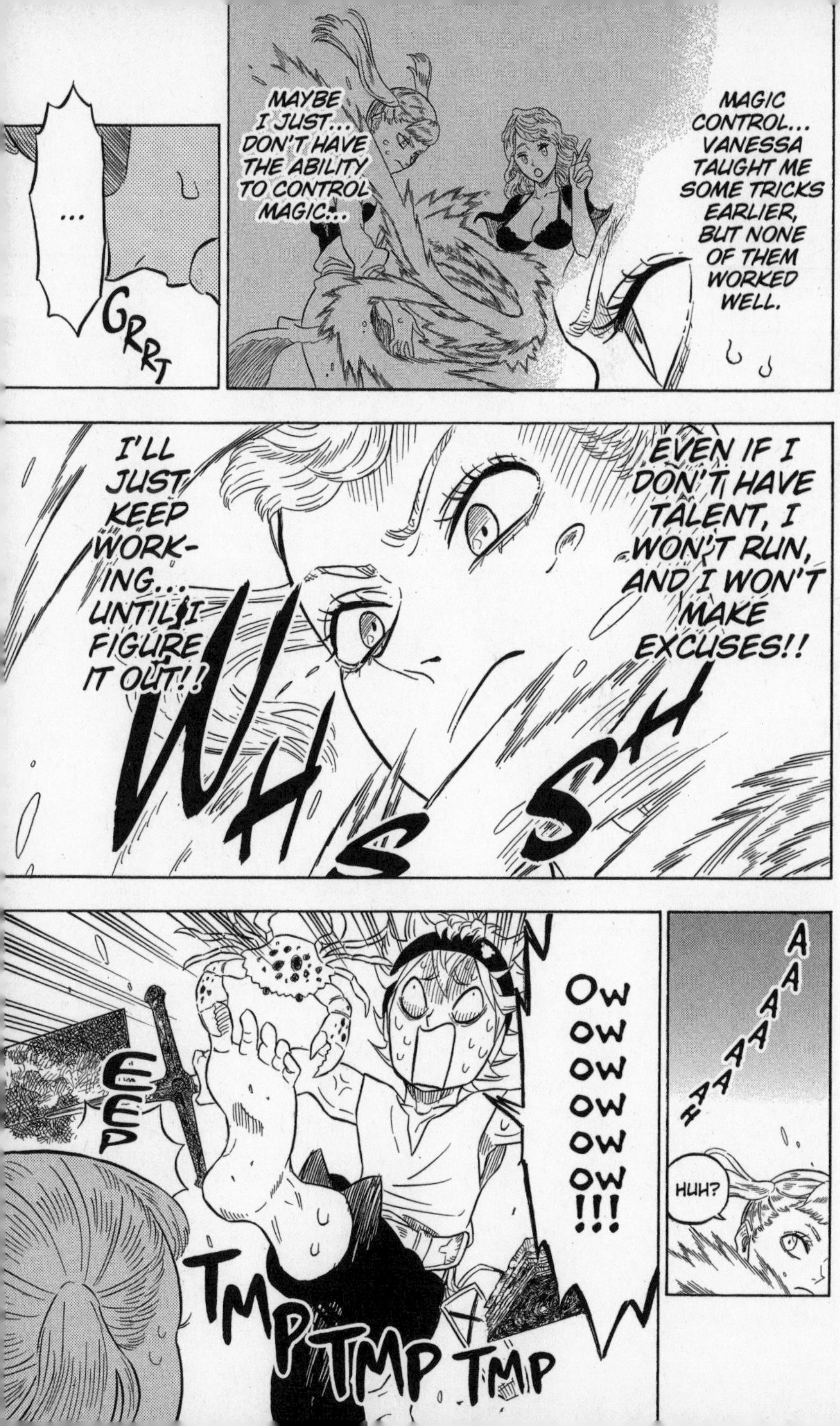
MAGIC CONTROL... VANESSA TAUGHT ME SOME TRICKS EARLIER, BUT NONE OF THEM WORKED WELL.
MAYBE I JUST... DON'T HAVE THE ABILITY TO CONTROL MAGIC...
...
GRRRT
EVEN IF I DON'T HAVE TALENT, I WON'T RUN, AND I WON'T MAKE EXCUSES!!
I'LL JUST KEEP WORKING... UNTIL I FIGURE IT OUT!!
WHSSH
AAAAAAAH
HUH?
OW OW OW OW OW OW!!!
EEEP
TMP TMP TMP TMP

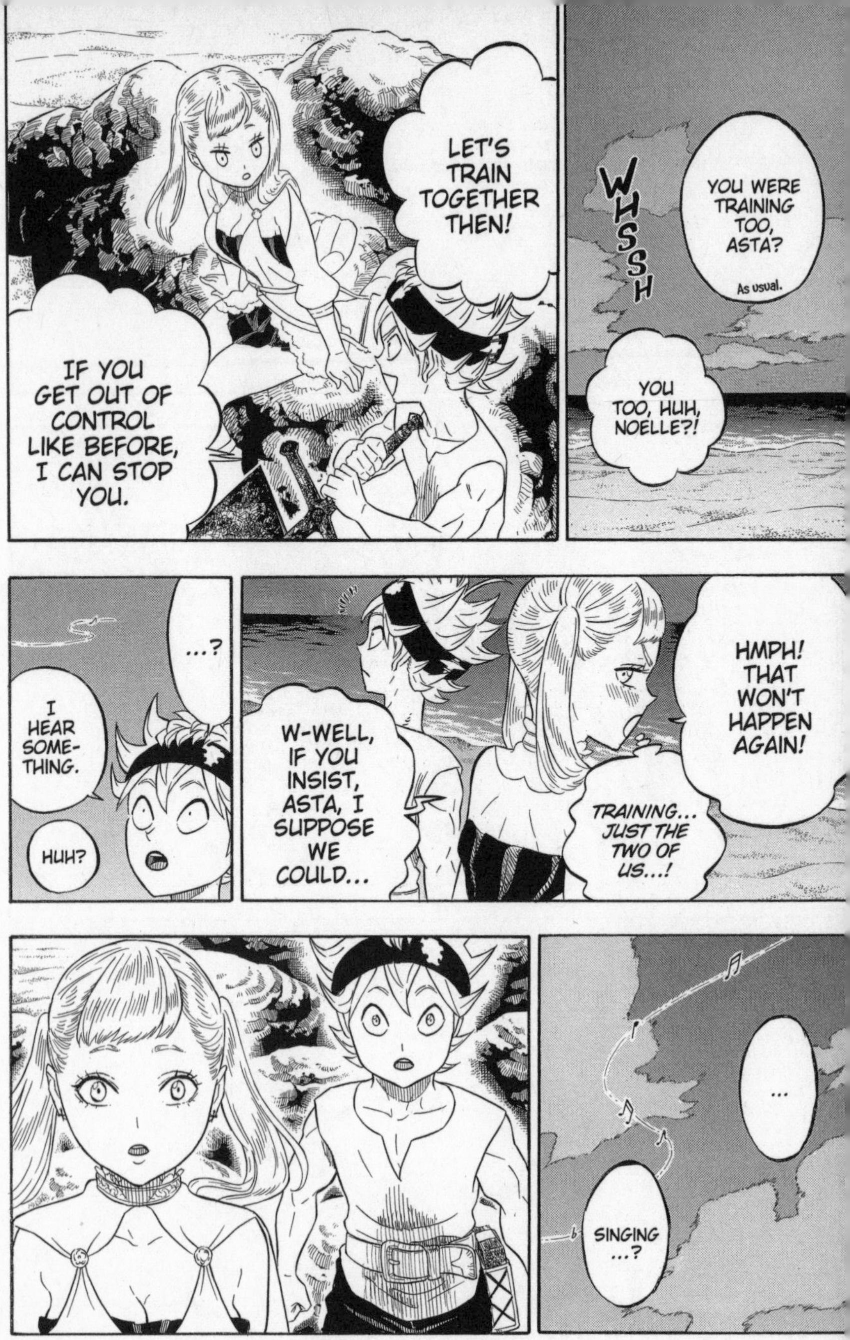
YOU WERE TRAINING TOO, ASTA?
As usual.
WHSSH
YOU TOO, HUH, NOELLE?!
LET'S TRAIN TOGETHER THEN!
IF YOU GET OUT OF CONTROL LIKE BEFORE, I CAN STOP YOU.
HMPH! THAT WON'T HAPPEN AGAIN!
TRAINING... JUST THE TWO OF US...!
W-WELL, IF YOU INSIST, ASTA, I SUPPOSE WE COULD...
...?
I HEAR SOMETHING.
HUH?
...
SINGING ...?

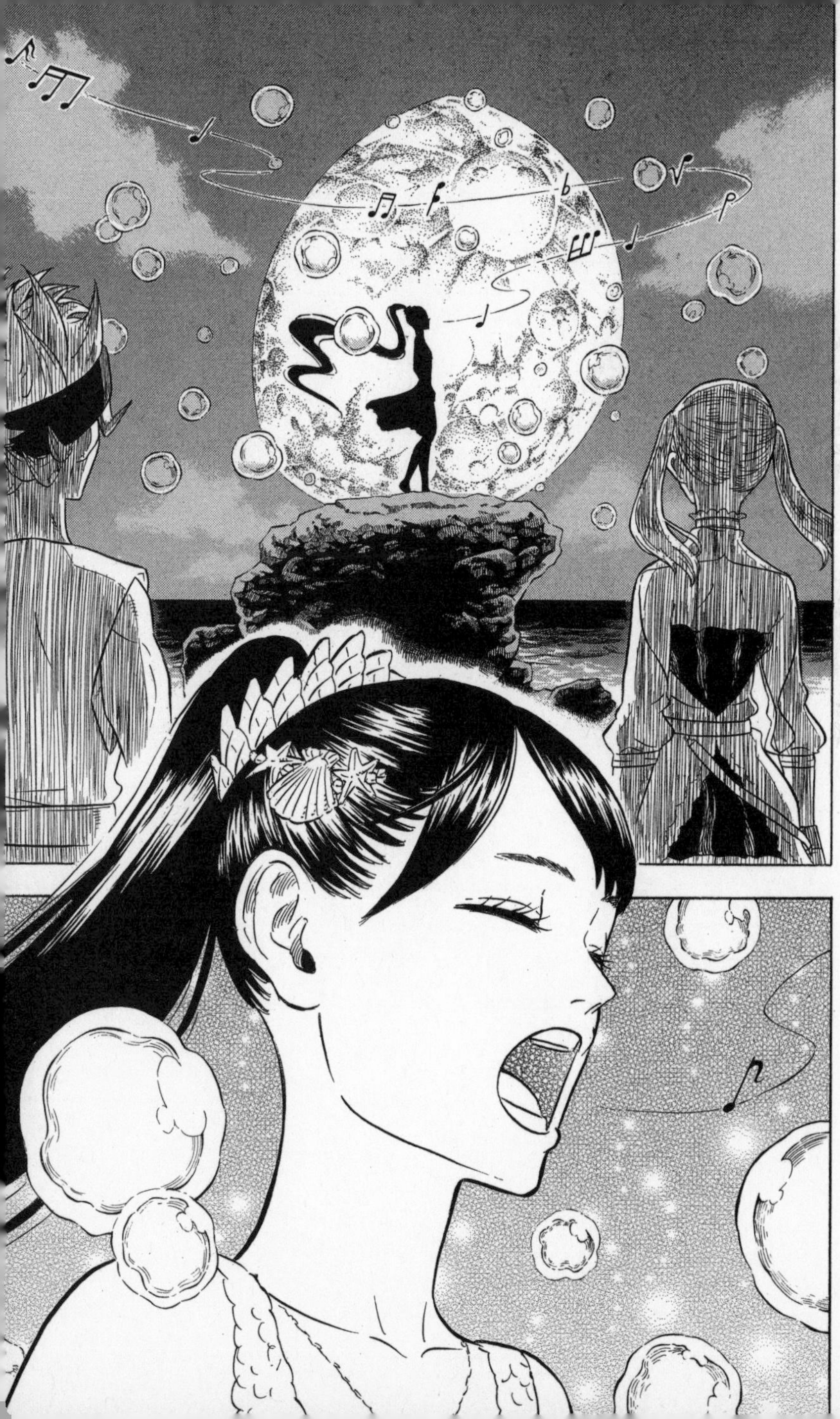

# Jack the Ripper

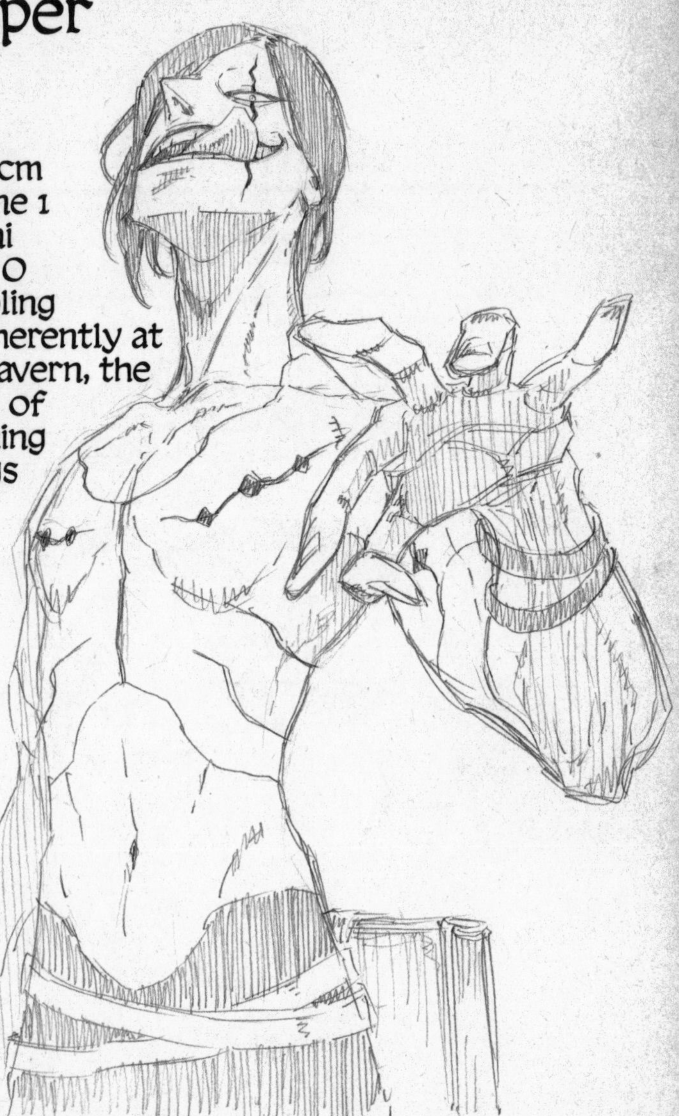

Age: 28
Height: 197 cm
Birthday: June 1
Sign: Gemini
Blood Type: O
Likes: Rambling incoherently at the tavern, the thrill of slashing things

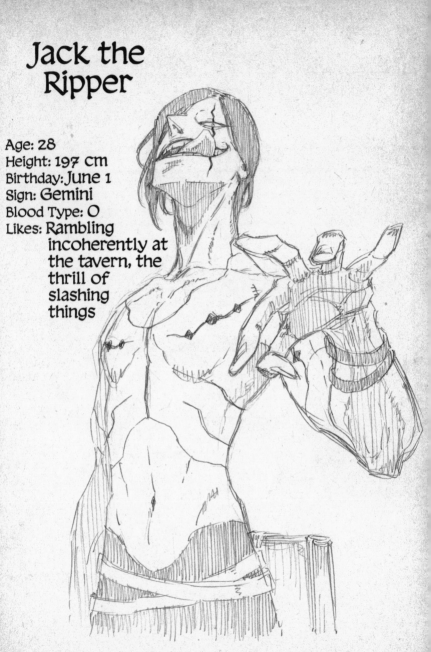

Character Profile

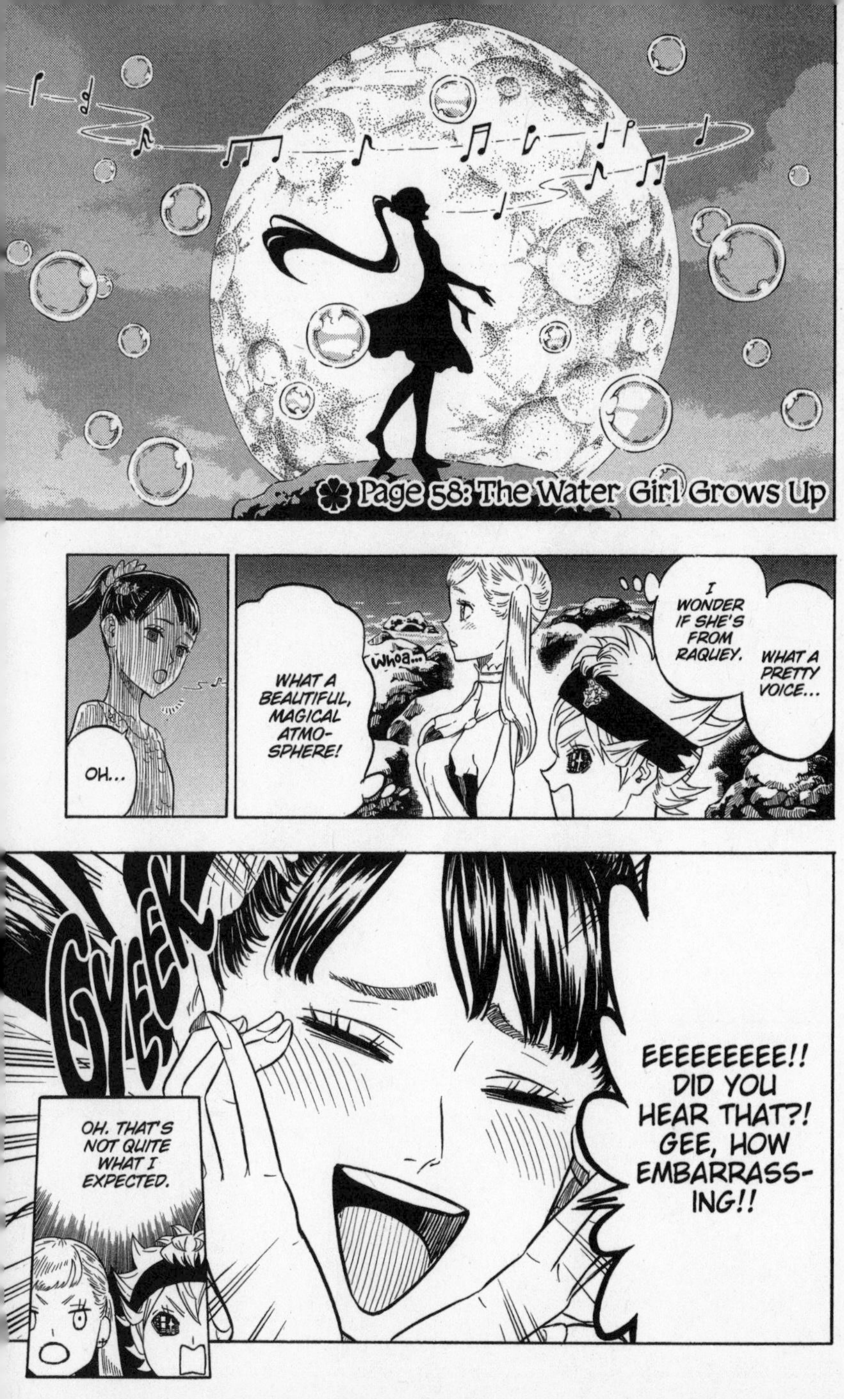
Page 58: The Water Girl Grows Up
I WONDER IF SHE'S FROM RAQUEY.
WHAT A PRETTY VOICE...
Whoa...
WHAT A BEAUTIFUL, MAGICAL ATMO-SPHERE!
OH...
EEEEEEEEE!! DID YOU HEAR THAT?! GEE, HOW EMBARRASS-ING!!
GYEEK
OH. THAT'S NOT QUITE WHAT I EXPECTED.

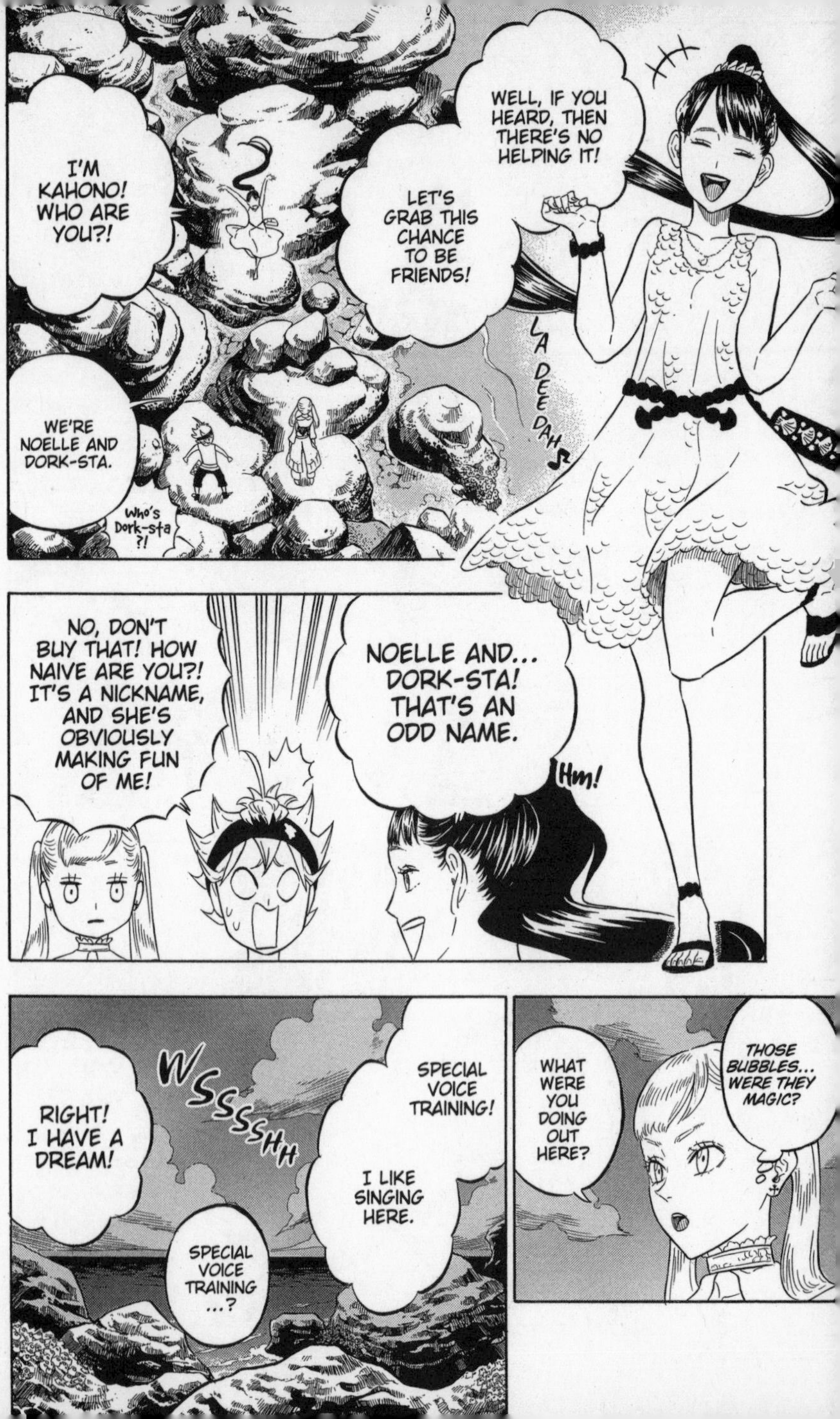
WELL, IF YOU HEARD, THEN THERE'S NO HELPING IT!
LET'S GRAB THIS CHANCE TO BE FRIENDS!
LA DEE DAH
I'M KAHONO! WHO ARE YOU?!
WE'RE NOELLE AND DORK-STA.
Who's Dork-sta ?!
NOELLE AND... DORK-STA! THAT'S AN ODD NAME.
Hm!
NO, DON'T BUY THAT! HOW NAIVE ARE YOU?! IT'S A NICKNAME, AND SHE'S OBVIOUSLY MAKING FUN OF ME!
THOSE BUBBLES... WERE THEY MAGIC?
WHAT WERE YOU DOING OUT HERE?
SPECIAL VOICE TRAINING!
I LIKE SINGING HERE.
WSSSSHH
SPECIAL VOICE TRAINING ...?
RIGHT! I HAVE A DREAM!

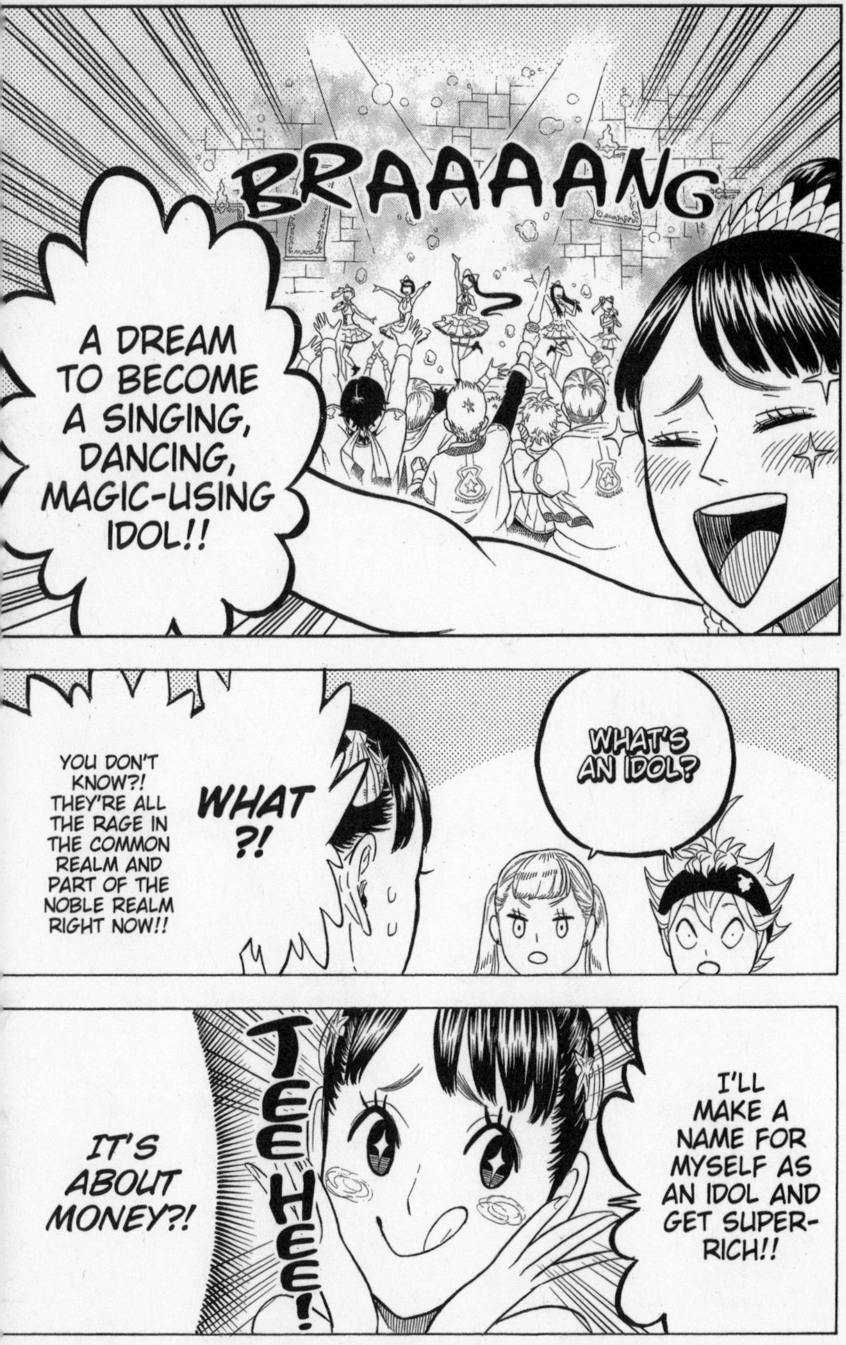
BRAAAANG
A DREAM TO BECOME A SINGING, DANCING, MAGIC-USING IDOL!!
WHAT'S AN IDOL?
WHAT?!
YOU DON'T KNOW?! THEY'RE ALL THE RAGE IN THE COMMON REALM AND PART OF THE NOBLE REALM RIGHT NOW!!
I'LL MAKE A NAME FOR MYSELF AS AN IDOL AND GET SUPER-RICH!!
TEEHEE!
IT'S ABOUT MONEY?!

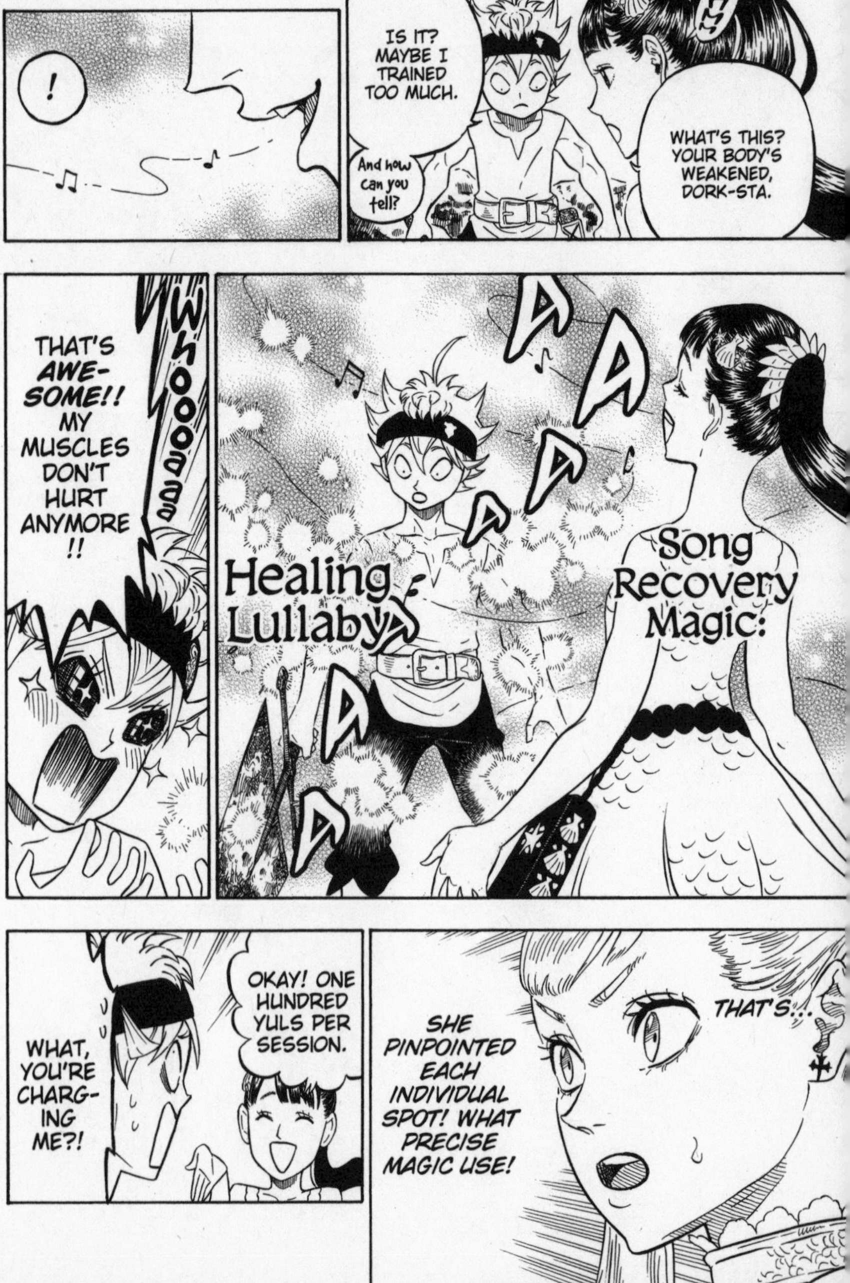
WHAT'S THIS? YOUR BODY'S WEAKENED, DORK-STA.
IS IT? MAYBE I TRAINED TOO MUCH.
And how can you tell?
!
Song Recovery Magic:
Healing Lullaby
THAT'S AWESOME!! MY MUSCLES DON'T HURT ANYMORE!!
THAT'S...
SHE PINPOINTED EACH INDIVIDUAL SPOT! WHAT PRECISE MAGIC USE!
OKAY! ONE HUNDRED YULS PER SESSION.
WHAT, YOU'RE CHARGING ME?!

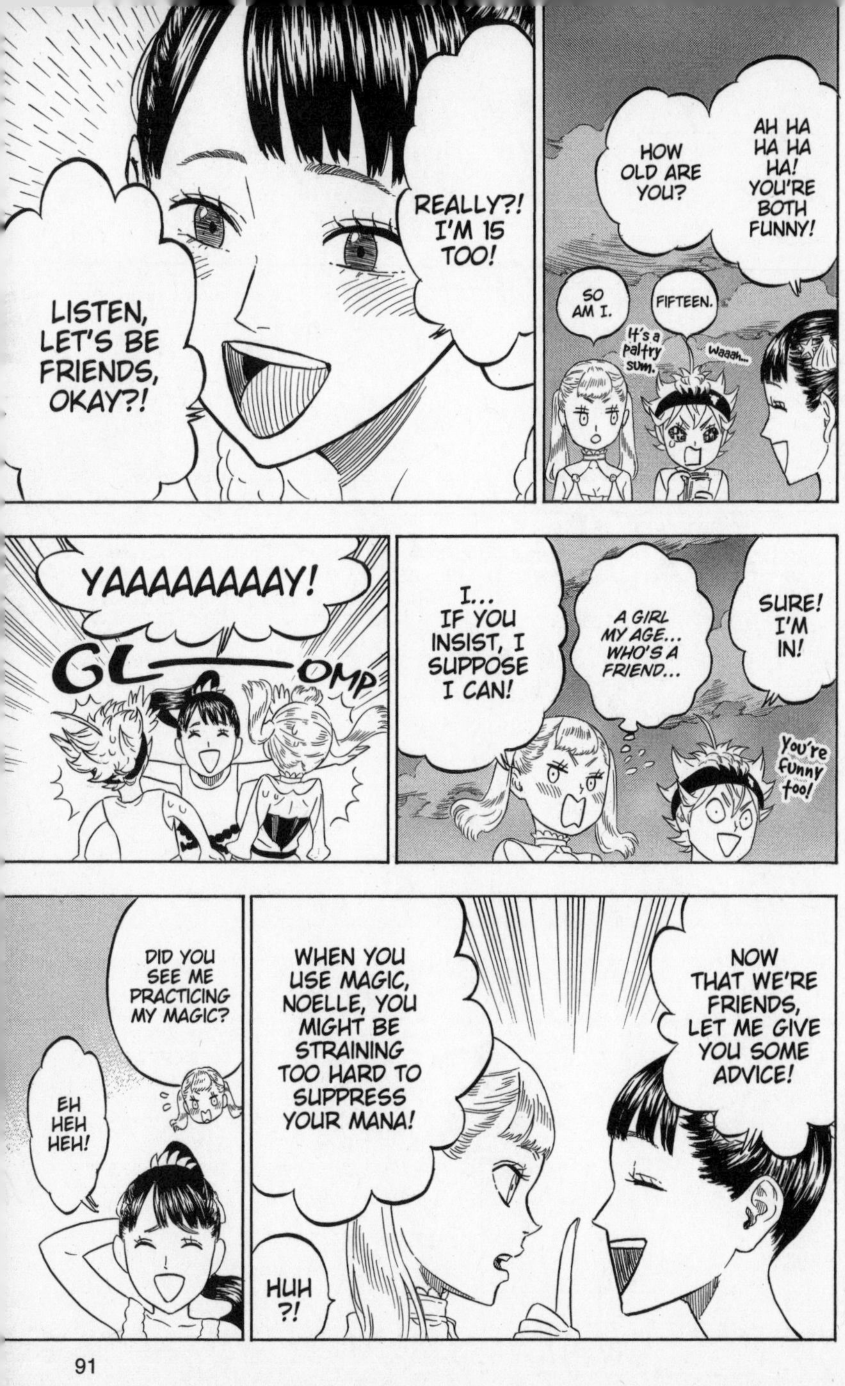
AH HA HA HA HA! YOU'RE BOTH FUNNY!
HOW OLD ARE YOU?
FIFTEEN.
SO AM I.
Waaah...
It's a paltry sum.
REALLY?! I'M 15 TOO!
LISTEN, LET'S BE FRIENDS, OKAY?!
SURE! I'M IN!
You're funny too!
A GIRL MY AGE... WHO'S A FRIEND...
I... IF YOU INSIST, I SUPPOSE I CAN!
YAAAAAAAAY!
GL—OMP
NOW THAT WE'RE FRIENDS, LET ME GIVE YOU SOME ADVICE!
WHEN YOU USE MAGIC, NOELLE, YOU MIGHT BE STRAINING TOO HARD TO SUPPRESS YOUR MANA!
HUH?!
DID YOU SEE ME PRACTICING MY MAGIC?
EH HEH HEH!

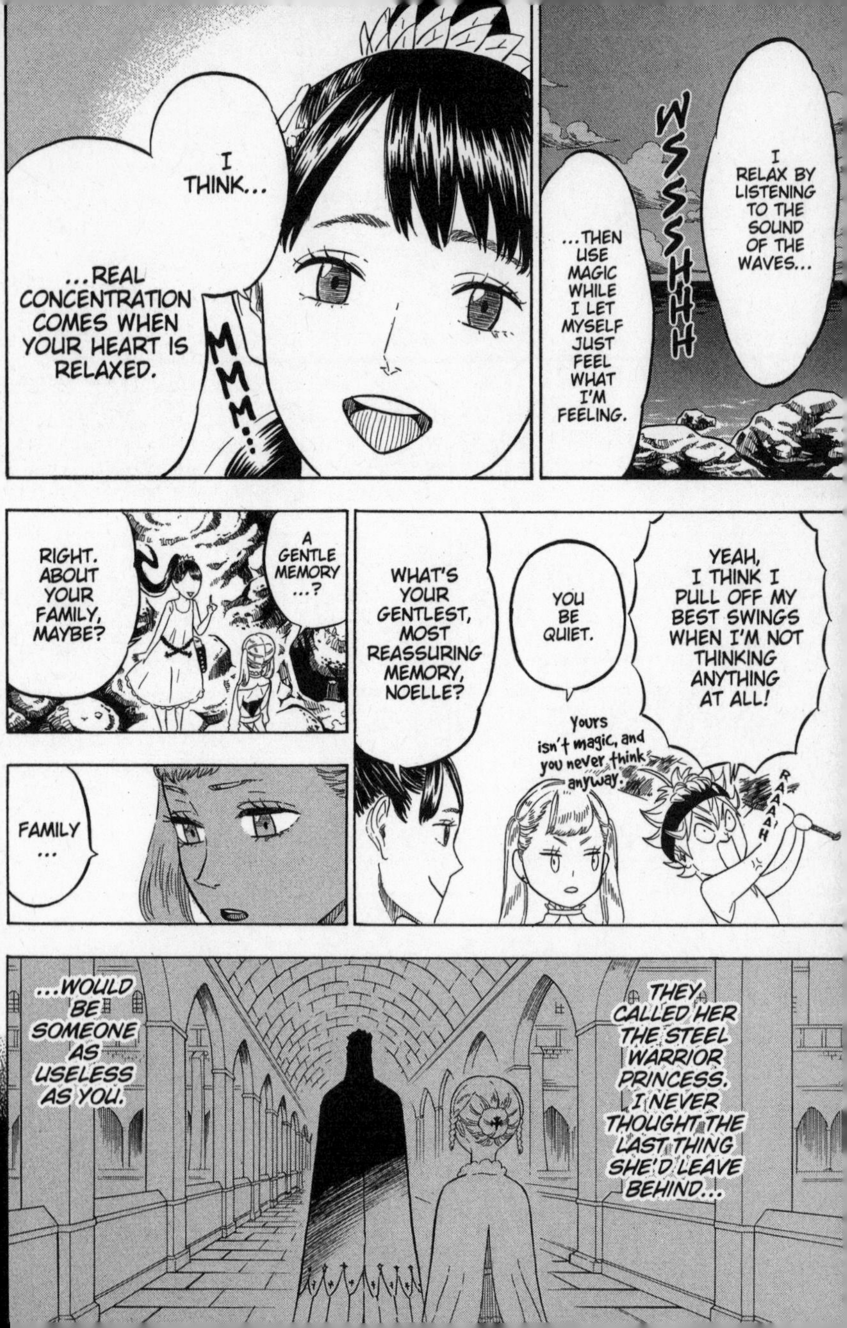
I RELAX BY LISTENING TO THE SOUND OF THE WAVES...
WSSSHHH
...THEN USE MAGIC WHILE I LET MYSELF JUST FEEL WHAT I'M FEELING.
I THINK...
...REAL CONCENTRATION COMES WHEN YOUR HEART IS RELAXED.
MMM...!
YEAH, I THINK I PULL OFF MY BEST SWINGS WHEN I'M NOT THINKING ANYTHING AT ALL!
RAAAAH
YOU BE QUIET.
Yours isn't magic, and you never think anyway.
WHAT'S YOUR GENTLEST, MOST REASSURING MEMORY, NOELLE?
A GENTLE MEMORY ...?
RIGHT. ABOUT YOUR FAMILY, MAYBE?
FAMILY ...
THEY CALLED HER THE STEEL WARRIOR PRINCESS. I NEVER THOUGHT THE LAST THING SHE'D LEAVE BEHIND...
...WOULD BE SOMEONE AS USELESS AS YOU.

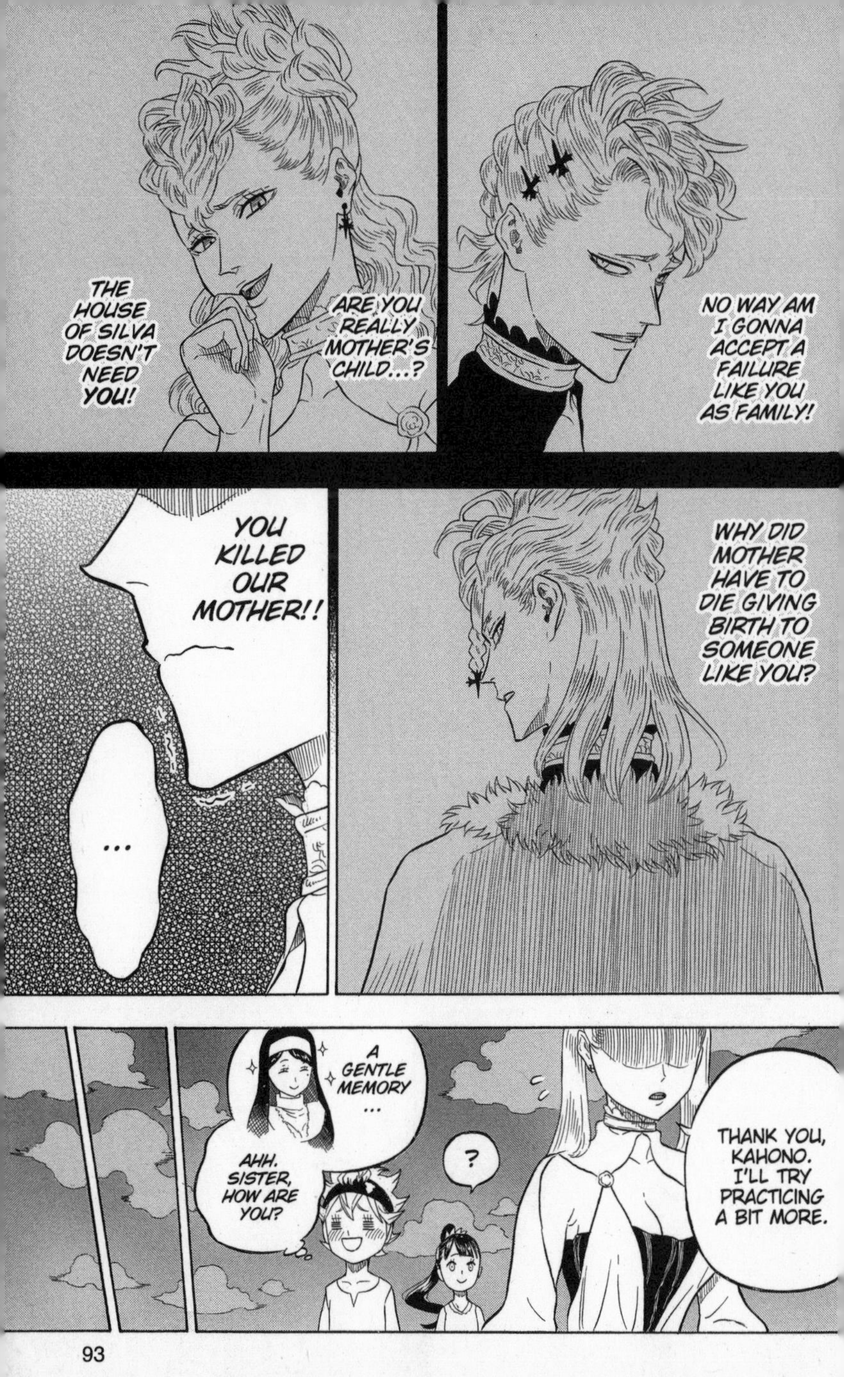
NO WAY AM I GONNA ACCEPT A FAILURE LIKE YOU AS FAMILY!
ARE YOU REALLY MOTHER'S CHILD...?
THE HOUSE OF SILVA DOESN'T NEED YOU!
WHY DID MOTHER HAVE TO DIE GIVING BIRTH TO SOMEONE LIKE YOU?
YOU KILLED OUR MOTHER!!
...
THANK YOU, KAHONO. I'LL TRY PRACTICING A BIT MORE.
?
A GENTLE MEMORY...
AHH. SISTER, HOW ARE YOU?

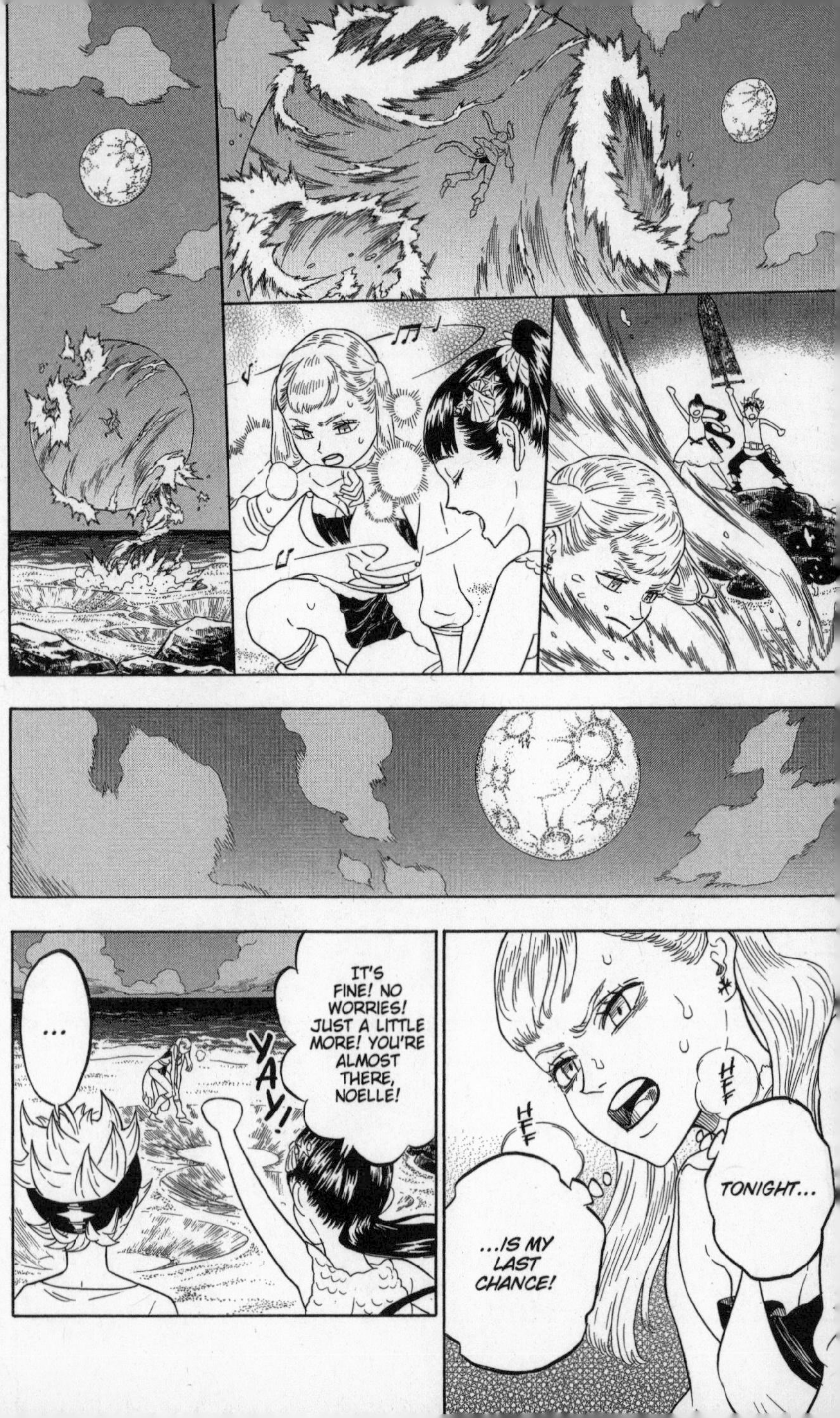
HEF
HEF
TONIGHT...
...IS MY LAST CHANCE!
IT'S FINE! NO WORRIES! JUST A LITTLE MORE! YOU'RE ALMOST THERE, NOELLE!
YAY!
...

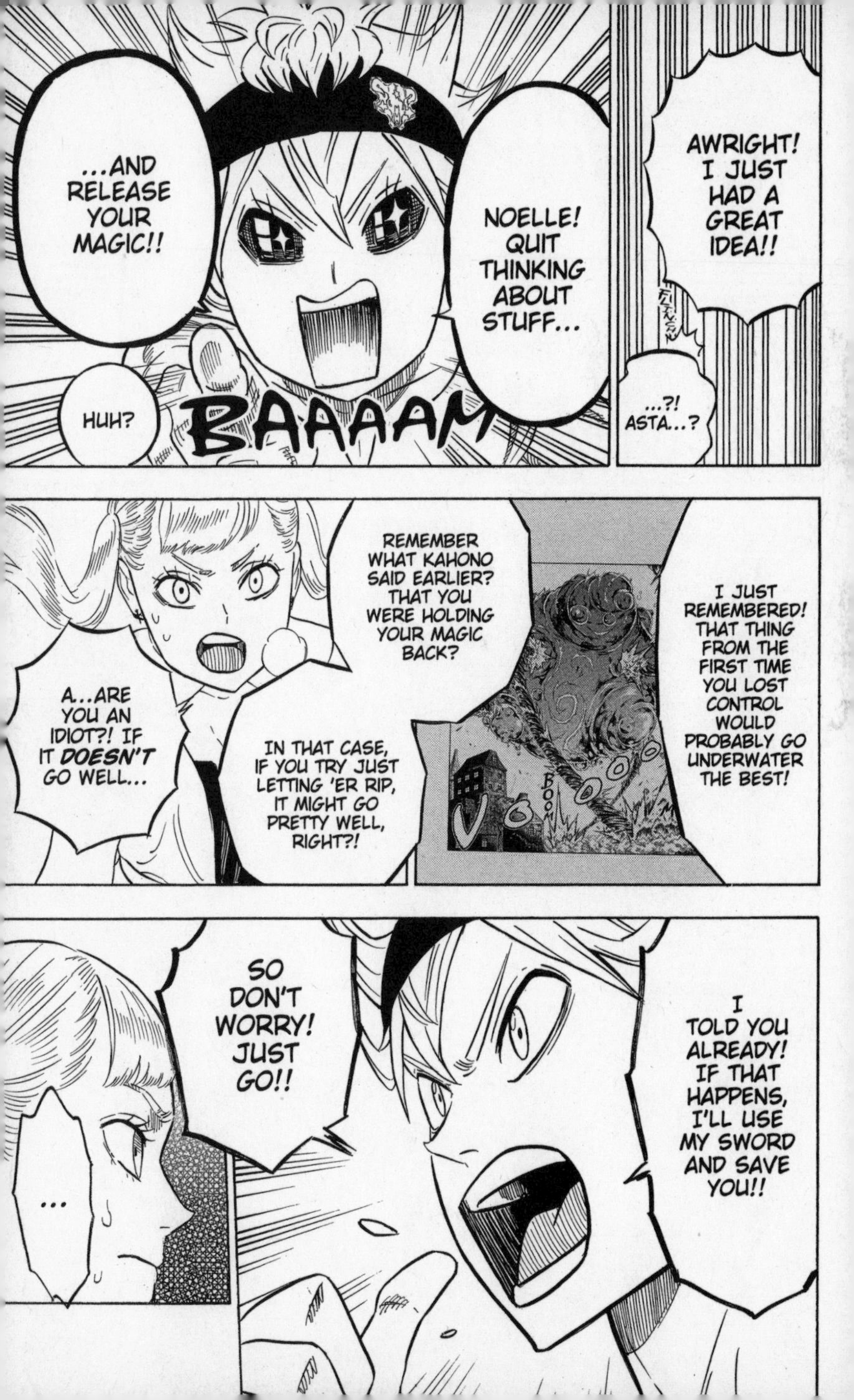
AWRIGHT! I JUST HAD A GREAT IDEA!!
...?! ASTA...?
NOELLE! QUIT THINKING ABOUT STUFF...
...AND RELEASE YOUR MAGIC!!
BAAAAM
HUH?
I JUST REMEMBERED! THAT THING FROM THE FIRST TIME YOU LOST CONTROL WOULD PROBABLY GO UNDERWATER THE BEST!
BOOM
REMEMBER WHAT KAHONO SAID EARLIER? THAT YOU WERE HOLDING YOUR MAGIC BACK?
IN THAT CASE, IF YOU TRY JUST LETTING 'ER RIP, IT MIGHT GO PRETTY WELL, RIGHT?!
A...ARE YOU AN IDIOT?! IF IT ***DOESN'T*** GO WELL...
I TOLD YOU ALREADY! IF THAT HAPPENS, I'LL USE MY SWORD AND SAVE YOU!!
SO DON'T WORRY! JUST GO!!
...

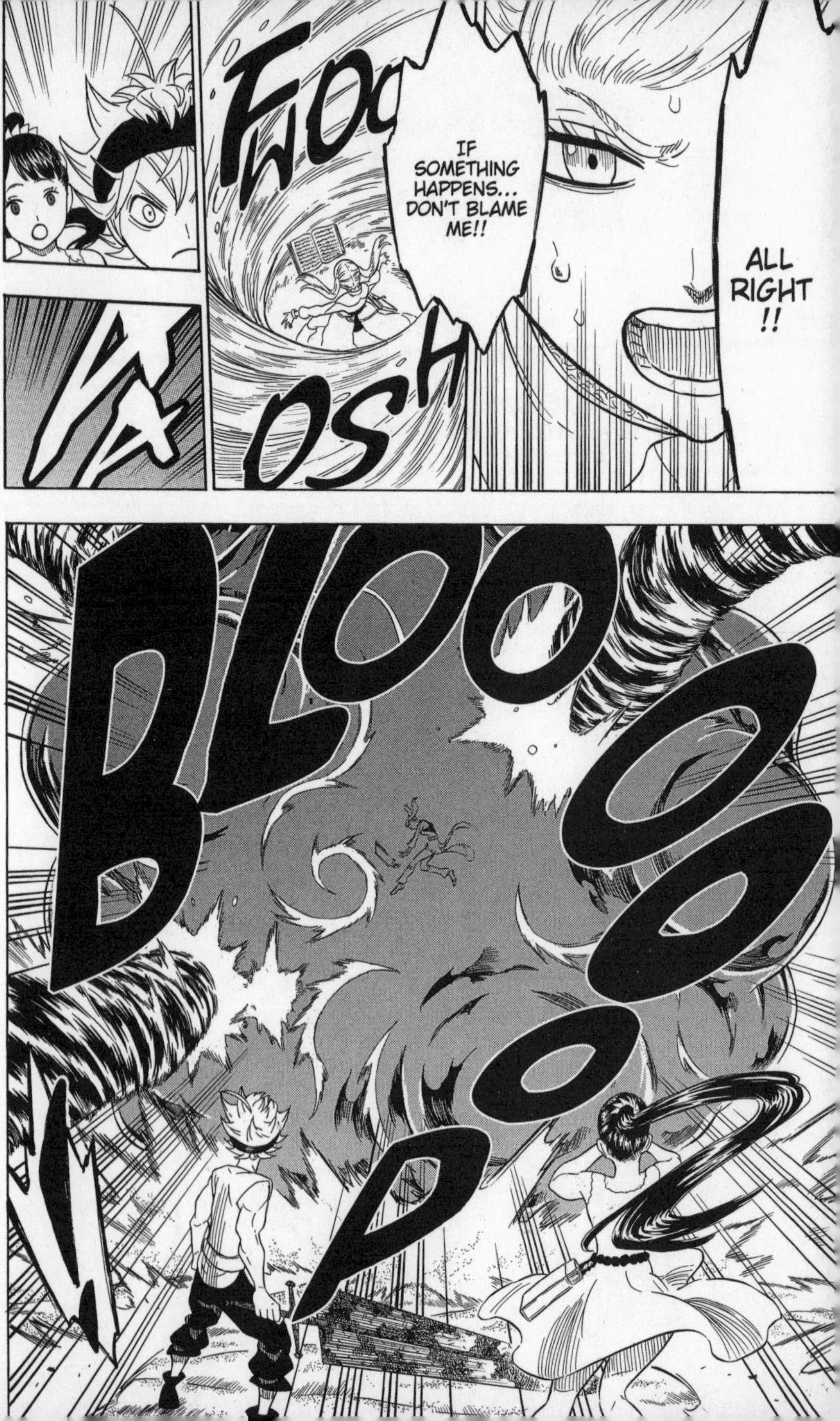
ALL RIGHT!!
IF SOMETHING HAPPENS... DON'T BLAME ME!!
FWOOOSH
BLOOOOOOM

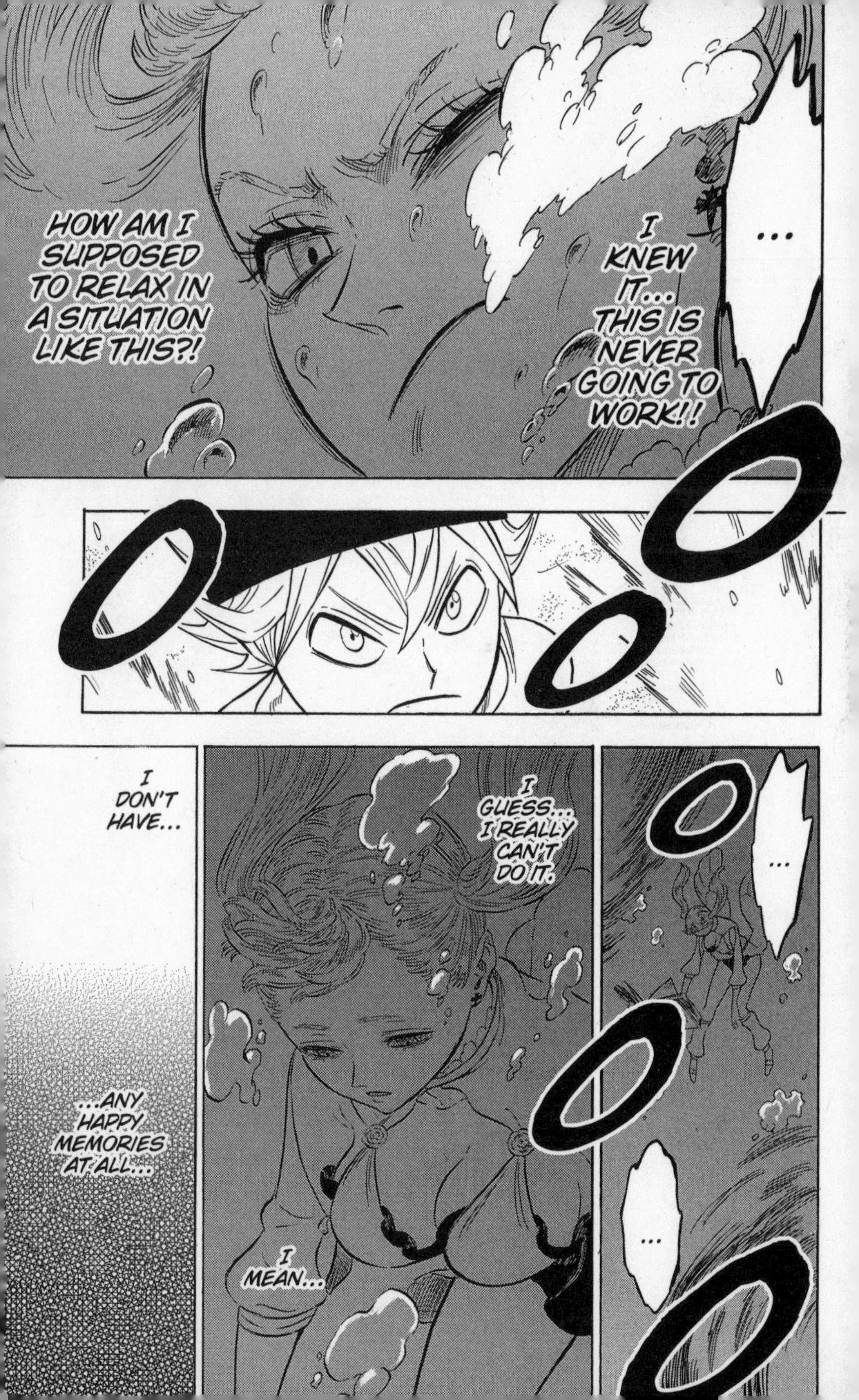
...
I KNEW IT... THIS IS NEVER GOING TO WORK!!
HOW AM I SUPPOSED TO RELAX IN A SITUATION LIKE THIS?!
...
...
I GUESS... I REALLY CAN'T DO IT.
I MEAN...
I DON'T HAVE...
...ANY HAPPY MEMORIES AT ALL...

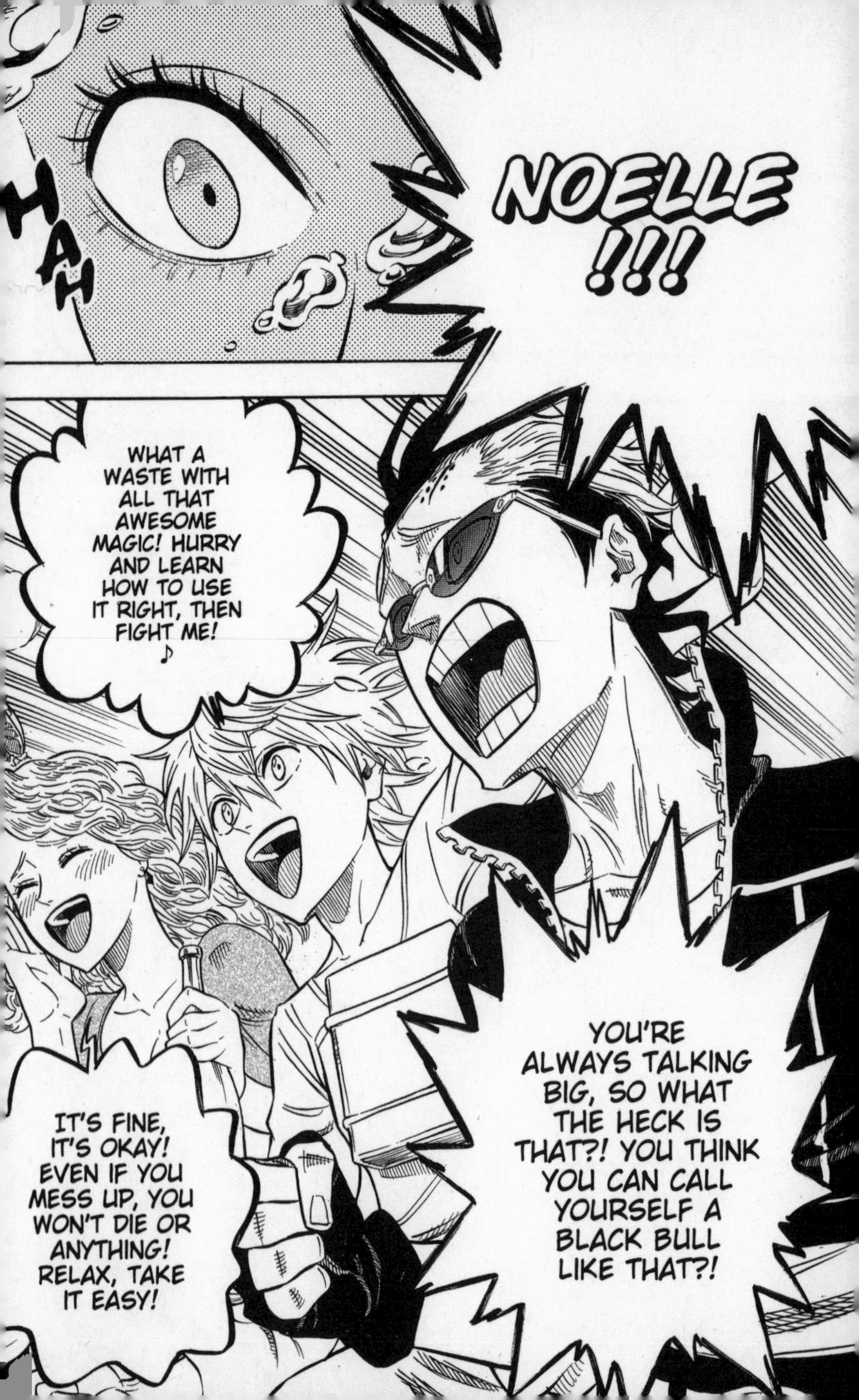
NOELLE!!!
HAH
YOU'RE ALWAYS TALKING BIG, SO WHAT THE HECK IS THAT?! YOU THINK YOU CAN CALL YOURSELF A BLACK BULL LIKE THAT?!
WHAT A WASTE WITH ALL THAT AWESOME MAGIC! HURRY AND LEARN HOW TO USE IT RIGHT, THEN FIGHT ME! ♪
IT'S FINE, IT'S OKAY! EVEN IF YOU MESS UP, YOU WON'T DIE OR ANYTHING! RELAX, TAKE IT EASY!

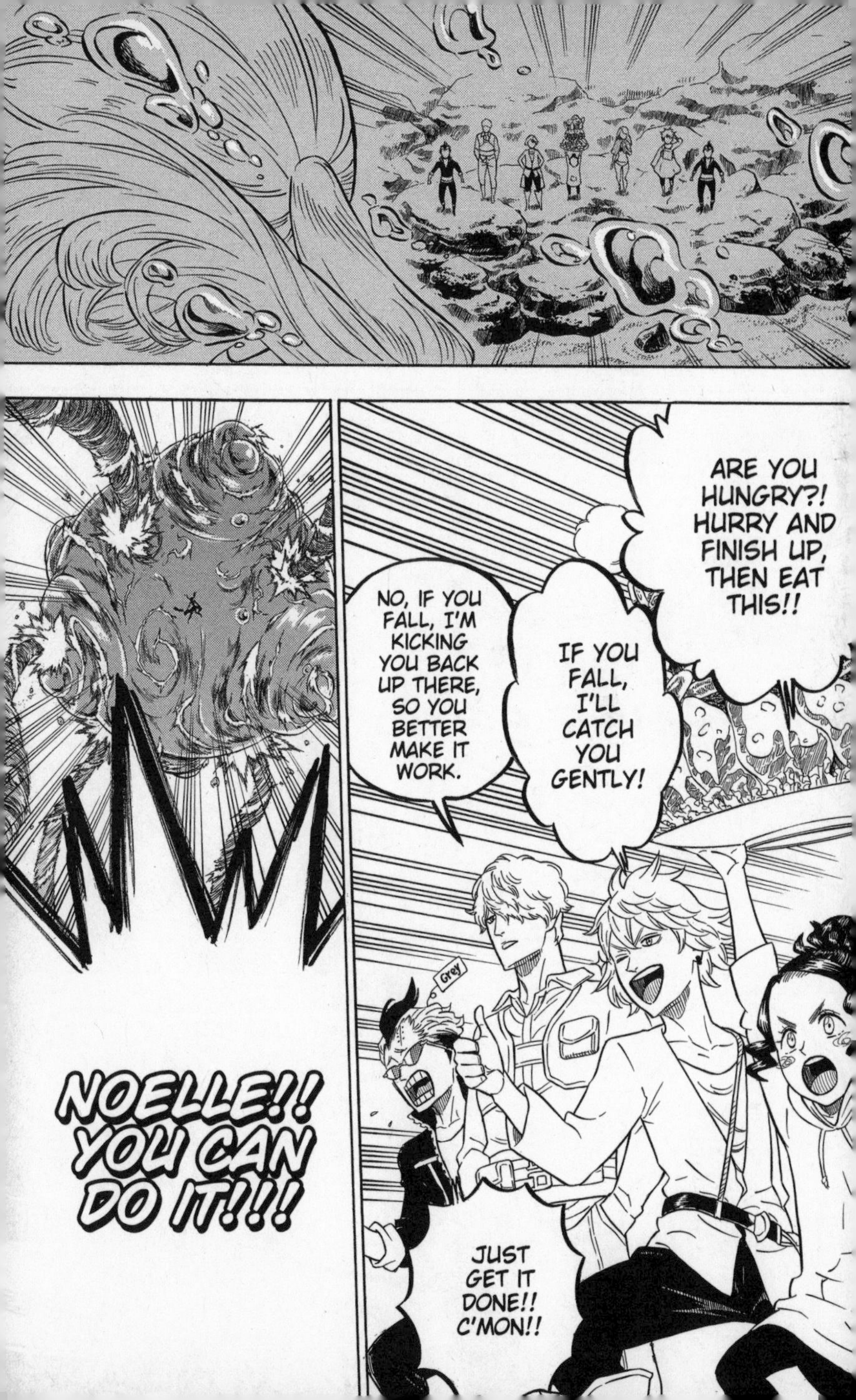
ARE YOU HUNGRY?! HURRY AND FINISH UP, THEN EAT THIS!!
IF YOU FALL, I'LL CATCH YOU GENTLY!
NO, IF YOU FALL, I'M KICKING YOU BACK UP THERE, SO YOU BETTER MAKE IT WORK.
Grey
JUST GET IT DONE!! C'MON!!
NOELLE!! YOU CAN DO IT!!!

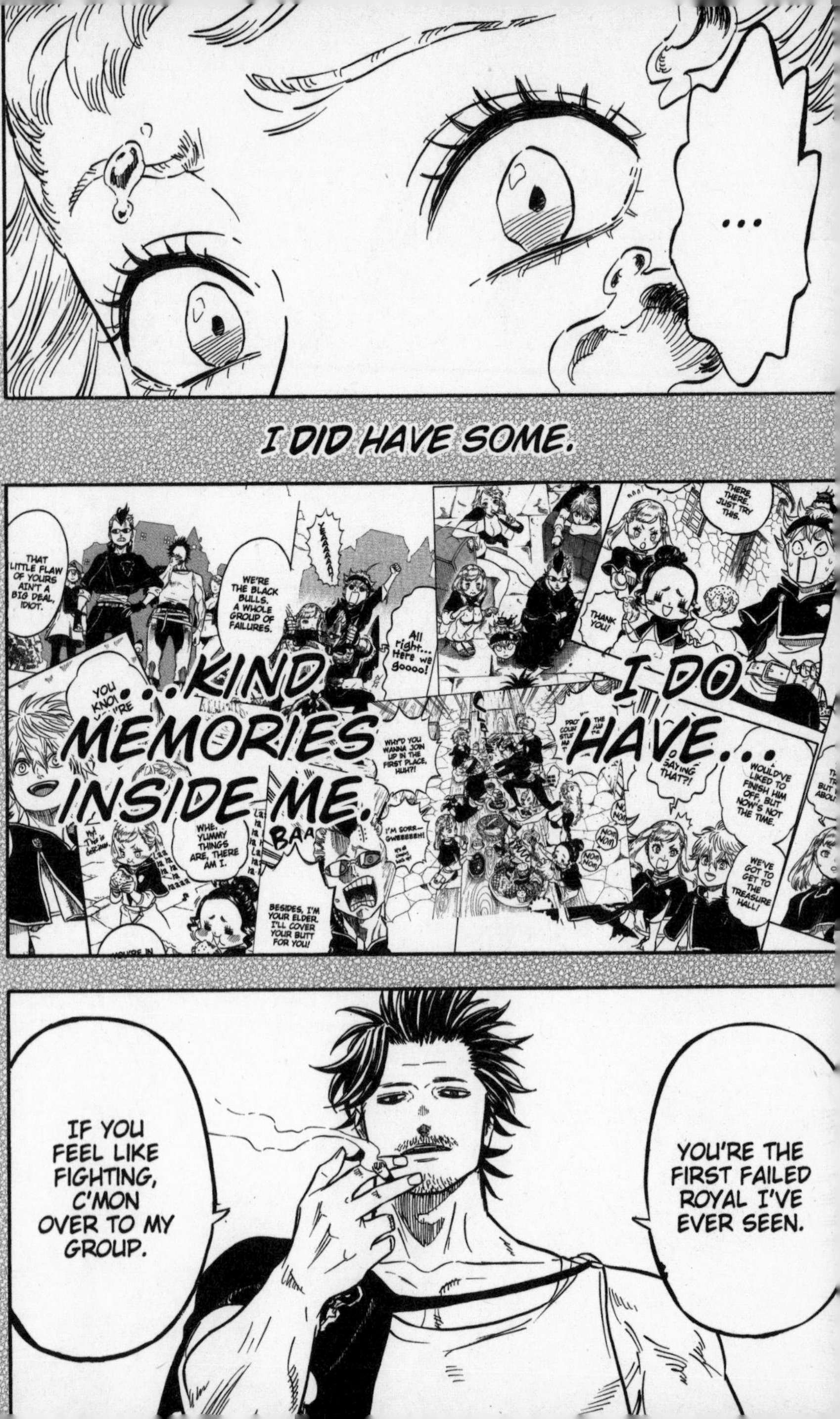
...
I DID HAVE SOME.
I DO HAVE...
...KIND MEMORIES INSIDE ME.
THERE, THERE. JUST TRY THIS.
THANK YOU!
All right... Here we goooo!
WE'RE THE BLACK BULLS. A WHOLE GROUP OF FAILURES.
THAT LITTLE FLAW OF YOURS AIN'T A BIG DEAL, IDIOT.
WOULD'VE LIKED TO FINISH HIM OFF, BUT NOW'S NOT THE TIME.
WE'VE GOT TO GET TO THE TREASURE HALL!
SAYING THAT?!
Nom Nom
Nom Nom
WHY'D YOU WANNA JOIN UP IN THE FIRST PLACE, HUH?!
I'M SORR— GWEEEEEH!
BESIDES, I'M YOUR ELDER. I'LL COVER YOUR BUTT FOR YOU!
BAA
WHE, YUMMY THINGS ARE, THERE AM I.
YOU'RE THE FIRST FAILED ROYAL I'VE EVER SEEN.
IF YOU FEEL LIKE FIGHTING, C'MON OVER TO MY GROUP.

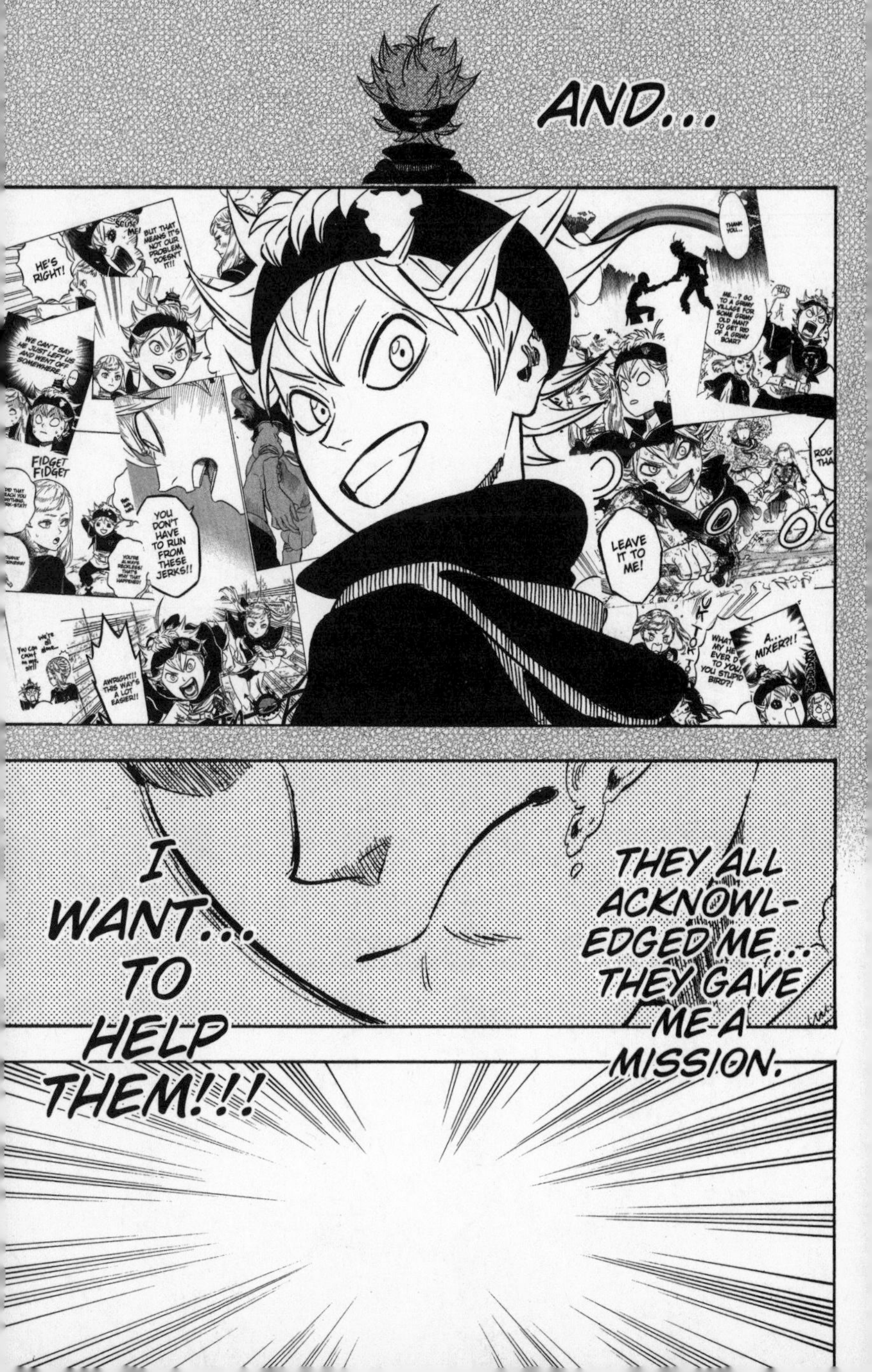
AND...
THANK YOU...
ME...? GO TO A GRIMY VILLAGE FOR SOME GRIMY OLD MAN TO GET RID OF A GRIMY BOAR?
LEAVE IT TO ME!
A... MIXER?!!
TOK TOK
BUT THAT MEANS IT'S NOT OUR PROBLEM, DOESN'T IT!!
'SCUSE ME!
HE'S RIGHT!
WE CAN'T SAY HE JUST LEFT US AND WENT OFF SOMEWHERE...
YOU DON'T HAVE TO RUN FROM THESE JERKS!!
YOU'RE ALWAYS RECKLESS! THAT'S WHY THAT HAPPENED!
FIDGET FIDGET
AWRIGHT!! THIS WAY'S A LOT EASIER!!
We're all done...
You can count on me, sir!!
THEY ALL ACKNOWLEDGED ME... THEY GAVE ME A MISSION.
I WANT... TO HELP THEM!!!

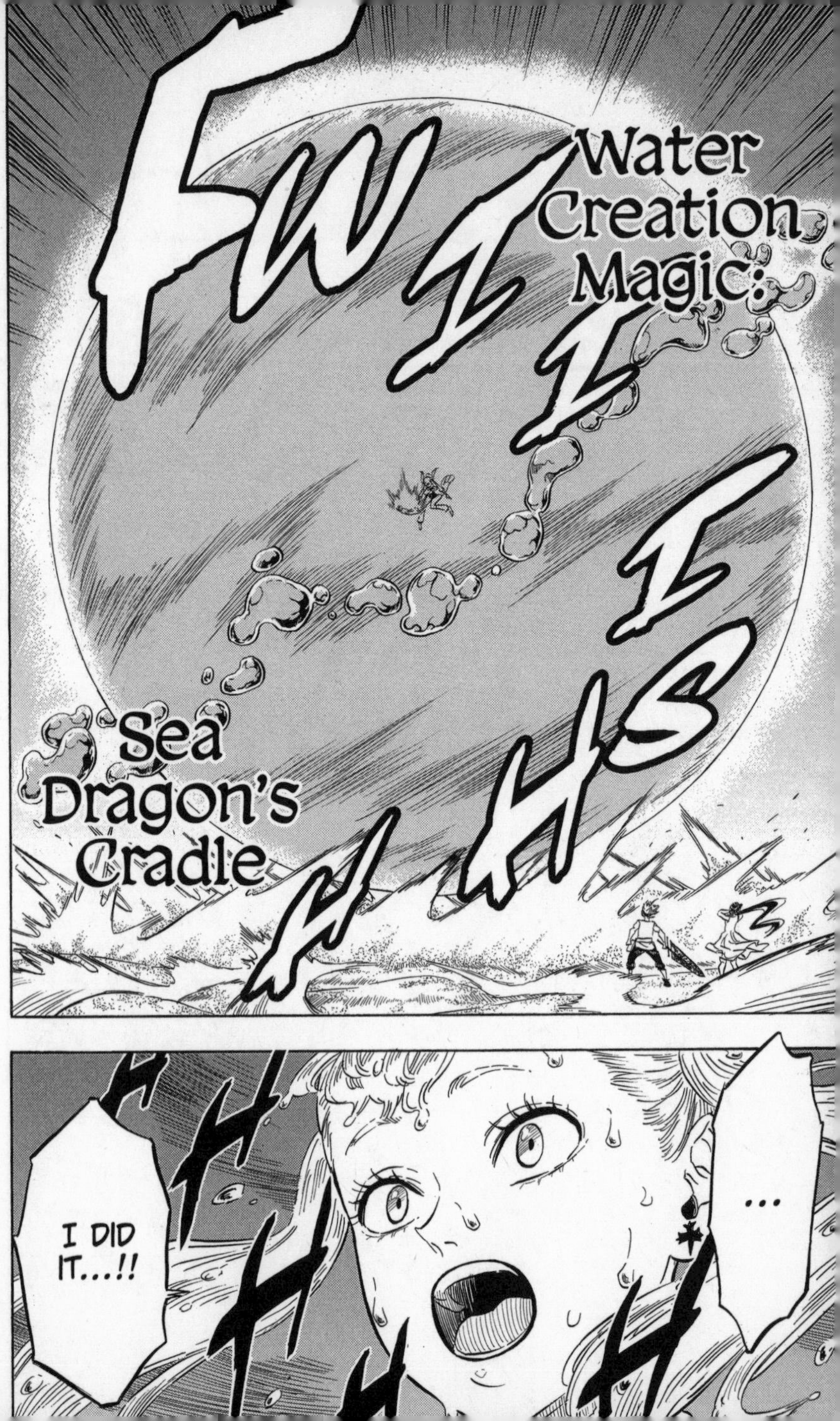
Water Creation Magic:
Sea Dragon's Cradle
...
I DID IT...!!

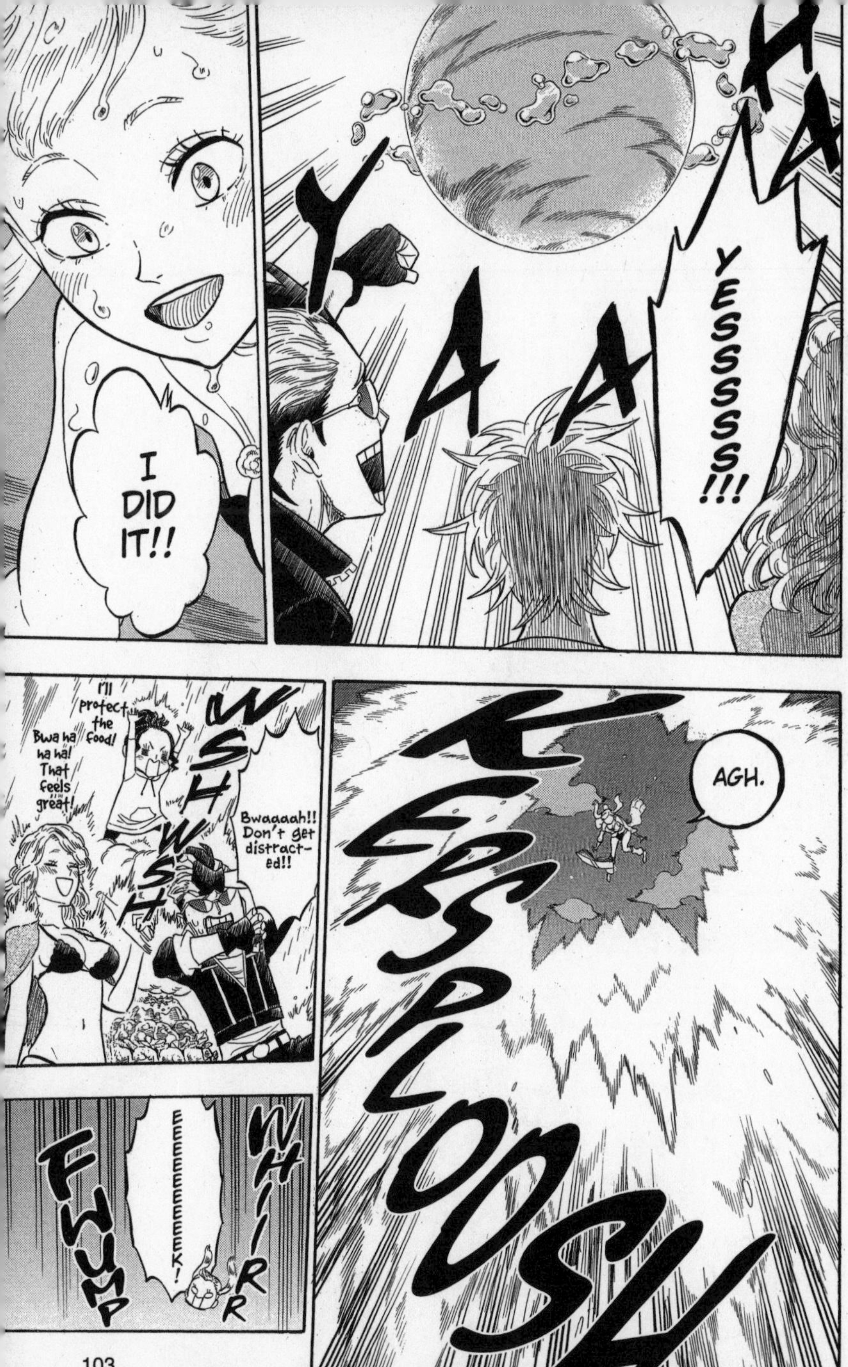
HA
YAA
YESSSSSS!!!
I DID IT!!
KRSPLOOSH
AGH.
WSHWSH
Bwaaaah!! Don't get distract-ed!!
I'll protect the food!
Bwa ha ha ha! That feels great!
WHIIRR
EEEEEEEEEEK!
FWUMP

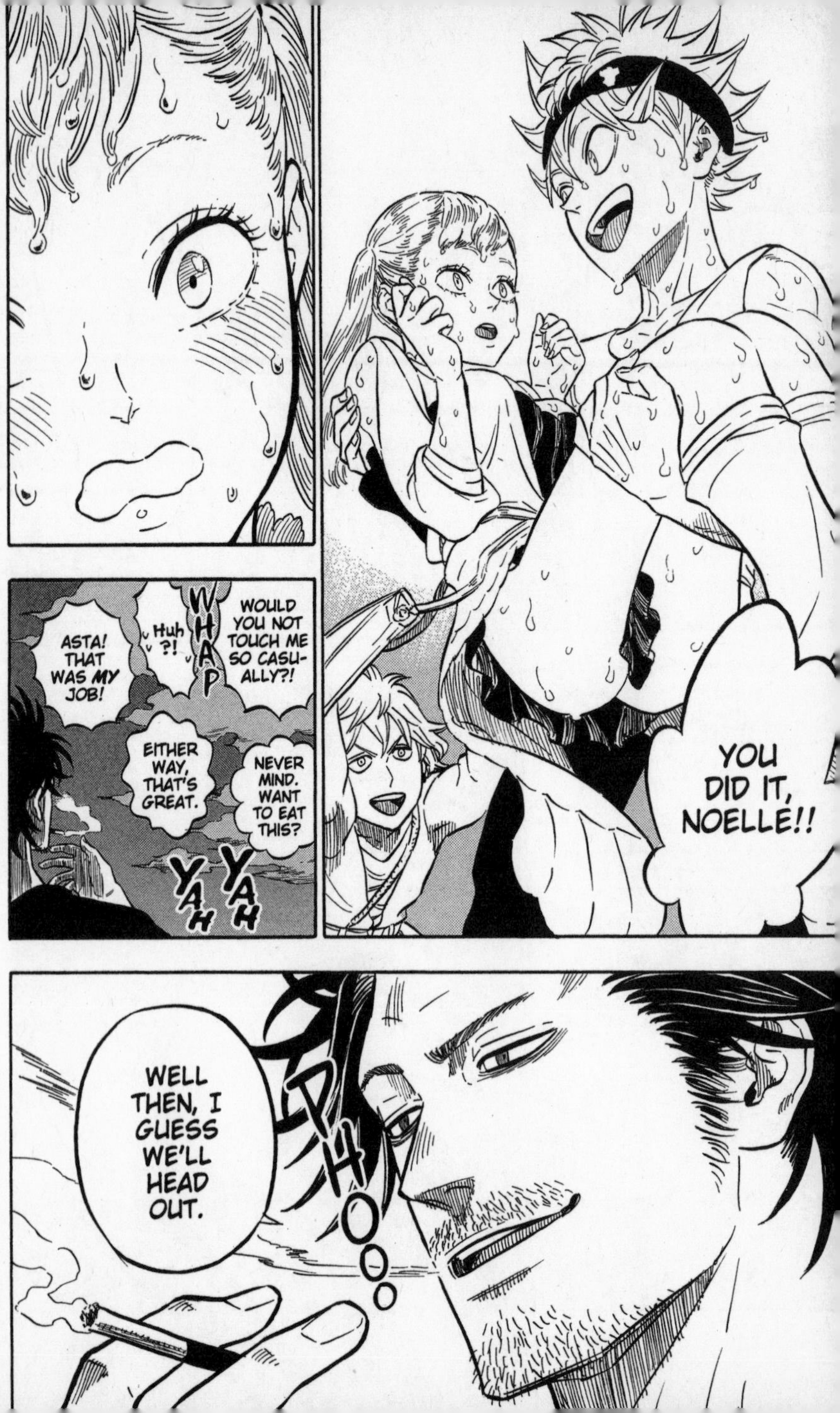
YOU DID IT, NOELLE!!
WOULD YOU NOT TOUCH ME SO CASUALLY?!
WHAP
Huh ?!
ASTA! THAT WAS MY JOB!
NEVER MIND. WANT TO EAT THIS?
EITHER WAY, THAT'S GREAT.
YAH YAH
WELL THEN, I GUESS WE'LL HEAD OUT.
PHOOO

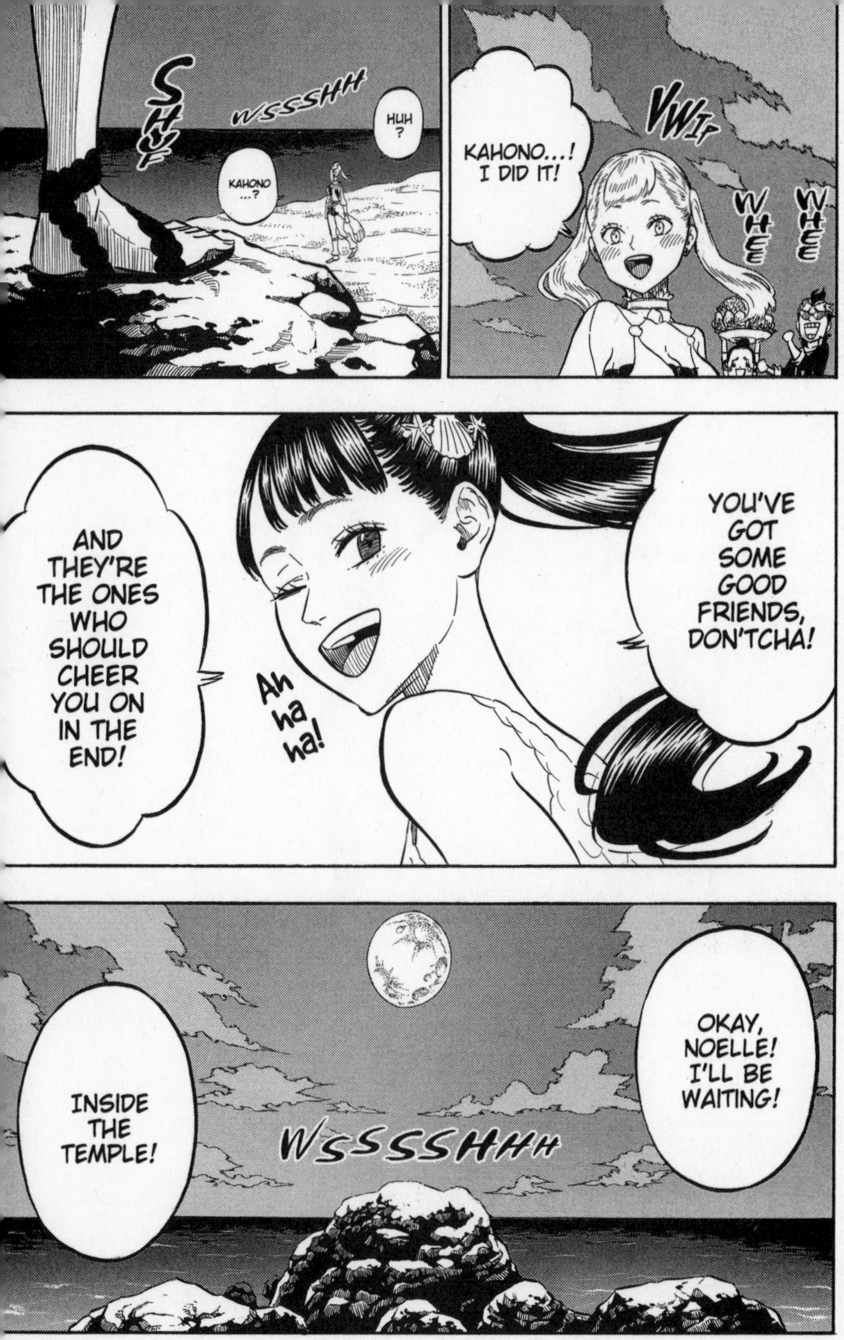
KAHONO...! I DID IT!
VWIr
WHEE
WHEE
HUH ?
WSSSHH
SHUF
KAHONO ...?
YOU'VE GOT SOME GOOD FRIENDS, DON'TCHA!
Ah ha ha!
AND THEY'RE THE ONES WHO SHOULD CHEER YOU ON IN THE END!
OKAY, NOELLE! I'LL BE WAITING!
WSSSSHHH
INSIDE THE TEMPLE!

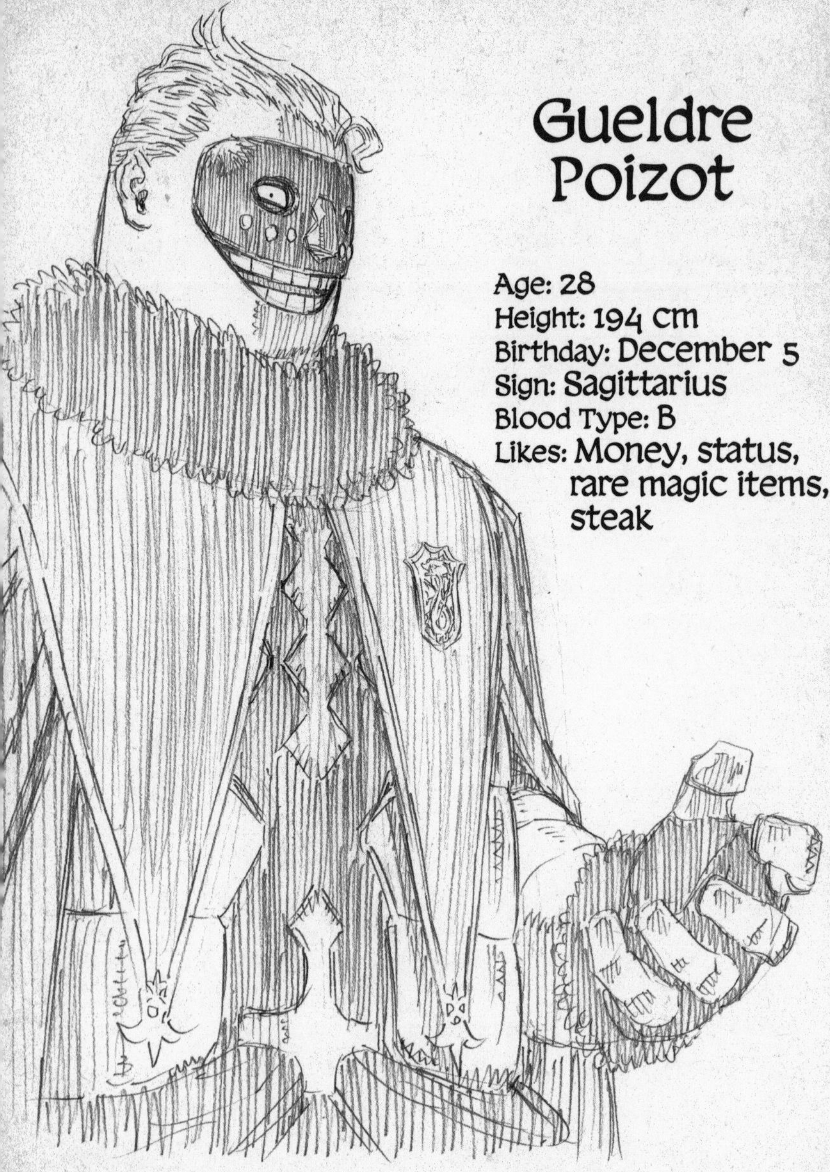

# Gueldre Poizot

Age: 28
Height: 194 cm
Birthday: December 5
Sign: Sagittarius
Blood Type: B
Likes: Money, status, rare magic items, steak

Character Profile

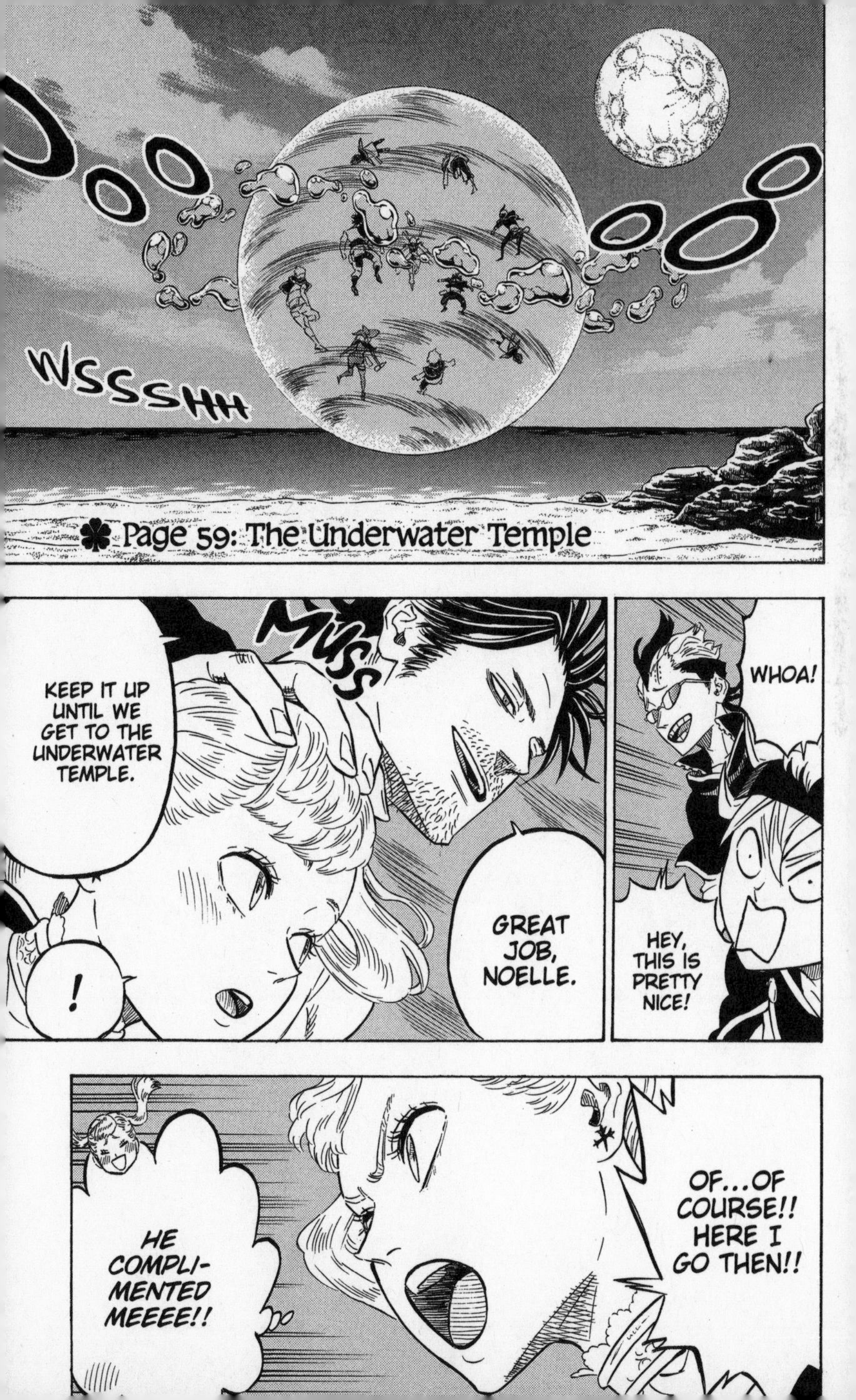
WSSSHH
Page 59: The Underwater Temple
WHOA!
HEY, THIS IS PRETTY NICE!
MUSS
KEEP IT UP UNTIL WE GET TO THE UNDERWATER TEMPLE.
GREAT JOB, NOELLE.
!
OF...OF COURSE!! HERE I GO THEN!!
HE COMPLI-MENTED MEEEE!!

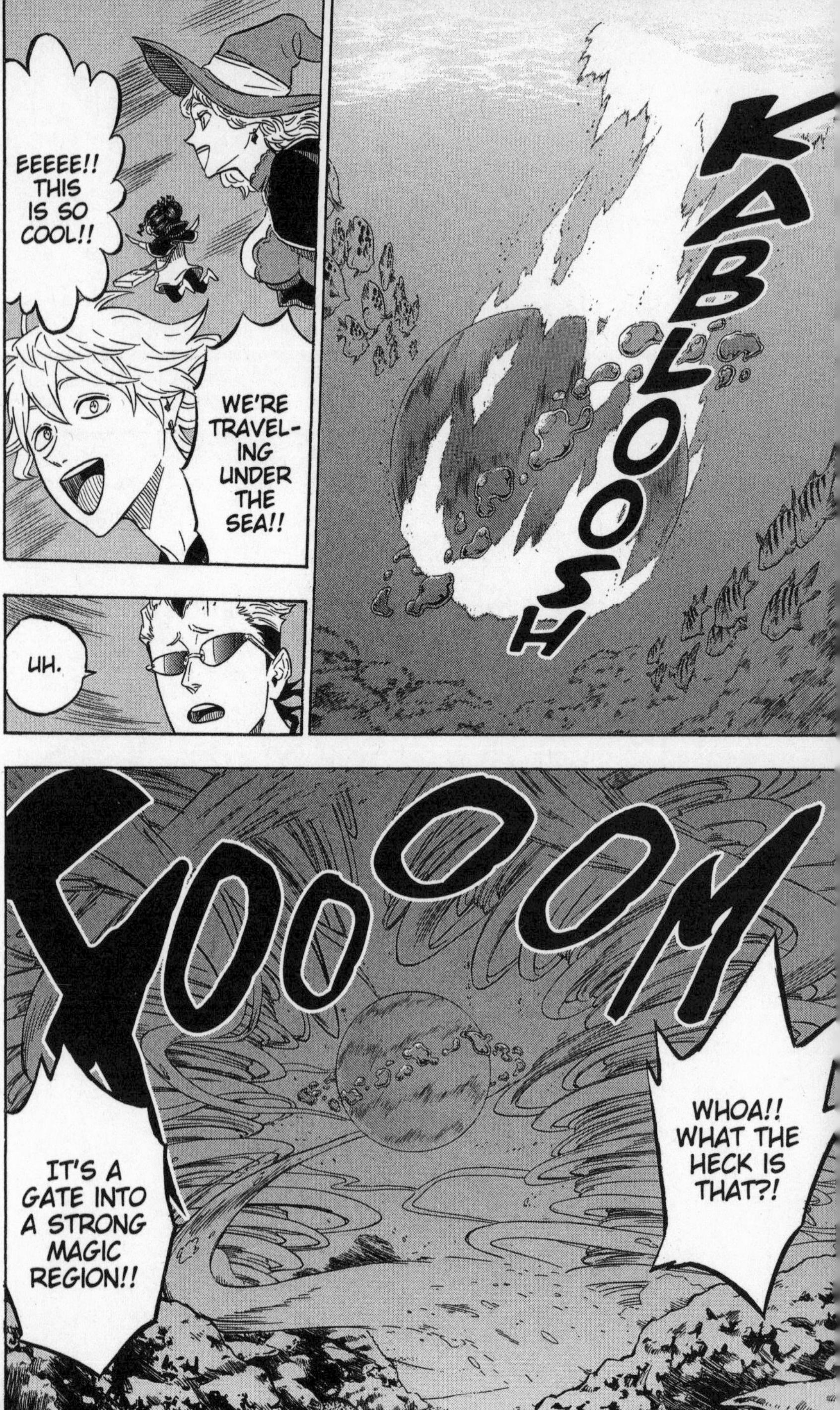
KABLOOSH
EEEEE!! THIS IS SO COOL!!
WE'RE TRAVEL-ING UNDER THE SEA!!
UH.
VOOOOM
WHOA!! WHAT THE HECK IS THAT?!
IT'S A GATE INTO A STRONG MAGIC REGION!!

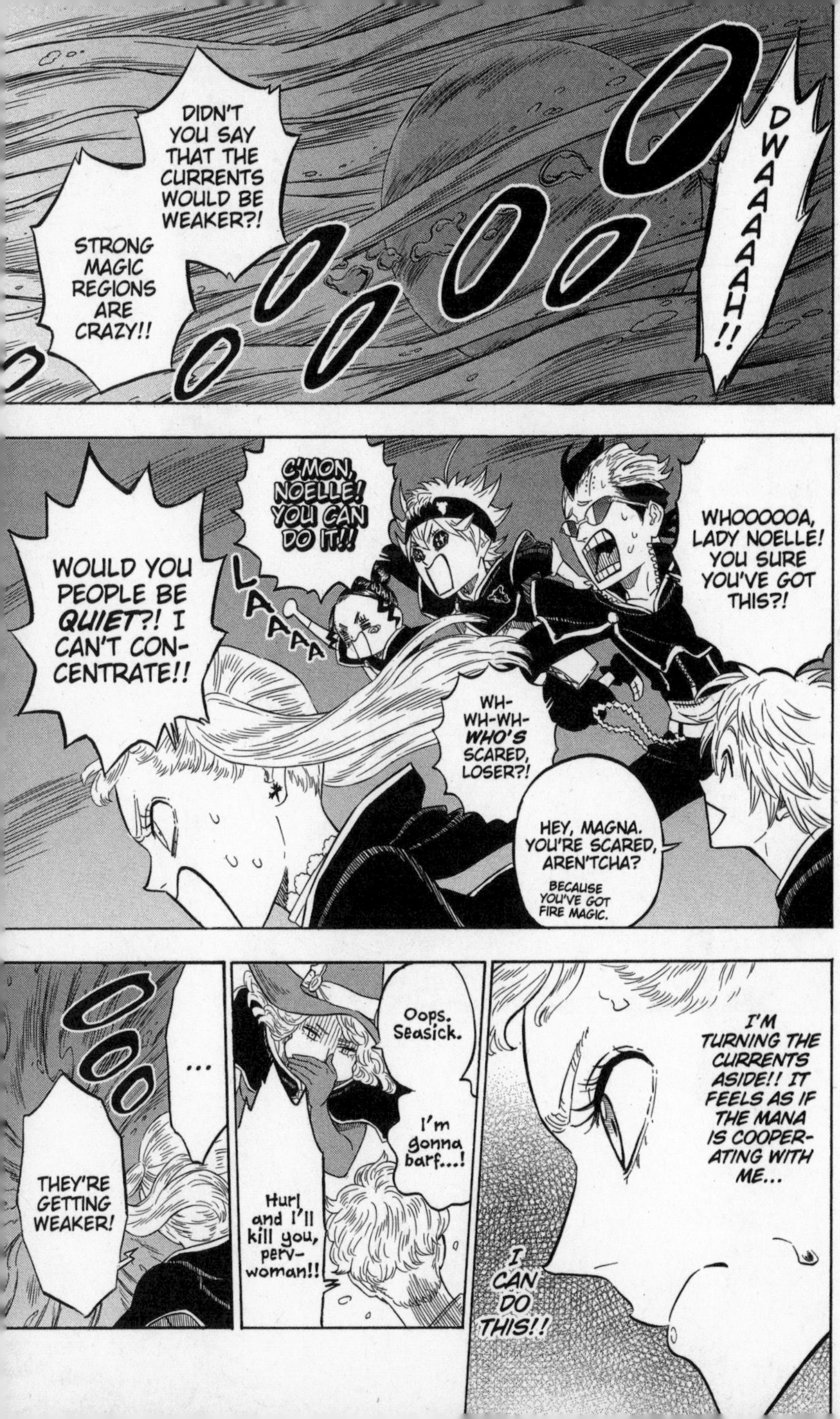
DWAAAAAAH!!
DIDN'T YOU SAY THAT THE CURRENTS WOULD BE WEAKER?!
STRONG MAGIC REGIONS ARE CRAZY!!
WHOOOOOA, LADY NOELLE! YOU SURE YOU'VE GOT THIS?!
C'MON, NOELLE! YOU CAN DO IT!!
WOULD YOU PEOPLE BE *QUIET*?! I CAN'T CON-CENTRATE!!
LAAAAA
HEY, MAGNA. YOU'RE SCARED, AREN'TCHA?
BECAUSE YOU'VE GOT FIRE MAGIC.
WH-WH-WH-*WHO'S* SCARED, LOSER?!
I'M TURNING THE CURRENTS ASIDE!! IT FEELS AS IF THE MANA IS COOPER-ATING WITH ME...
I CAN DO THIS!!
Oops. Seasick.
I'm gonna barf...!
Hurl, and I'll kill you, perv-woman!!
OOO
...
THEY'RE GETTING WEAKER!

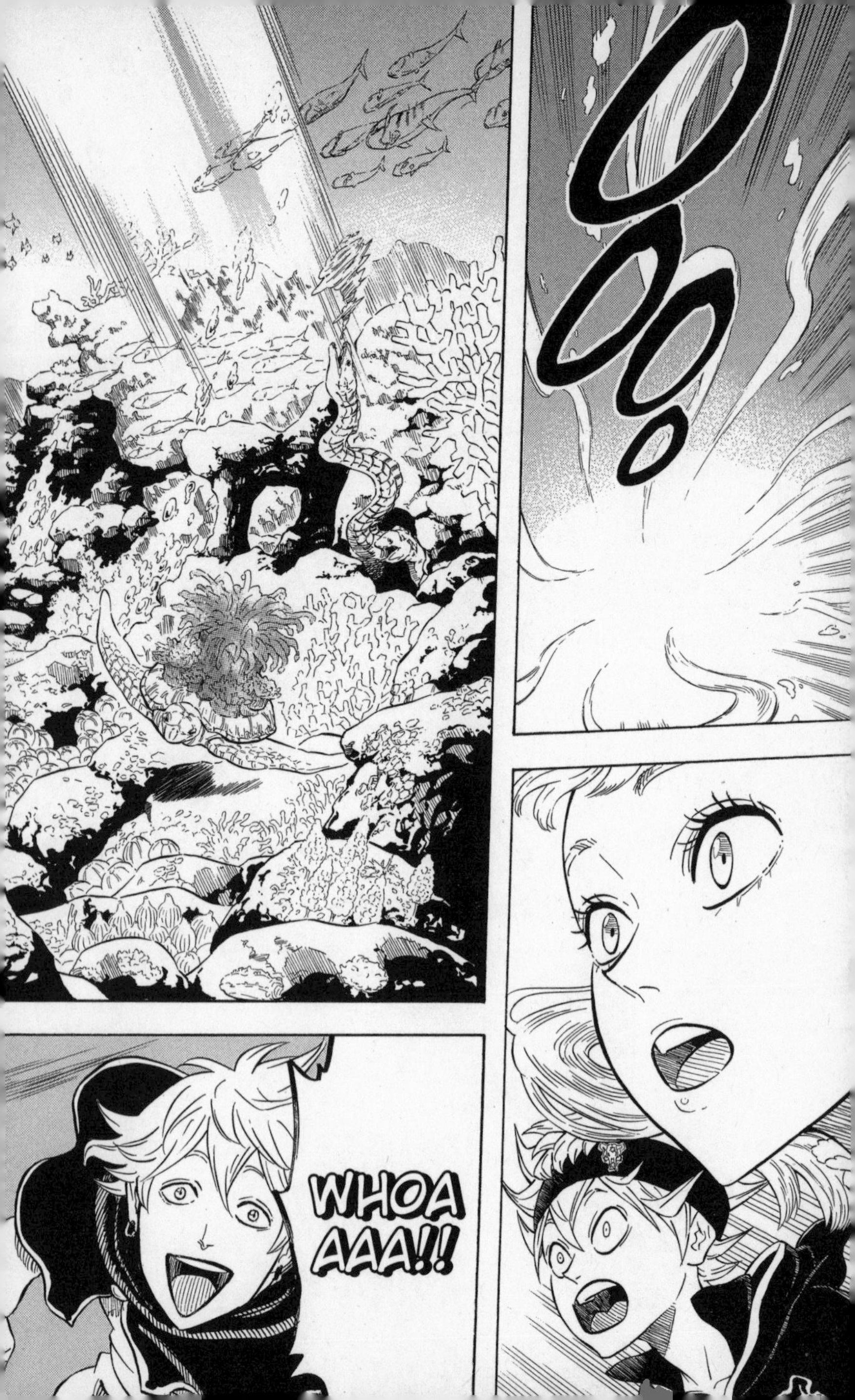
WHOA AAA!!

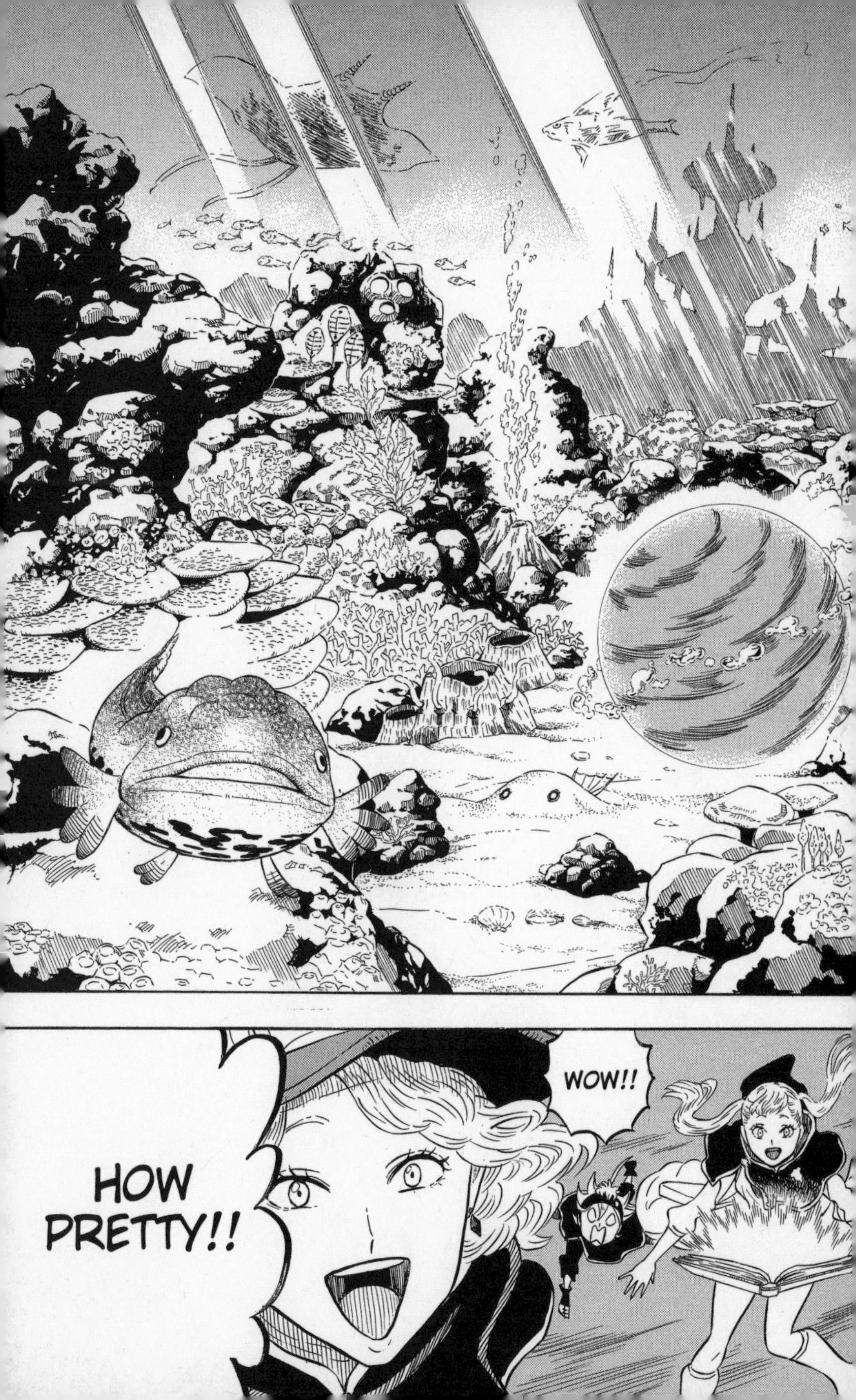
WOW!!
HOW PRETTY!!

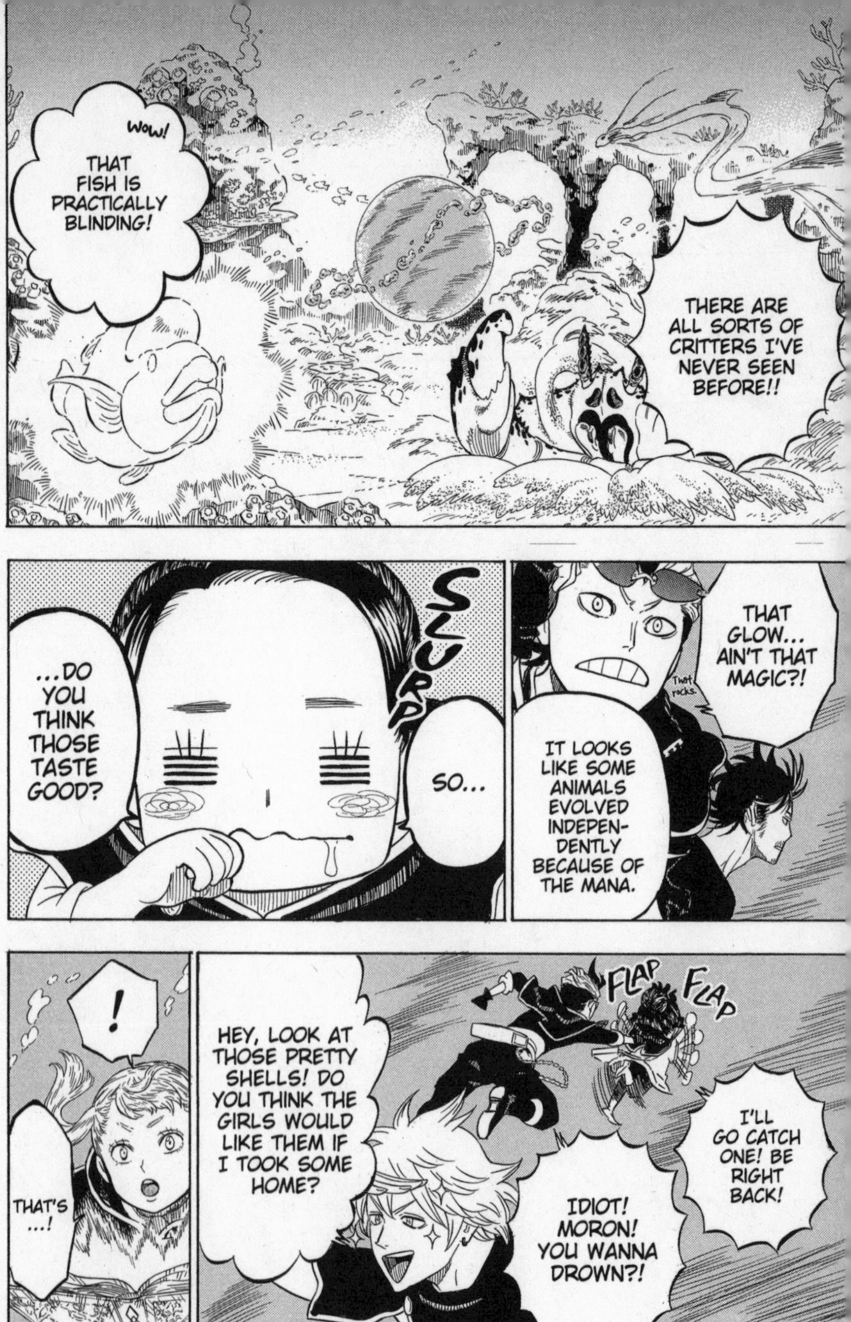
THERE ARE ALL SORTS OF CRITTERS I'VE NEVER SEEN BEFORE!!
WOW!
THAT FISH IS PRACTICALLY BLINDING!
THAT GLOW... AIN'T THAT MAGIC?!
That rocks.
IT LOOKS LIKE SOME ANIMALS EVOLVED INDEPEN-DENTLY BECAUSE OF THE MANA.
SLURP
SO...
...DO YOU THINK THOSE TASTE GOOD?
FLAP FLAP
I'LL GO CATCH ONE! BE RIGHT BACK!
HEY, LOOK AT THOSE PRETTY SHELLS! DO YOU THINK THE GIRLS WOULD LIKE THEM IF I TOOK SOME HOME?
IDIOT! MORON! YOU WANNA DROWN?!
!
THAT'S ...!

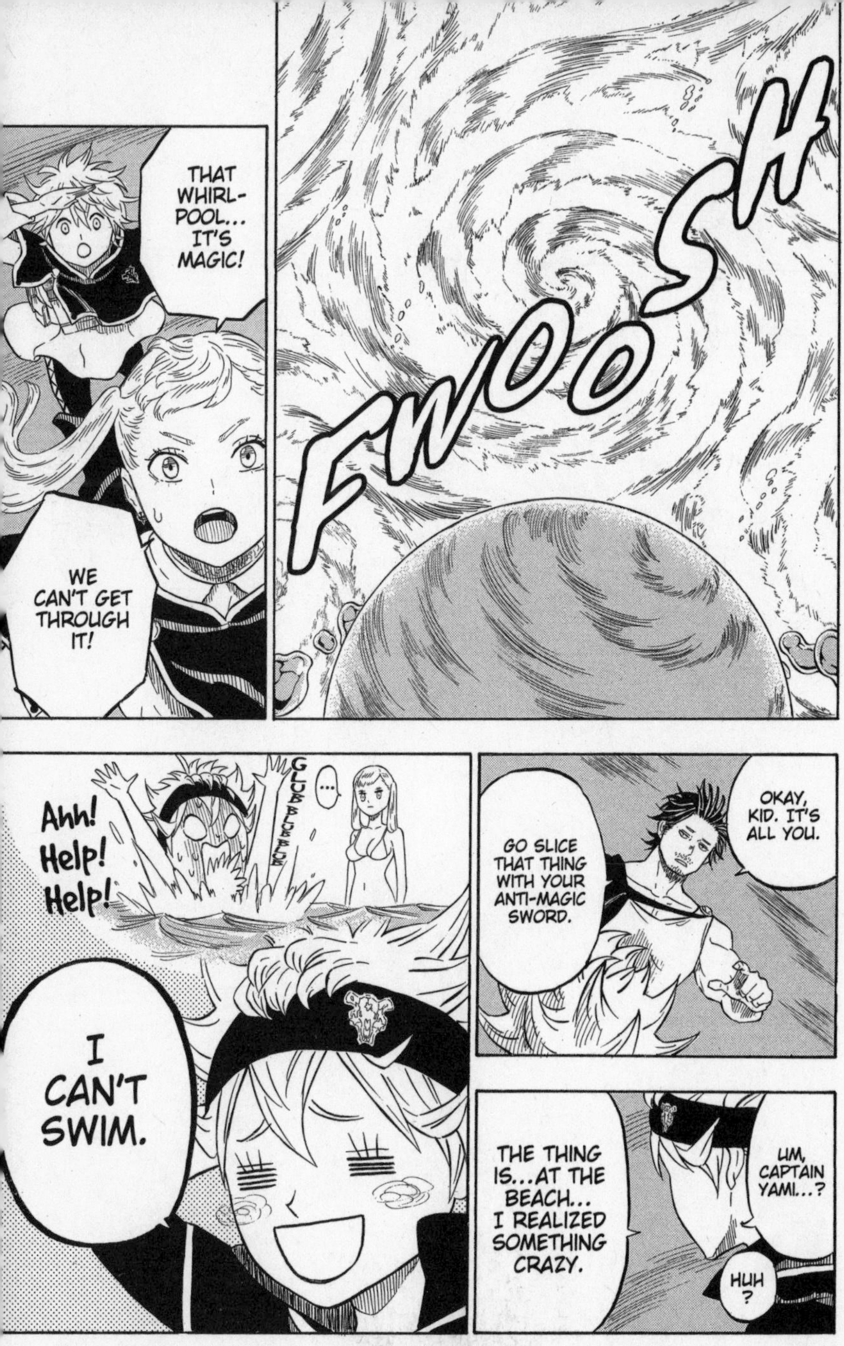
FWOOSH
THAT WHIRL-POOL... IT'S MAGIC!
WE CAN'T GET THROUGH IT!
OKAY, KID. IT'S ALL YOU.
GO SLICE THAT THING WITH YOUR ANTI-MAGIC SWORD.
UM, CAPTAIN YAMI...?
THE THING IS...AT THE BEACH... I REALIZED SOMETHING CRAZY.
HUH?
...
GLUB BLUB BLUB
Ahh! Help! Help!
I CAN'T SWIM.

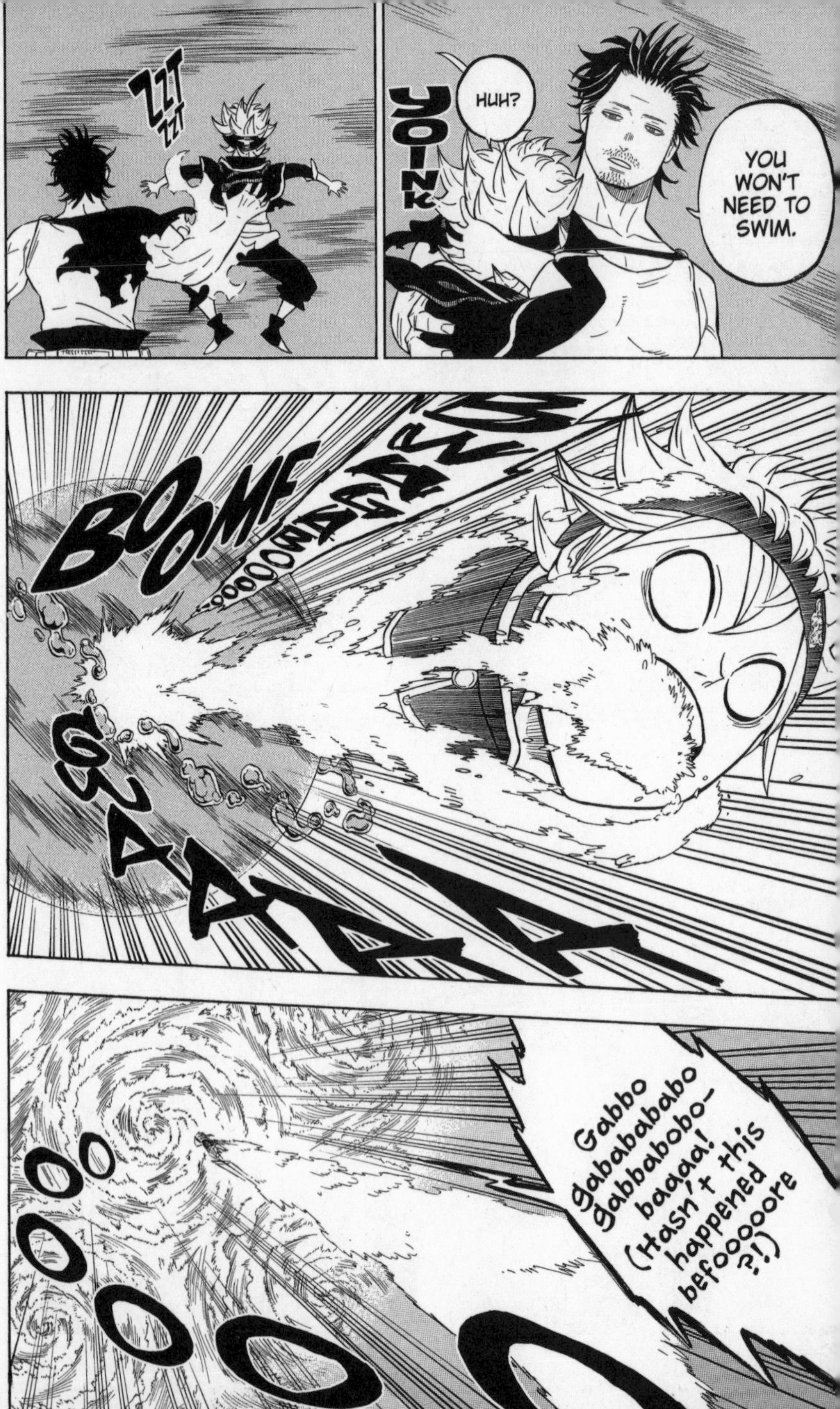
YOU WON'T NEED TO SWIM.
HUH?
YOINK
ZZT ZZT
BOOMF
GUAAAA
Gabbo gabababo gabbabobo-baaaa! (Hasn't this happened befoooooore?!)
OOOOOO

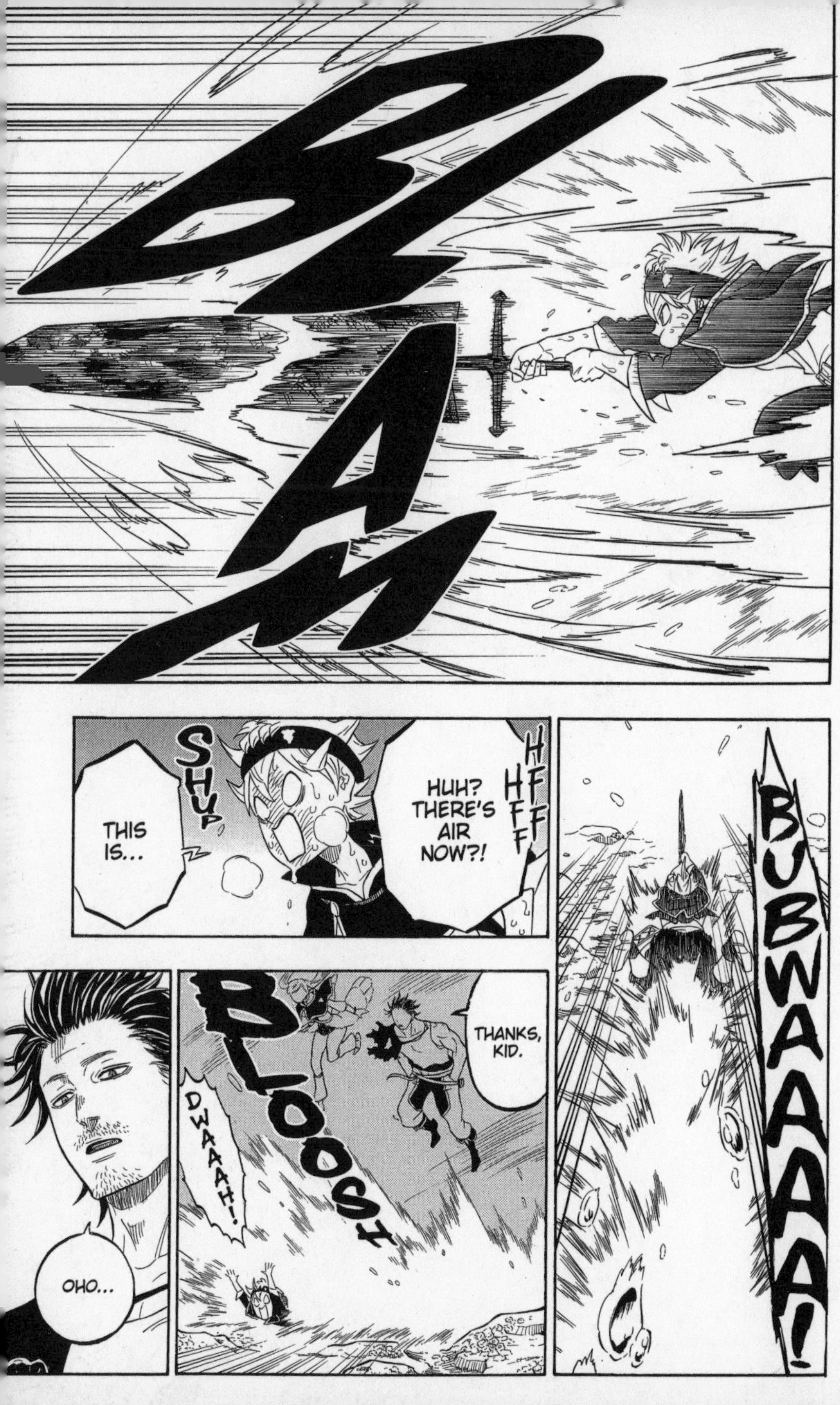
BAM
BUBWAAAA!
HFF HFF
HUH? THERE'S AIR NOW?!
SHUP
THIS IS...
THANKS, KID.
BLOOSH
DWAAAH!
OHO...

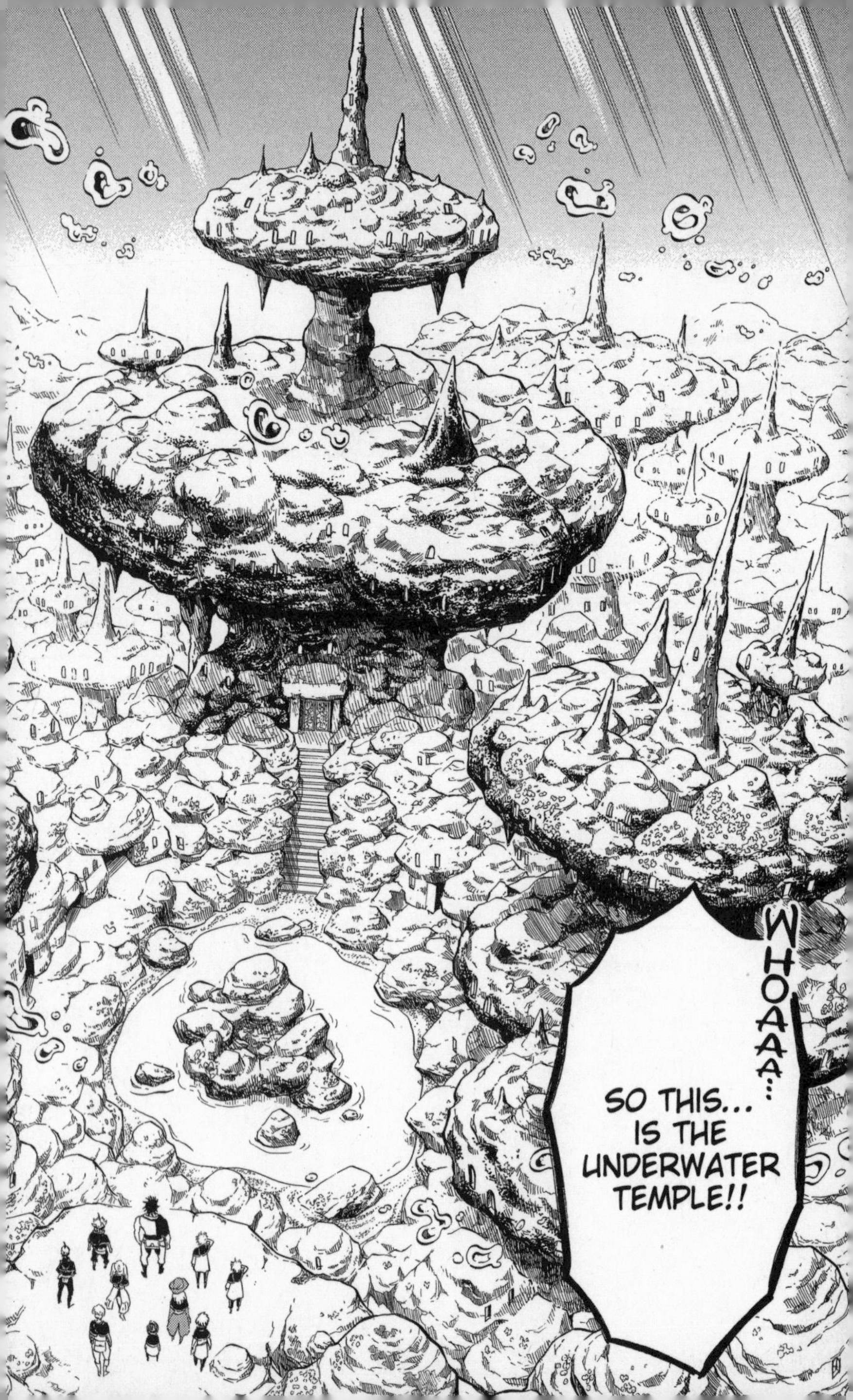
WHOAAA...
SO THIS... IS THE UNDERWATER TEMPLE!!

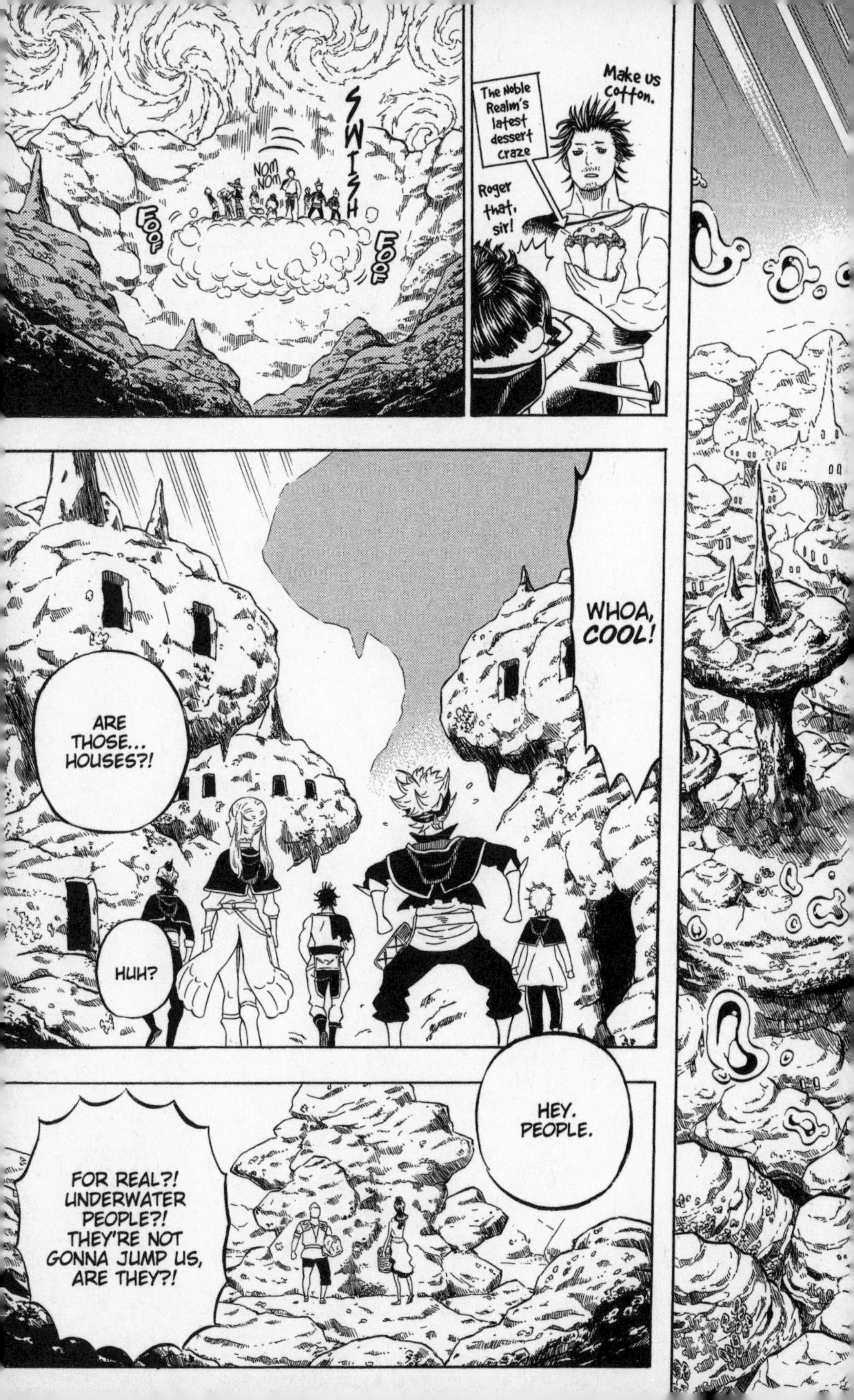
Make us cotton.
The Noble Realm's latest dessert craze
Roger that, sir!
SWISH
NOM NOM
FOOF
FOOF
WHOA, COOL!
ARE THOSE... HOUSES?!
HUH?
HEY. PEOPLE.
FOR REAL?! UNDERWATER PEOPLE?! THEY'RE NOT GONNA JUMP US, ARE THEY?!

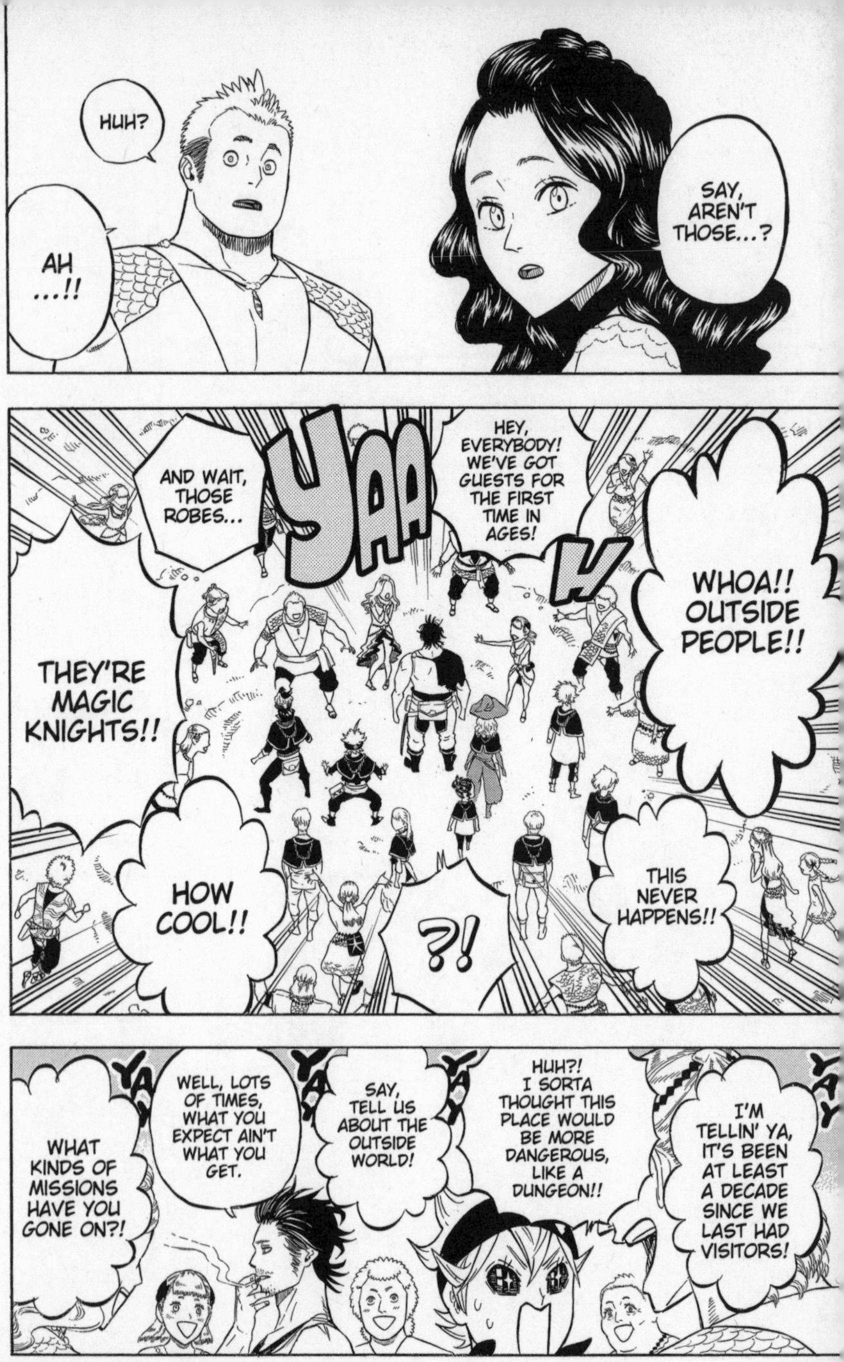
SAY, AREN'T THOSE...?
HUH?
AH ...!!
WHOA!! OUTSIDE PEOPLE!!
HEY, EVERYBODY! WE'VE GOT GUESTS FOR THE FIRST TIME IN AGES!
YAAAH
AND WAIT, THOSE ROBES...
THEY'RE MAGIC KNIGHTS!!
THIS NEVER HAPPENS!!
?!
HOW COOL!!
YAY
I'M TELLIN' YA, IT'S BEEN AT LEAST A DECADE SINCE WE LAST HAD VISITORS!
HUH?! I SORTA THOUGHT THIS PLACE WOULD BE MORE DANGEROUS, LIKE A DUNGEON!!
SAY, TELL US ABOUT THE OUTSIDE WORLD!
WELL, LOTS OF TIMES, WHAT YOU EXPECT AIN'T WHAT YOU GET.
WHAT KINDS OF MISSIONS HAVE YOU GONE ON?!

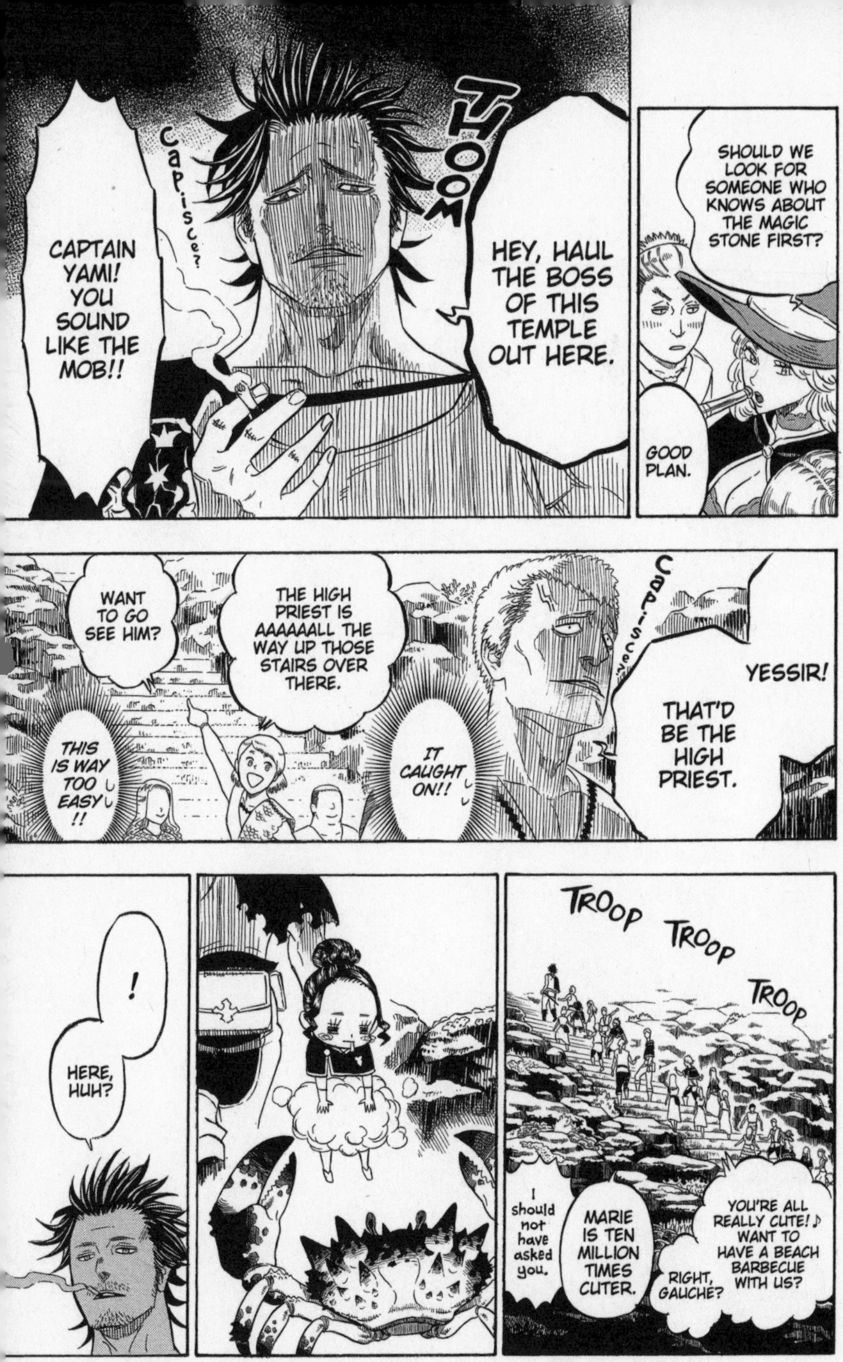
SHOULD WE LOOK FOR SOMEONE WHO KNOWS ABOUT THE MAGIC STONE FIRST?
GOOD PLAN.
THOOM
HEY, HAUL THE BOSS OF THIS TEMPLE OUT HERE.
Capisce?
CAPTAIN YAMI! YOU SOUND LIKE THE MOB!!
Capisce?
YESSIR!
THAT'D BE THE HIGH PRIEST.
IT CAUGHT ON!!
THE HIGH PRIEST IS AAAAAALL THE WAY UP THOSE STAIRS OVER THERE.
WANT TO GO SEE HIM?
THIS IS WAY TOO EASY!!
TROOP
TROOP
TROOP
YOU'RE ALL REALLY CUTE!♪ WANT TO HAVE A BEACH BARBECUE WITH US?
RIGHT, GAUCHE?
MARIE IS TEN MILLION TIMES CUTER.
I should not have asked you.
!
HERE, HUH?

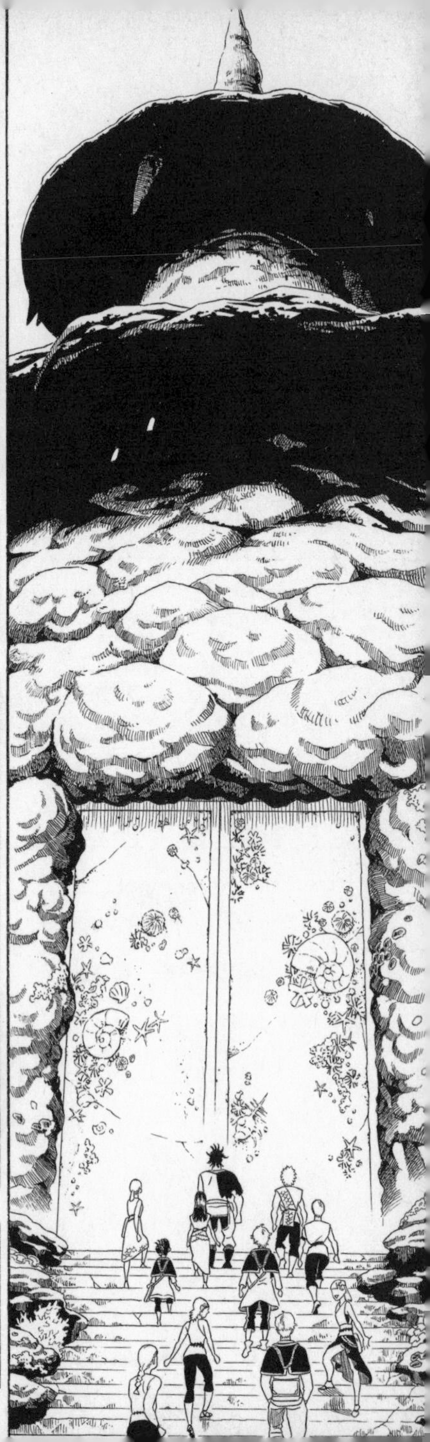

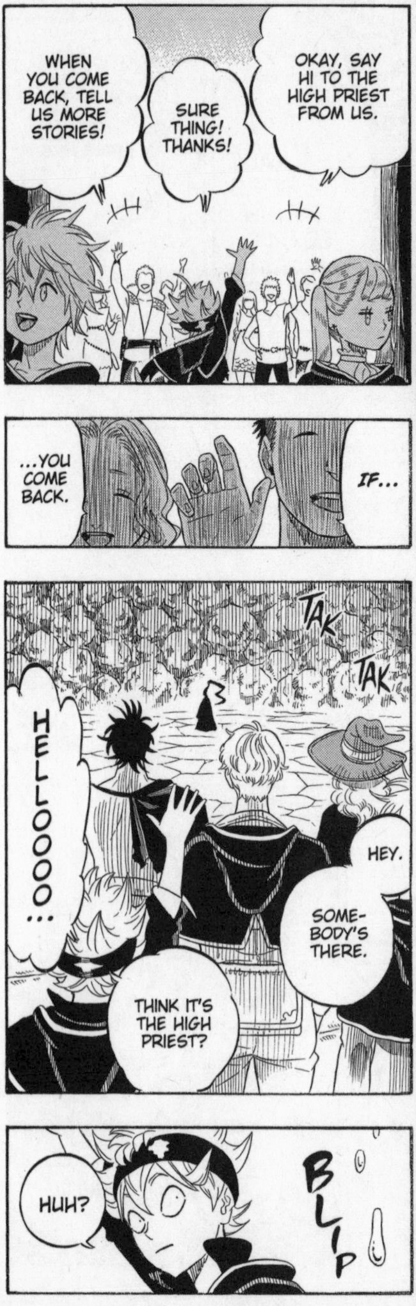
OKAY, SAY HI TO THE HIGH PRIEST FROM US.
SURE THING! THANKS!
WHEN YOU COME BACK, TELL US MORE STORIES!
IF...
...YOU COME BACK.
TAK TAK
HELLOOOO...
HEY.
SOMEBODY'S THERE.
THINK IT'S THE HIGH PRIEST?
BLIP
HUH?

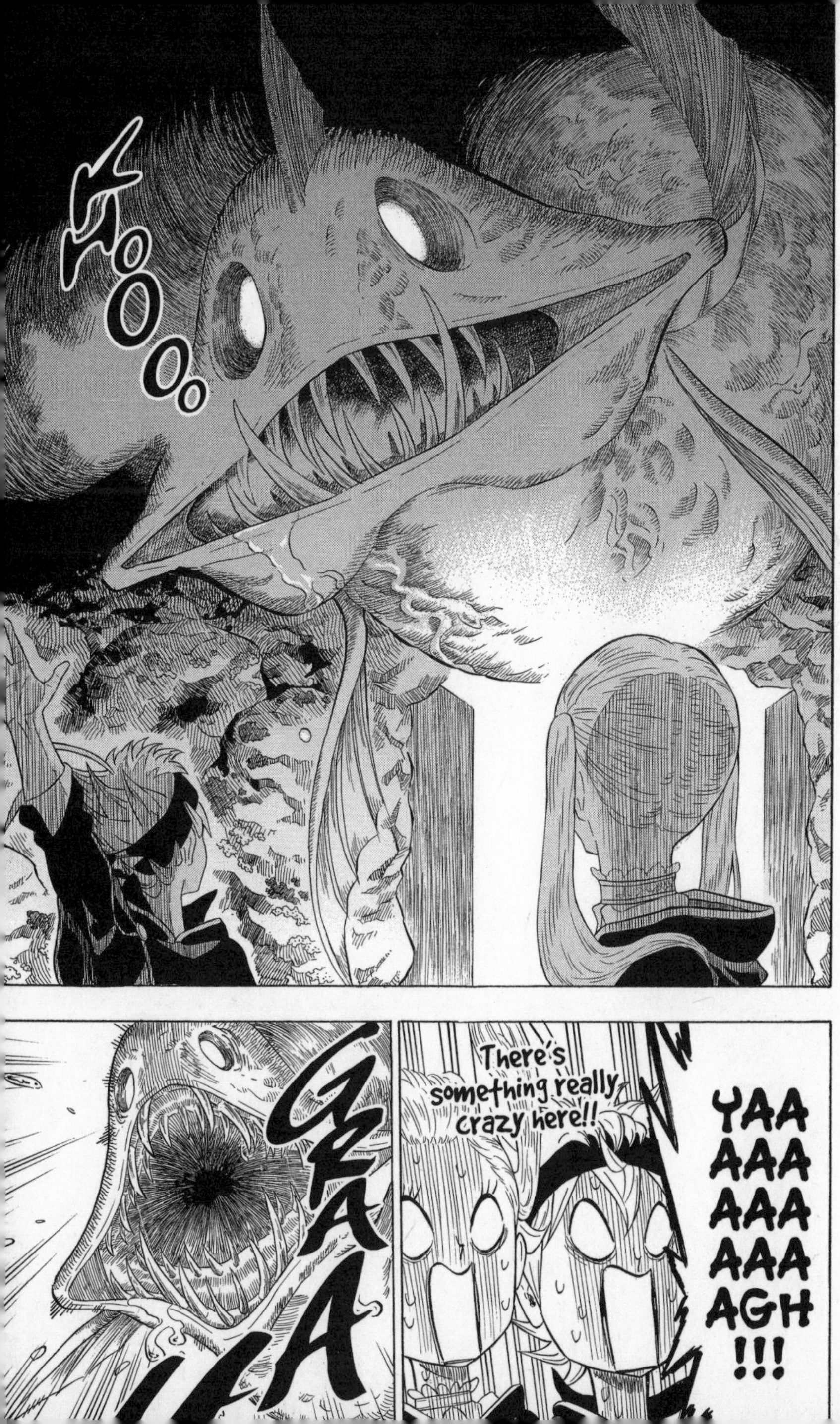
YAAAAAAAAAAAAGH!!!
There's something really crazy here!!

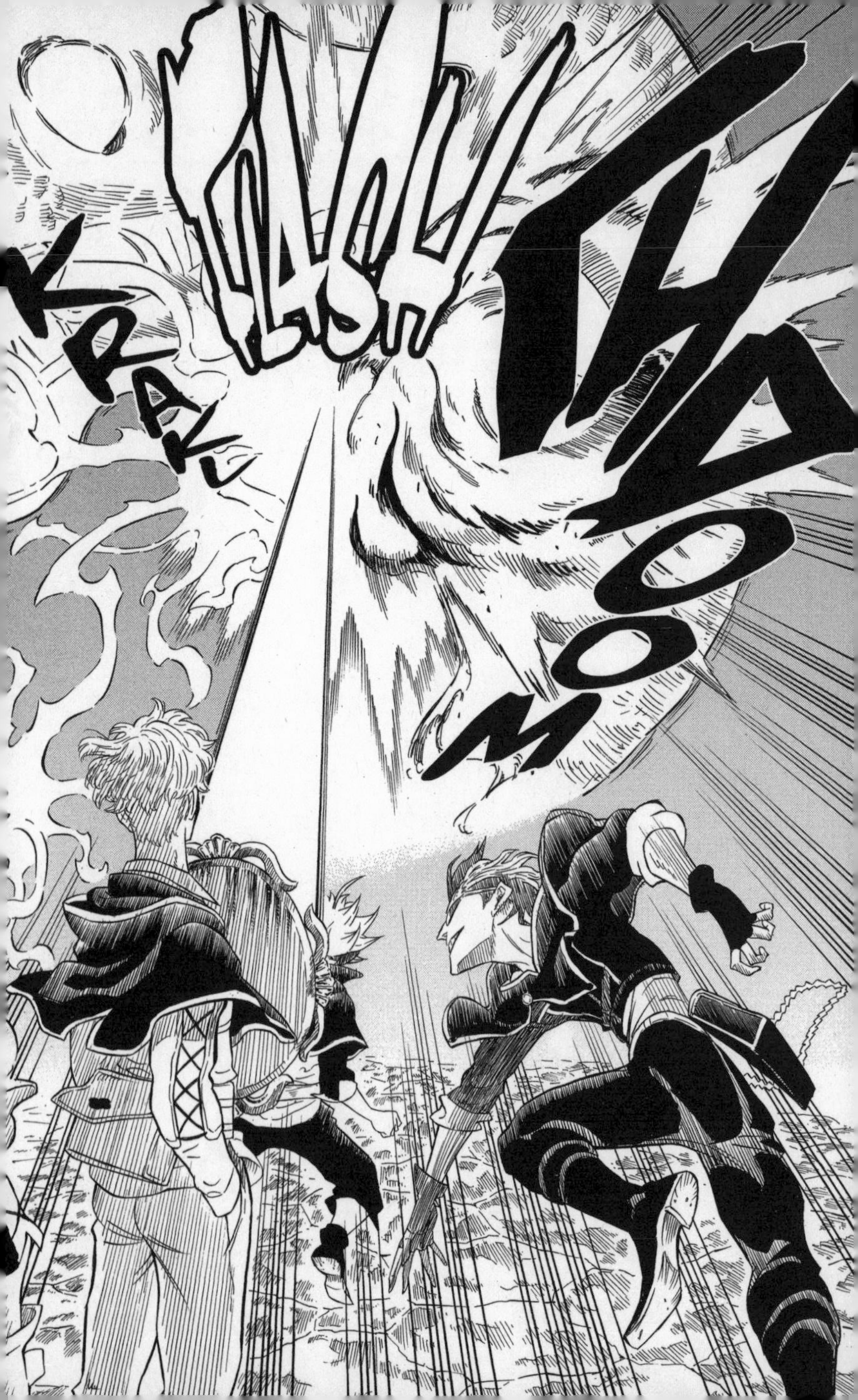
KRAK!
WHOOM

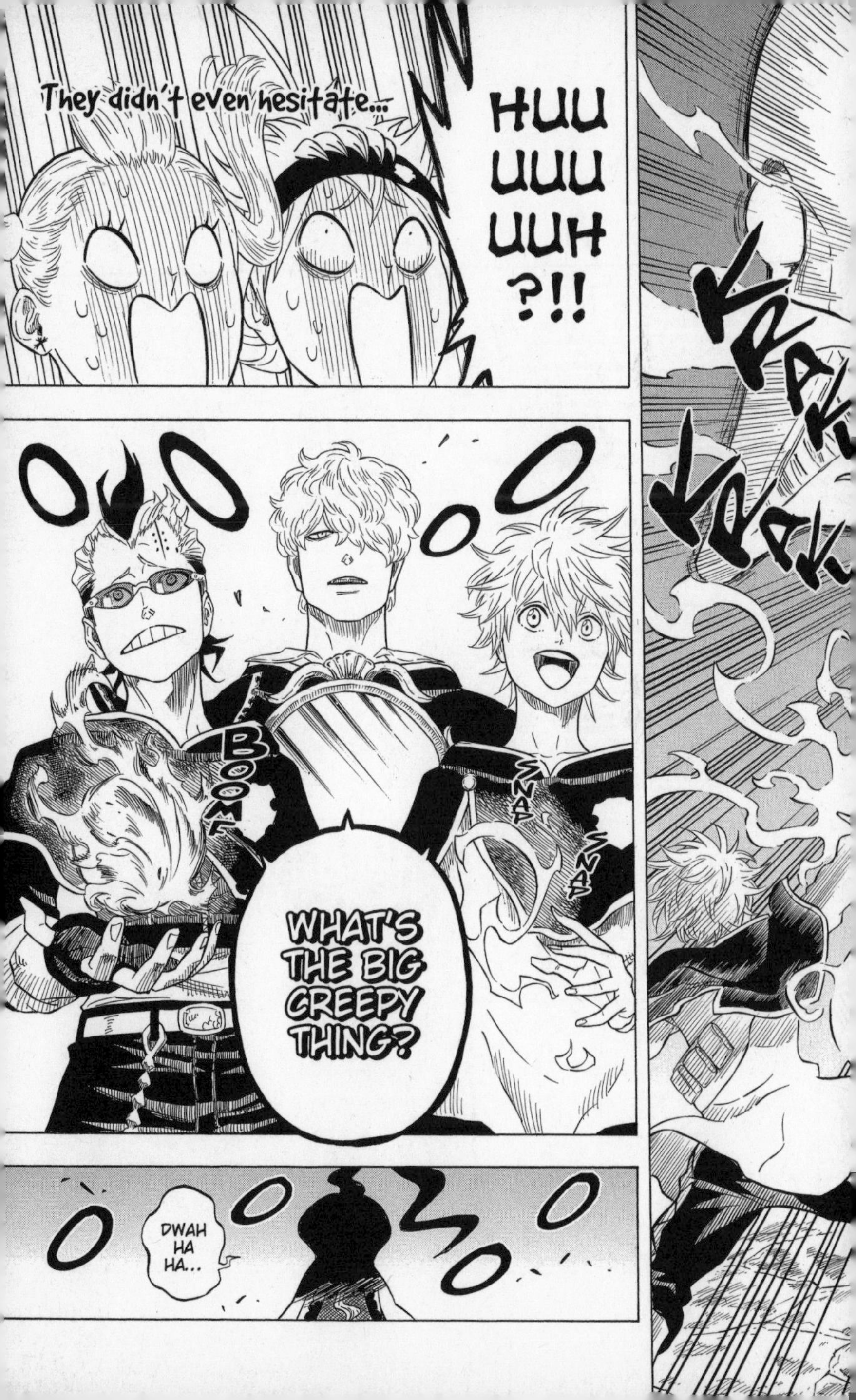
KRAK
KRAK
HUUUUUUUH?!!
They didn't even hesitate...
O O
O O
SNAP
SNAP
BOOMF
WHAT'S THE BIG CREEPY THING?
O O
O O O
DWAH HA HA...

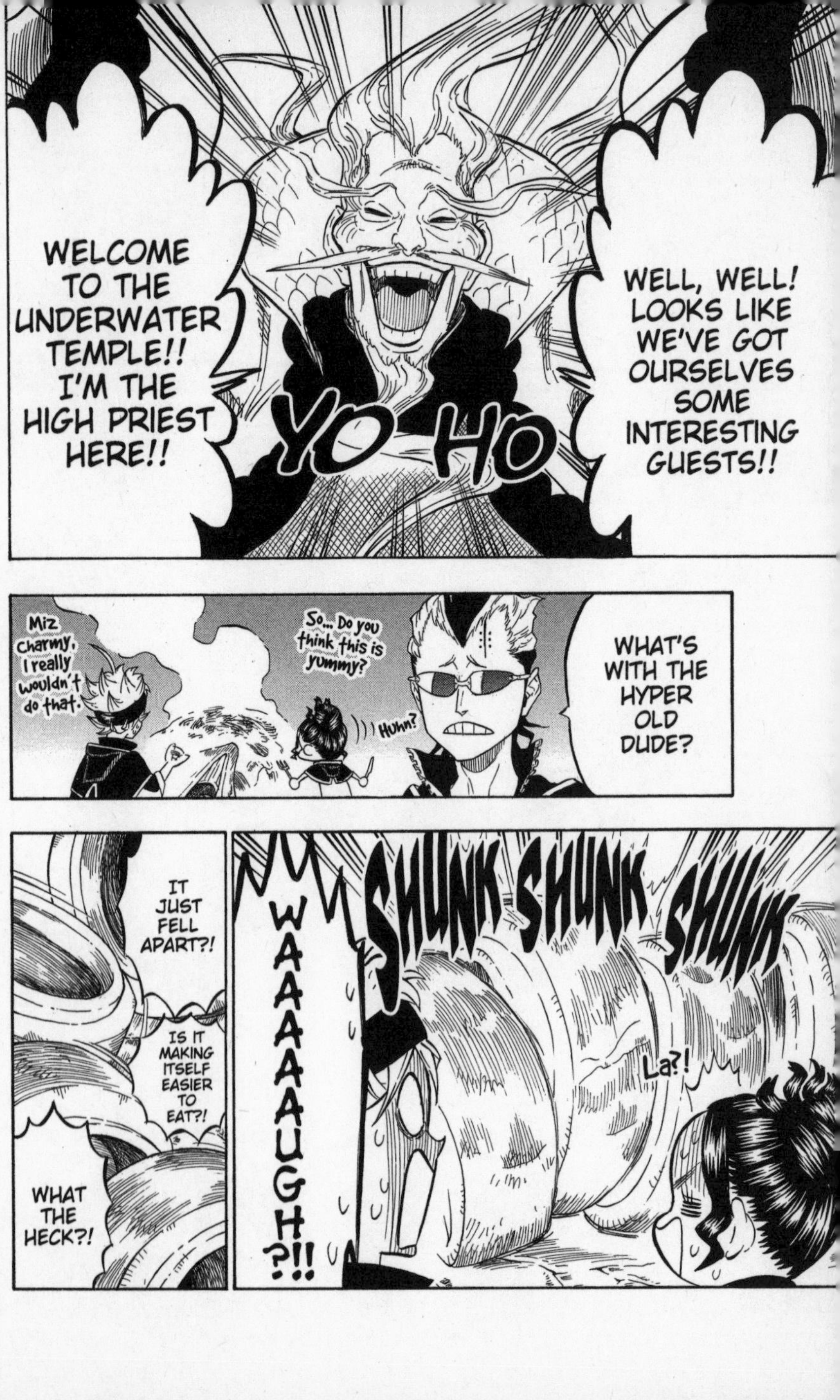
WELL, WELL! LOOKS LIKE WE'VE GOT OURSELVES SOME INTERESTING GUESTS!!
YO HO
WELCOME TO THE UNDERWATER TEMPLE!! I'M THE HIGH PRIEST HERE!!
WHAT'S WITH THE HYPER OLD DUDE?
Huhn?
So... Do you think this is yummy?
Miz Charmy, I really wouldn't do that.
SHUNK SHUNK SHUNK
La?!
WAAAAAUGH?!!
IT JUST FELL APART?!
IS IT MAKING ITSELF EASIER TO EAT?!
WHAT THE HECK?!

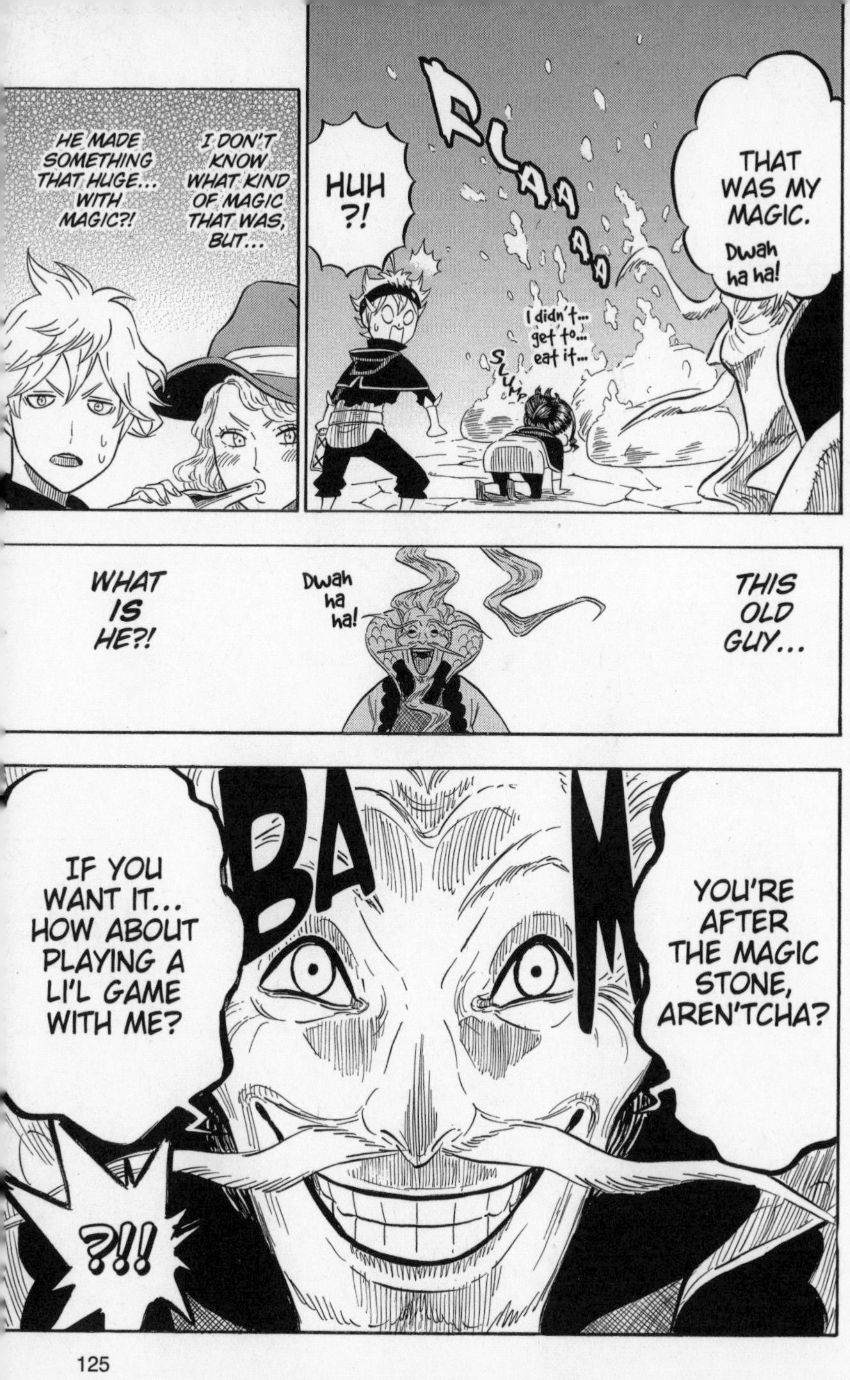
THAT WAS MY MAGIC.
Dwah ha ha!
RLAAAAA
HUH?!
I didn't... get to... eat it...
SLUMP
I DON'T KNOW WHAT KIND OF MAGIC THAT WAS, BUT...
HE MADE SOMETHING THAT HUGE... WITH MAGIC?!
THIS OLD GUY...
Dwah ha ha!
WHAT IS HE?!
YOU'RE AFTER THE MAGIC STONE, AREN'TCHA?
BAM
IF YOU WANT IT... HOW ABOUT PLAYING A LI'L GAME WITH ME?
?!!

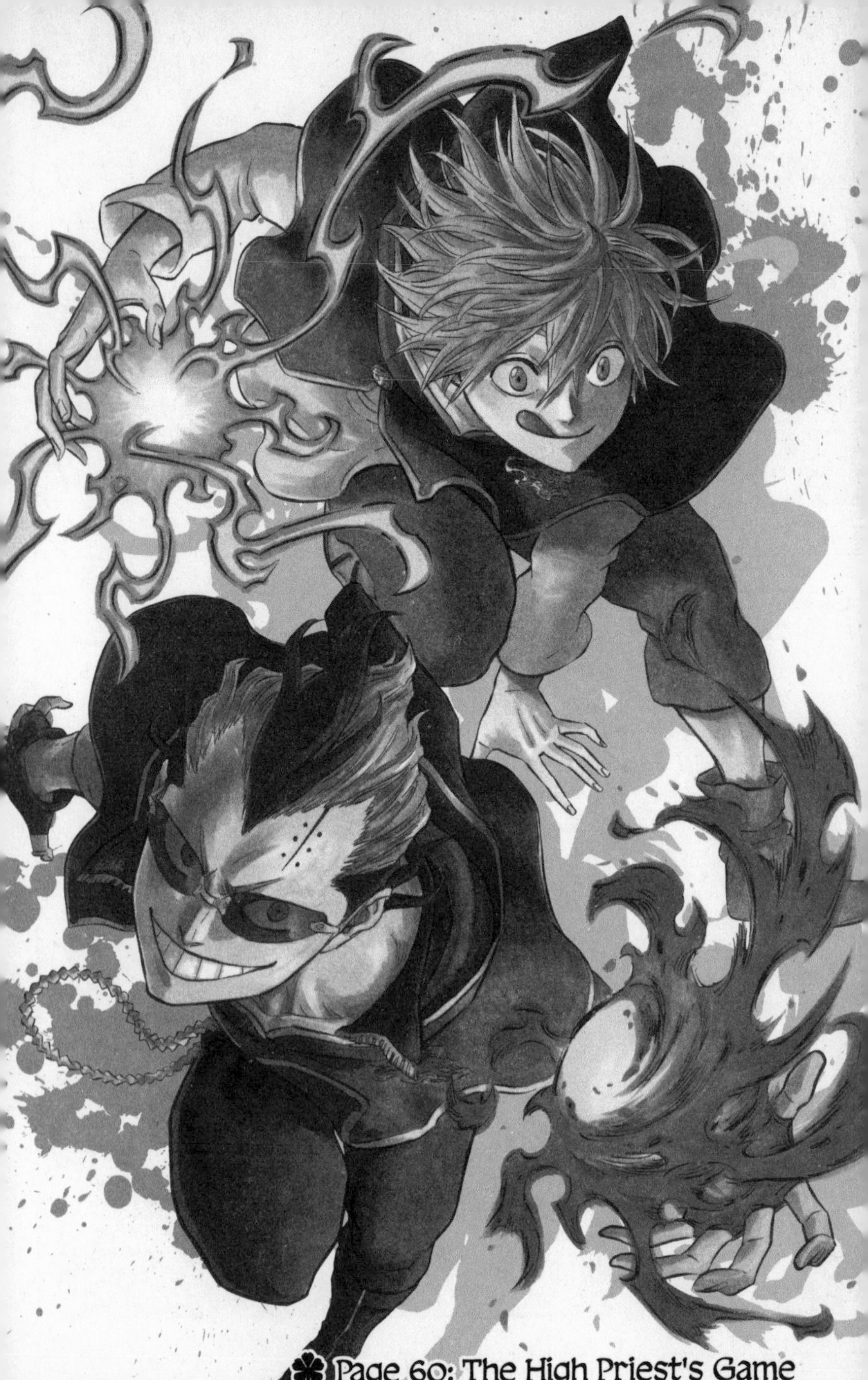

## Page 60: The High Priest's Game

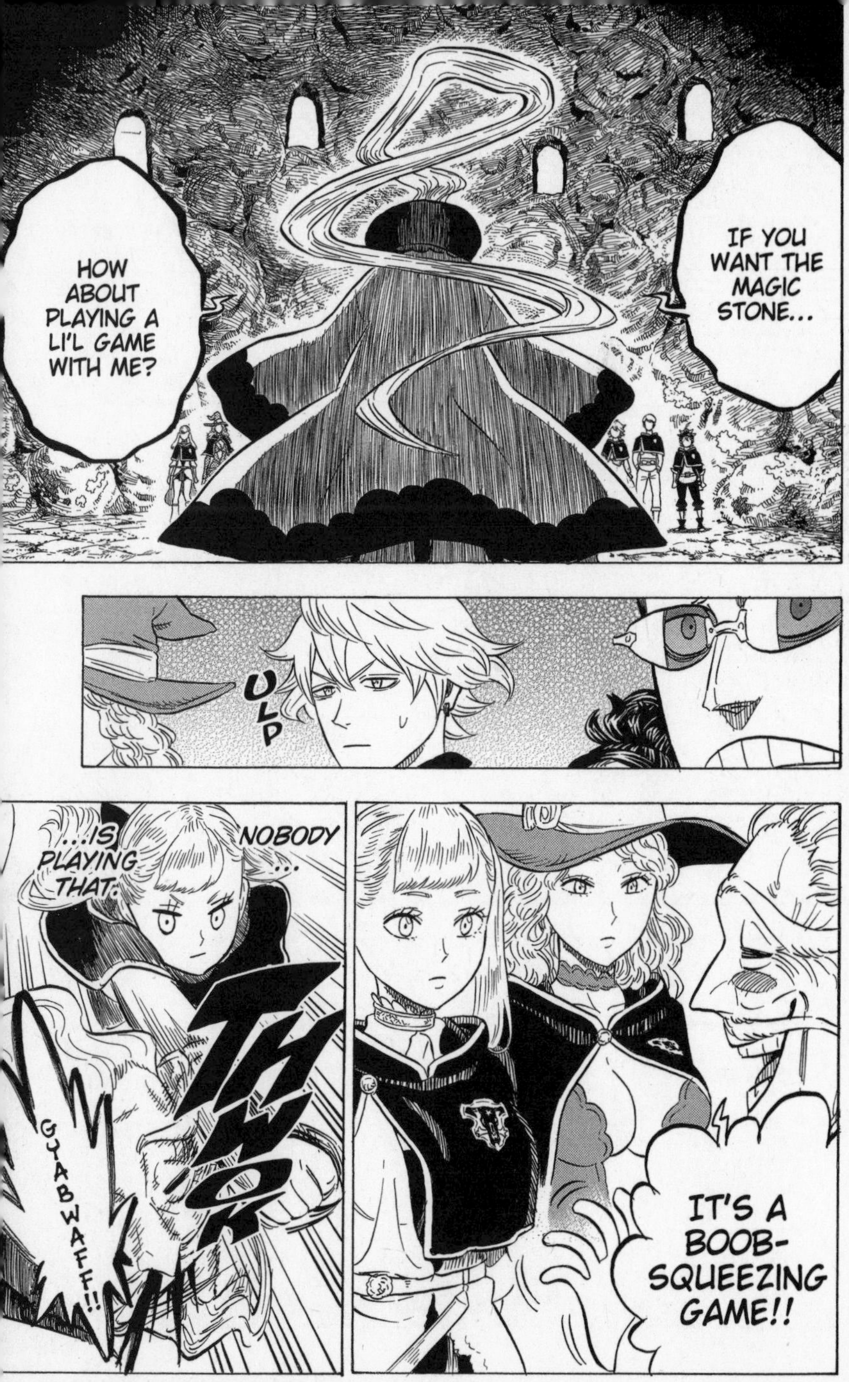
IF YOU WANT THE MAGIC STONE...
HOW ABOUT PLAYING A LI'L GAME WITH ME?
ULP
IT'S A BOOB-SQUEEZING GAME!!
NOBODY...
...IS PLAYING THAT.
GYABWAFF!!

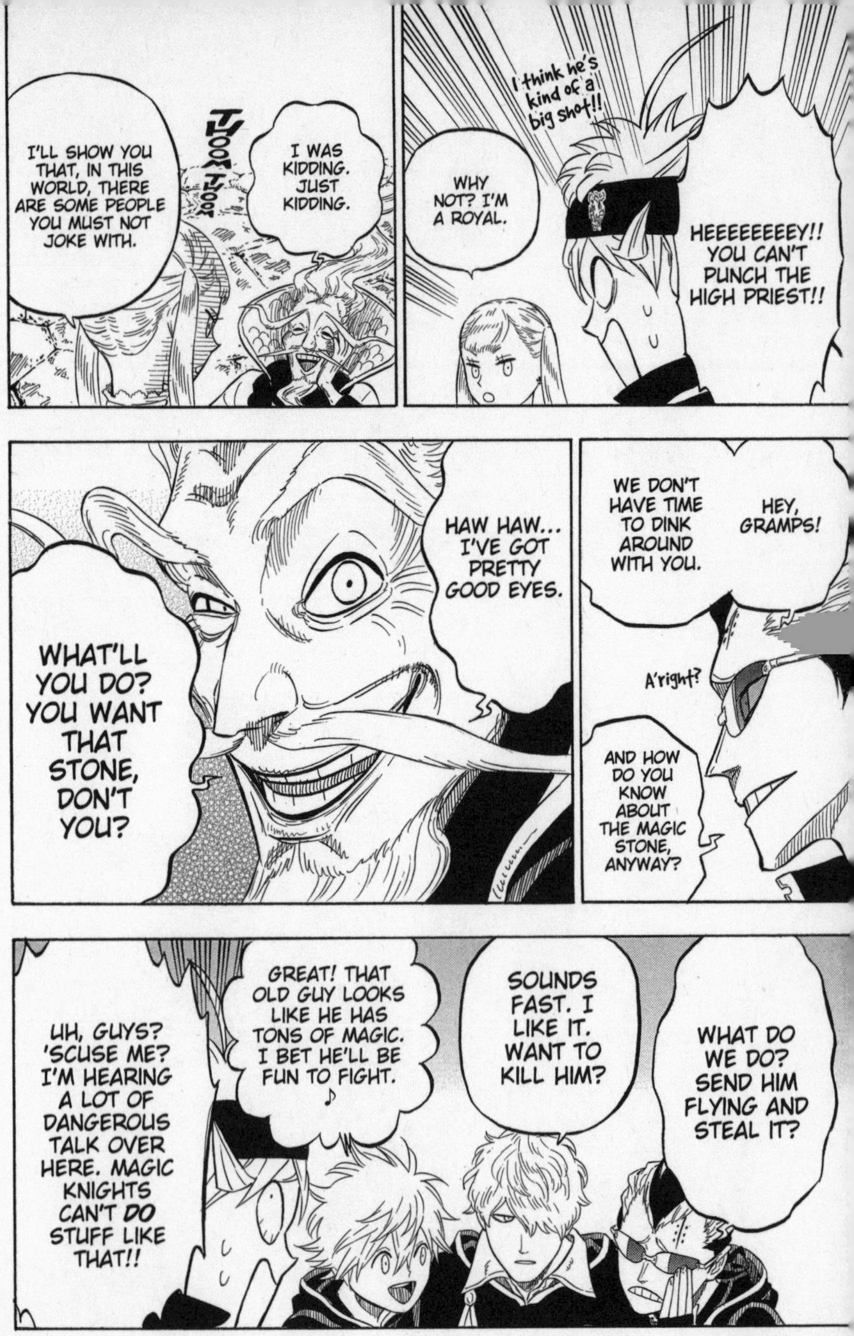
HEEEEEEEEY!! YOU CAN'T PUNCH THE HIGH PRIEST!!
I think he's kind of a big shot!!
WHY NOT? I'M A ROYAL.
I WAS KIDDING. JUST KIDDING.
TJOOM TJOOM
I'LL SHOW YOU THAT, IN THIS WORLD, THERE ARE SOME PEOPLE YOU MUST NOT JOKE WITH.
HEY, GRAMPS!
WE DON'T HAVE TIME TO DINK AROUND WITH YOU.
A'right?
AND HOW DO YOU KNOW ABOUT THE MAGIC STONE, ANYWAY?
HAW HAW... I'VE GOT PRETTY GOOD EYES.
WHAT'LL YOU DO? YOU WANT THAT STONE, DON'T YOU?
WHAT DO WE DO? SEND HIM FLYING AND STEAL IT?
SOUNDS FAST. I LIKE IT. WANT TO KILL HIM?
GREAT! THAT OLD GUY LOOKS LIKE HE HAS TONS OF MAGIC. I BET HE'LL BE FUN TO FIGHT. ♪
UH, GUYS? 'SCUSE ME? I'M HEARING A LOT OF DANGEROUS TALK OVER HERE. MAGIC KNIGHTS CAN'T DO STUFF LIKE THAT!!

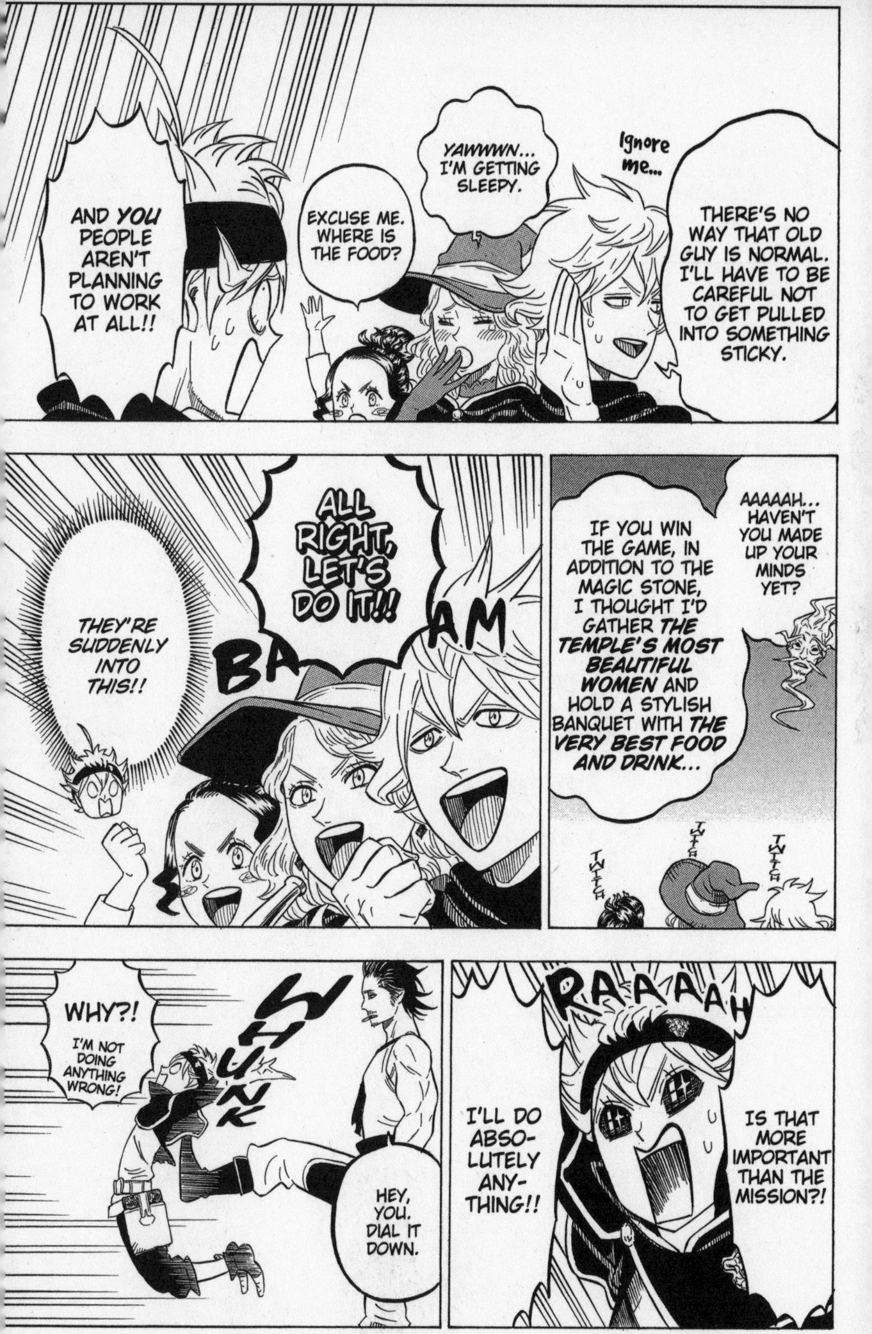
THERE'S NO WAY THAT OLD GUY IS NORMAL. I'LL HAVE TO BE CAREFUL NOT TO GET PULLED INTO SOMETHING STICKY.
Ignore me...
YAWWWN... I'M GETTING SLEEPY.
EXCUSE ME. WHERE IS THE FOOD?
AND YOU PEOPLE AREN'T PLANNING TO WORK AT ALL!!
AAAAAH... HAVEN'T YOU MADE UP YOUR MINDS YET?
IF YOU WIN THE GAME, IN ADDITION TO THE MAGIC STONE, I THOUGHT I'D GATHER THE TEMPLE'S MOST BEAUTIFUL WOMEN AND HOLD A STYLISH BANQUET WITH THE VERY BEST FOOD AND DRINK...
TWITCH
TWITCH
TWITCH
ALL RIGHT, LET'S DO IT!!
BAAM
THEY'RE SUDDENLY INTO THIS!!
RAAAAAH
IS THAT MORE IMPORTANT THAN THE MISSION?!
I'LL DO ABSO-LUTELY ANY-THING!!
WHUNK
HEY, YOU. DIAL IT DOWN.
WHY?!
I'M NOT DOING ANYTHING WRONG!

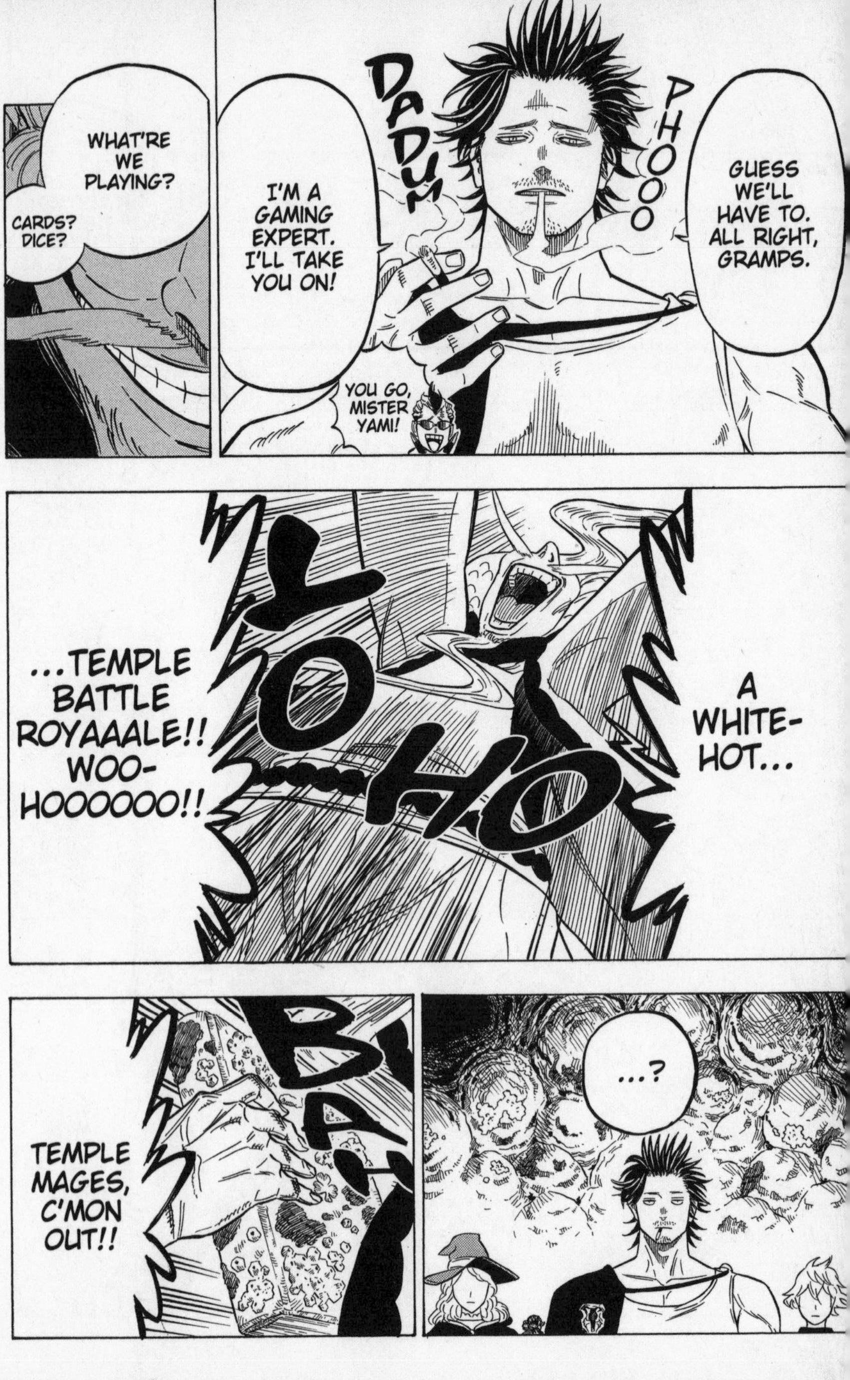
GUESS WE'LL HAVE TO. ALL RIGHT, GRAMPS.
PHOOOO
DADUM
I'M A GAMING EXPERT. I'LL TAKE YOU ON!
YOU GO, MISTER YAMI!
WHAT'RE WE PLAYING?
CARDS? DICE?
A WHITE-HOT...
YOHO
...TEMPLE BATTLE ROYAAALE!! WOO-HOOOOOO!!
...?
BA
TEMPLE MAGES, C'MON OUT!!

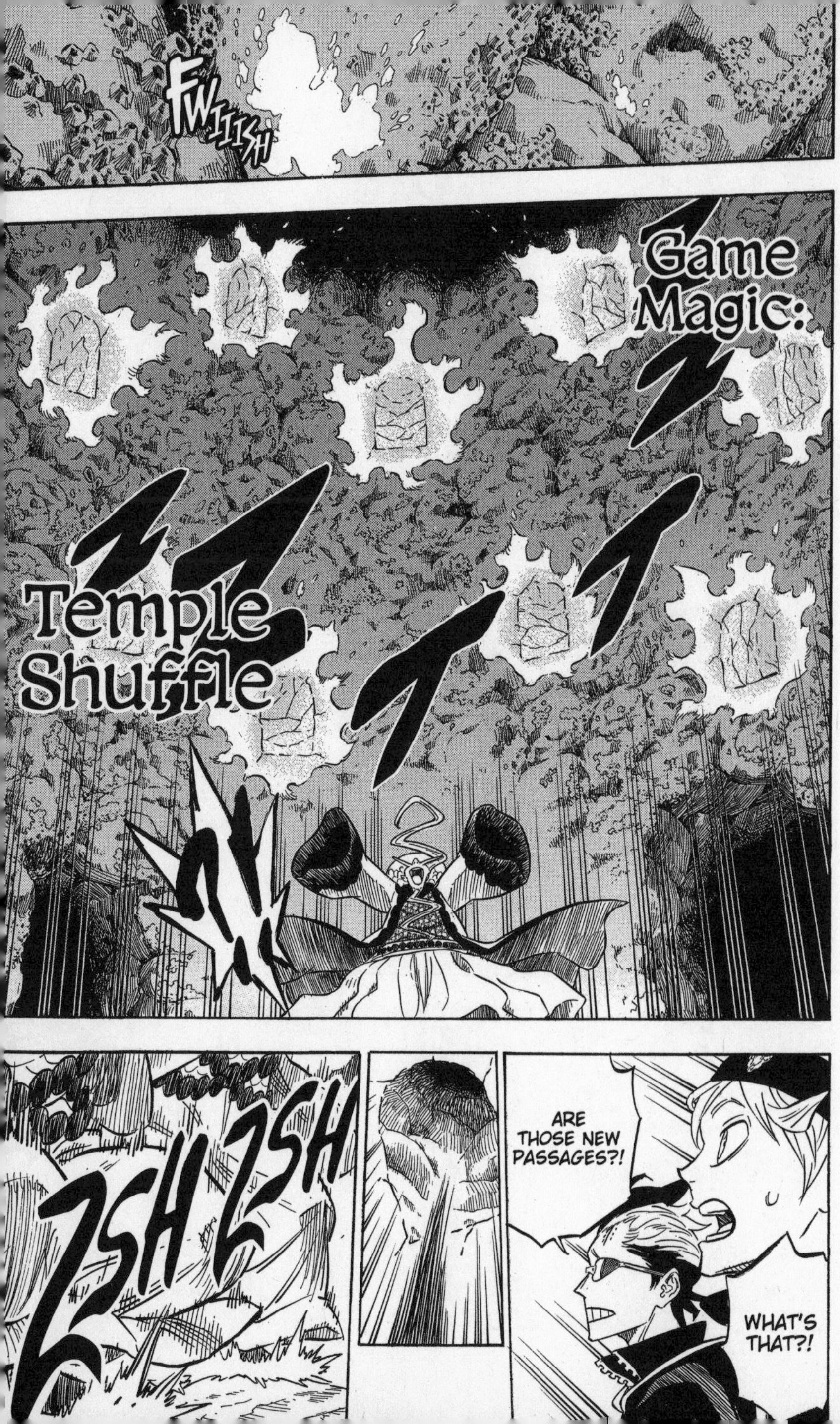
FWIIISH
Game Magic:
Temple Shuffle
ARE THOSE NEW PASSAGES?!
WHAT'S THAT?!
ZSH
ZSH

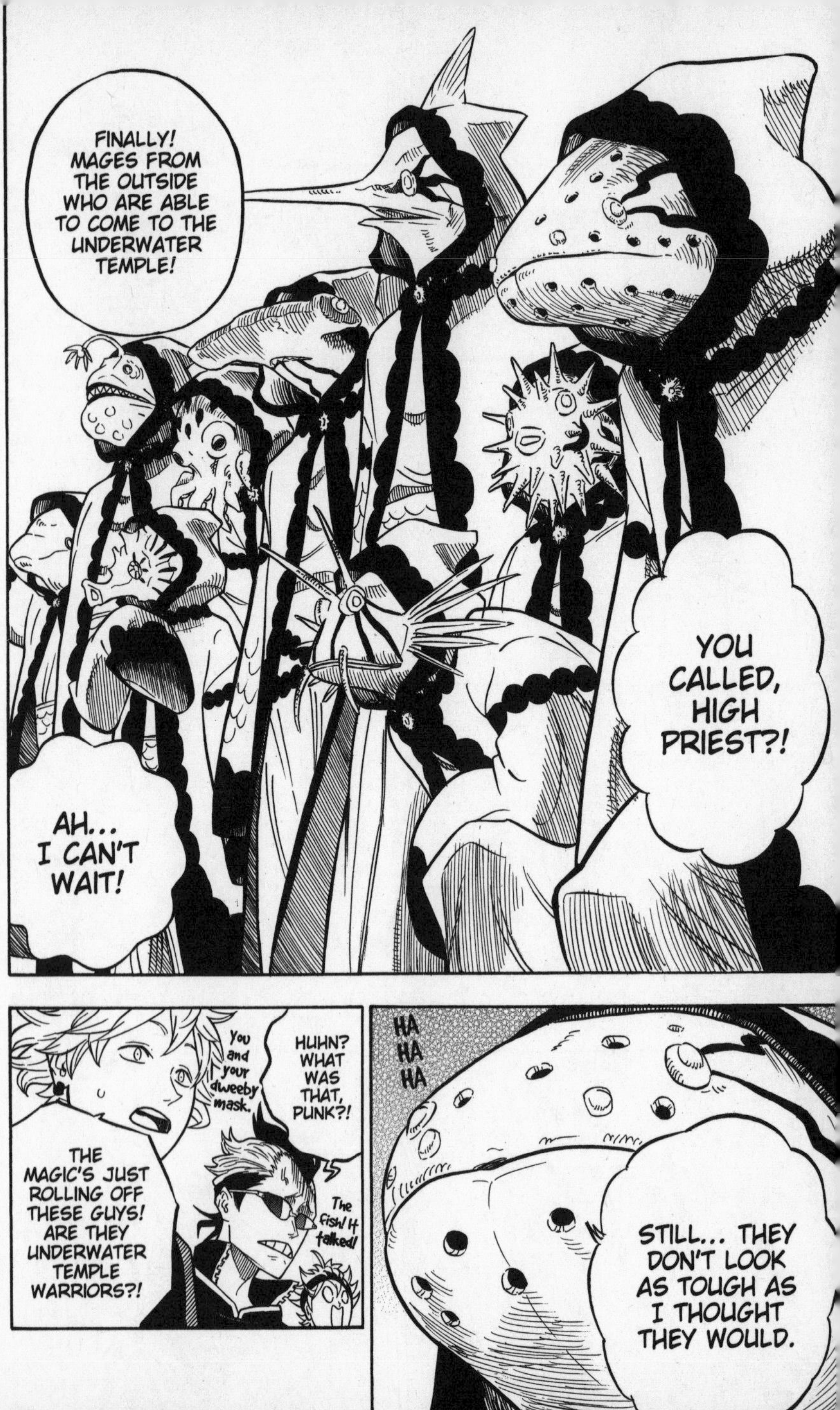
FINALLY! MAGES FROM THE OUTSIDE WHO ARE ABLE TO COME TO THE UNDERWATER TEMPLE!
YOU CALLED, HIGH PRIEST?!
AH... I CAN'T WAIT!
HA HA HA
STILL... THEY DON'T LOOK AS TOUGH AS I THOUGHT THEY WOULD.
HUHN? WHAT WAS THAT, PUNK?!
You and your dweeby mask.
THE MAGIC'S JUST ROLLING OFF THESE GUYS! ARE THEY UNDERWATER TEMPLE WARRIORS?!
The fish! It talked!

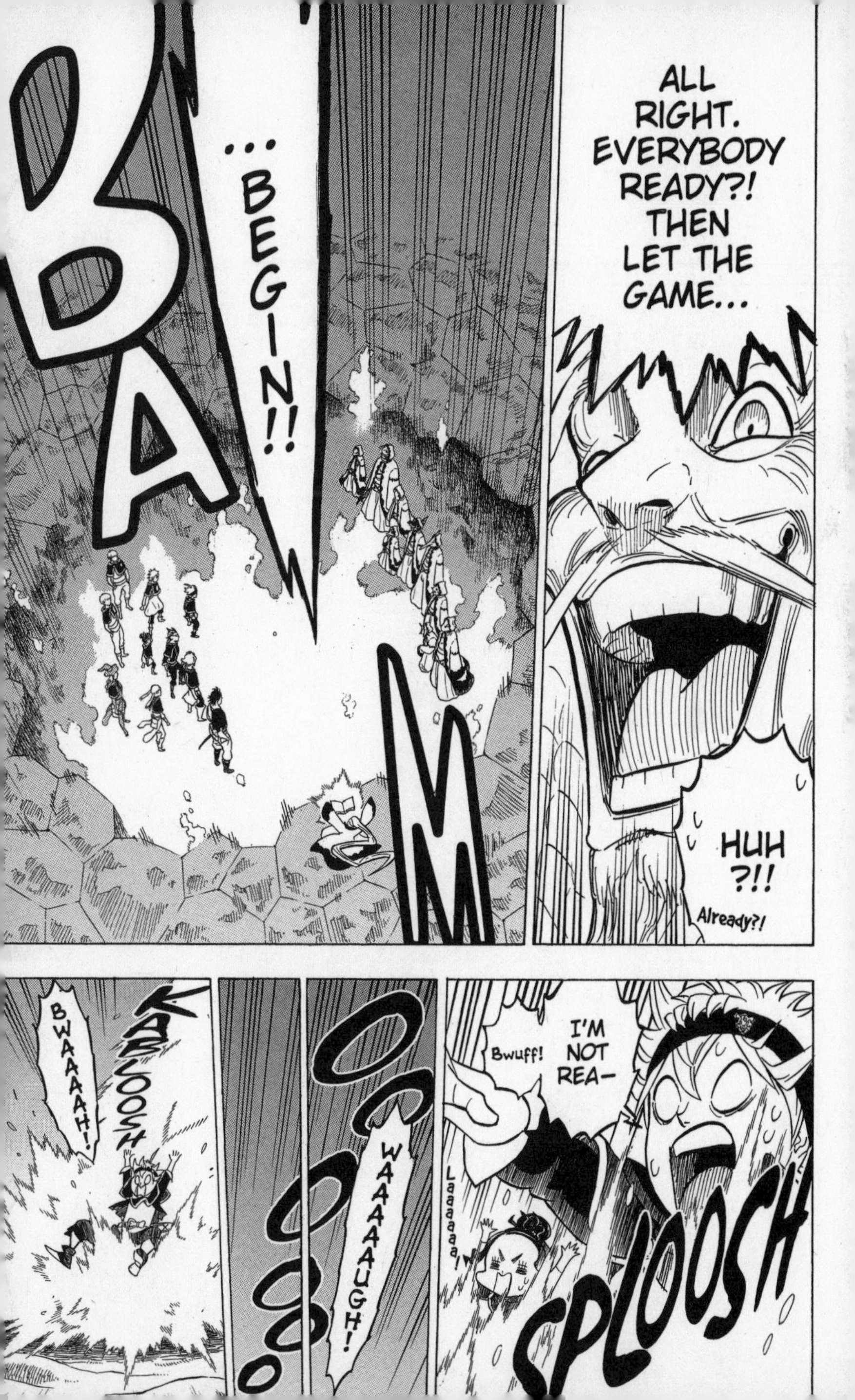
ALL RIGHT. EVERYBODY READY?! THEN LET THE GAME...
HUH?!!
Already?!
...BEGIN!!
BAAM
I'M NOT REA-
Bwuff!
Laaaaaa!
CPLOOSH!
WAAAAAAUGH!
OOOOOO
KABLOOSH
BWAAAAAH!

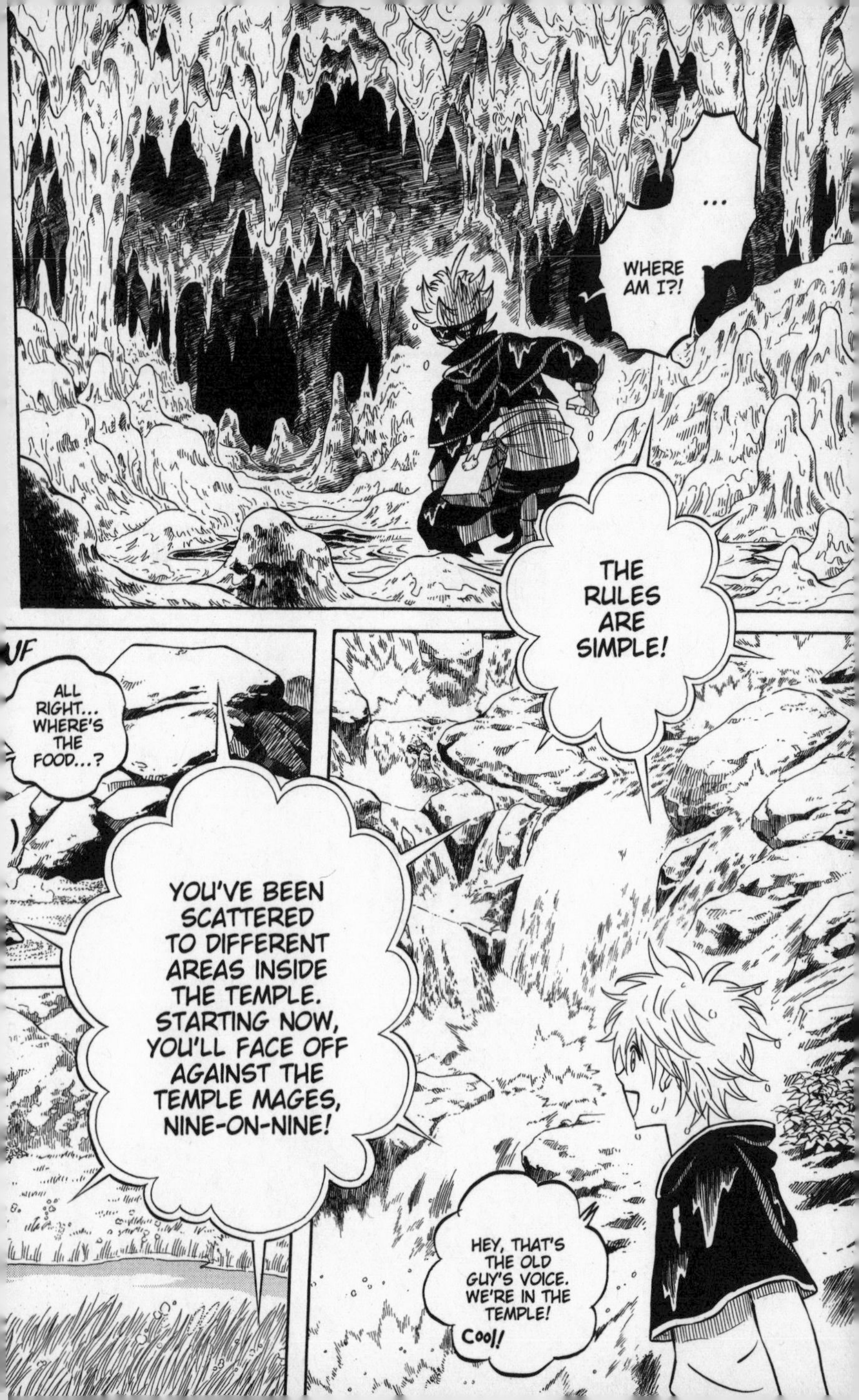
...
WHERE AM I?!
THE RULES ARE SIMPLE!
YOU'VE BEEN SCATTERED TO DIFFERENT AREAS INSIDE THE TEMPLE. STARTING NOW, YOU'LL FACE OFF AGAINST THE TEMPLE MAGES, NINE-ON-NINE!
HEY, THAT'S THE OLD GUY'S VOICE. WE'RE IN THE TEMPLE!
COOL!
ALL RIGHT... WHERE'S THE FOOD...?

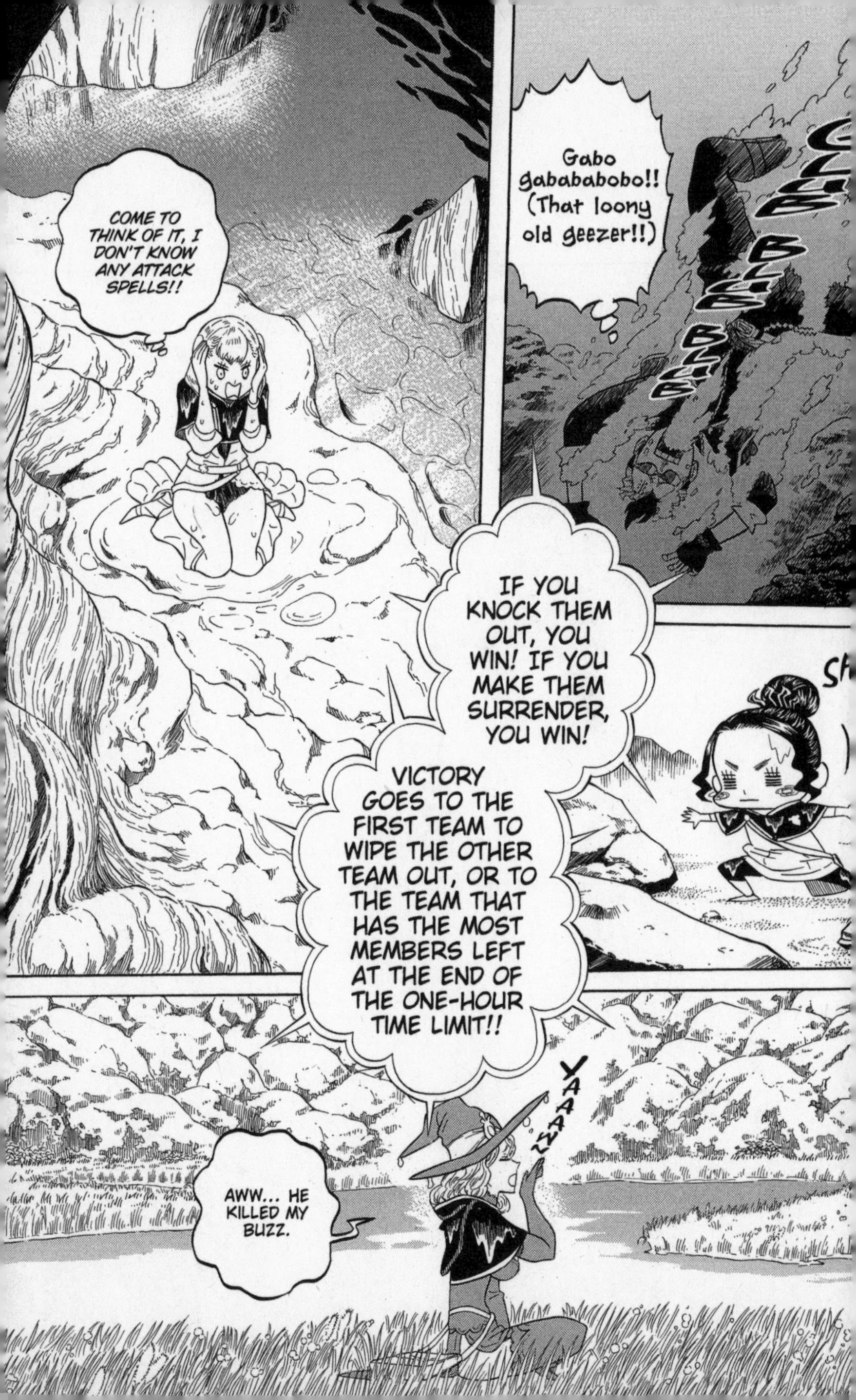
Gabo gababababobo!! (That loony old geezer!!)
GLUB BLUB BLUB
IF YOU KNOCK THEM OUT, YOU WIN! IF YOU MAKE THEM SURRENDER, YOU WIN!
COME TO THINK OF IT, I DON'T KNOW ANY ATTACK SPELLS!!
VICTORY GOES TO THE FIRST TEAM TO WIPE THE OTHER TEAM OUT, OR TO THE TEAM THAT HAS THE MOST MEMBERS LEFT AT THE END OF THE ONE-HOUR TIME LIMIT!!
YAAAAWN
AWW... HE KILLED MY BUZZ.

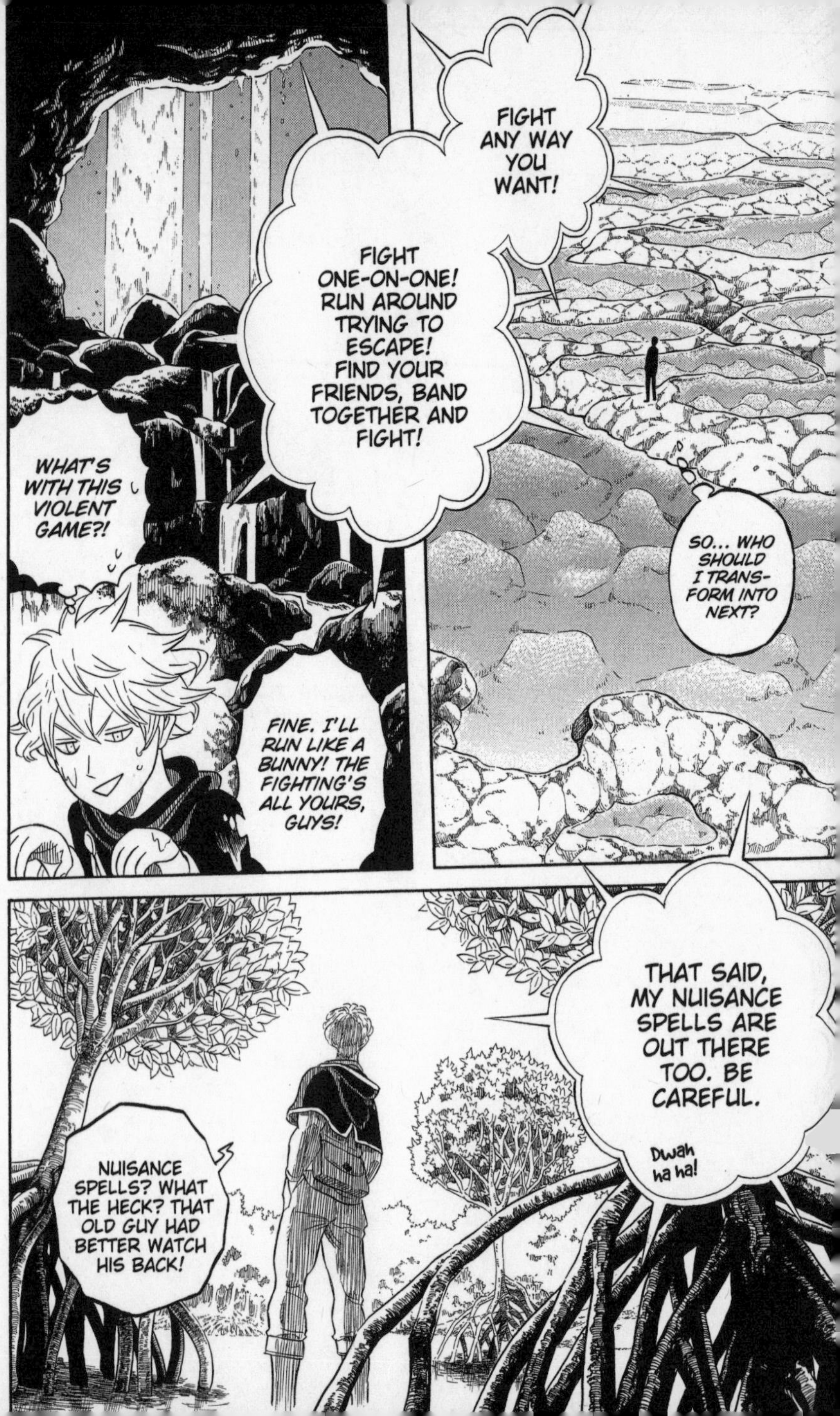
FIGHT ANY WAY YOU WANT!
FIGHT ONE-ON-ONE! RUN AROUND TRYING TO ESCAPE! FIND YOUR FRIENDS, BAND TOGETHER AND FIGHT!
SO... WHO SHOULD I TRANSFORM INTO NEXT?
WHAT'S WITH THIS VIOLENT GAME?!
FINE. I'LL RUN LIKE A BUNNY! THE FIGHTING'S ALL YOURS, GUYS!
THAT SAID, MY NUISANCE SPELLS ARE OUT THERE TOO. BE CAREFUL.
Dwah ha ha!
NUISANCE SPELLS? WHAT THE HECK? THAT OLD GUY HAD BETTER WATCH HIS BACK!

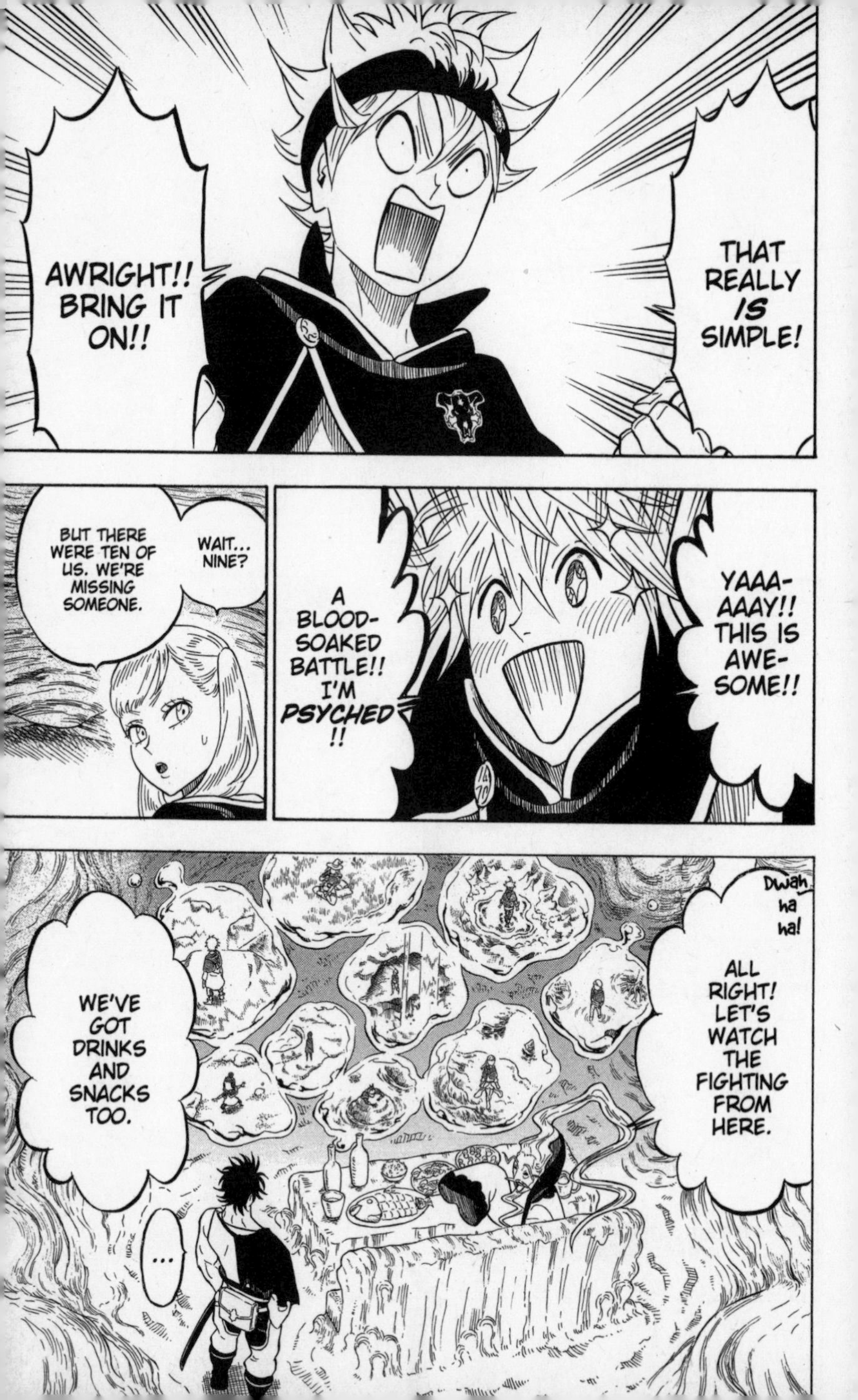
THAT REALLY *IS* SIMPLE!
AWRIGHT!! BRING IT ON!!
YAAA-AAAY!! THIS IS AWE-SOME!!
A BLOOD-SOAKED BATTLE!! I'M *PSYCHED*!!
BUT THERE WERE TEN OF US. WE'RE MISSING SOMEONE.
WAIT... NINE?
Dwah ha ha!
ALL RIGHT! LET'S WATCH THE FIGHTING FROM HERE.
WE'VE GOT DRINKS AND SNACKS TOO.
...

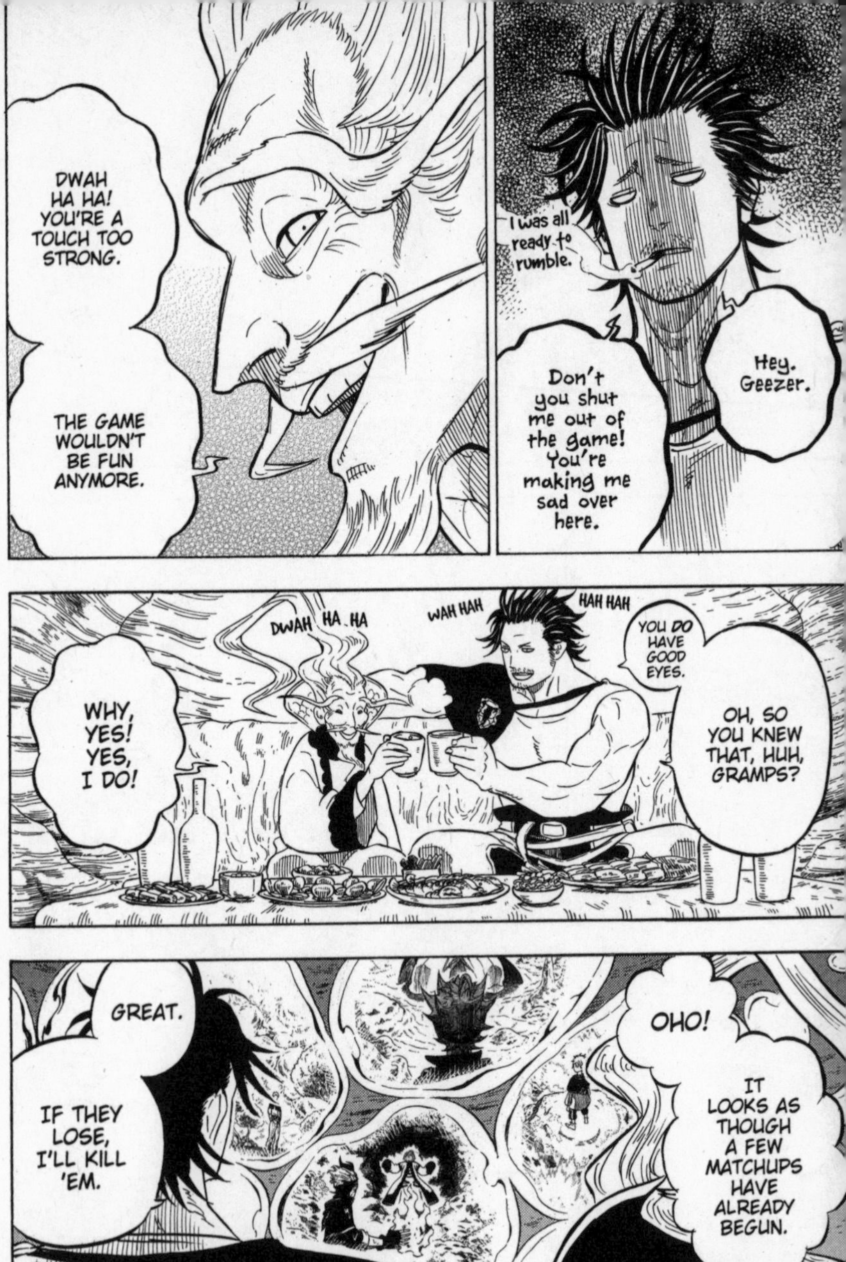
I was all ready to rumble.
Hey. Geezer.
Don't you shut me out of the game! You're making me sad over here.
DWAH HA HA! YOU'RE A TOUCH TOO STRONG.
THE GAME WOULDN'T BE FUN ANYMORE.
HAH HAH
WAH HAH
OH, SO YOU KNEW THAT, HUH, GRAMPS?
YOU DO HAVE GOOD EYES.
DWAH HA HA
WHY, YES! YES, I DO!
OHO!
IT LOOKS AS THOUGH A FEW MATCHUPS HAVE ALREADY BEGUN.
GREAT.
IF THEY LOSE, I'LL KILL 'EM.

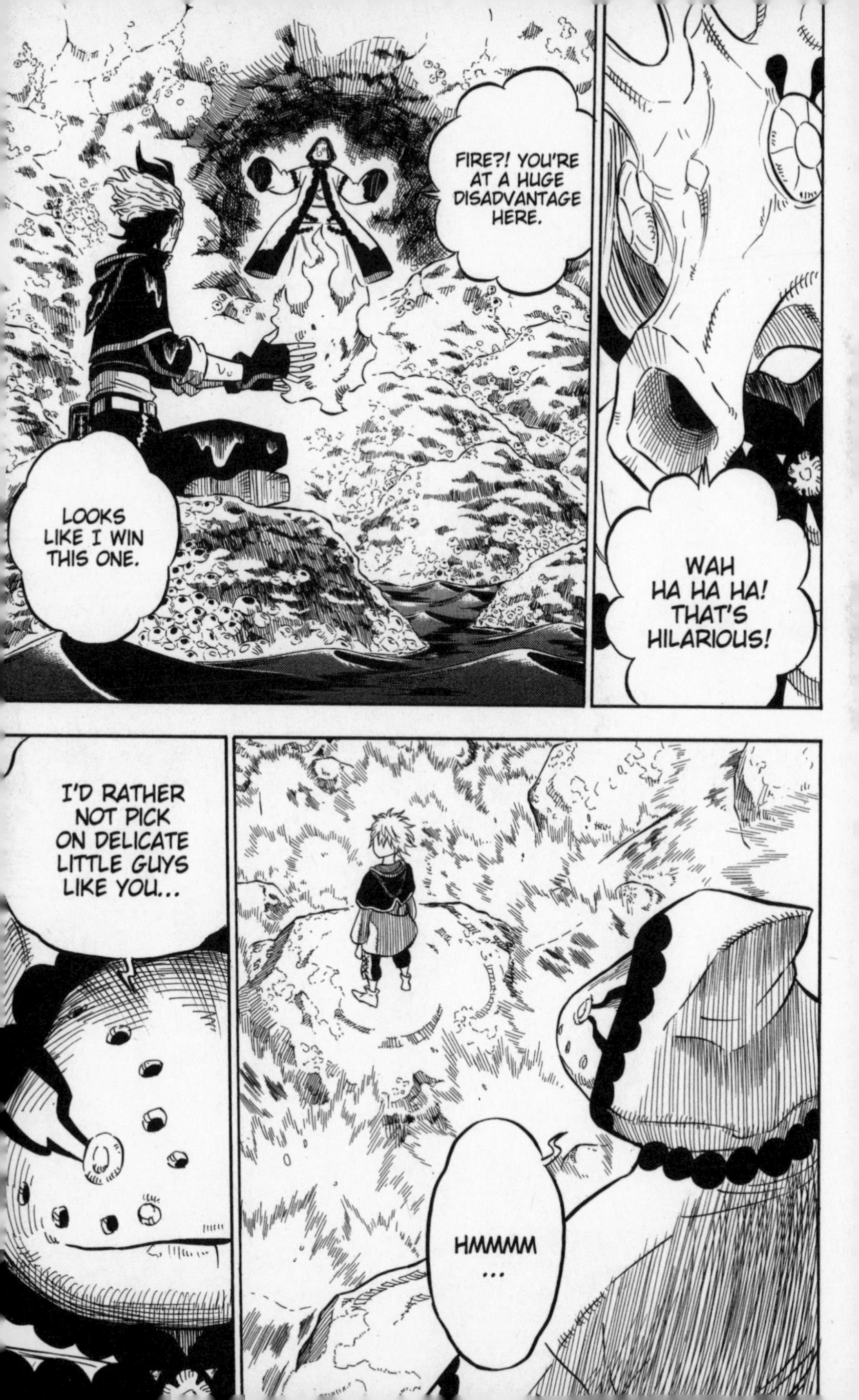
WAH HA HA HA! THAT'S HILARIOUS!
FIRE?! YOU'RE AT A HUGE DISADVANTAGE HERE.
LOOKS LIKE I WIN THIS ONE.
HMMMM...
I'D RATHER NOT PICK ON DELICATE LITTLE GUYS LIKE YOU...

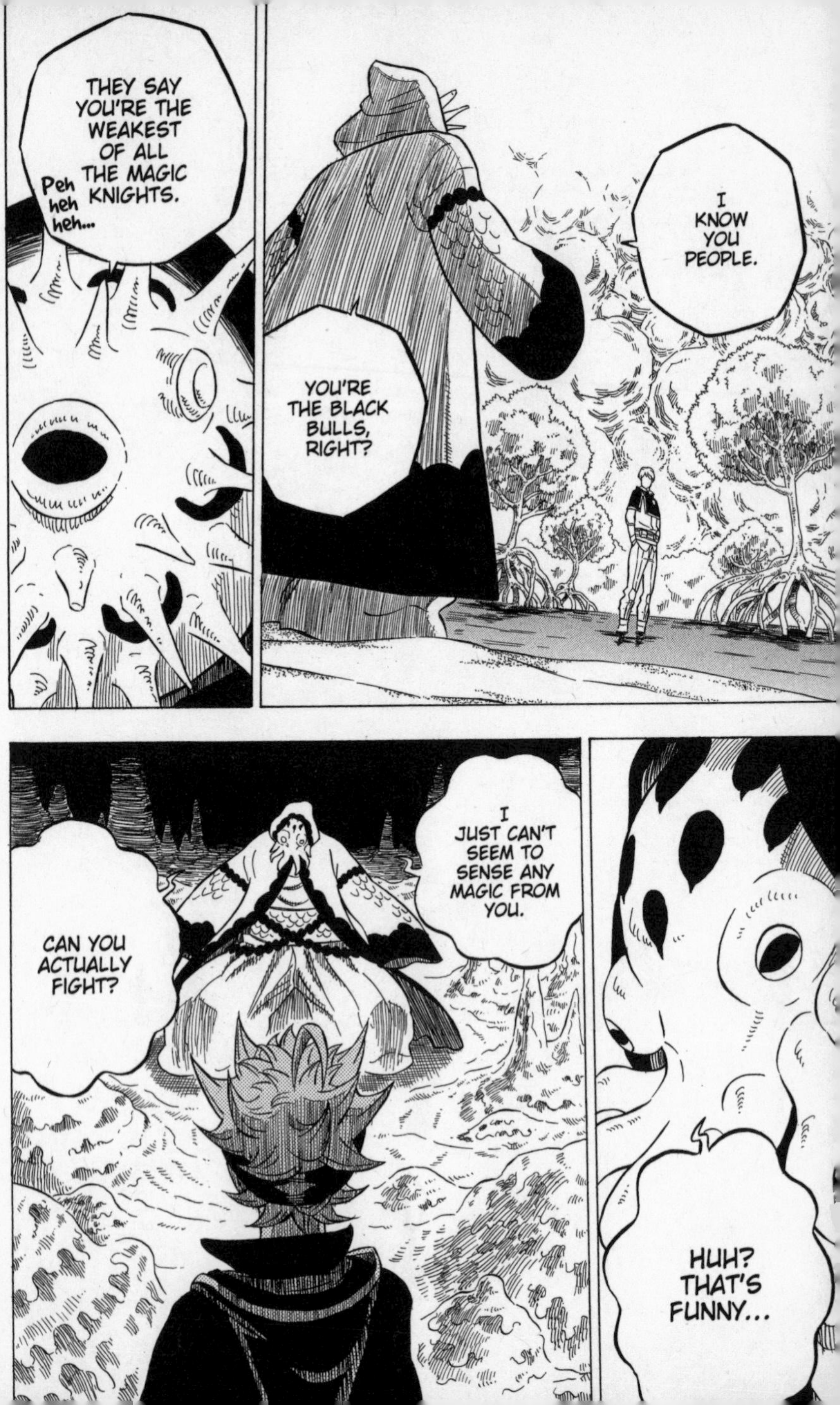
I KNOW YOU PEOPLE.
YOU'RE THE BLACK BULLS, RIGHT?
THEY SAY YOU'RE THE WEAKEST OF ALL THE MAGIC KNIGHTS.
Peh heh heh...
HUH? THAT'S FUNNY...
I JUST CAN'T SEEM TO SENSE ANY MAGIC FROM YOU.
CAN YOU ACTUALLY FIGHT?

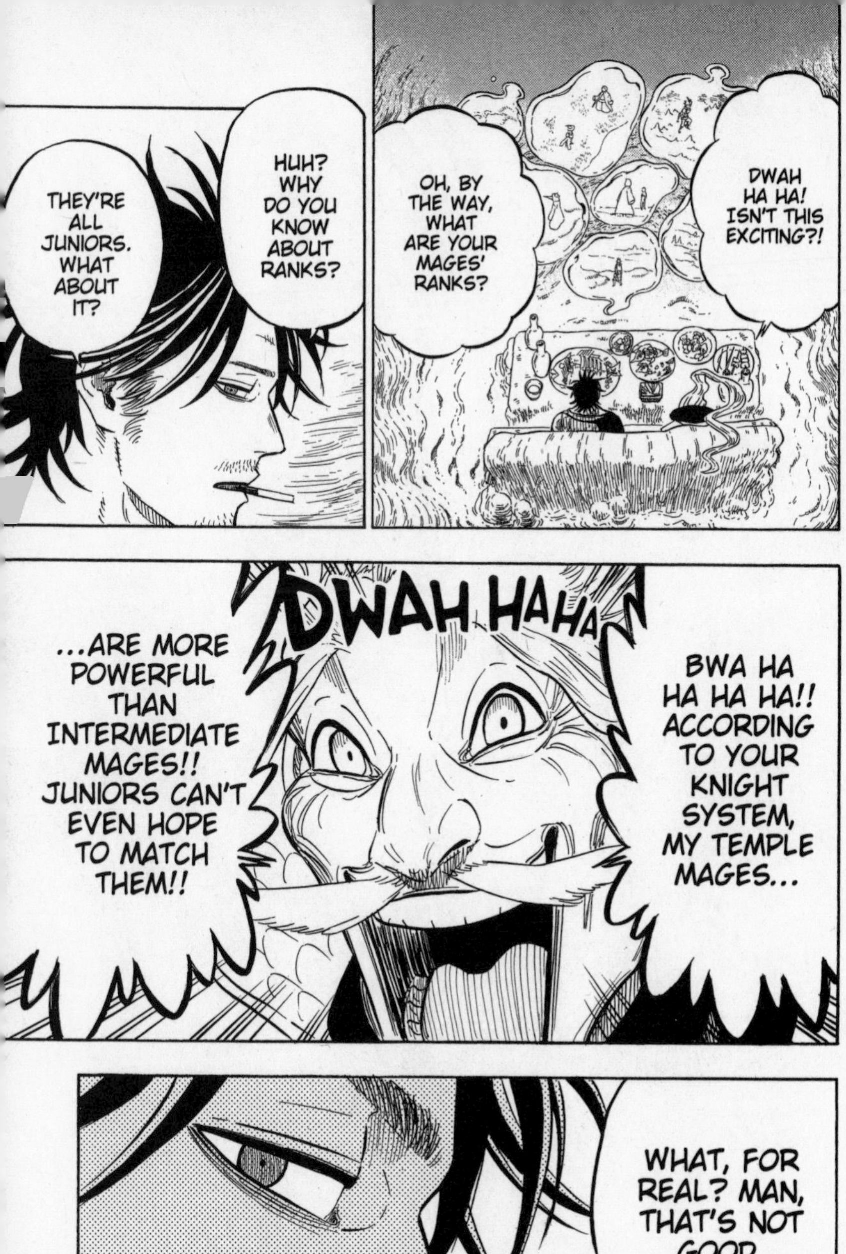
DWAH HA HA! ISN'T THIS EXCITING?!
OH, BY THE WAY, WHAT ARE YOUR MAGES' RANKS?
HUH? WHY DO YOU KNOW ABOUT RANKS?
THEY'RE ALL JUNIORS. WHAT ABOUT IT?
DWAH HAHA
BWA HA HA HA HA!! ACCORDING TO YOUR KNIGHT SYSTEM, MY TEMPLE MAGES...
...ARE MORE POWERFUL THAN INTERMEDIATE MAGES!! JUNIORS CAN'T EVEN HOPE TO MATCH THEM!!
WHAT, FOR REAL? MAN, THAT'S NOT GOOD.

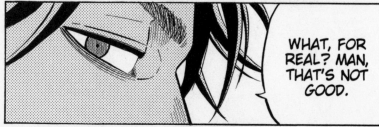

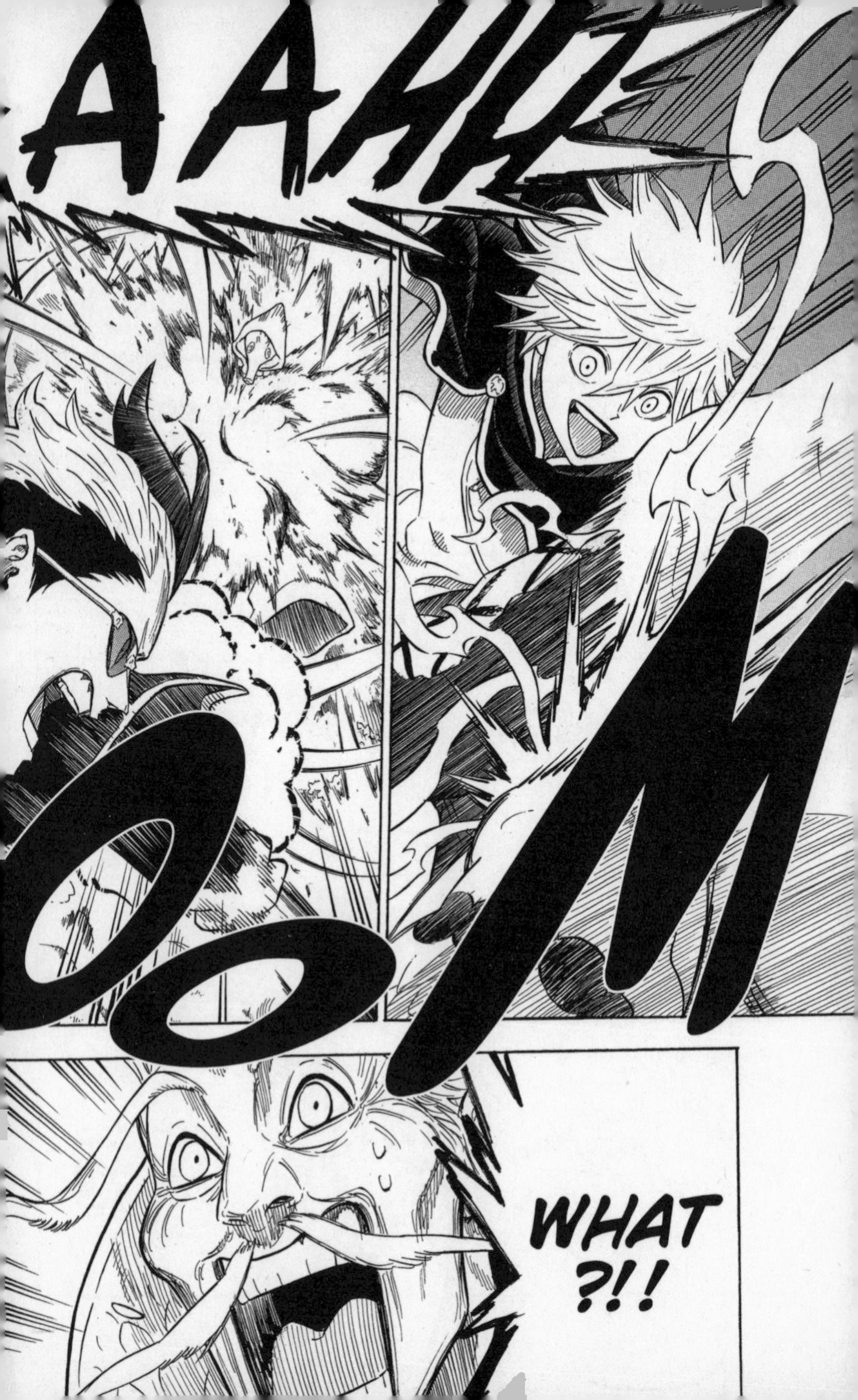

AAHH
BOOM
WHAT ?!!

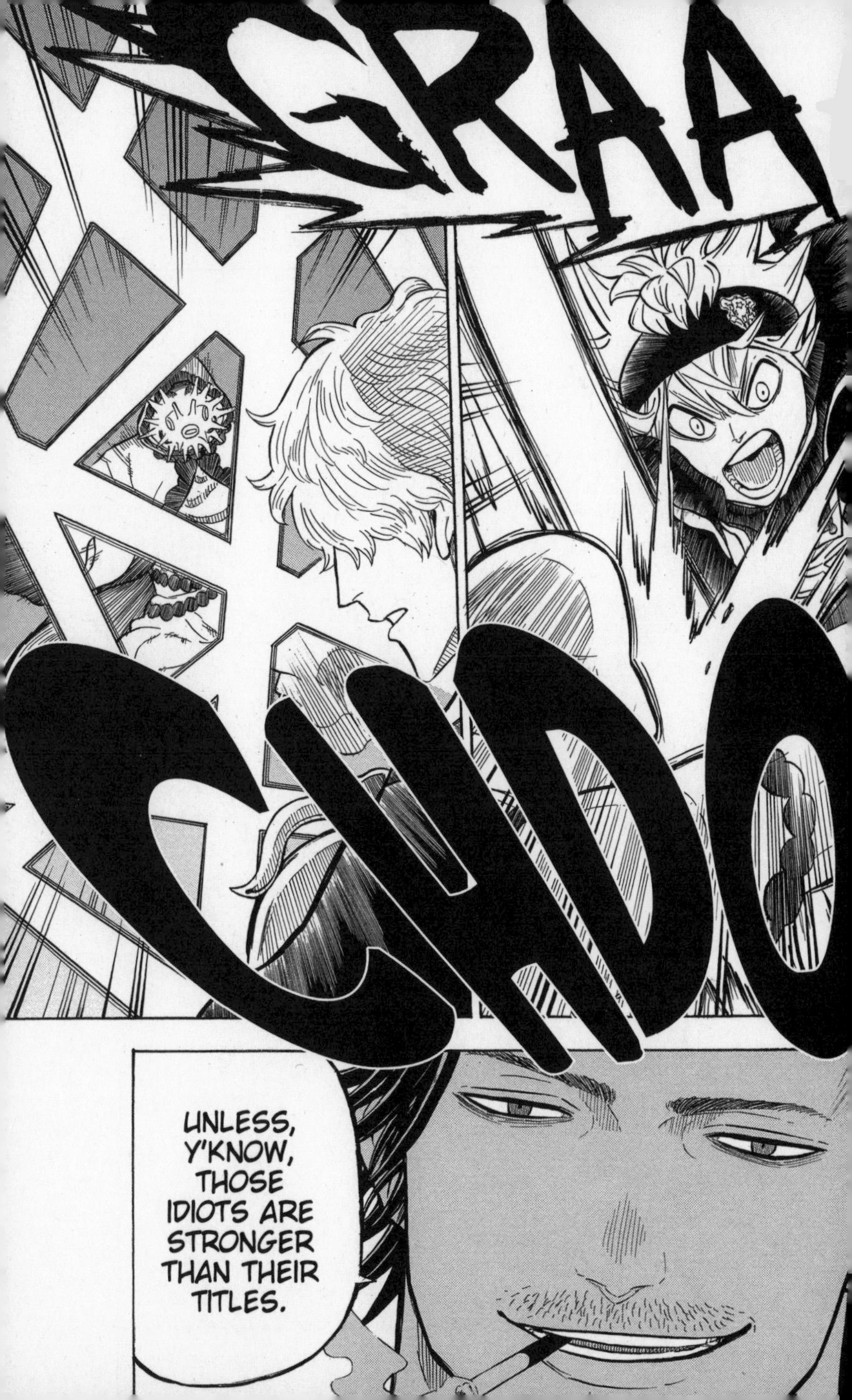
GRAA
CHDO
UNLESS, Y'KNOW, THOSE IDIOTS ARE STRONGER THAN THEIR TITLES.

# Theresa Rapual

Age: 65
Height: 162 cm
Birthday: March 28
Sign: Aries
Blood Type: O
Likes: Pumpkin soup, the children at the church

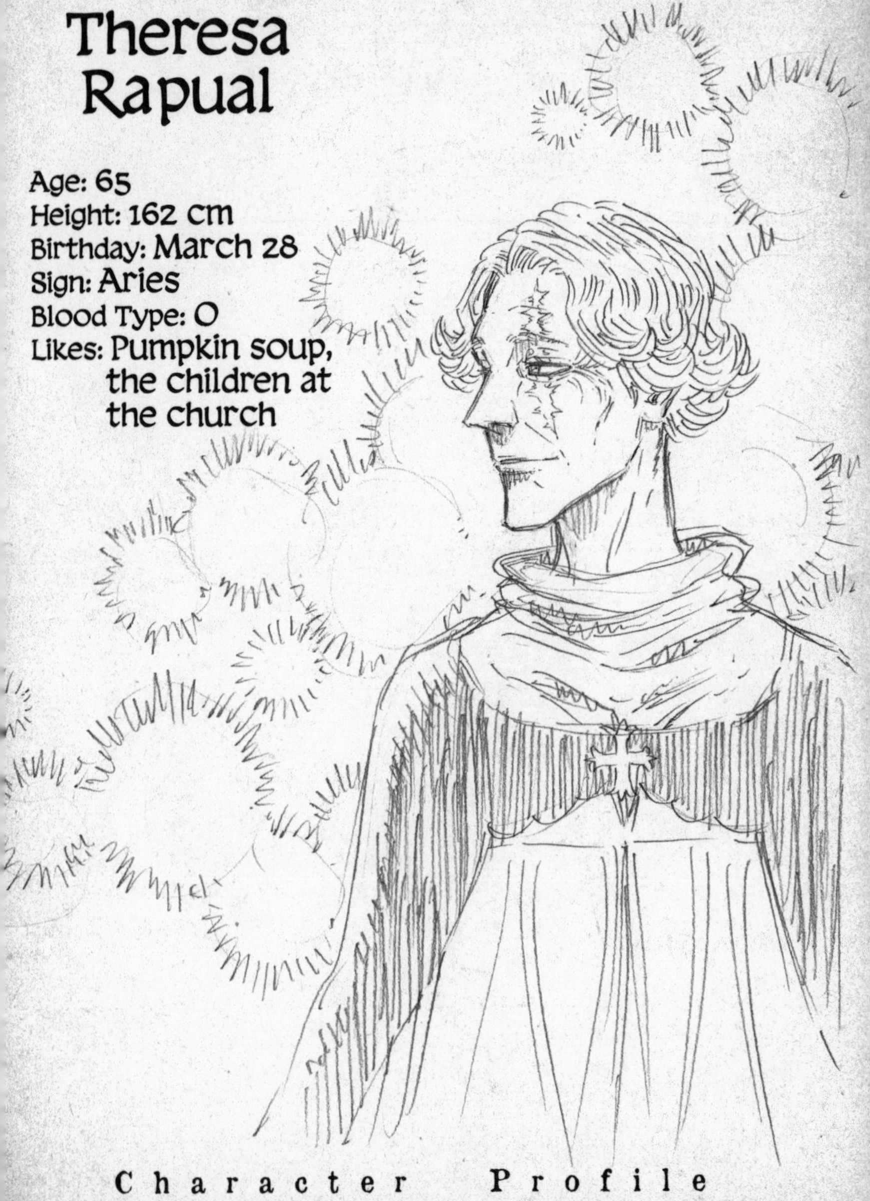

Character Profile

# ✤ Page 61: Temple Battle Royale

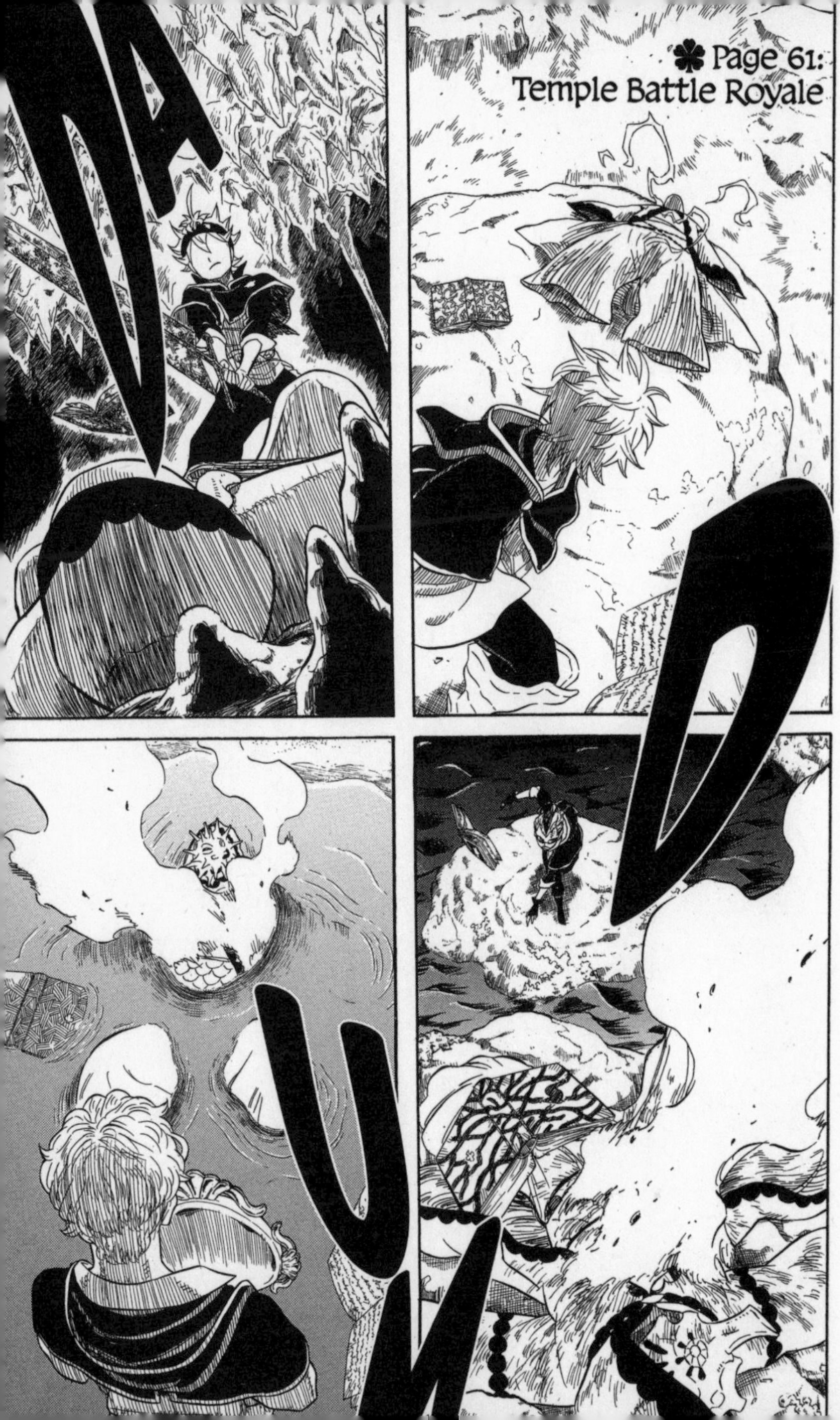

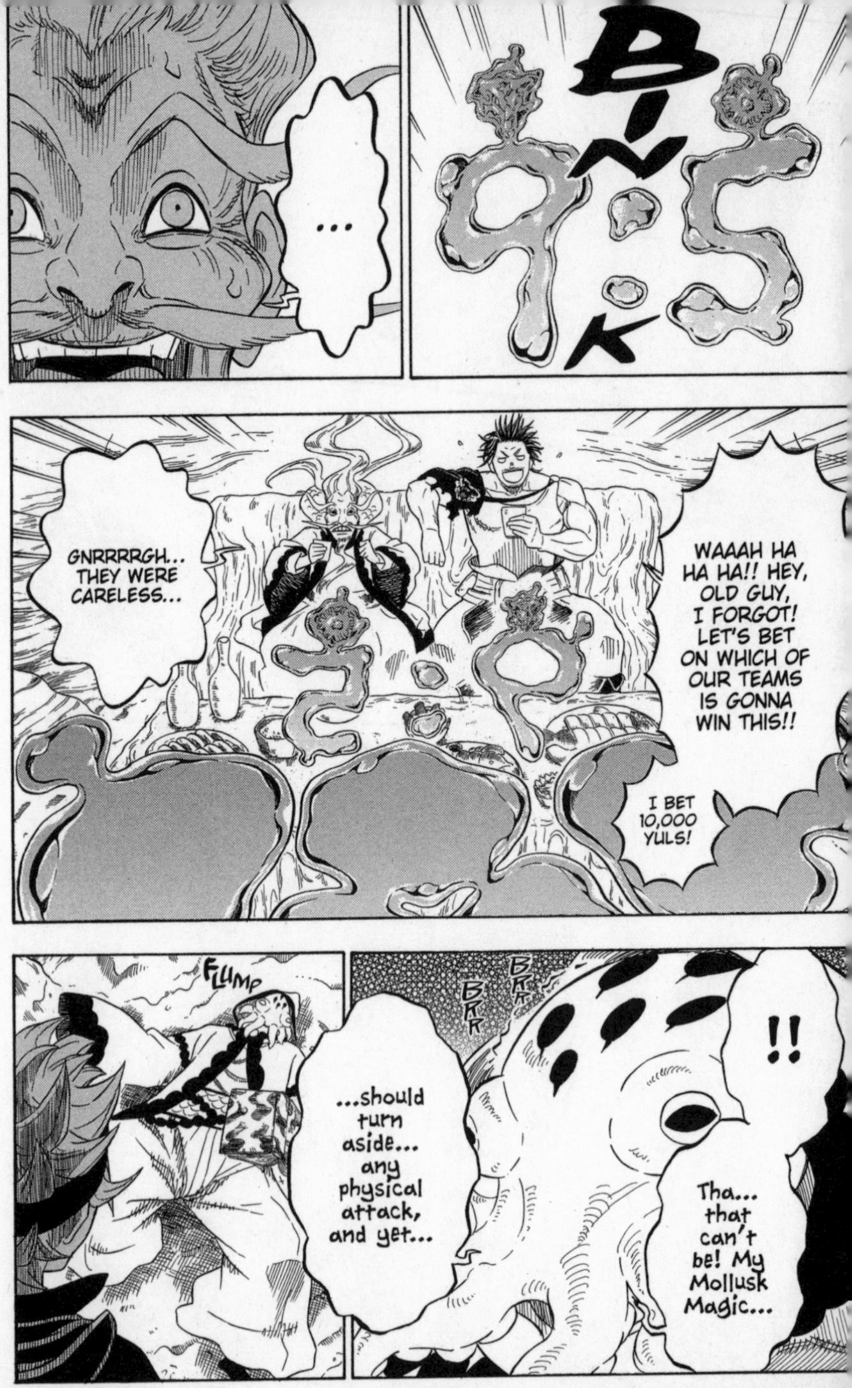
BINK
...
WAAAH HA HA!! HEY, OLD GUY, I FORGOT! LET'S BET ON WHICH OF OUR TEAMS IS GONNA WIN THIS!!
I BET 10,000 YULS!
GNRRRRGH... THEY WERE CARELESS...
BRR BRR
!!
Tha... that can't be! My Mollusk Magic...
FLUMP
...should turn aside... any physical attack, and yet...

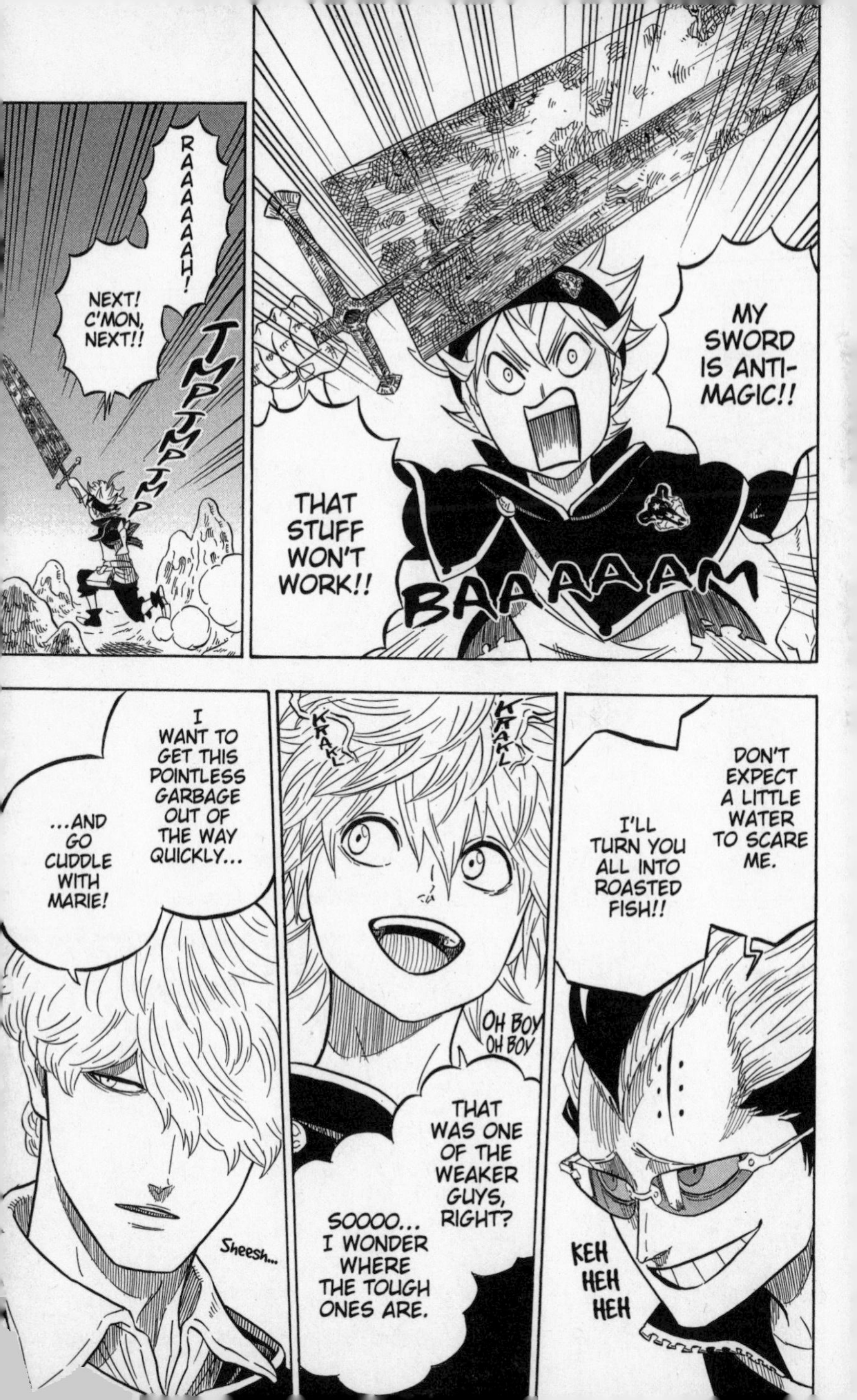
MY SWORD IS ANTI-MAGIC!!
THAT STUFF WON'T WORK!!
BAAAAAM
RAAAAAAAH!
NEXT! C'MON, NEXT!!
TMPTMPTMP
DON'T EXPECT A LITTLE WATER TO SCARE ME.
I'LL TURN YOU ALL INTO ROASTED FISH!!
KEH HEH HEH
KRAKL
KRAKL
OH BOY OH BOY
THAT WAS ONE OF THE WEAKER GUYS, RIGHT?
SOOOO... I WONDER WHERE THE TOUGH ONES ARE.
I WANT TO GET THIS POINTLESS GARBAGE OUT OF THE WAY QUICKLY...
...AND GO CUDDLE WITH MARIE!
Sheesh...

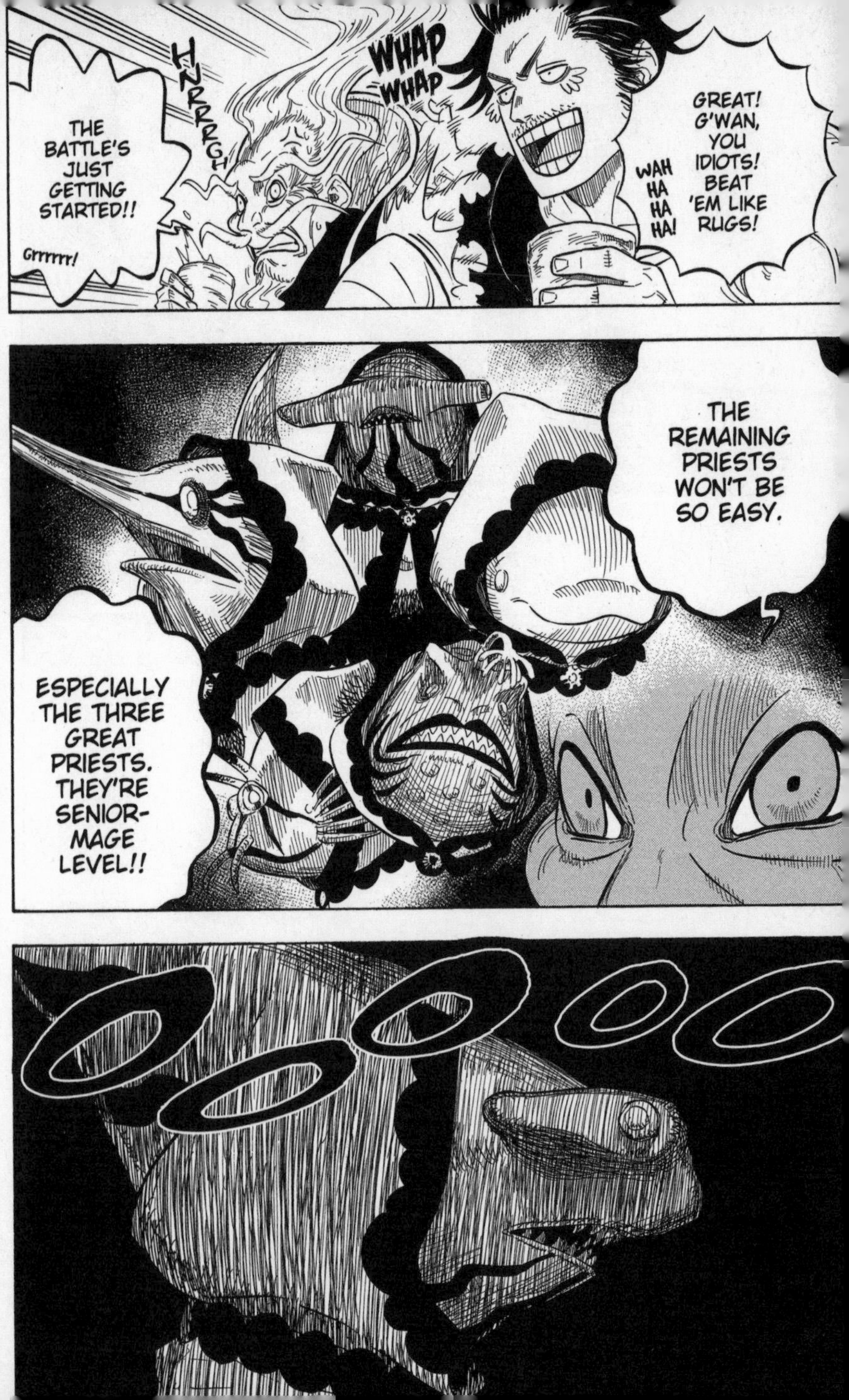
GREAT! G'WAN, YOU IDIOTS! BEAT 'EM LIKE RUGS!
WAH HA HA HA!
WHAP WHAP
HNRRRGH
THE BATTLE'S JUST GETTING STARTED!!
Grrrrrr!
THE REMAINING PRIESTS WON'T BE SO EASY.
ESPECIALLY THE THREE GREAT PRIESTS. THEY'RE SENIOR-MAGE LEVEL!!

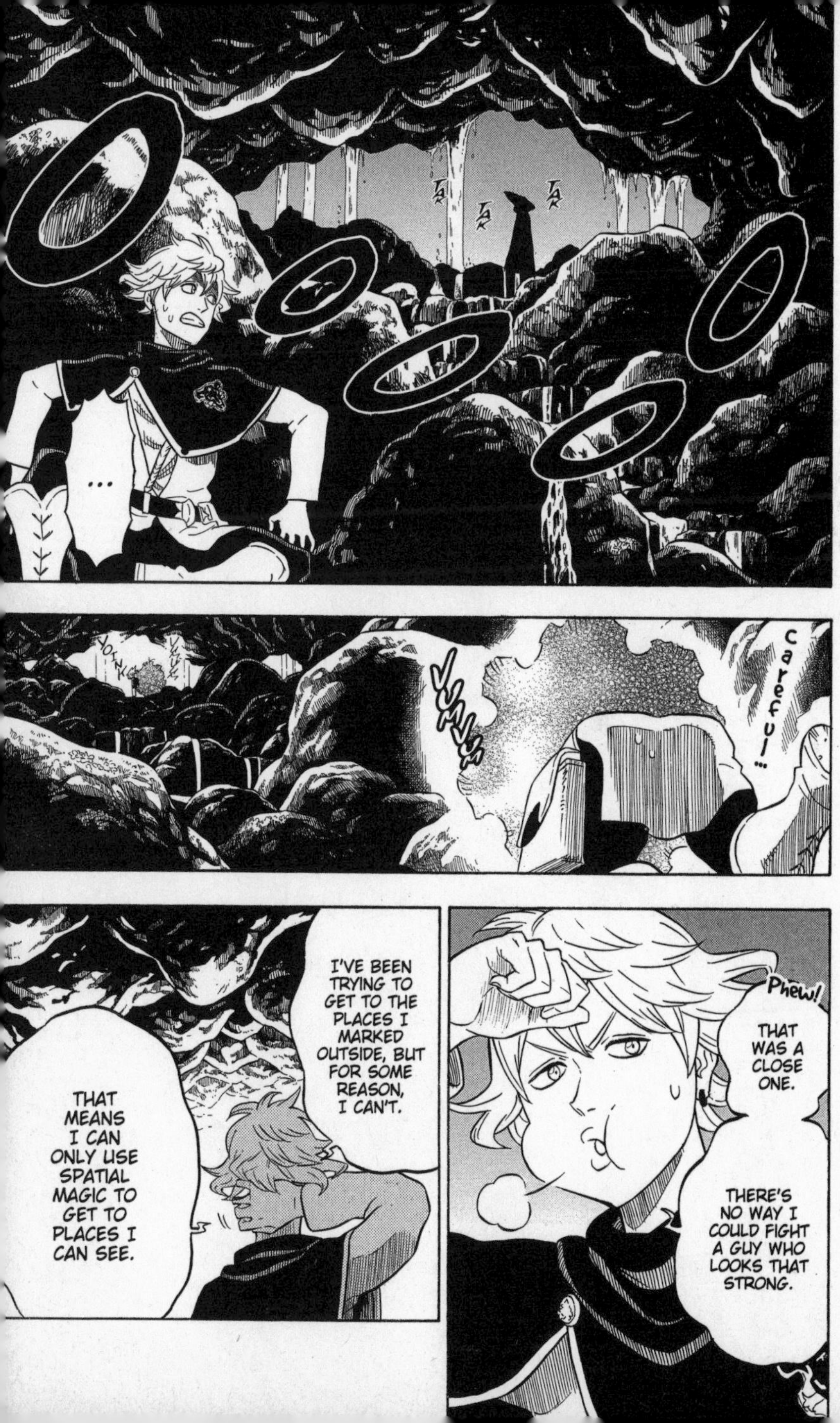
...
Careful!...
Phew!
THAT WAS A CLOSE ONE.
THERE'S NO WAY I COULD FIGHT A GUY WHO LOOKS THAT STRONG.
I'VE BEEN TRYING TO GET TO THE PLACES I MARKED OUTSIDE, BUT FOR SOME REASON, I CAN'T.
THAT MEANS I CAN ONLY USE SPATIAL MAGIC TO GET TO PLACES I CAN SEE.

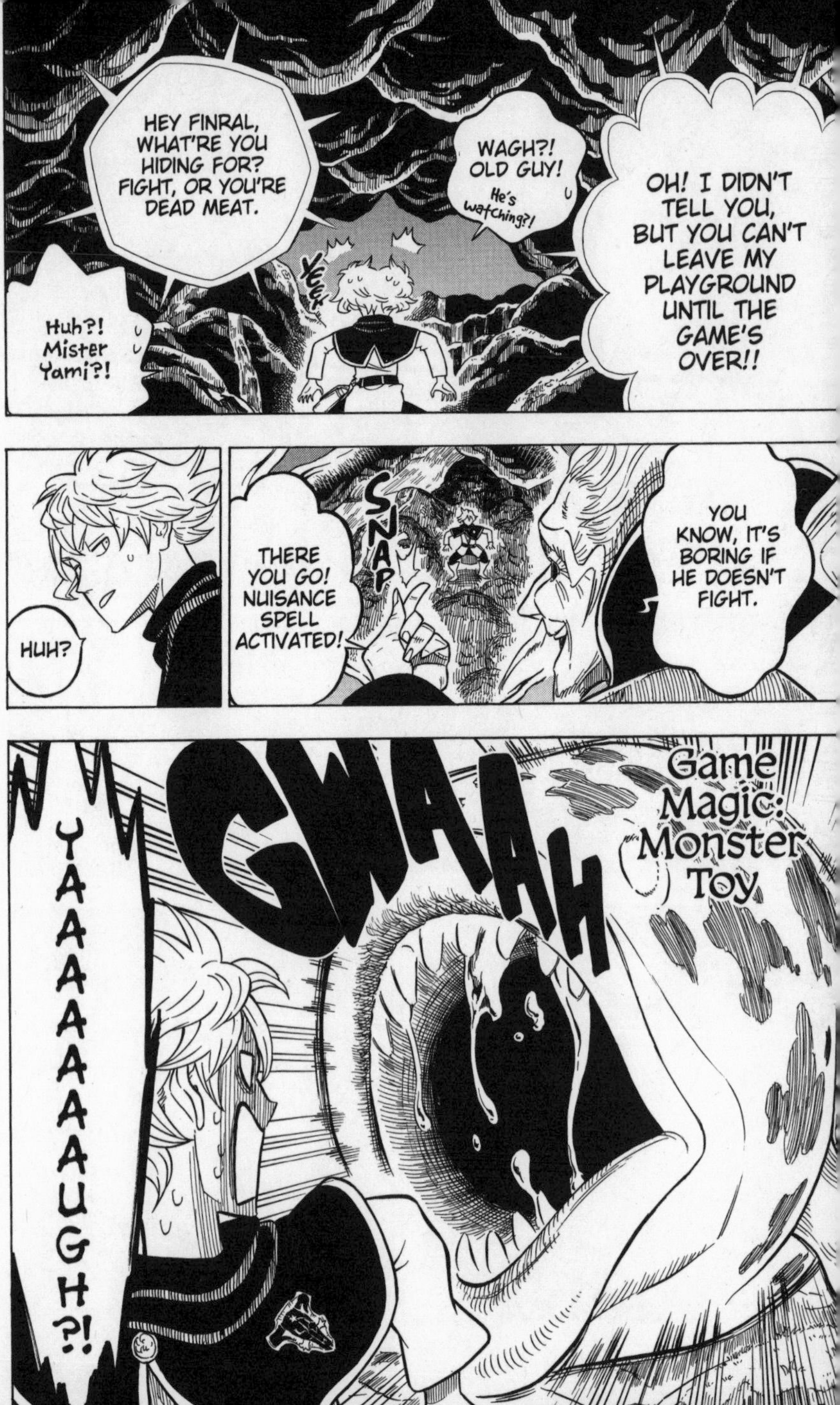
OH! I DIDN'T TELL YOU, BUT YOU CAN'T LEAVE MY PLAYGROUND UNTIL THE GAME'S OVER!!
WAGH?! OLD GUY!
He's watching?!
HEY FINRAL, WHAT'RE YOU HIDING FOR? FIGHT, OR YOU'RE DEAD MEAT.
Huh?! Mister Yami?!
YOU KNOW, IT'S BORING IF HE DOESN'T FIGHT.
SNAP
THERE YOU GO! NUISANCE SPELL ACTIVATED!
HUH?
Game Magic: Monster Toy
GWAAAH
YAAAAAAAAAAUGH?!

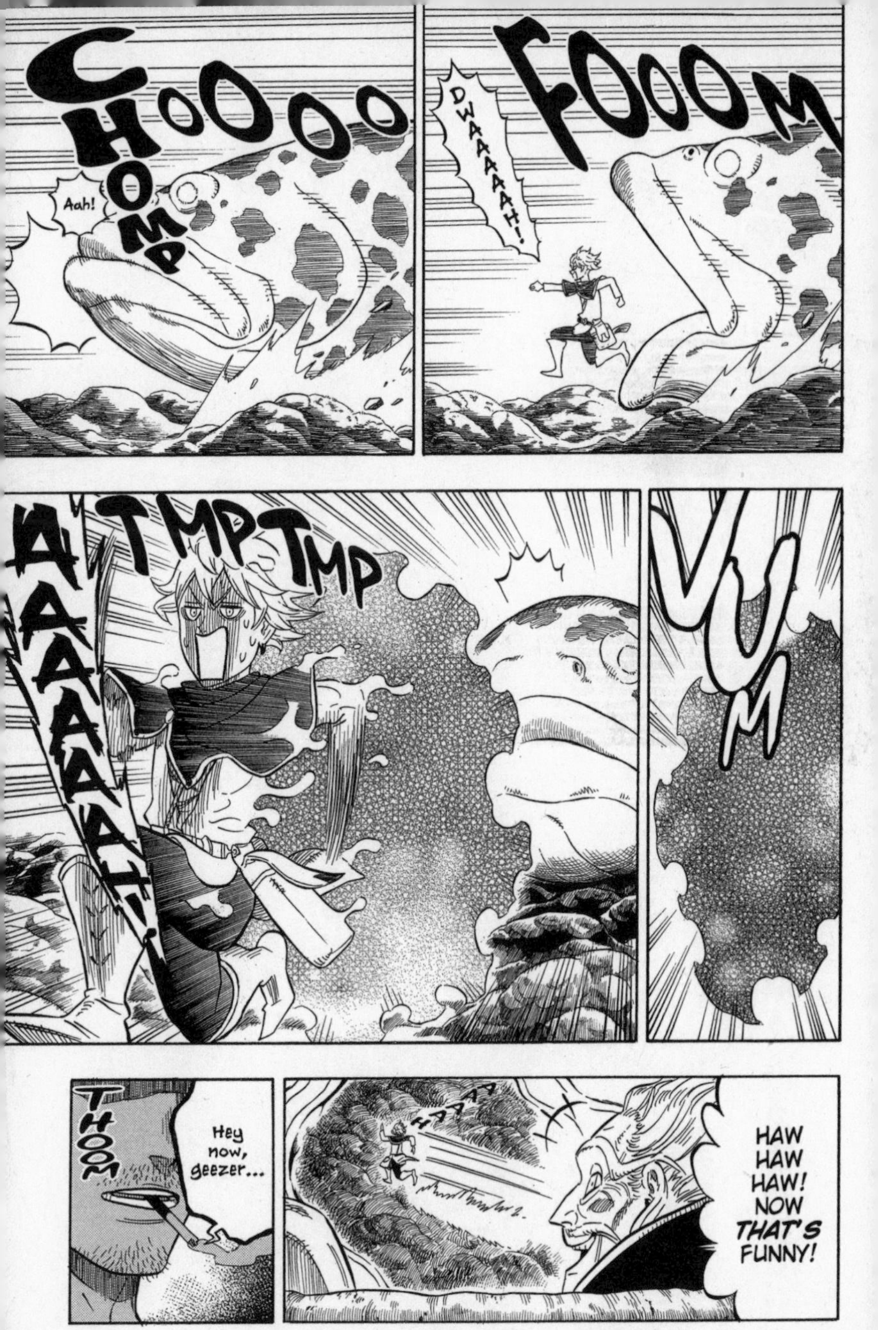
FOOOM
DWAAAAAAH!
CHOOOOOMP
Aah!
VUUM
TMP TMP
AAAAAAAH!
HAW HAW HAW! NOW *THAT'S* FUNNY!
HAAAA
THOOM
Hey now, geezer...

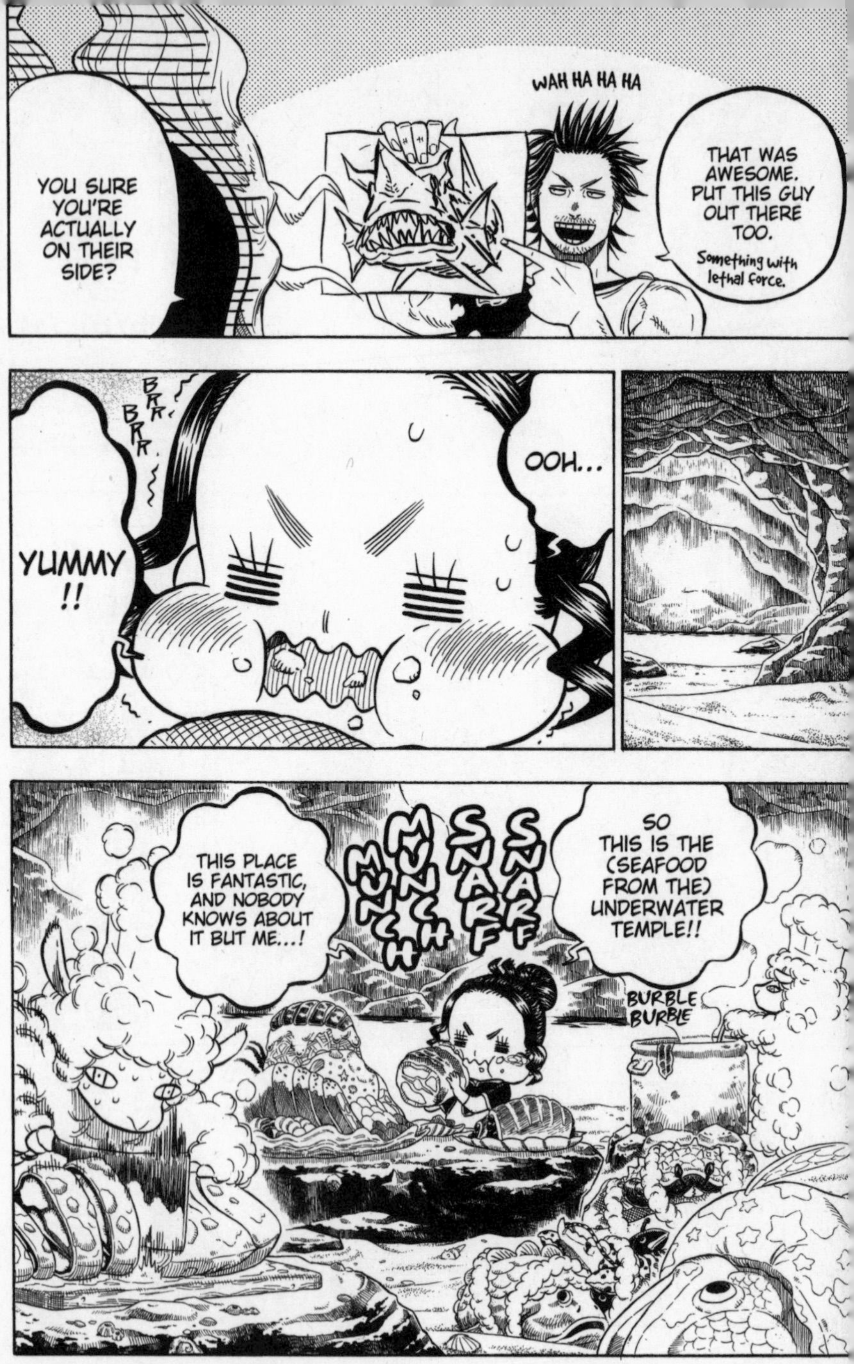
WAH HA HA HA
THAT WAS AWESOME. PUT THIS GUY OUT THERE TOO.
Something with lethal force.
YOU SURE YOU'RE ACTUALLY ON THEIR SIDE?
OOH...
BRR BRR
YUMMY!!
SO THIS IS THE (SEAFOOD FROM THE) UNDERWATER TEMPLE!!
SNARF SNARF
MUNCH MUNCH
BURBLE BURBLE
THIS PLACE IS FANTASTIC, AND NOBODY KNOWS ABOUT IT BUT ME...!

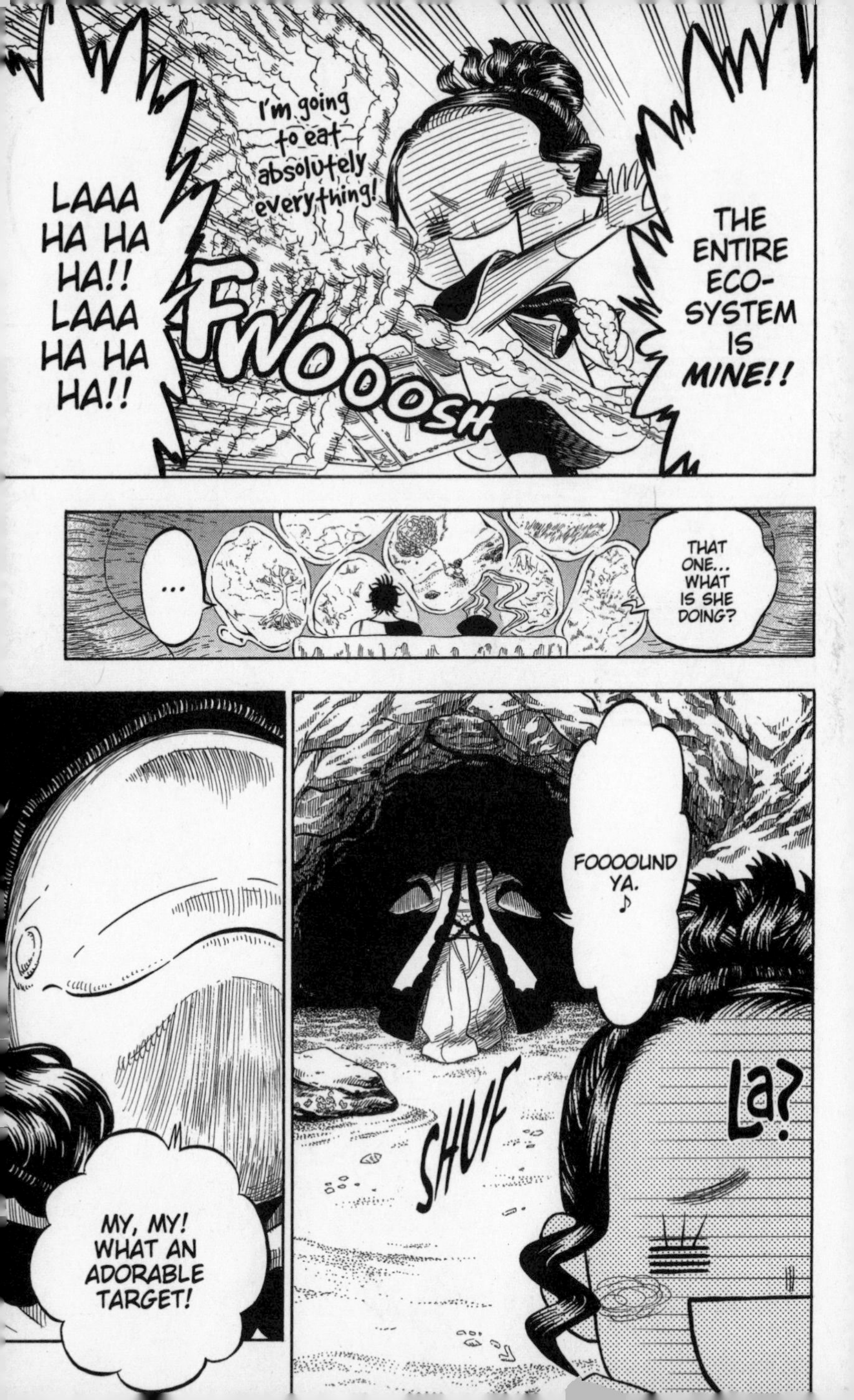
THE ENTIRE ECO-SYSTEM IS MINE!!
I'm going to eat absolutely everything!
LAAA HA HA HA!! LAAA HA HA HA!!
FWOOOOSH
THAT ONE... WHAT IS SHE DOING?
...
FOOOOUND YA. ♪
La?
SHUF
MY, MY! WHAT AN ADORABLE TARGET!

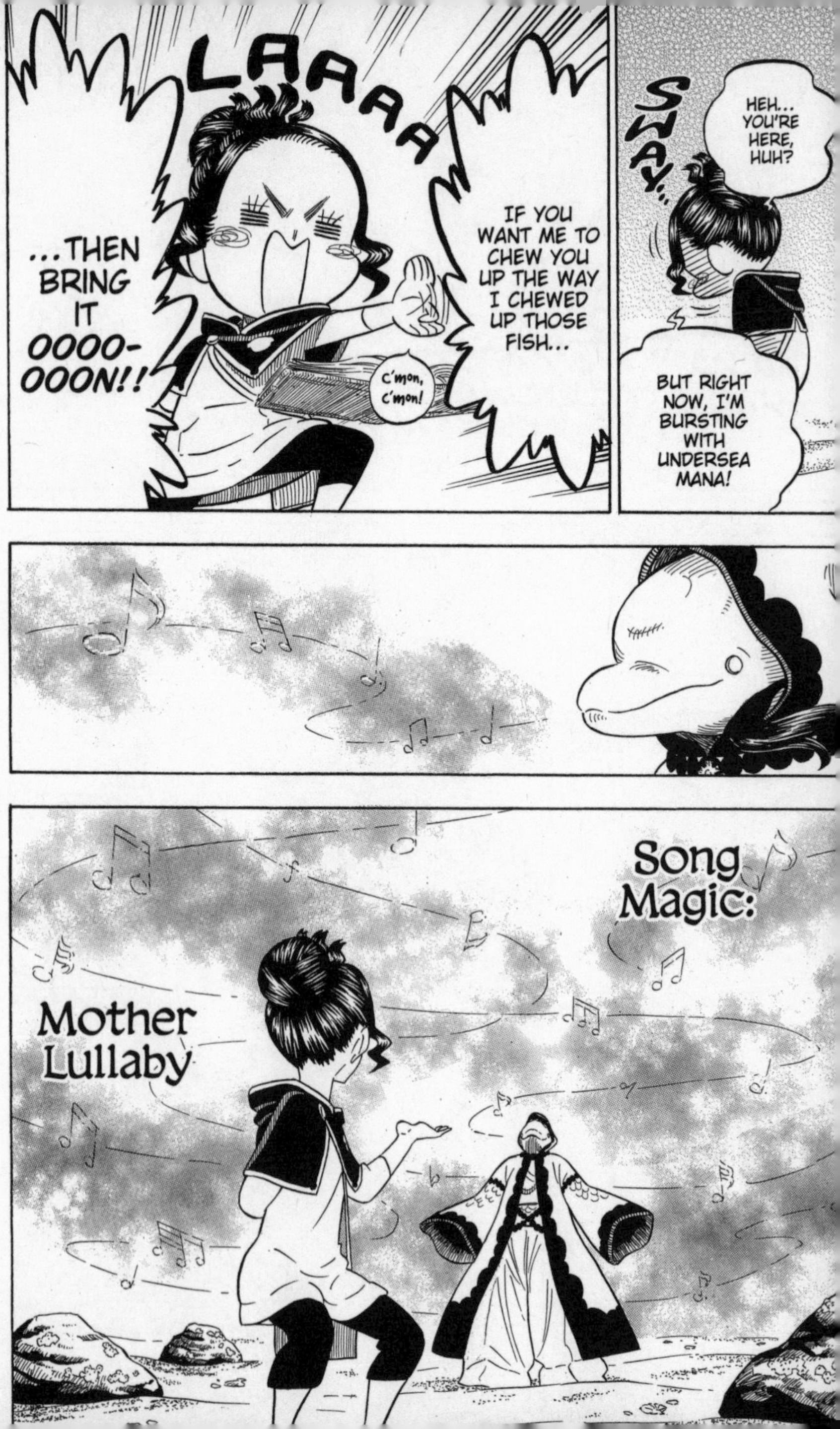
SWAY...
HEH... YOU'RE HERE, HUH?
BUT RIGHT NOW, I'M BURSTING WITH UNDERSEA MANA!
LAAAAA
IF YOU WANT ME TO CHEW YOU UP THE WAY I CHEWED UP THOSE FISH...
C'mon, c'mon!
...THEN BRING IT OOOO-OOON!!
Song Magic:
Mother Lullaby

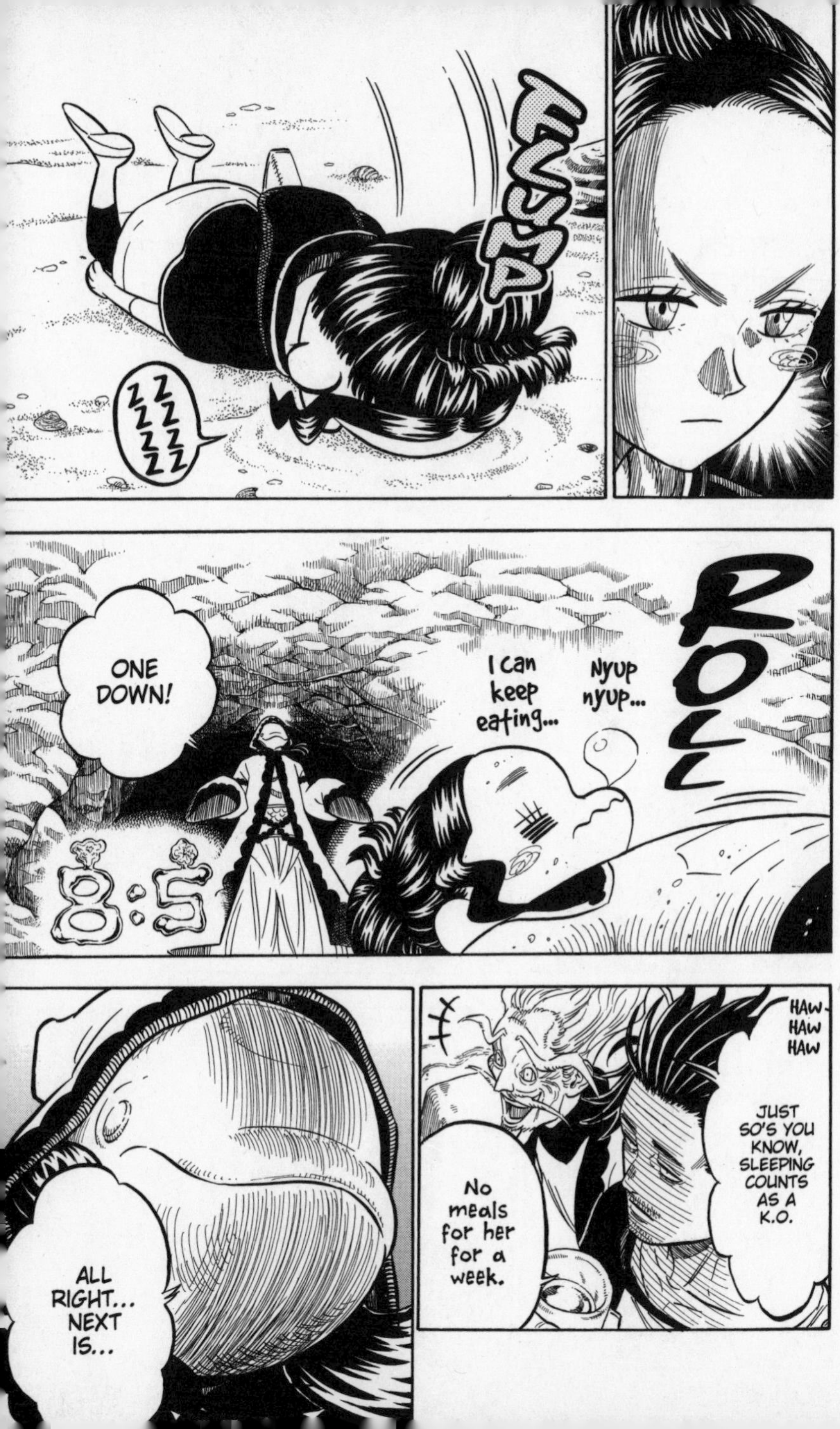
FLUMP
ZZZZZZZZ
ROLL
Nyup nyup...
I can keep eating...
ONE DOWN!
8:5
HAW HAW HAW
JUST SO'S YOU KNOW, SLEEPING COUNTS AS A K.O.
No meals for her for a week.
ALL RIGHT... NEXT IS...

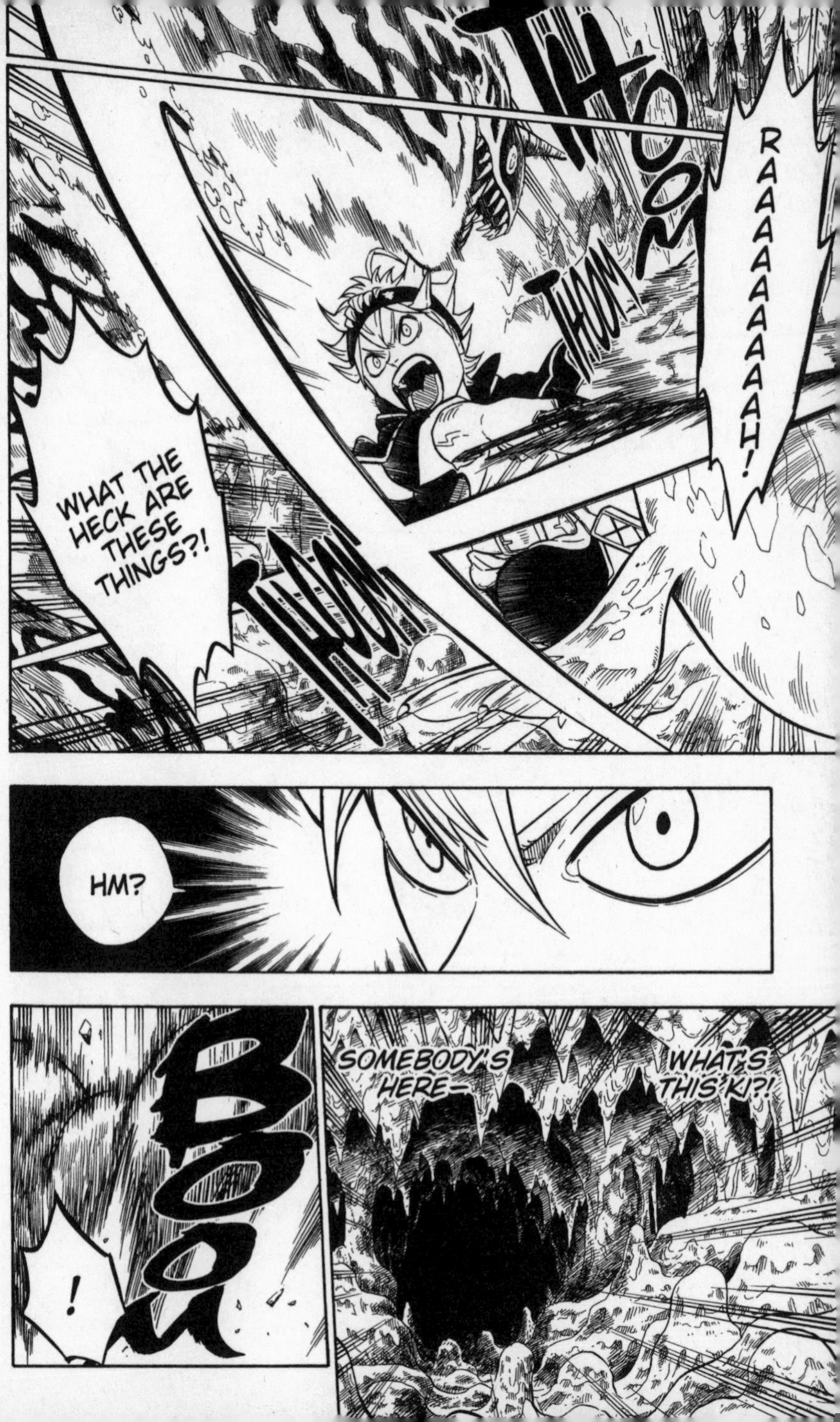
RAAAAAAAAAH!
THOOM
THOM
THOOM
WHAT THE HECK ARE THESE THINGS?!
HM?
WHAT'S THIS KI?!
SOMEBODY'S HERE—
!

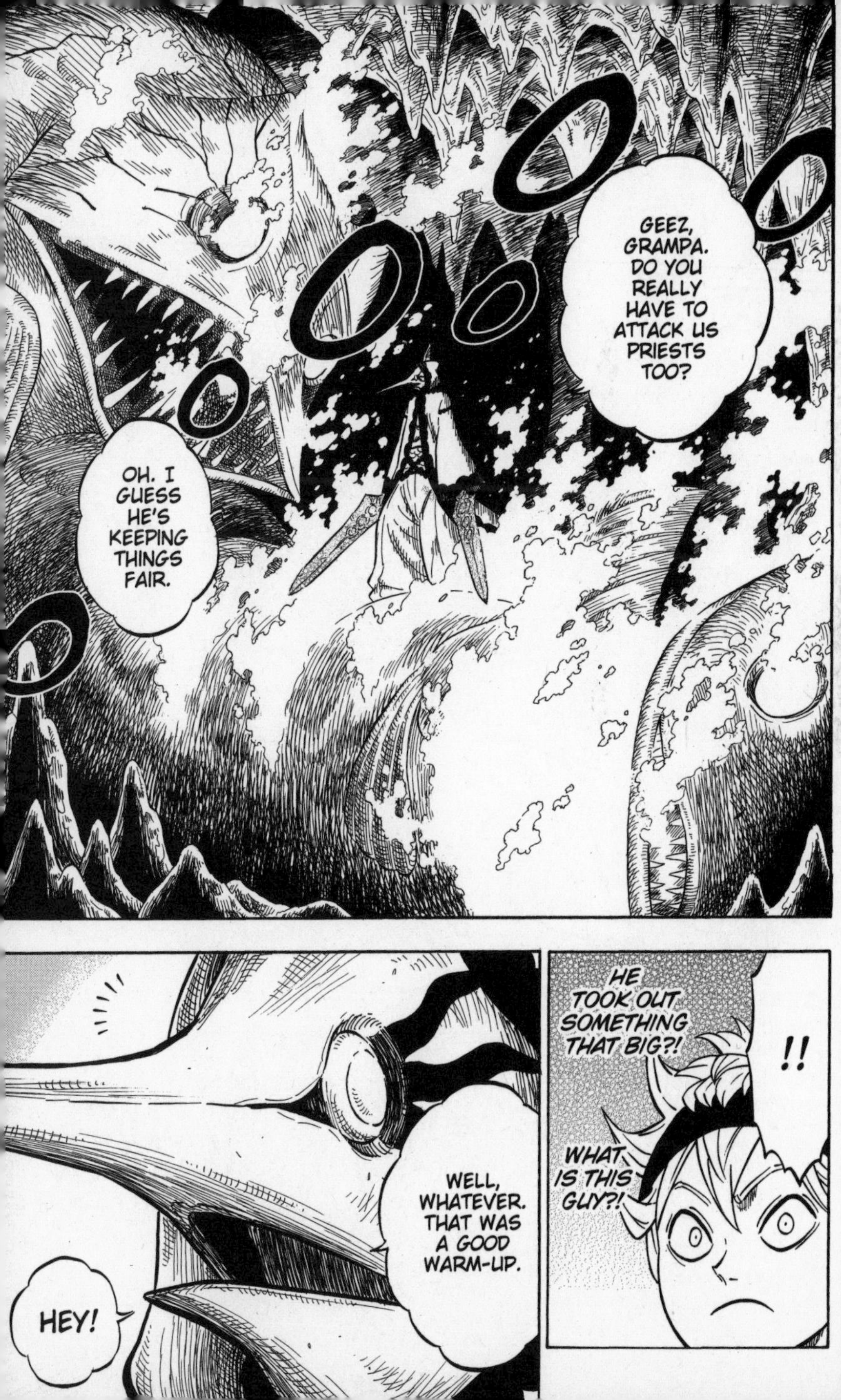
GEEZ, GRAMPA. DO YOU REALLY HAVE TO ATTACK US PRIESTS TOO?
OH. I GUESS HE'S KEEPING THINGS FAIR.
HE TOOK OUT SOMETHING THAT BIG?!
!!
WHAT IS THIS GUY?!
WELL, WHATEVER. THAT WAS A GOOD WARM-UP.
HEY!

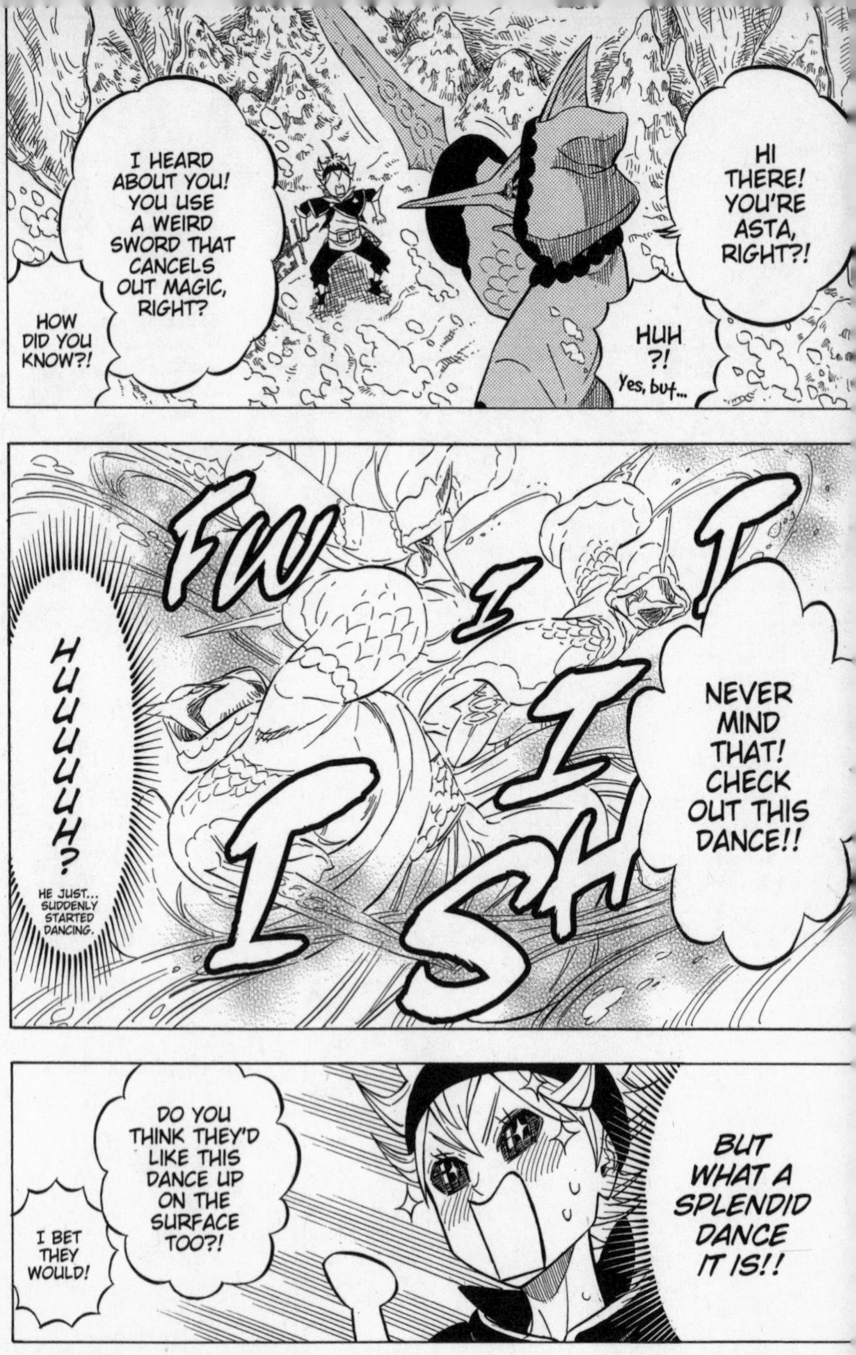
HI THERE! YOU'RE ASTA, RIGHT?!
HUH?! Yes, but...
I HEARD ABOUT YOU! YOU USE A WEIRD SWORD THAT CANCELS OUT MAGIC, RIGHT?
HOW DID YOU KNOW?!
NEVER MIND THAT! CHECK OUT THIS DANCE!!
FWIIIISH
HUUUUUUH?
HE JUST... SUDDENLY STARTED DANCING.
BUT WHAT A SPLENDID DANCE IT IS!!
DO YOU THINK THEY'D LIKE THIS DANCE UP ON THE SURFACE TOO?!
I BET THEY WOULD!

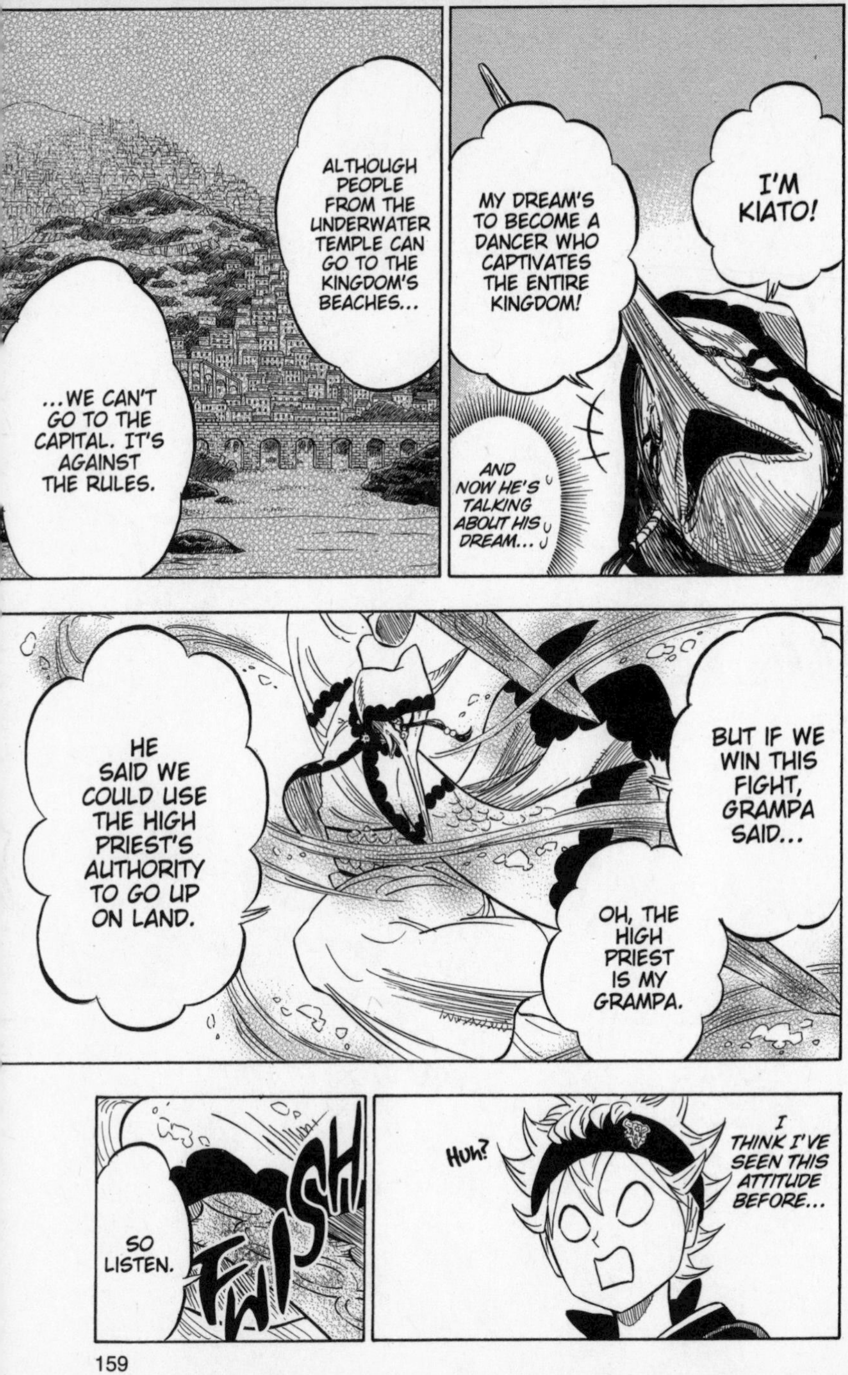
I'M KIATO!
MY DREAM'S TO BECOME A DANCER WHO CAPTIVATES THE ENTIRE KINGDOM!
AND NOW HE'S TALKING ABOUT HIS DREAM...
ALTHOUGH PEOPLE FROM THE UNDERWATER TEMPLE CAN GO TO THE KINGDOM'S BEACHES...
...WE CAN'T GO TO THE CAPITAL. IT'S AGAINST THE RULES.
BUT IF WE WIN THIS FIGHT, GRAMPA SAID...
OH, THE HIGH PRIEST IS MY GRAMPA.
HE SAID WE COULD USE THE HIGH PRIEST'S AUTHORITY TO GO UP ON LAND.
I THINK I'VE SEEN THIS ATTITUDE BEFORE...
HUH?
FWISH!
SO LISTEN.

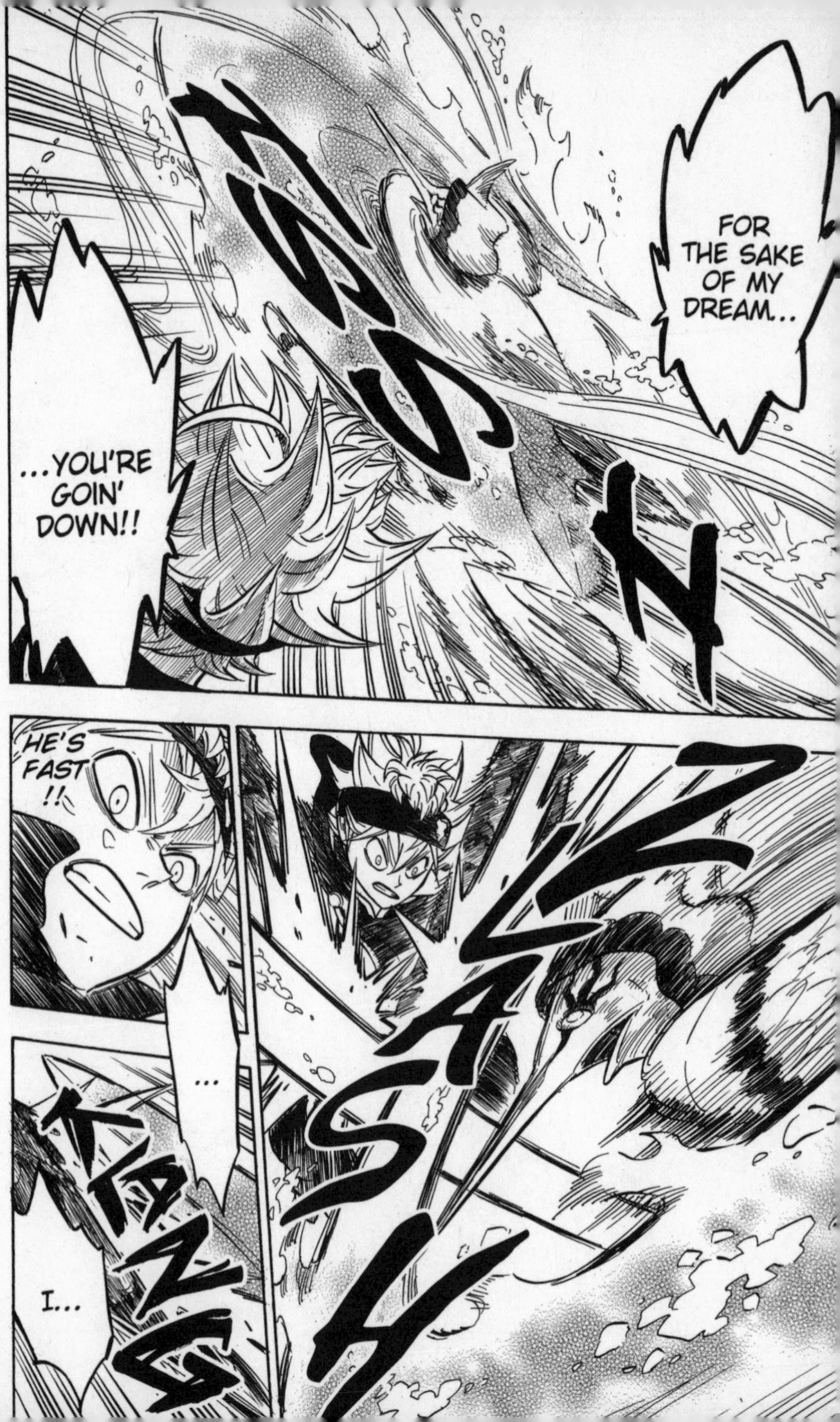
FOR THE SAKE OF MY DREAM...
...YOU'RE GOIN' DOWN!!
HE'S FAST!!
...
I...

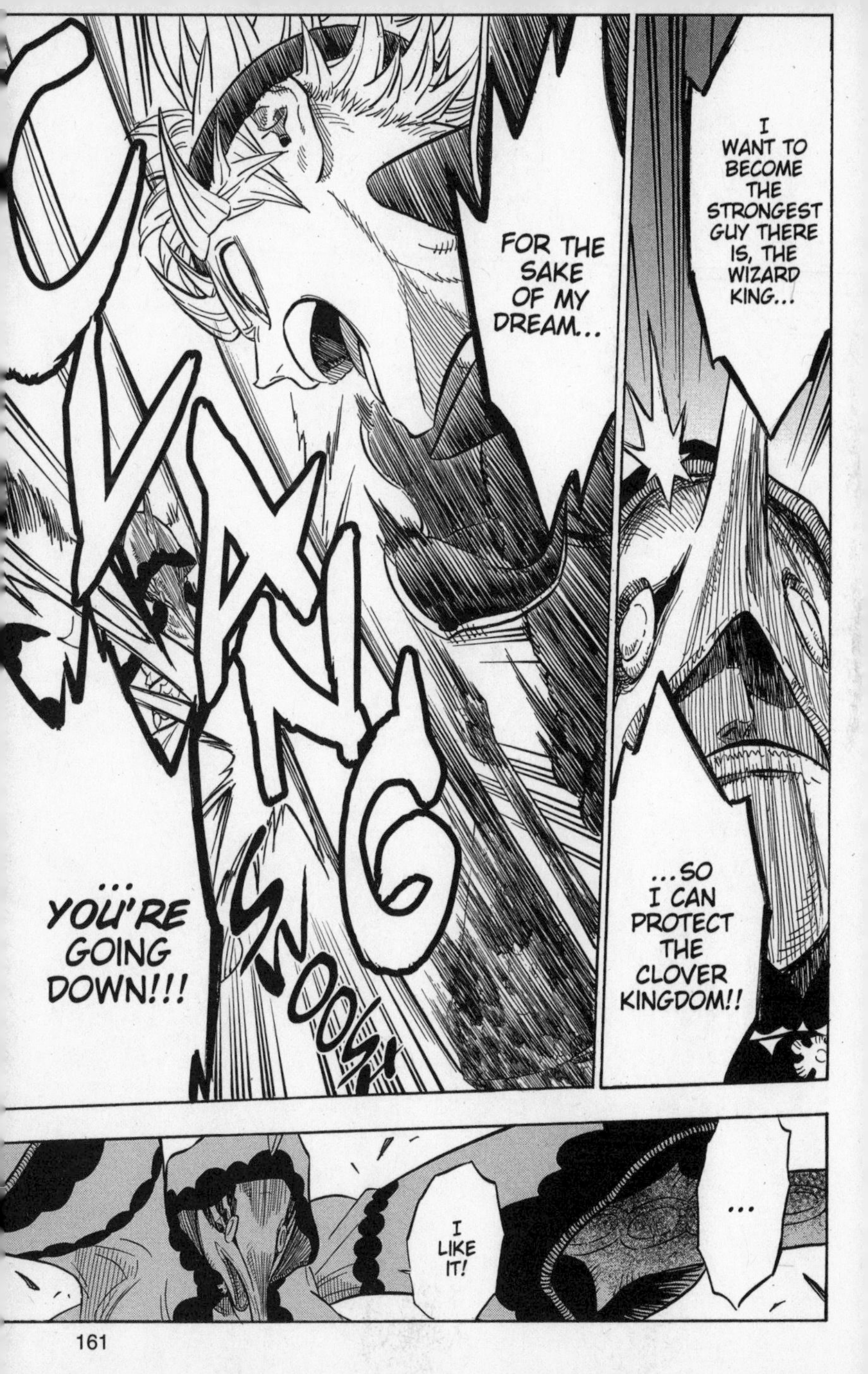
I WANT TO BECOME THE STRONGEST GUY THERE IS, THE WIZARD KING...
...SO I CAN PROTECT THE CLOVER KINGDOM!!
FOR THE SAKE OF MY DREAM...
... YOU'RE GOING DOWN!!!
...
I LIKE IT!

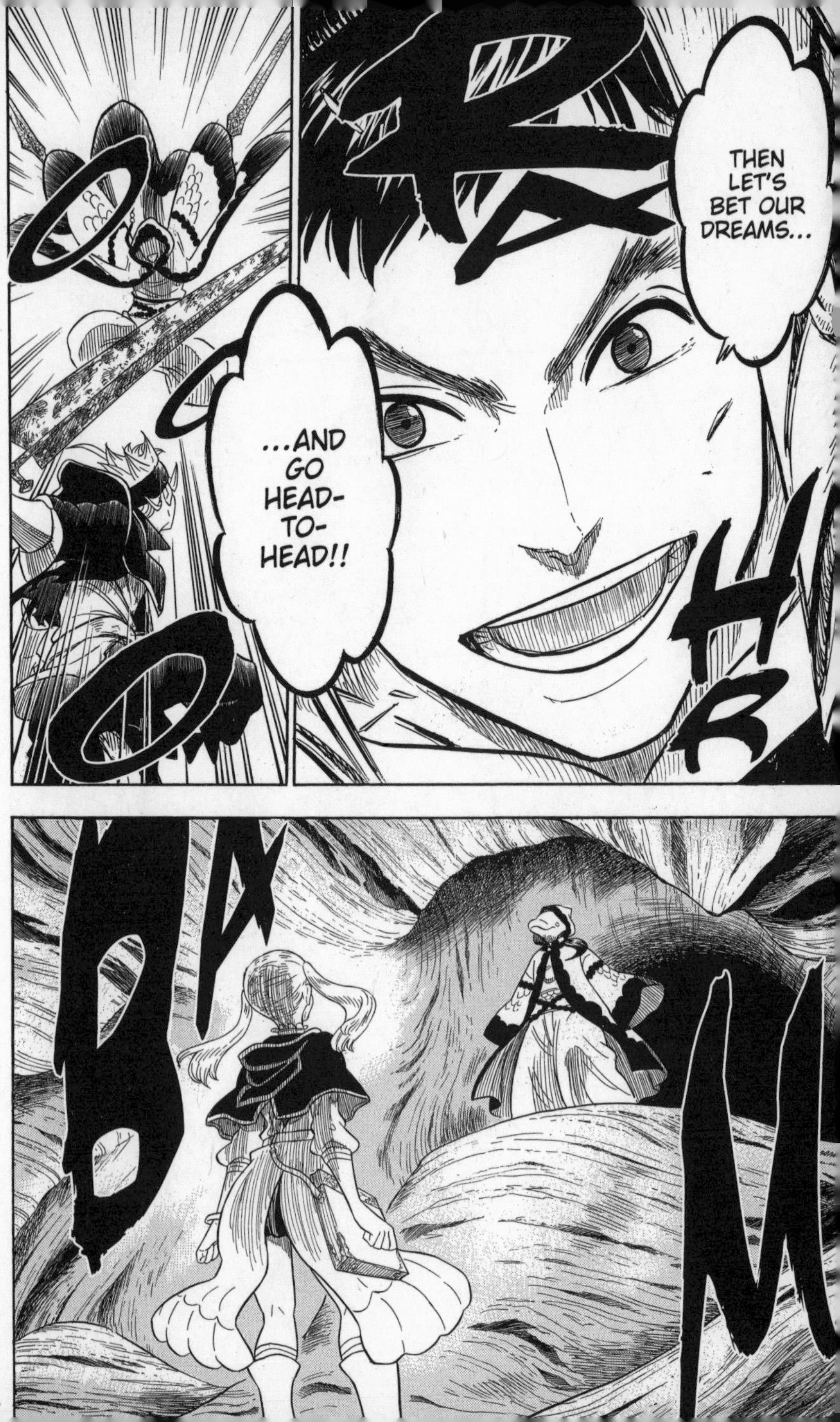
THEN LET'S BET OUR DREAMS...
...AND GO HEAD-TO-HEAD!!

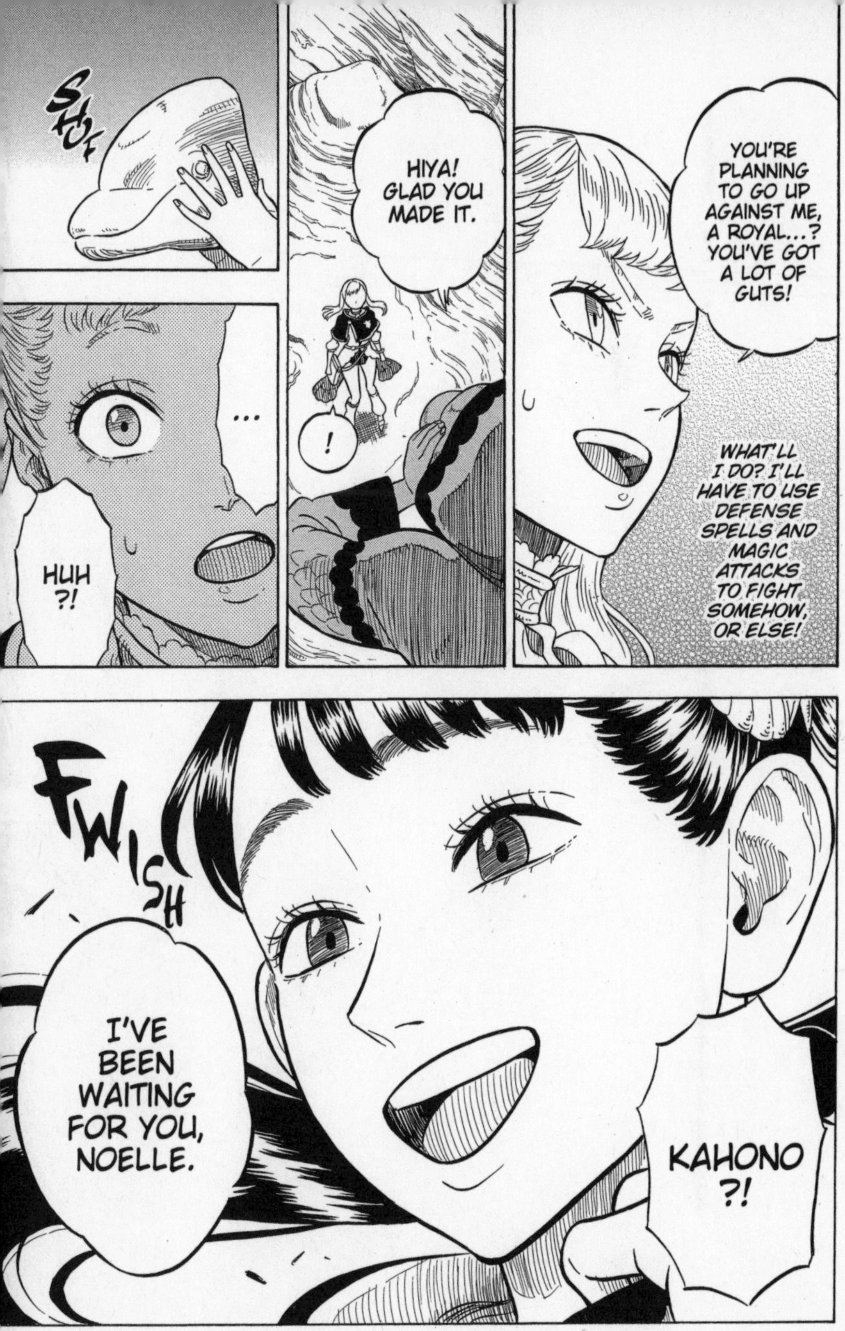
YOU'RE PLANNING TO GO UP AGAINST ME, A ROYAL...? YOU'VE GOT A LOT OF GUTS!
WHAT'LL I DO? I'LL HAVE TO USE DEFENSE SPELLS AND MAGIC ATTACKS TO FIGHT SOMEHOW, OR ELSE!
HIYA! GLAD YOU MADE IT.
!
SHOK
...
HUH?!
FWISH
I'VE BEEN WAITING FOR YOU, NOELLE.
KAHONO?!

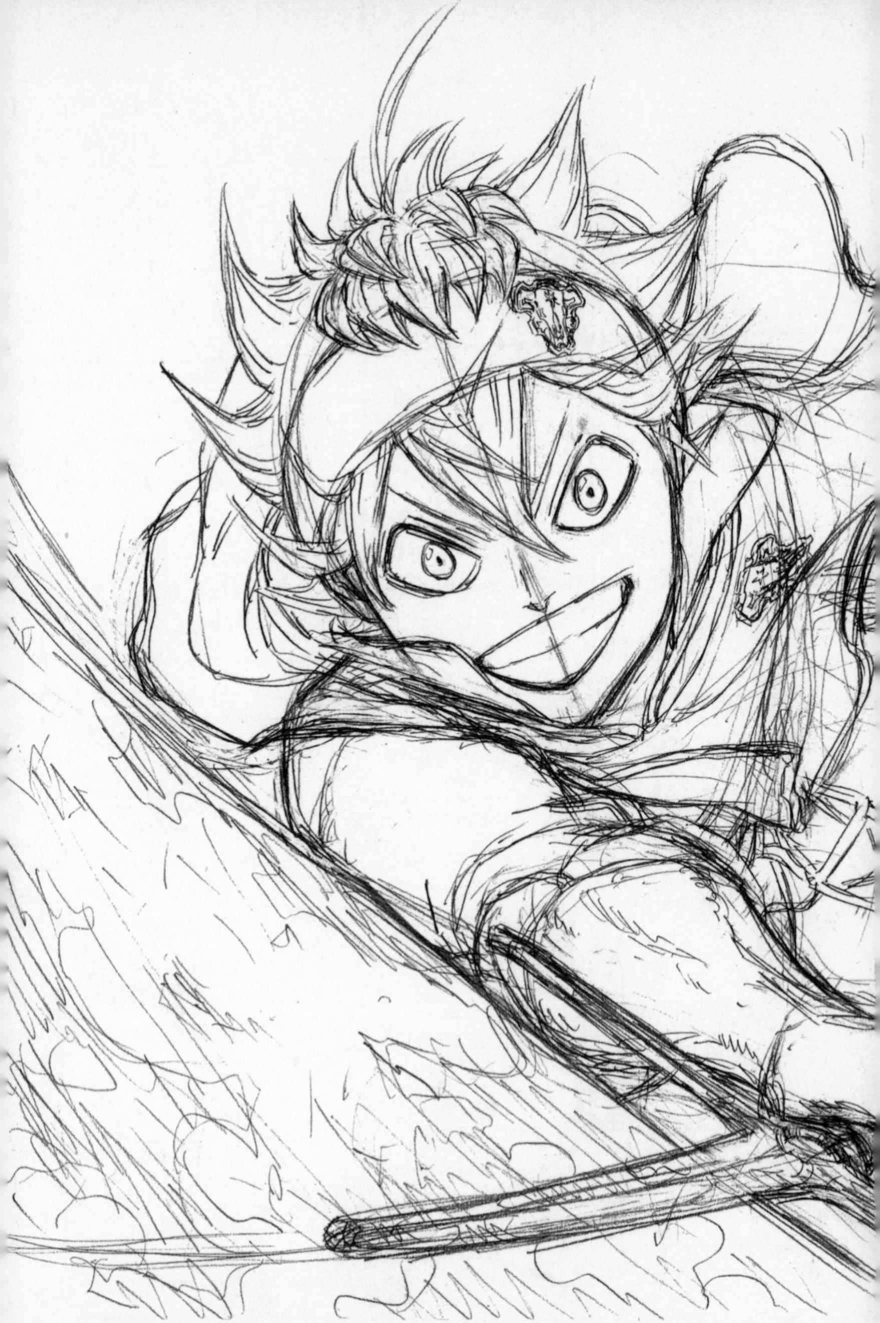

Cover for *Weekly Shonen Jump* 2016 Issue #14/Sketch

# ❀ Page 62: Rule of the Strong

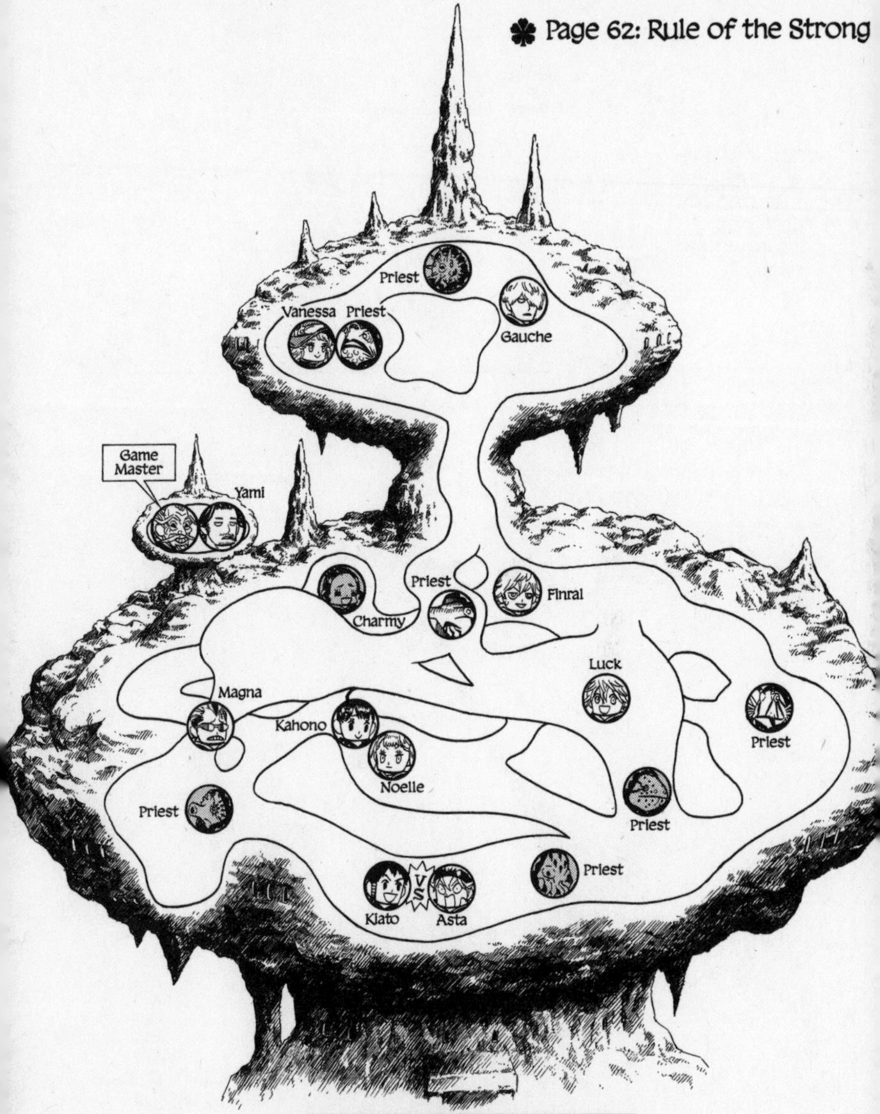

Priest
Vanessa
Priest
Gauche
Game Master
Yami
Priest
Finral
Charmy
Luck
Magna
Kahono
Priest
Noelle
Priest
Priest
Priest
VS
Kiato
Asta


## Temple Battle Royale Rules

① A team battle, nine-on-nine. All combat methods allowed.
② Victory goes to the first team to annihilate the other team by knocking members out or making them surrender, or to the team that has the most members left at the end of the one-hour time limit.
③ The game master is able to activate "nuisance spells" within the temple.
④ No one can leave the temple until the game is over.

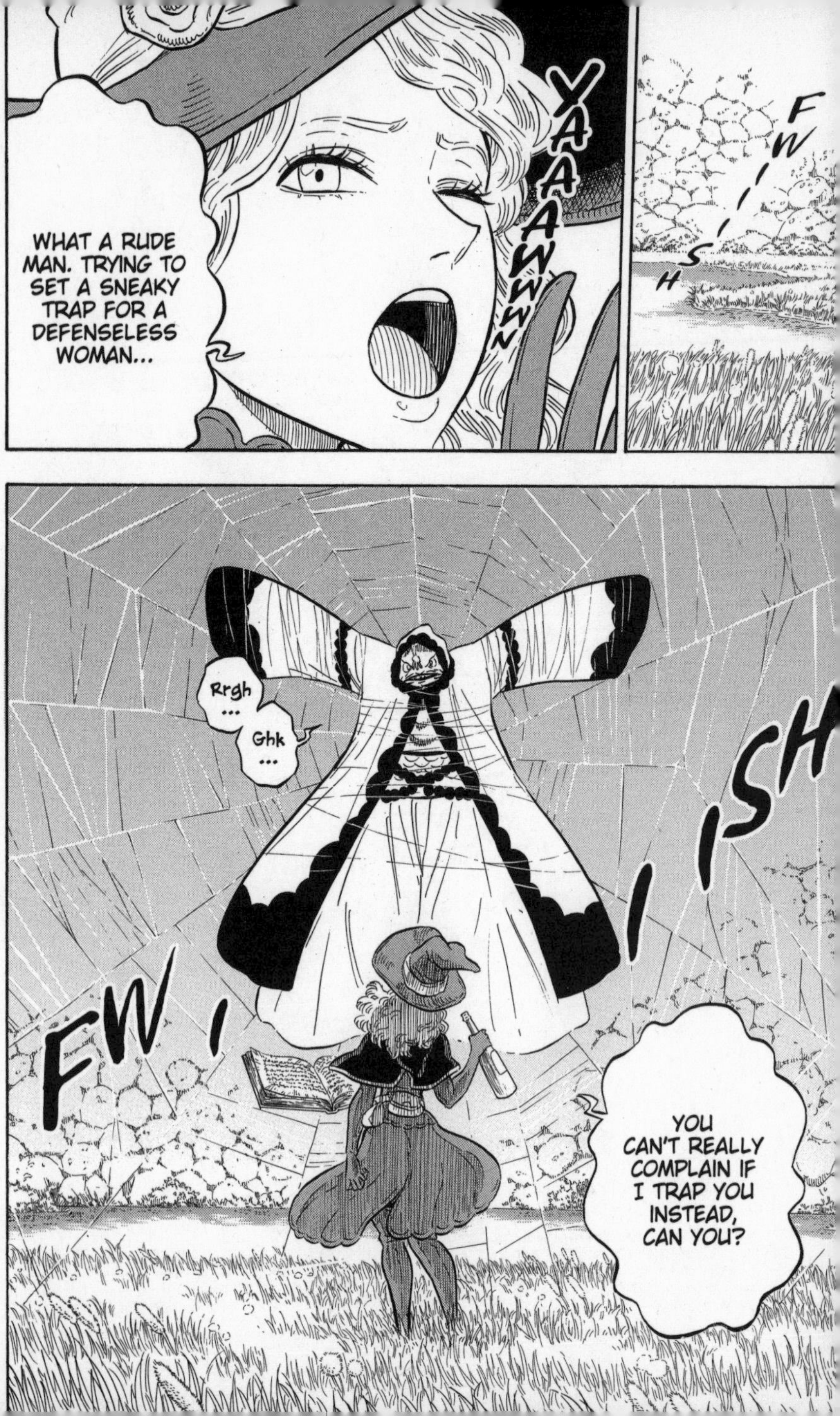
FWIISH
YAAAWWN
WHAT A RUDE MAN. TRYING TO SET A SNEAKY TRAP FOR A DEFENSELESS WOMAN...
FWIISH
Rrgh...
Ghk...
YOU CAN'T REALLY COMPLAIN IF I TRAP YOU INSTEAD, CAN YOU?

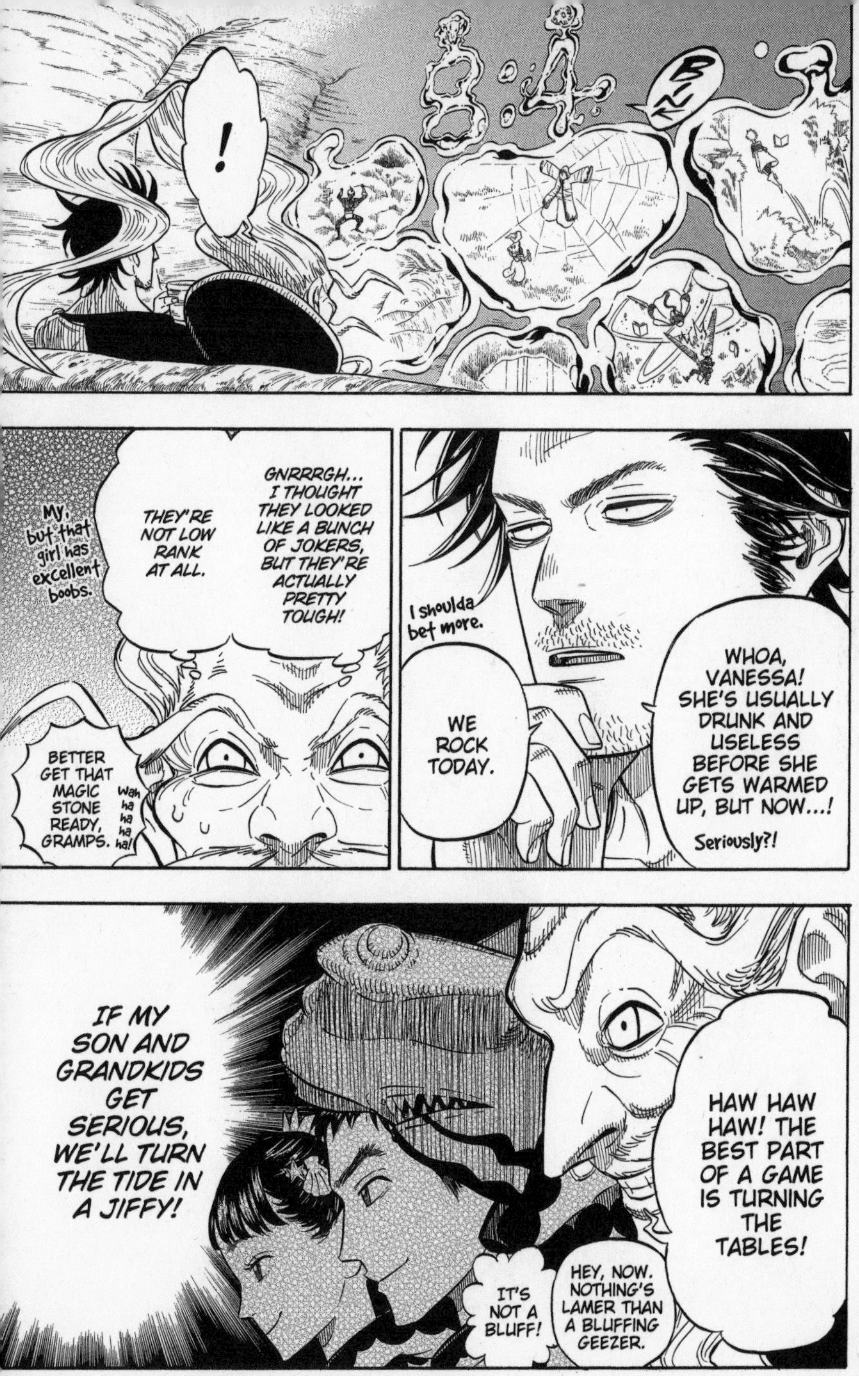
BLINK
8:4
!
WHOA, VANESSA! SHE'S USUALLY DRUNK AND USELESS BEFORE SHE GETS WARMED UP, BUT NOW...!
Seriously?!
I shoulda bet more.
WE ROCK TODAY.
GNRRRGH... I THOUGHT THEY LOOKED LIKE A BUNCH OF JOKERS, BUT THEY'RE ACTUALLY PRETTY TOUGH!
THEY'RE NOT LOW RANK AT ALL.
My, but that girl has excellent boobs.
Wah ha ha ha ha!
BETTER GET THAT MAGIC STONE READY, GRAMPS.
HAW HAW HAW! THE BEST PART OF A GAME IS TURNING THE TABLES!
HEY, NOW. NOTHING'S LAMER THAN A BLUFFING GEEZER.
IT'S NOT A BLUFF!
IF MY SON AND GRANDKIDS GET SERIOUS, WE'LL TURN THE TIDE IN A JIFFY!

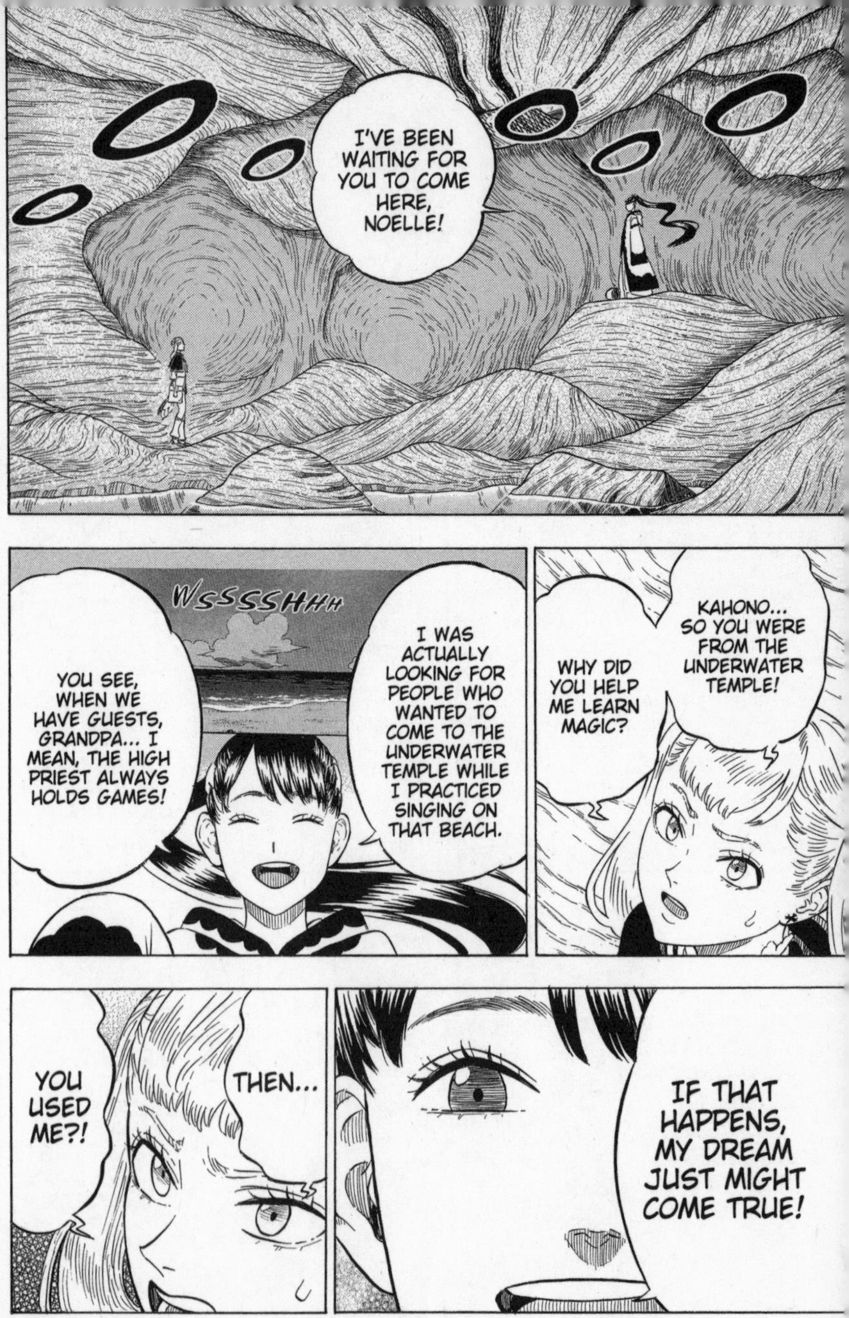
I'VE BEEN WAITING FOR YOU TO COME HERE, NOELLE!
KAHONO... SO YOU WERE FROM THE UNDERWATER TEMPLE!
WHY DID YOU HELP ME LEARN MAGIC?
WSSSSHHH
I WAS ACTUALLY LOOKING FOR PEOPLE WHO WANTED TO COME TO THE UNDERWATER TEMPLE WHILE I PRACTICED SINGING ON THAT BEACH.
YOU SEE, WHEN WE HAVE GUESTS, GRANDPA... I MEAN, THE HIGH PRIEST ALWAYS HOLDS GAMES!
IF THAT HAPPENS, MY DREAM JUST MIGHT COME TRUE!
THEN...
YOU USED ME?!

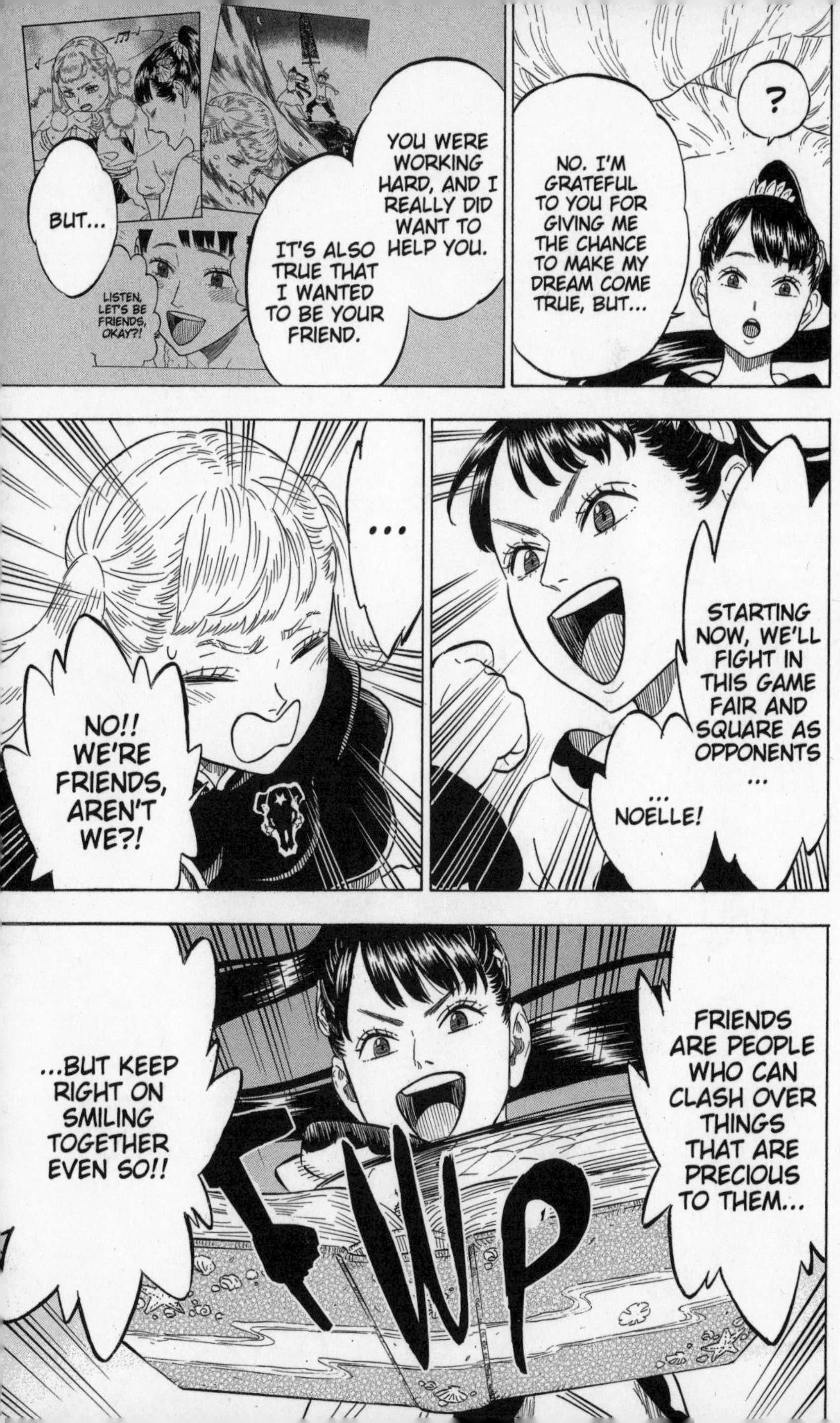
?
NO. I'M GRATEFUL TO YOU FOR GIVING ME THE CHANCE TO MAKE MY DREAM COME TRUE, BUT...
YOU WERE WORKING HARD, AND I REALLY DID WANT TO HELP YOU.
IT'S ALSO TRUE THAT I WANTED TO BE YOUR FRIEND.
BUT...
LISTEN, LET'S BE FRIENDS, OKAY?!
STARTING NOW, WE'LL FIGHT IN THIS GAME FAIR AND SQUARE AS OPPONENTS ...
... NOELLE!
...
NO!! WE'RE FRIENDS, AREN'T WE?!
FRIENDS ARE PEOPLE WHO CAN CLASH OVER THINGS THAT ARE PRECIOUS TO THEM...
...BUT KEEP RIGHT ON SMILING TOGETHER EVEN SO!!
FWP

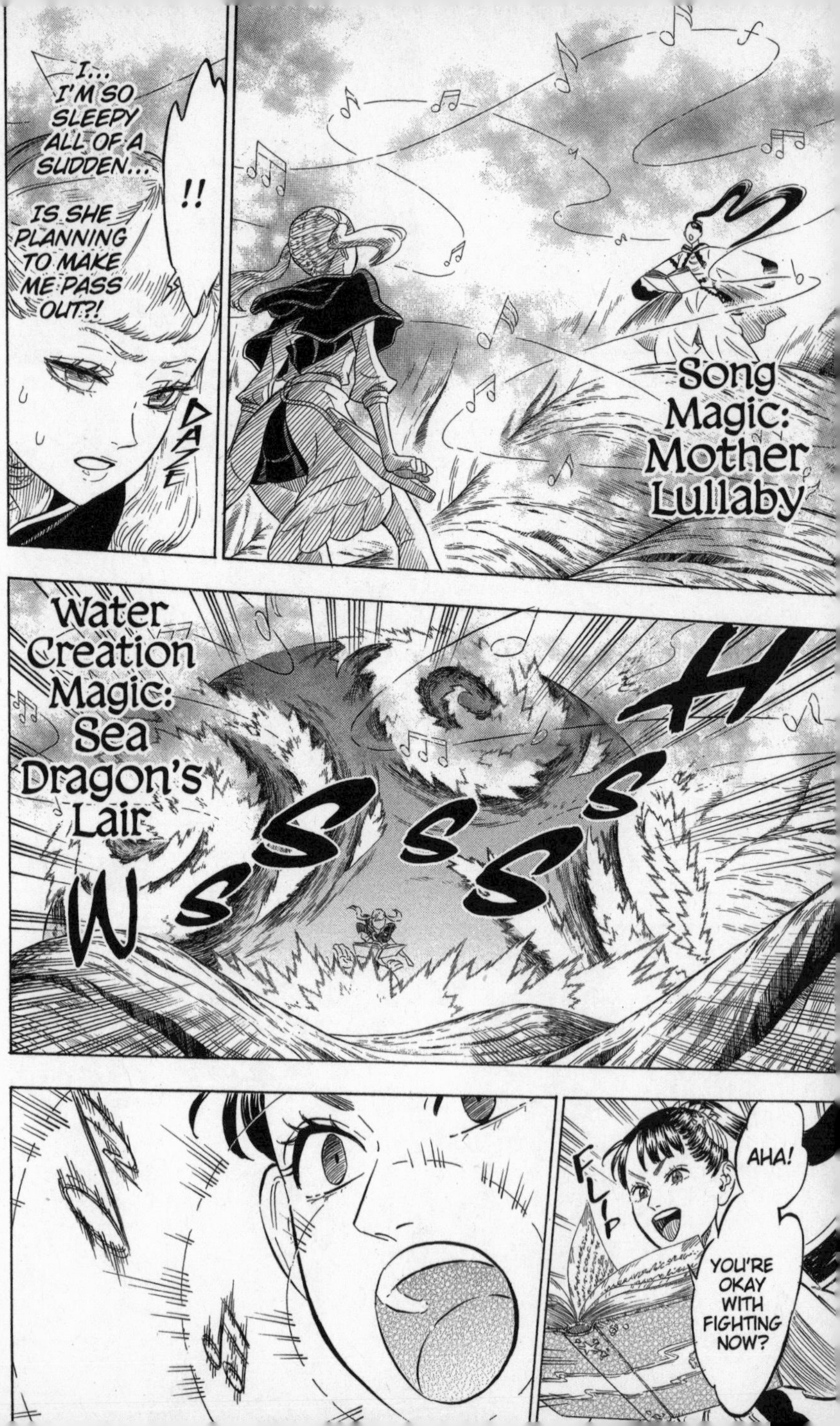
Song Magic: Mother Lullaby
!!
I... I'M SO SLEEPY ALL OF A SUDDEN...
IS SHE PLANNING TO MAKE ME PASS OUT?!
DAZE
Water Creation Magic: Sea Dragon's Lair
WSSSSSSSH
AHA!
FLIP
YOU'RE OKAY WITH FIGHTING NOW?

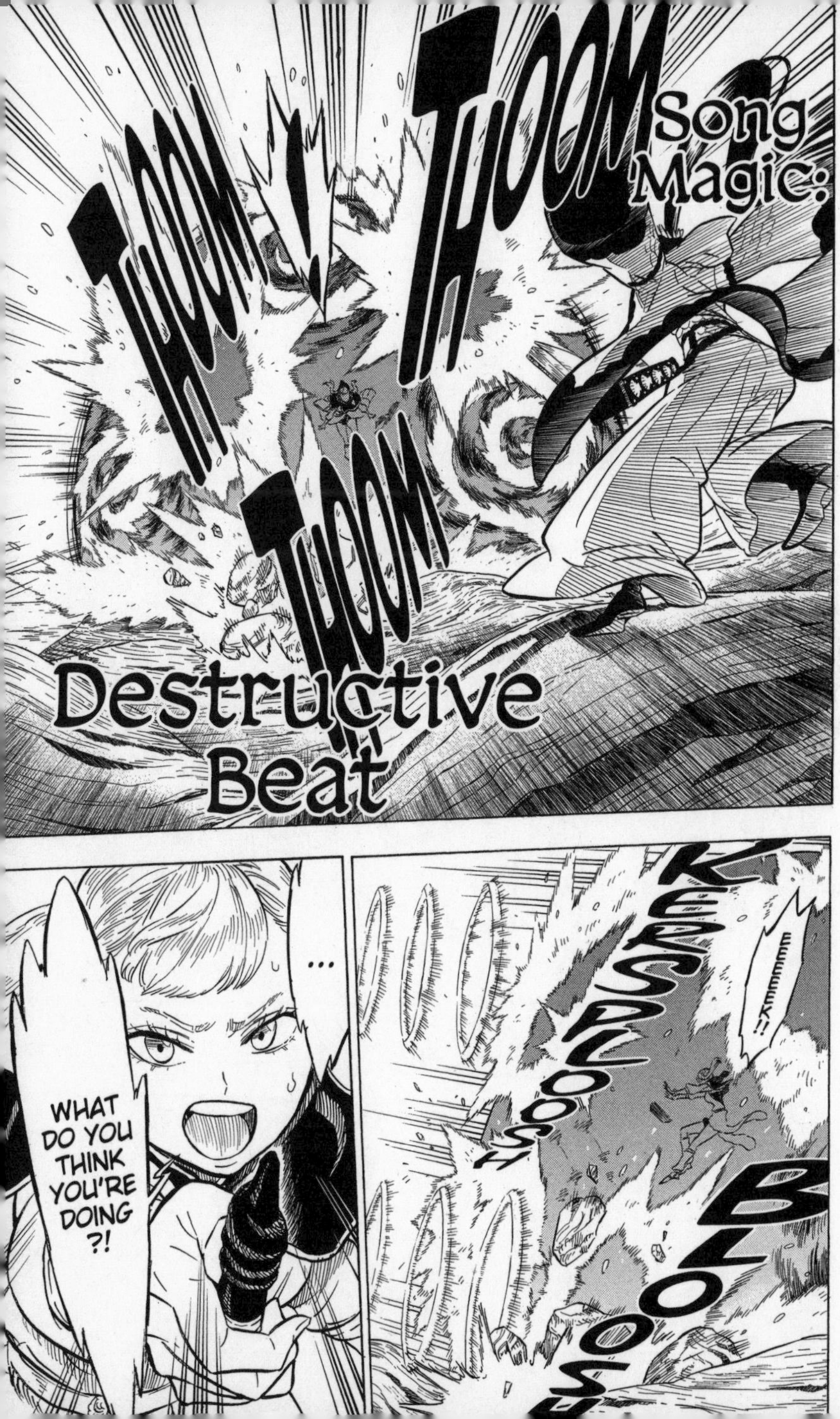
THOOM
THOOM
THOOM
Song Magic:
Destructive Beat
KERSPLOOOSH
EEEEEK!!
BLOOOSH
...
WHAT DO YOU THINK YOU'RE DOING?!

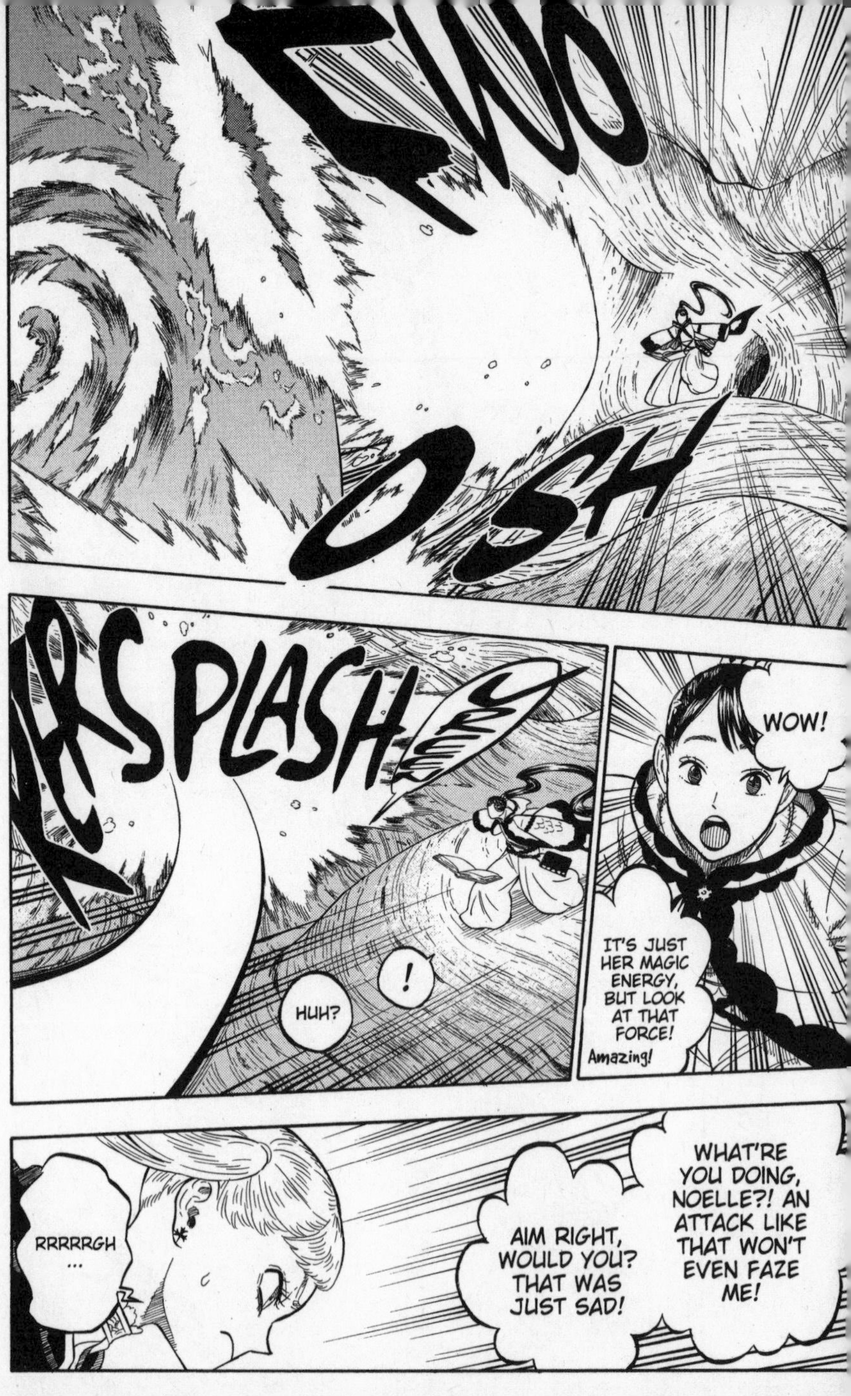
FWOOSH
WOW!
IT'S JUST HER MAGIC ENERGY, BUT LOOK AT THAT FORCE!
Amazing!
SPLASH
!
HUH?
WHAT'RE YOU DOING, NOELLE?! AN ATTACK LIKE THAT WON'T EVEN FAZE ME!
AIM RIGHT, WOULD YOU? THAT WAS JUST SAD!
RRRRRGH ...

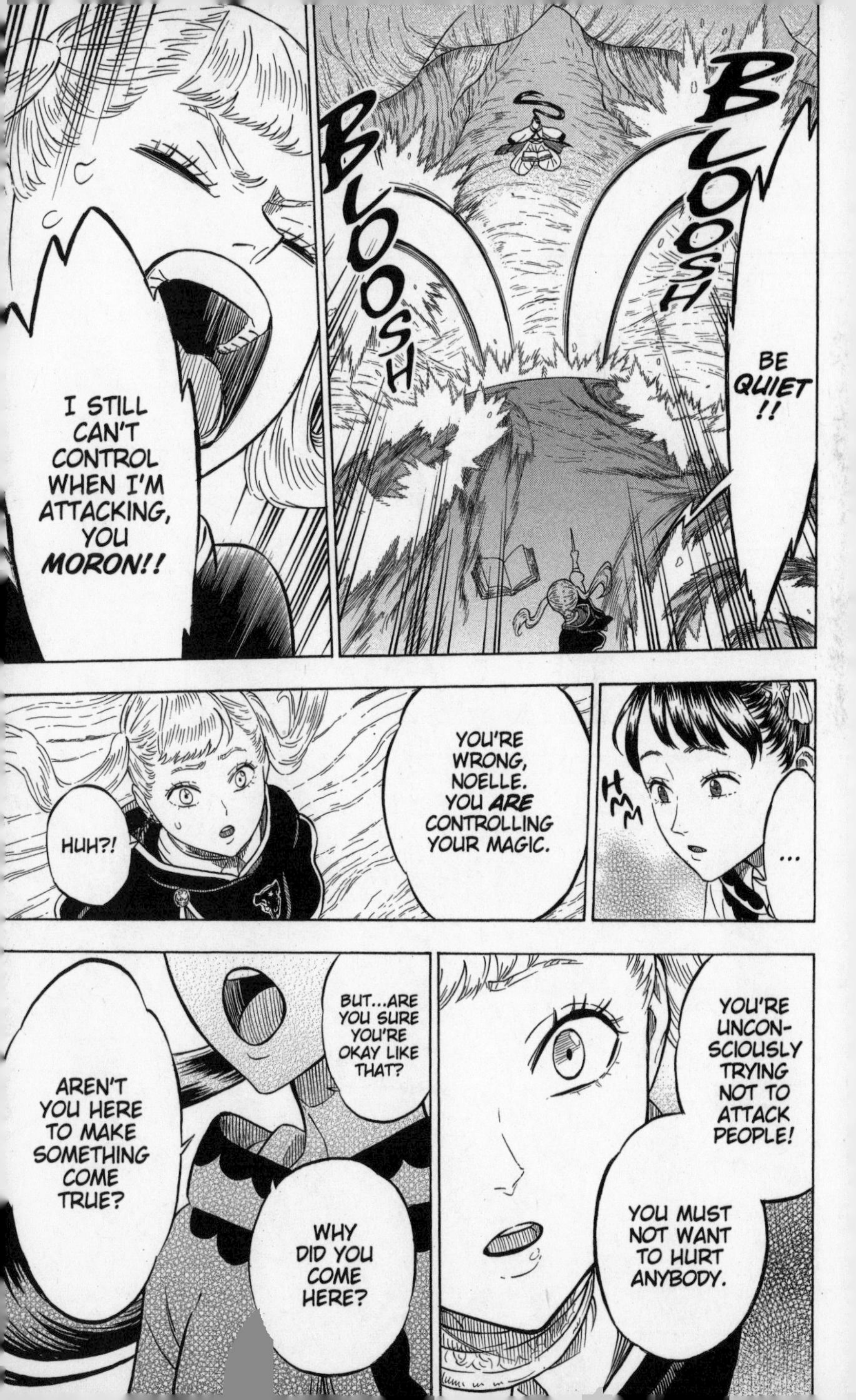
BLOOSH
BLOOSH
BE QUIET!!
I STILL CAN'T CONTROL WHEN I'M ATTACKING, YOU MORON!!
HMM
...
YOU'RE WRONG, NOELLE. YOU ARE CONTROLLING YOUR MAGIC.
HUH?!
YOU'RE UNCONSCIOUSLY TRYING NOT TO ATTACK PEOPLE!
YOU MUST NOT WANT TO HURT ANYBODY.
BUT...ARE YOU SURE YOU'RE OKAY LIKE THAT?
AREN'T YOU HERE TO MAKE SOMETHING COME TRUE?
WHY DID YOU COME HERE?

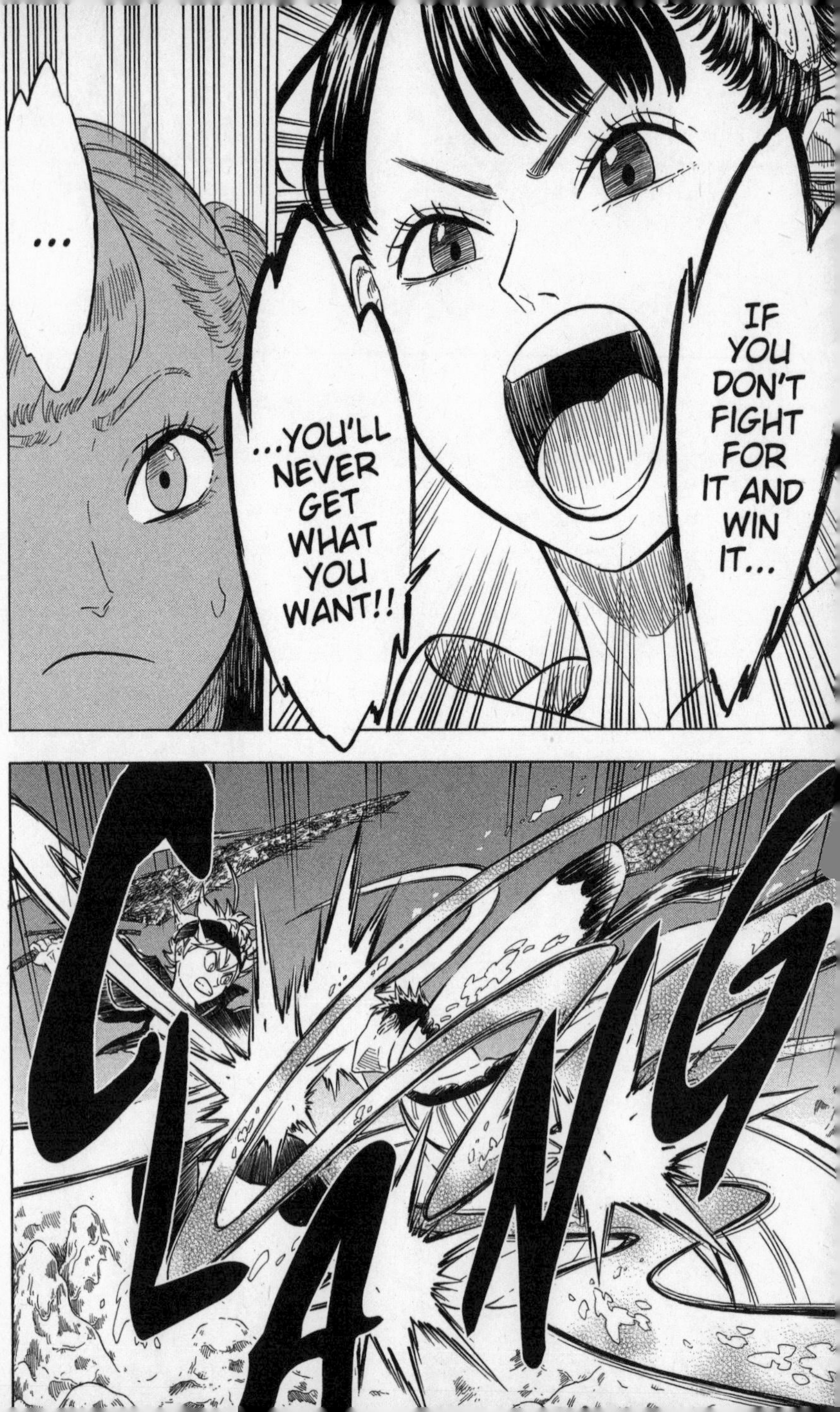
IF YOU DON'T FIGHT FOR IT AND WIN IT...
...YOU'LL NEVER GET WHAT YOU WANT!!
...
CLANG

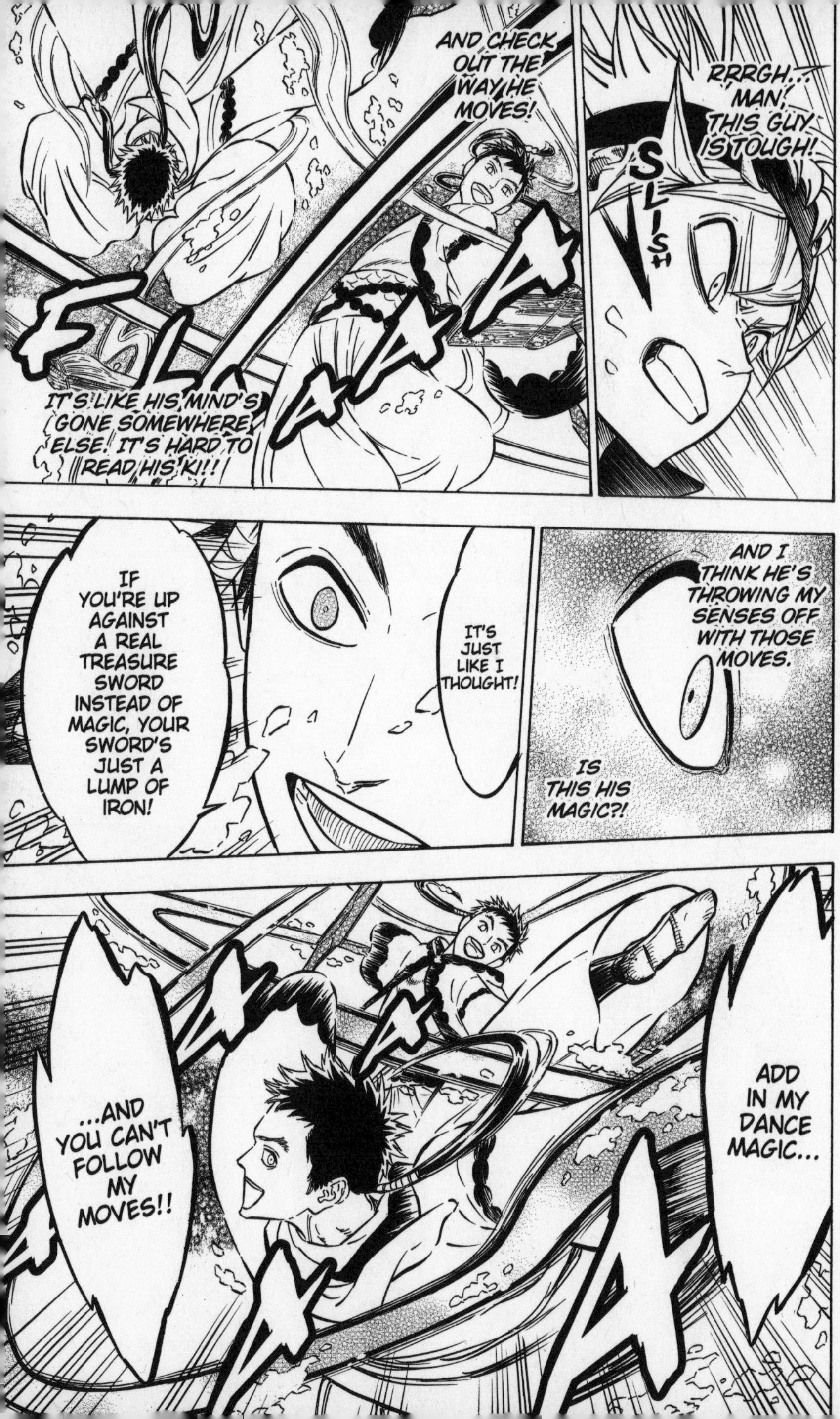
RRRGH... MAN, THIS GUY IS TOUGH!
SLISH
AND CHECK OUT THE WAY HE MOVES!
IT'S LIKE HIS MIND'S GONE SOMEWHERE ELSE. IT'S HARD TO READ HIS KI!!
AND I THINK HE'S THROWING MY SENSES OFF WITH THOSE MOVES.
IS THIS HIS MAGIC?!
IT'S JUST LIKE I THOUGHT!
IF YOU'RE UP AGAINST A REAL TREASURE SWORD INSTEAD OF MAGIC, YOUR SWORD'S JUST A LUMP OF IRON!
ADD IN MY DANCE MAGIC...
...AND YOU CAN'T FOLLOW MY MOVES!!

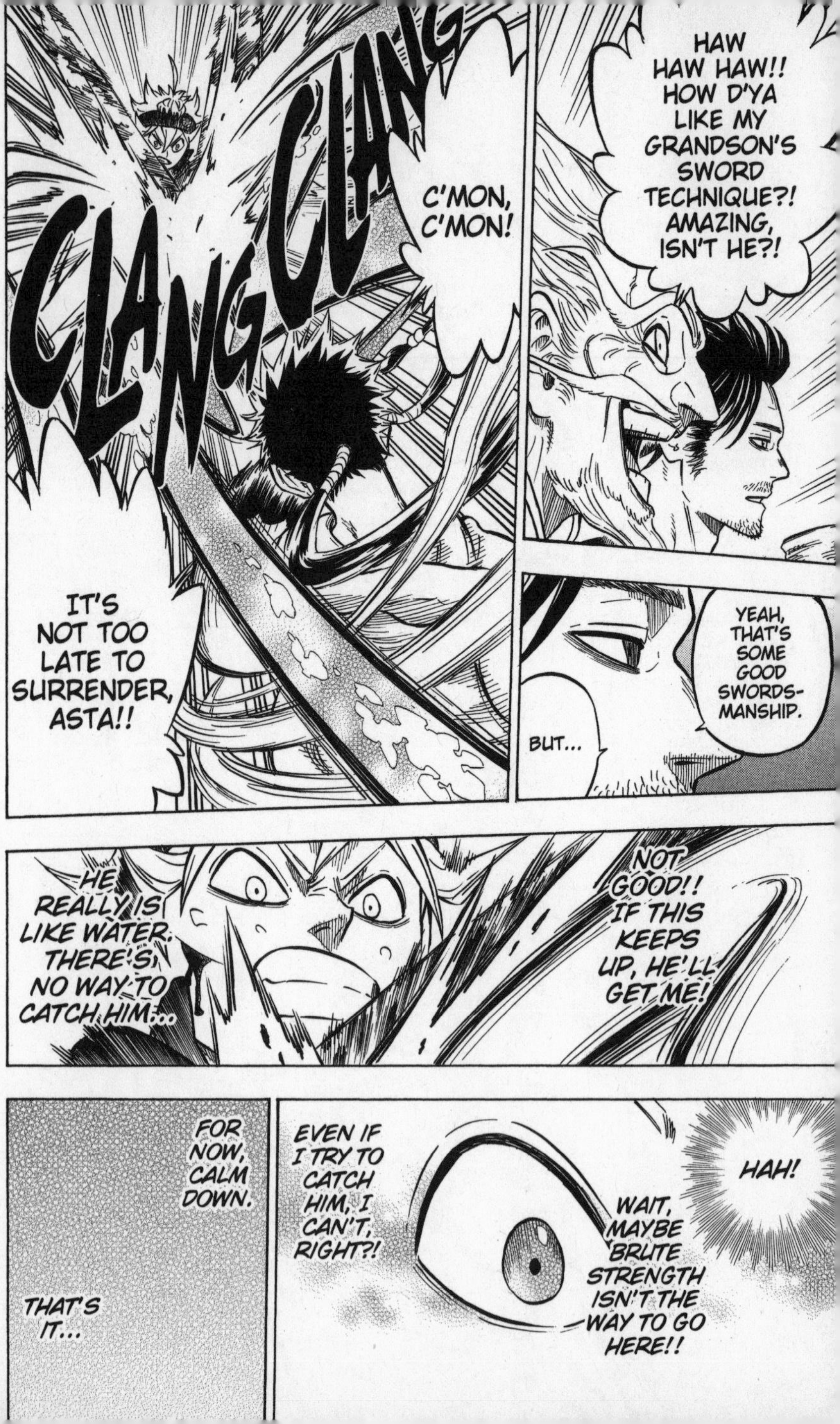
HAW HAW HAW!! HOW D'YA LIKE MY GRANDSON'S SWORD TECHNIQUE?! AMAZING, ISN'T HE?!
YEAH, THAT'S SOME GOOD SWORDS-MANSHIP.
BUT...
C'MON, C'MON!
CLANG CLANG
IT'S NOT TOO LATE TO SURRENDER, ASTA!!
NOT GOOD!! IF THIS KEEPS UP, HE'LL GET ME!
HE REALLY IS LIKE WATER. THERE'S NO WAY TO CATCH HIM...
HAH!
WAIT, MAYBE BRUTE STRENGTH ISN'T THE WAY TO GO HERE!!
EVEN IF I TRY TO CATCH HIM, I CAN'T, RIGHT?!
FOR NOW, CALM DOWN.
THAT'S IT...

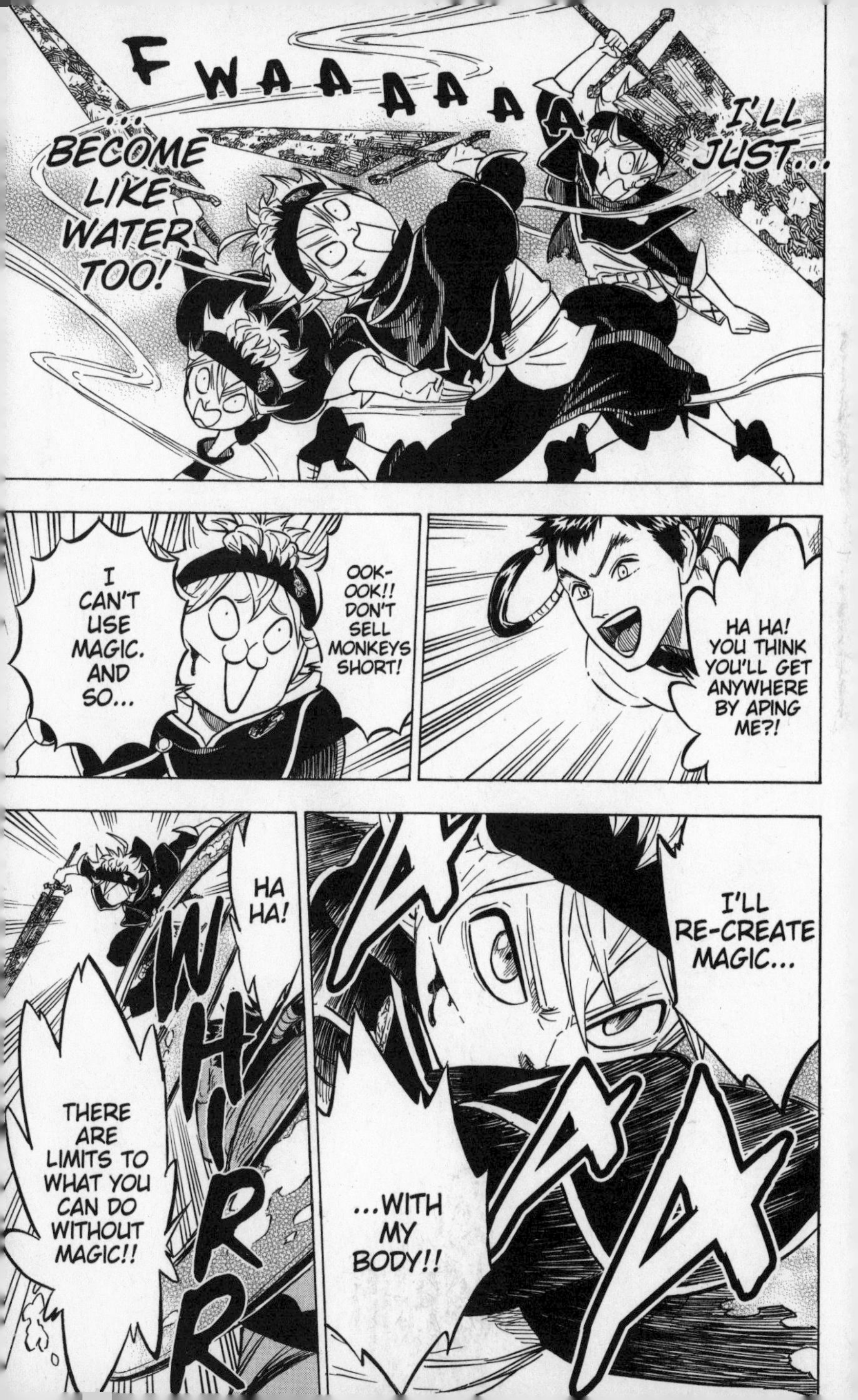
I'LL JUST...
FWAAAAAA
...BECOME LIKE WATER TOO!
HA HA! YOU THINK YOU'LL GET ANYWHERE BY APING ME?!
OOK-OOK!! DON'T SELL MONKEYS SHORT!
I CAN'T USE MAGIC. AND SO...
I'LL RE-CREATE MAGIC...
...WITH MY BODY!!
HA HA!
WHIRR
THERE ARE LIMITS TO WHAT YOU CAN DO WITHOUT MAGIC!!

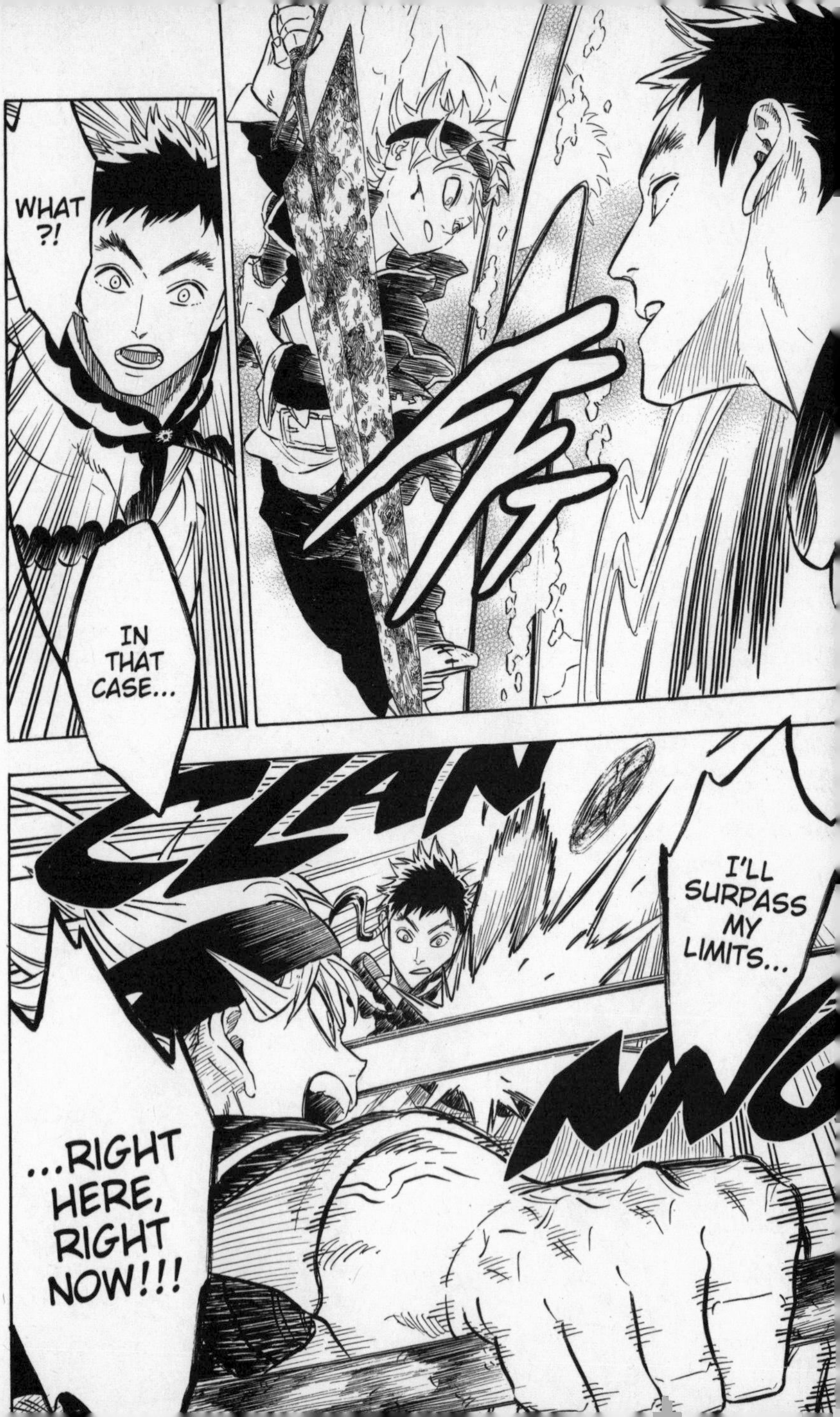
WHAT ?!
IN THAT CASE...
I'LL SURPASS MY LIMITS...
CLAN
NNG
...RIGHT HERE, RIGHT NOW!!!

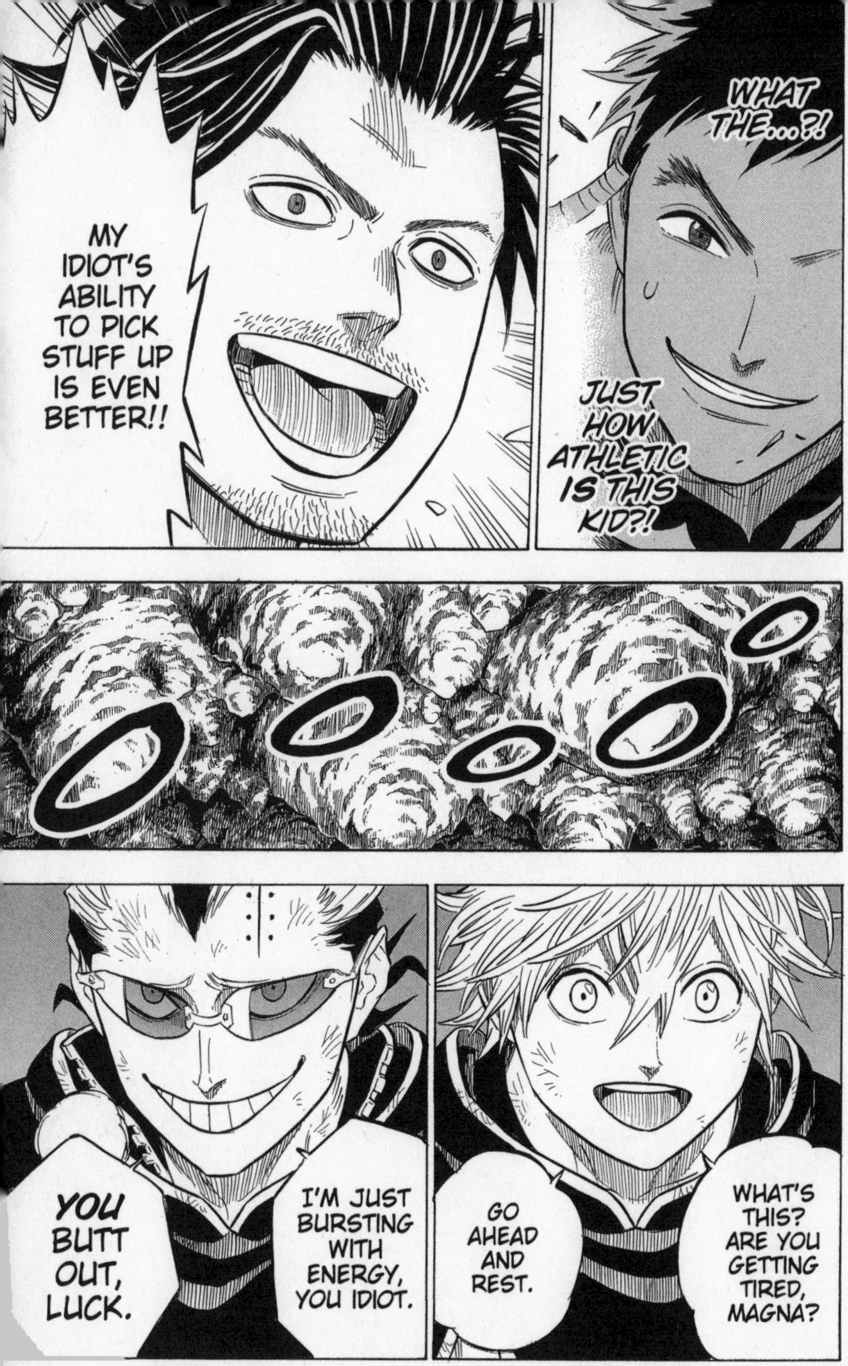
WHAT THE...?!
JUST HOW ATHLETIC IS THIS KID?!
MY IDIOT'S ABILITY TO PICK STUFF UP IS EVEN BETTER!!
WHAT'S THIS? ARE YOU GETTING TIRED, MAGNA?
GO AHEAD AND REST.
I'M JUST BURSTING WITH ENERGY, YOU IDIOT.
YOU BUTT OUT, LUCK.

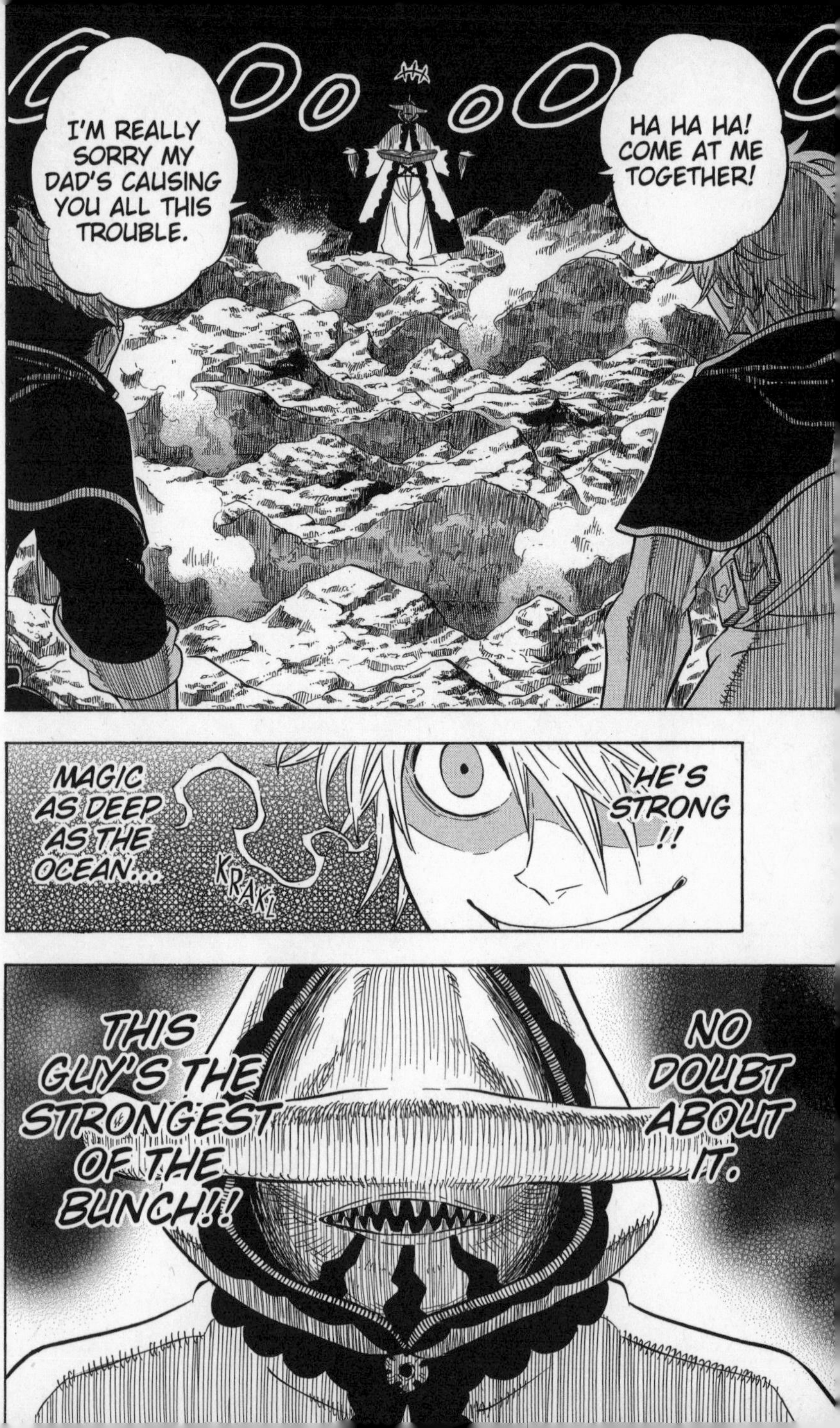
HA HA HA! COME AT ME TOGETHER!
I'M REALLY SORRY MY DAD'S CAUSING YOU ALL THIS TROUBLE.
HE'S STRONG!!
KRAKL
MAGIC AS DEEP AS THE OCEAN...
NO DOUBT ABOUT IT.
THIS GUY'S THE STRONGEST OF THE BUNCH!!

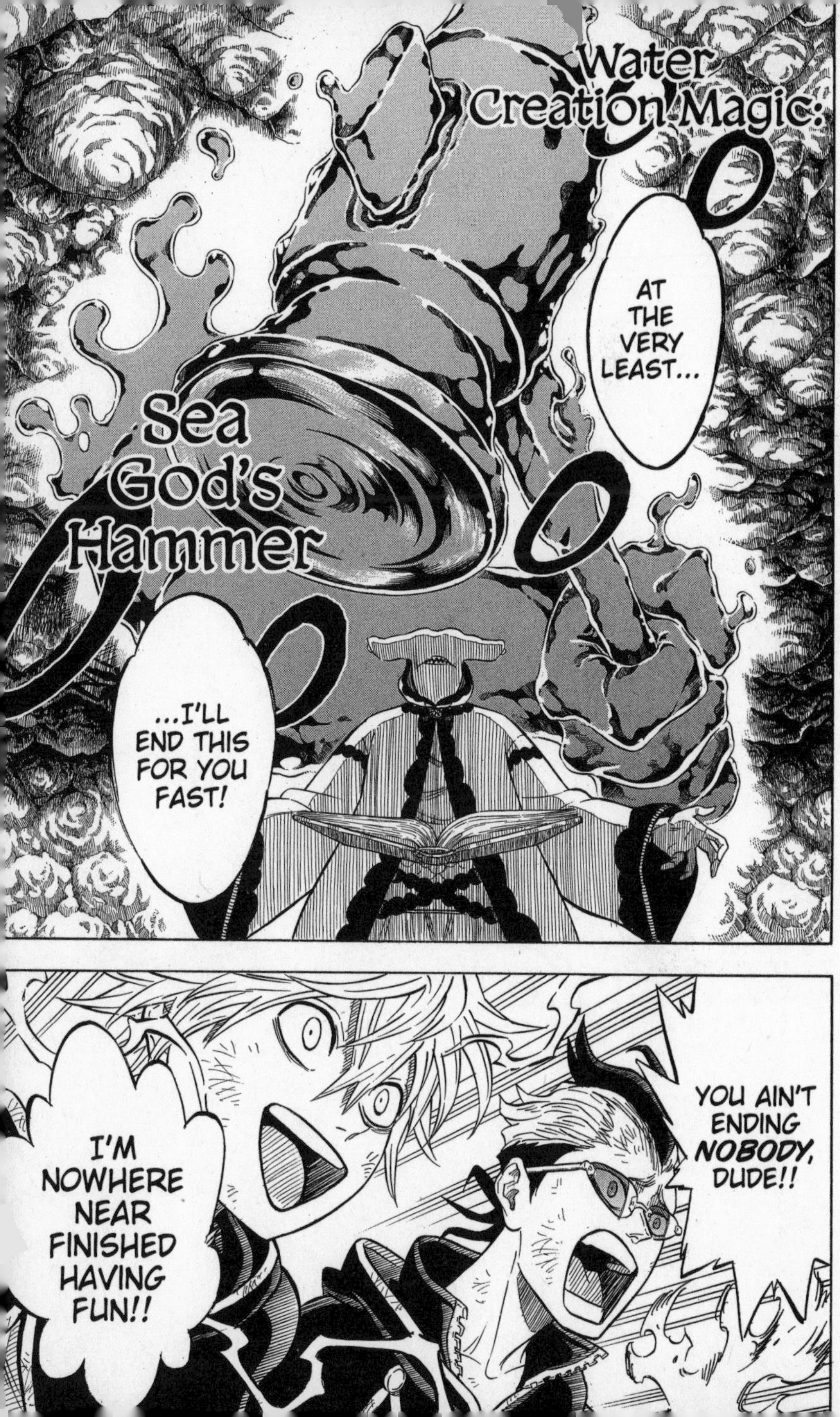
Water Creation Magic:
AT THE VERY LEAST...
Sea God's Hammer
...I'LL END THIS FOR YOU FAST!
YOU AIN'T ENDING NOBODY, DUDE!!
I'M NOWHERE NEAR FINISHED HAVING FUN!!

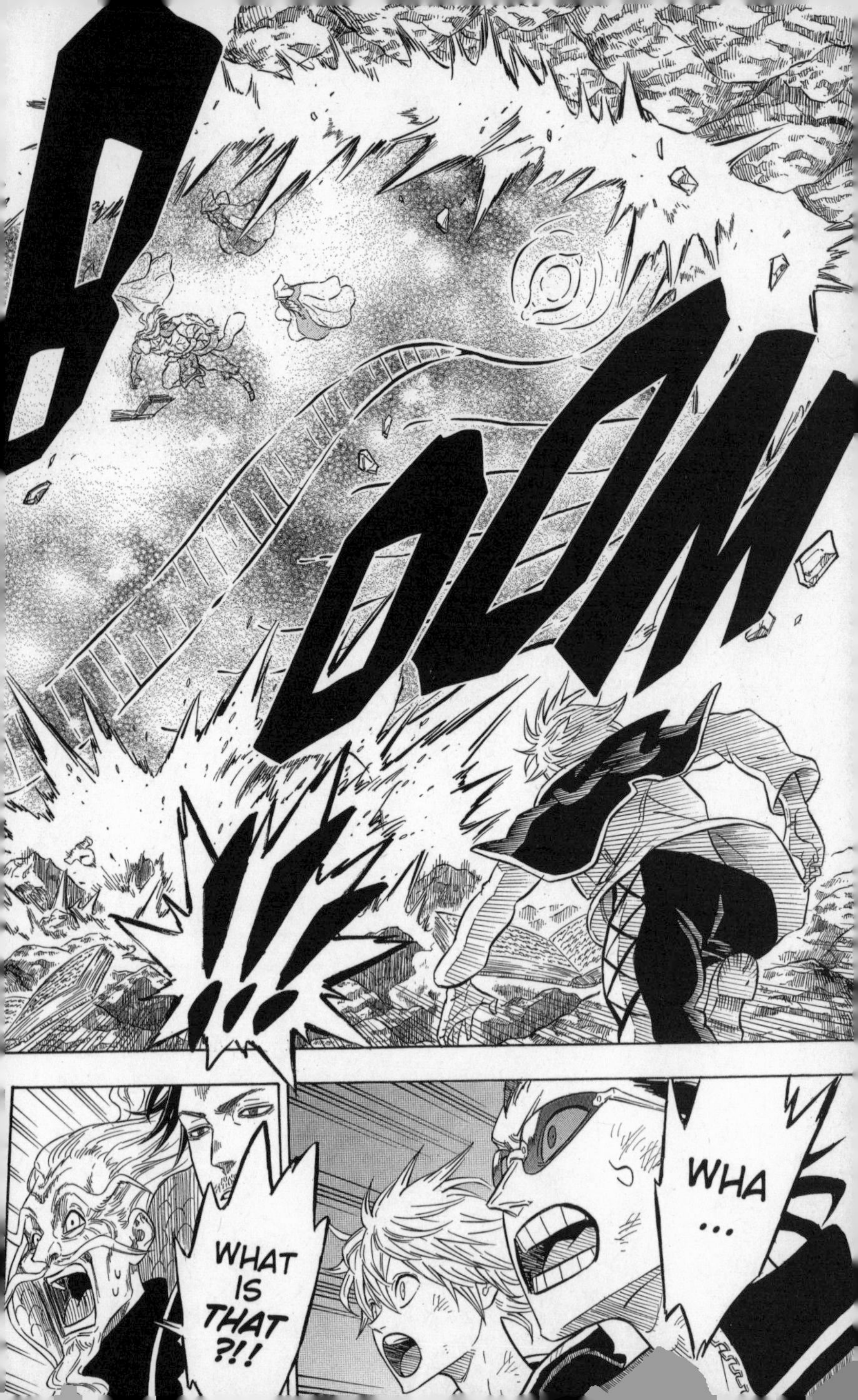
BOOM
!!
WHA...
WHAT IS THAT?!!

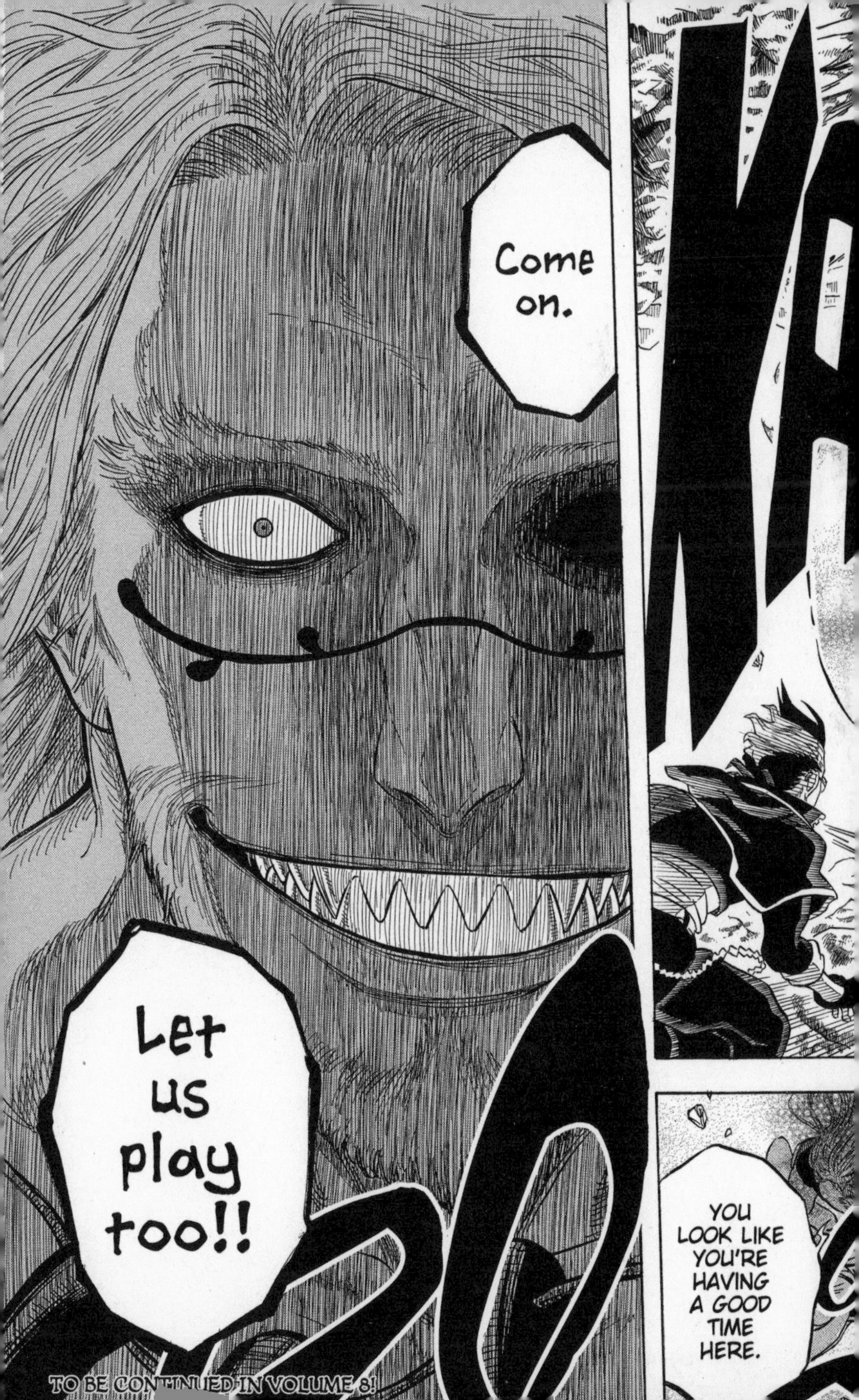
YOU LOOK LIKE YOU'RE HAVING A GOOD TIME HERE.
Come on.
Let us play too!!
TO BE CONTINUED IN VOLUME 8!

# The Assorted Questions Brigade

Good day! Good evening! Good morning! It's time for the letters corner. We got some good questions this time too, so here come the answers.

Q: At the Magic Knight entrance exam, were the people next to the captains the second-strongest members, or were they completely unrelated? (Rabimaru, Hyogo)

A: They're people the captains randomly selected to accompany them that day. Yami took Finral to provide his transportation, Fuegoleon took his little brother Leopold, and Nozel took his younger sister Nebra (although her hairstyle was different).

Q: For your manga pages, do you do everything from inking to laying down tone by hand? Don't you use any digital tools at all? (Yuchan, Osaka)

A: At this point, it's all totally analog. Going digital for tone and coloring interests me, but this analog guy doesn't have enough time and courage for it.

Q: Is Nozel a lame guy who has a servant braid that front braid for him? Or is he a creepy guy who does it himself? (Well-Behaved Dog, Shizuoka)

A: The answer might be somewhere in this volume!

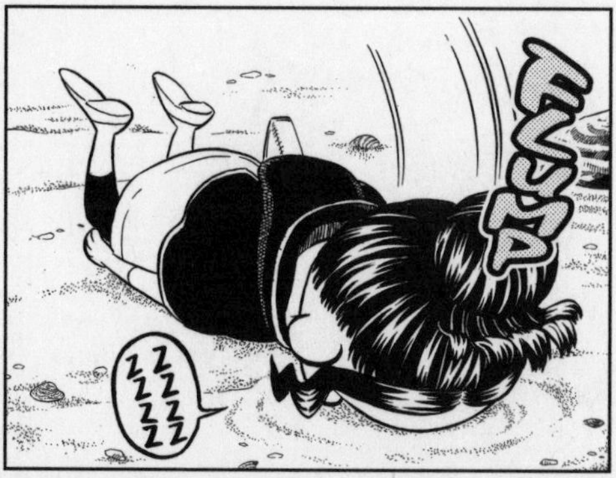
FLUMP
ZZZZ
ZZZZ

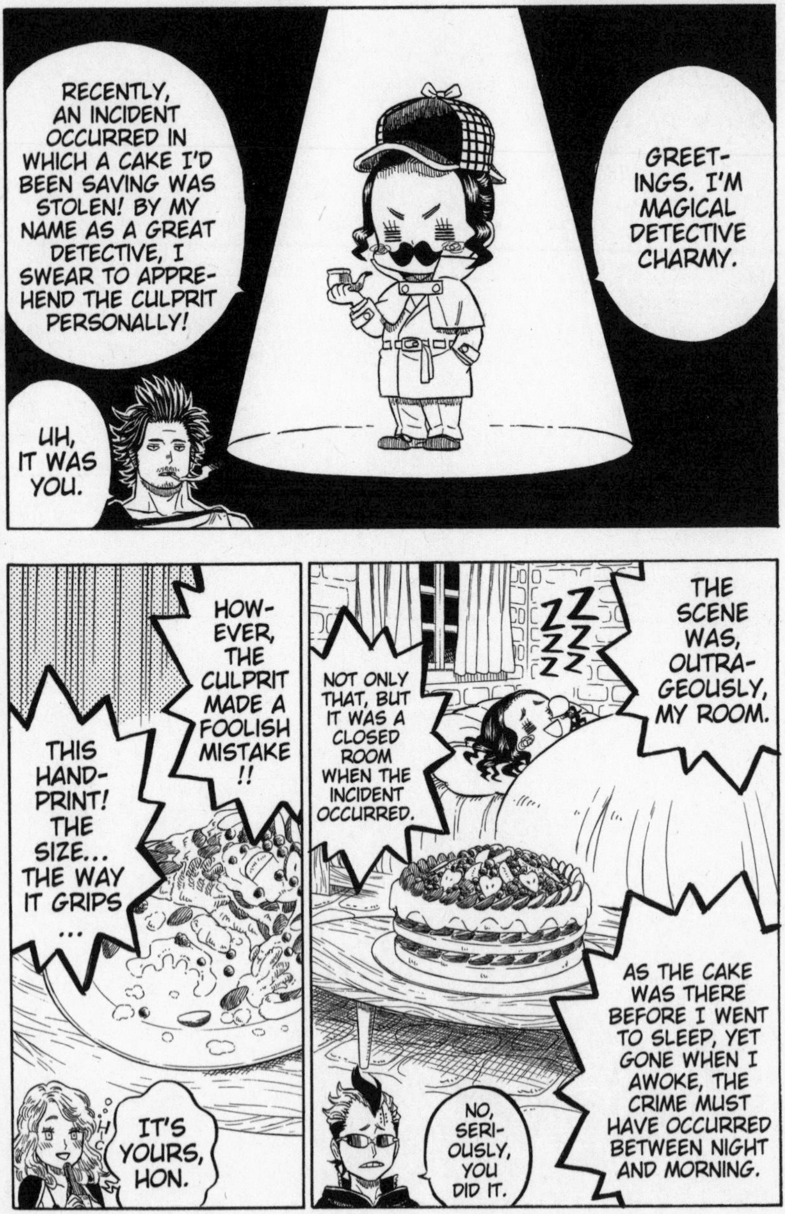
GREET-INGS. I'M MAGICAL DETECTIVE CHARMY.
RECENTLY, AN INCIDENT OCCURRED IN WHICH A CAKE I'D BEEN SAVING WAS STOLEN! BY MY NAME AS A GREAT DETECTIVE, I SWEAR TO APPRE-HEND THE CULPRIT PERSONALLY!
UH, IT WAS YOU.
THE SCENE WAS, OUTRA-GEOUSLY, MY ROOM.
ZZZ ZZZ
NOT ONLY THAT, BUT IT WAS A CLOSED ROOM WHEN THE INCIDENT OCCURRED.
AS THE CAKE WAS THERE BEFORE I WENT TO SLEEP, YET GONE WHEN I AWOKE, THE CRIME MUST HAVE OCCURRED BETWEEN NIGHT AND MORNING.
NO, SERI-OUSLY, YOU DID IT.
HOW-EVER, THE CULPRIT MADE A FOOLISH MISTAKE !!
THIS HAND-PRINT! THE SIZE... THE WAY IT GRIPS ...
HIC
IT'S YOURS, HON.

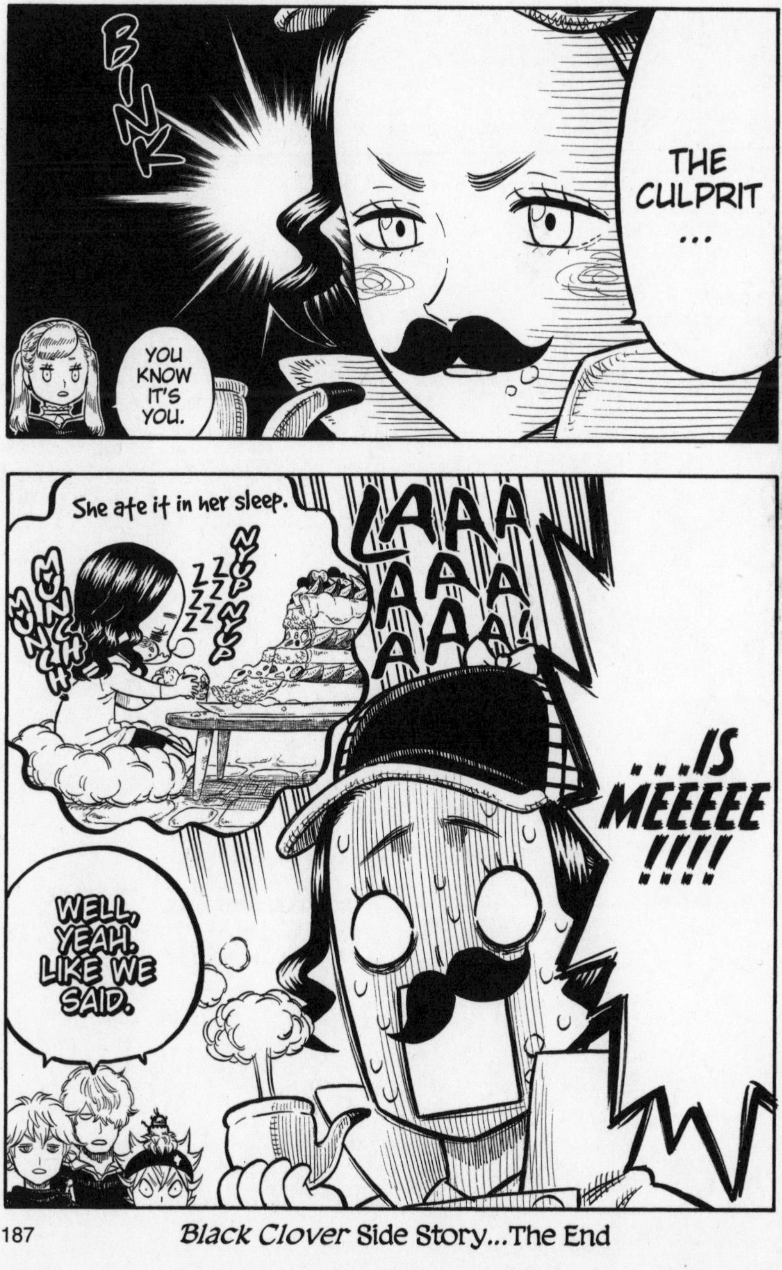
THE CULPRIT ...
BINK
YOU KNOW IT'S YOU.
LAAAAAAAAA!
...IS MEEEEE!!!!
She ate it in her sleep.
NYUP NYUP
ZZZZZZ
MUNCH MUNCH
WELL, YEAH. LIKE WE SAID.

*Black Clover* Side Story...The End

# The Blank Page Brigade

This volume's topic:
What's a shiny thing that happened to you recently?

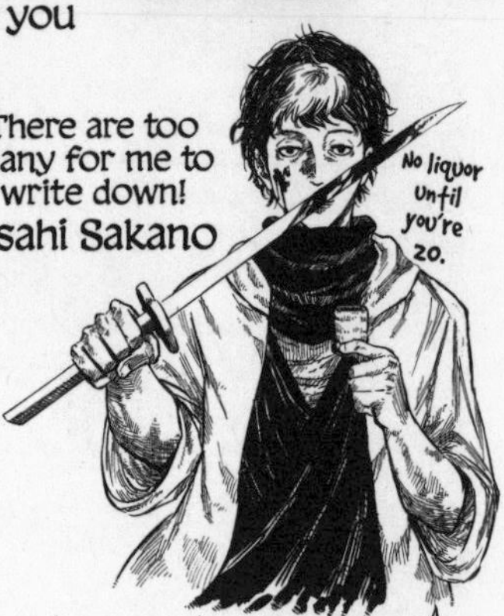
No liquor until you're 20.

There are too many for me to write down!
Asahi Sakano

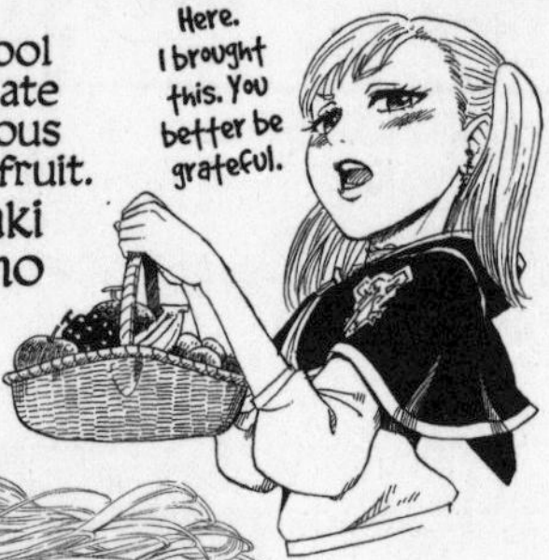
Here. I brought this. You better be grateful.

The drool when I ate a delicious piece of fruit.
Teruaki Mizuno

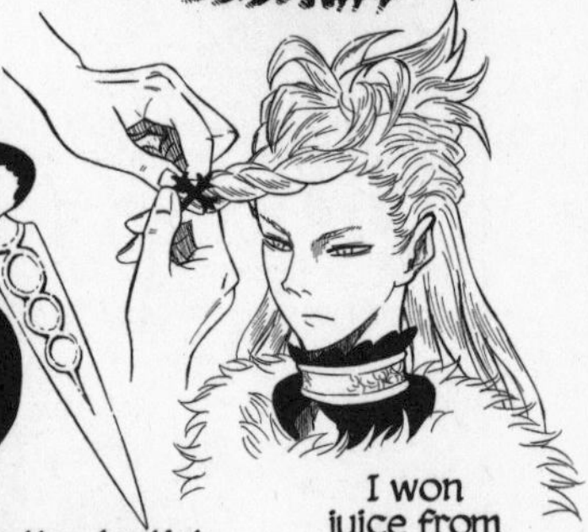

I won juice from a vending machine!
Hayato Gotō

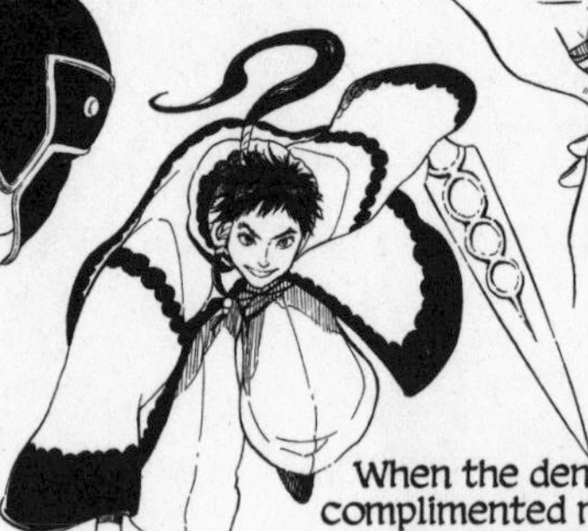

When the dentist complimented me on my teeth-brushing technique!
Genya Hori

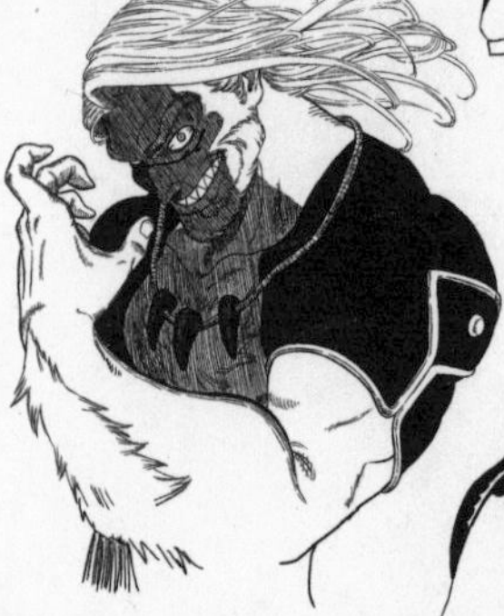

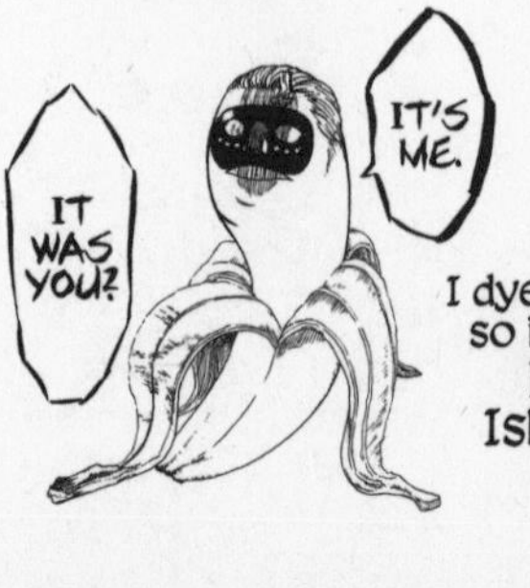
IT'S ME.
IT WAS YOU!?

I dyed my hair, so it's shiny.
Kōki Ishikawa

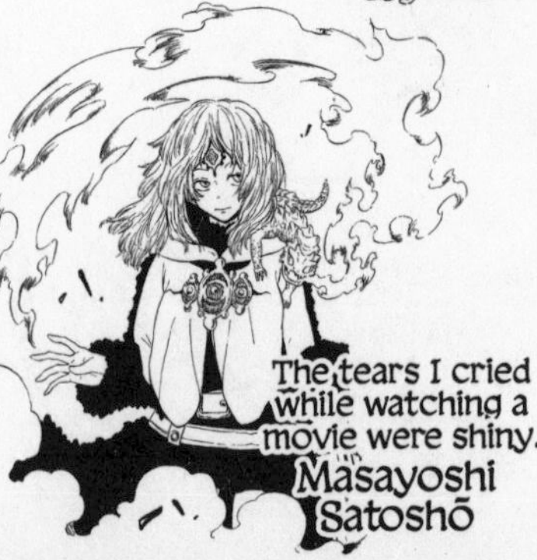

The tears I cried while watching a movie were shiny.
Masayoshi Satoshō

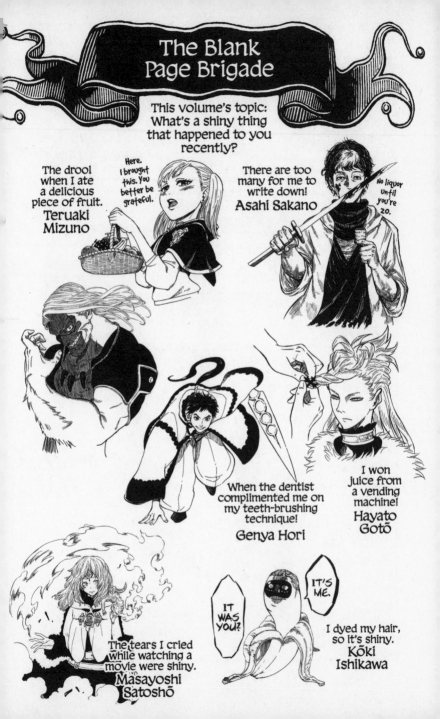

When I entered a drawing at a *yakiniku* place, and I won extra-special Korean barbecued short ribs. The meat juices were shiny.

©

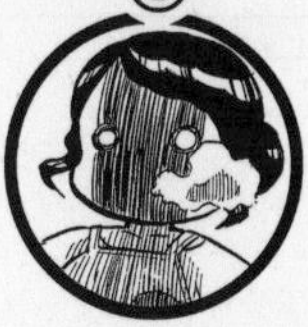

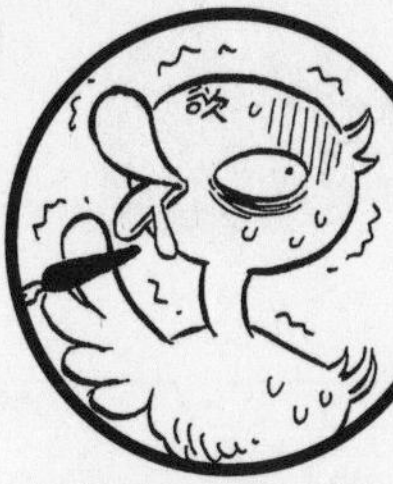

They exist side by side with work hell, but every day is shiny!

Captain Tabata

When I went out shopping while we were working on the manga, and the (female) clerk at the convenience store remembered me...

Editor Katayama

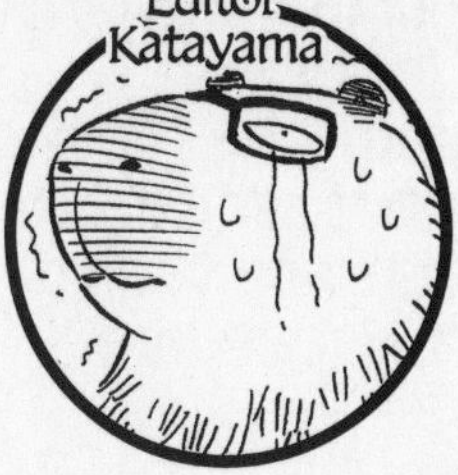

A shiny girls' night out near the train station.

Designer Iwai

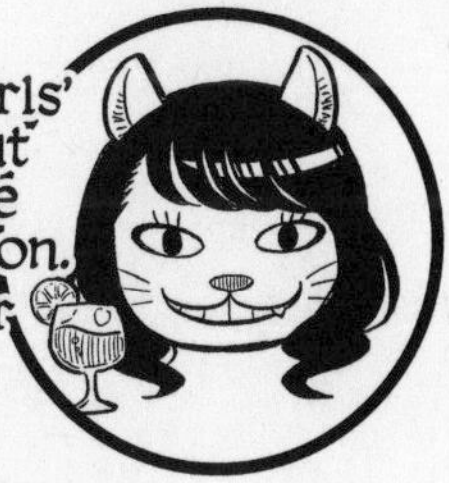

My face, when my daughter (one year, three months) spit on it...

Comics Editor Tomiyama

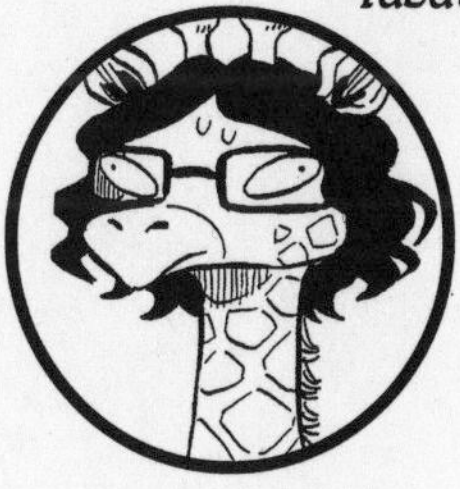

# AFTERWORD

Guess what?!

This volume goes on sale at the same time as the novel in Japan!!

Man oh man... Who'd have thought they'd release a novel for me? Thank you so much!

I'm deeply grateful to Johnny Onda Sensei, who expanded and deepened the world of *Black Clover* in fun, interesting and enthusiastic ways! He's obviously a fantastic guy.

Characters that will show up in the main story before long make appearances in the novel, so if you feel like it, absolutely check it out!!

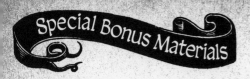

# Special Bonus Materials

Presenting early sketches of the priest mages who live in the Underwater Temple! The masks are grotesque, but what are their real faces like?!

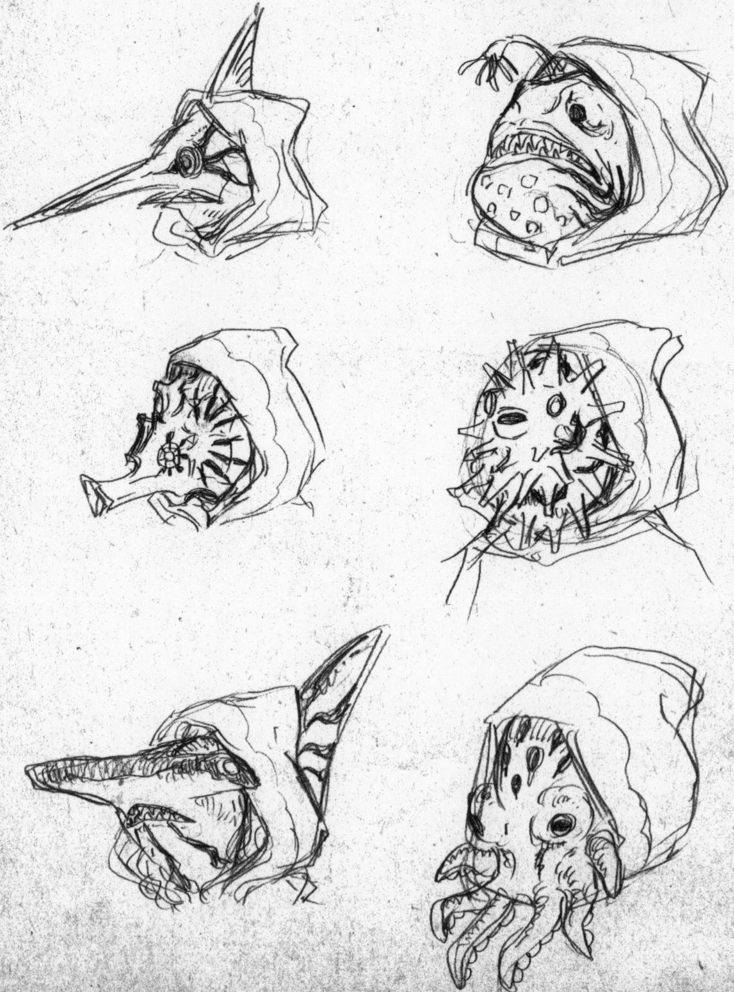

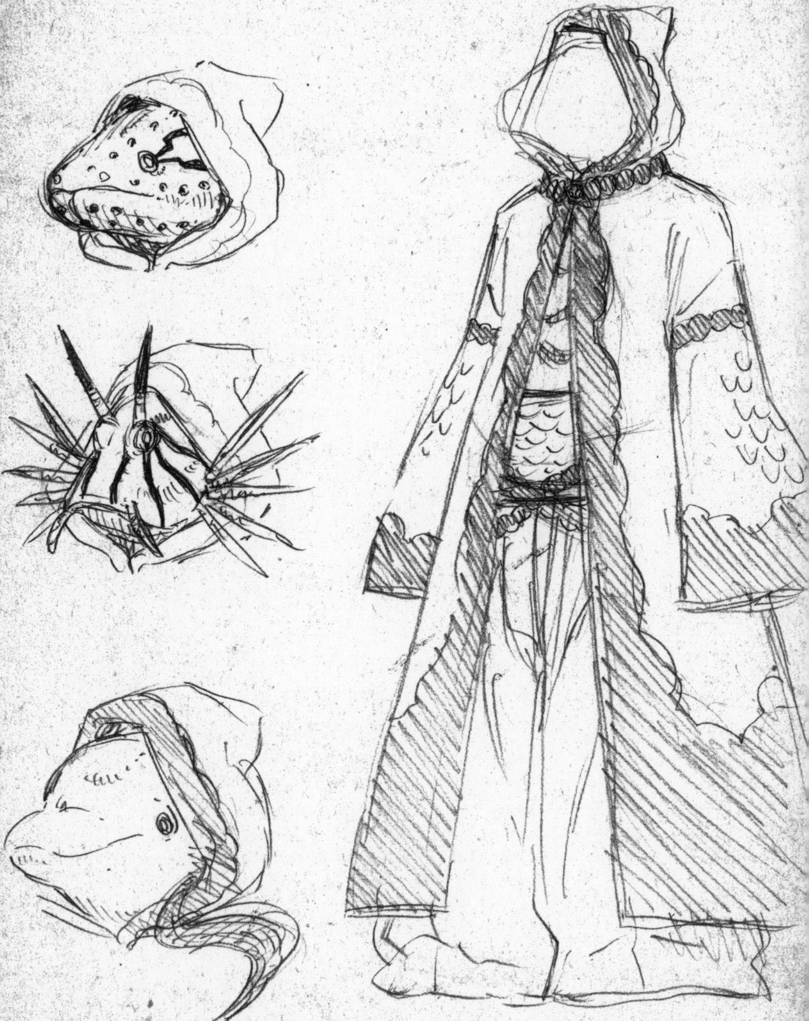

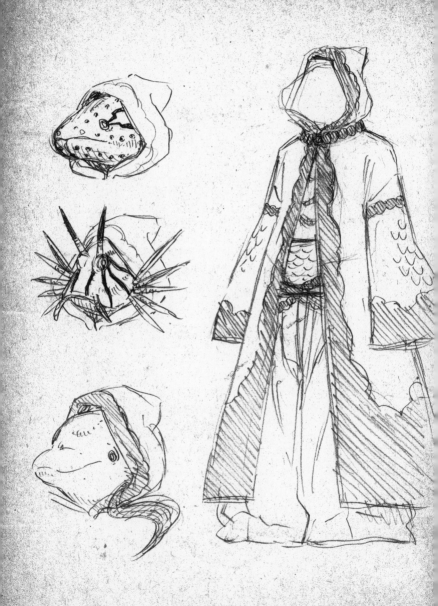

# YOU'RE READING
# THE WRONG WAY!

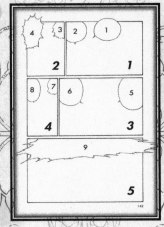

## BLACK CLOVER

reads from right to left, starting
in the upper-right corner. Japanese
is read from right to left, meaning
that action, sound effects, and
word-balloon order are completely
reversed from English order.